THE
POLITICAL JOURNAL
OF
George Bubb Dodington

George Bubb Doddington
Lord Melcombe.

A caricatura, but extremely like.
It was drawn by George Lord Townshend,
and engraved by Bartolozzi,
but falsely ascribed to Hogarth.
H.W.

THE DIARIST. Annotation is Horace Walpole's
(reproduced by courtesy of Lord Rothschild)

THE
POLITICAL JOURNAL
OF
George Bubb Dodington

EDITED BY

JOHN CARSWELL

AND

LEWIS ARNOLD DRALLE

OXFORD

AT THE CLARENDON PRESS

1965

Oxford University Press, Amen House, London E.C.4

GLASGOW NEW YORK TORONTO MELBOURNE WELLINGTON
BOMBAY CALCUTTA MADRAS KARACHI LAHORE DACCA
CAPE TOWN SALISBURY NAIROBI IBADAN ACCRA
KUALA LUMPUR HONG KONG

© *Oxford University Press 1965*

PRINTED IN GREAT BRITAIN
AT THE UNIVERSITY PRESS, OXFORD
BY VIVIAN RIDLER
PRINTER TO THE UNIVERSITY

PREFACE

THIS work, undertaken originally at the suggestion of the late Sir Lewis Namier, represents some nine years of transatlantic collaboration and considerable contributions besides those of the editors, both in Britain and in the United States. No doubt it will be found that much has been omitted: we can only hope, with Dr. Johnson, that it will be remembered that much has been performed.

We are especially grateful to Dr. William A. Jackson and the Houghton Library at Harvard University (in whose custody the main body of Dodington's surviving archives now is) for the greater part of our text. Other items we owe to the courtesy of the Marquess of Bute, whose librarian, Miss Catherine Armet, has been particularly helpful to us; the Trustees of the British Museum; Bodley's Librarian; and the Institute of Historical Research at the University of London, where the Secretary, Mr. E. L. C. Mullins, and Mr. John Brooke, made available their valuable collection of transcripts. Miss Mary Isabel Fry and the staff of the Huntington Library graciously opened to us the great resources of that institution.

Besides allowing us reference to Horace Walpole's annotations in his copy of Dodington's Diary, Lord Rothschild has kindly allowed us to reproduce Lord Lyttelton's caricature of the diarist. Authentic portraits of Dodington are few, and the 'striking likeness engraved by Angus' which appeared first in 1784 and has been reproduced frequently since (its most recent appearance being in a paperback of the Hervey Memoirs), must, we fear, after consultation with Mr. Romney Sedgwick, be rejected as trumped up.

Mrs. Mildred Dralle and Mrs. Ianthe Carswell have contributed so very much more than the usual wifely encouragement that they may both be said to have become members in full standing of the editorial team. None of which is advanced to excuse the editors from lapses in providing a text which they will only claim is more faithful than that published a hundred and eighty years ago.

J. C.
L. A. D.

London, England
Wichita, Kansas

CONTENTS

INTRODUCTION

In the diary of George Bubb Dodington one is confronted with an invaluable historical document and a ruined reputation. Faithfulness to the facts is in either case the cause. Day by day Dodington recorded his activities in the hope of justifying himself to posterity, and within twenty years of his death his diary was published as a monument to the corruption of his age and a contribution to the cause of parliamenary reform. It can now be seen as one of the cardinal documents of eighteenth-century politics.

The text published by Penruddock Wyndham in 1784 has remained, despite the survival of the holograph *Diary* now at Harvard,[1] the only one in print. It suffers from a number of defects: it is incomplete, and so fails to convey the full impact of a working politician's log-book; it is inaccurate—genteelisms intrude, entries are telescoped, and in detail hardly a line corresponds exactly with the original;[2] its slab-like page, and its allusions that could still be caught without help by the reader of 1784, make it difficult and tiresome today. Above all it lacks the actuality of the original. In the full *Diary*, interspersed with Dodington's ample accounts of his more important conversations written down within a few hours of their occurrence, briefer entries (in and between their lines) parade the whole procession that made up his world—noblemen and spies, journalists and painters, venal clergymen and election agents, princes and court ladies, ministers, officials, and country gentry. The cumulative effect of this detail is to convey the full texture of political life in the middle of the eighteenth century.

The *Diary* in its original form is the main feature of this edition. But we have aimed also at throwing the diarist's political life into higher relief by including correspondence and certain other papers which show the face he turned to the outer world and to his

---

[1] Harvard MS. Eng. 188*. The transcript from which the 1784 edition was made is in Mr. W. S. Lewis's collection at Farmington.

[2] As an example of telescoping compare the 1784 text following the news of George II's death with what D. actually wrote. The prejudice of Wyndham, who was an ally of Wyvill, may be judged not only from his preface, but by a number of disparaging notes by him on D.'s letters and papers.

colleagues; and have inserted this in chronological sequence so as to give as complete an account as is now possible of Dodington's career during the last fourteen years of his life.

When the *Diary* opens Dodington was moving into late middle age: he was 57, with a long political life behind him.[1] Although he was a thoroughly conventional politician his experience had been extensive and in some ways unusual. It certainly gave him, in his own eyes and those of others, a standing in the political world which the *Diary* takes for granted.

Like several other leading Georgian politicians Dodington was not especially well-born, but his family, like those of Walpole and Pelham, could claim the kind of established landed gentility that did not disdain official positions; and through his maternal grandmother, a Temple, he was connected with the celebrated 'cousinhood' itself.[2] His father was one Jeremiah Bubb, who is said to have been an apothecary but described himself as an Esquire of Foy, in Hereford, and appears to have been the son of another Jeremiah who sat for Carlisle in the Convention and the first Parliament of William III. George Bubb was thus the diarist's name from his birth in 1691 until 1720, when he assumed his mother's surname of Dodington,[3] in honour of his maternal uncle.

The Dodingtons were considerably higher in the social scale than the Bubbs, and possessed a pedigree stretching back to the twelfth century, together with considerable landed property in North Somerset. The diarist's maternal uncle George Dodington compiled an enormous fortune in politics and commerce under William III and Anne; and it was no doubt under his patronage that George Bubb received his education (Winchester, Exeter College Oxford, Lincoln's Inn, and the Grand Tour) and was brought into Parliament and the public service early in the Hanoverian era.

The uncle died in 1720, leaving his nephew the monuments of a successful whig politician's career—a large sum in cash and securities, a valuable Irish sinecure, a half-finished Vanbrugh palace

---

[1] A fuller account of D.'s career than can here be given is in Carswell, *The Old Cause* (1954).

[2] See Genealogical Table, p. xxvi.

[3] He was thus, and so always called himself, George Dodington. The inclusion of his old surname Bubb is therefore, strictly, incorrect: though he was never allowed to forget it by his enemies. It is possible, though uncertain, that the two Jeremiah Bubbs were, in fact, one and the same person. The information is meagre and contradictory.

at Tarrant Gunville in Dorset known as Eastbury, and considerable parliamentary influence. The foundations of Dodington as a politician therefore lay in the Augustan age, in its true sense of the first twenty years of the century, and in the West Country.

His first political experience, however, was in diplomacy, for in 1715, only a year after being brought into Parliament for the Treasury borough of Winchelsea, he was sent as Envoy to Spain, where he remained for two years. His success in negotiating, with the formidable Alberoni, the commercial treaty that governed Anglo-Spanish trade for the next thirty years, established his reputation. It also brought him the friendship of Paul Methuen, who, as the *Diary* shows, became his life-long political mentor.[1]

After a short period in opposition with Walpole as a supporter of the then Prince of Wales, Dodington followed his chief back into power and served for fifteen years (1724–39) as a Treasury Commissioner. In 1739 he broke with Walpole—the pretext was a quarrel over electoral influence at Weymouth—and broke the surface of political life as a leader in the alliance which overthrew the Robinocracy during the crisis of 1741–2. Two years later the Pelhams made him Treasurer of the Navy, the office his uncle had held in the days of the Junto. As such he served until the Peace of Aix la Chapelle brought an end to the War of the Austrian Succession and, for Dodington, the critical decision whether to continue in office or not, with which the *Diary* opens.

The *Diary* makes it clear that Dodington had an exaggerated idea of his importance in the political world; but even the truncated account of his career up to the age of 57 which has been given establishes that he had many of the qualifications for high office in the eighteenth century: wide experience in all three of the major spheres of government—foreign affairs, finance, and the navy; wealth; some reputation as a parliamentarian; and substantial parliamentary influence. His range of contacts was also exceptionally wide, extending, for instance, to city men such as John Bance, the dissenting clothier and banker, permanent officials such as John Scrope, and innumerable military and naval officers. His notes on Byng's cruise, the Rochefort raid, and the expedition of Braddock

---

[1] D.'s papers as Spanish Envoy are in British Museum Egerton MSS. 2170–5. He earned the respect, or at any rate the friendship, of Alberoni which continued even after the latter's fall (see *Seward's Anecdotes* (1804), vol. ii).

show that he could follow military operations intelligently and in detail, and that he had access to good sources of information.

Few commoners, and not many peers, could claim a more considerable electoral force than Dodington. Its core was the four-member borough of Weymouth and Melcombe, where the effectiveness of his control, shared with the local family of Tucker, earned a feeling tribute from the Duke of Newcastle. He himself sat for Bridgwater under an arrangement with the Poulet family[1] until the catastrophic defeat of 1754, and continued to have an interest there; and the *Diary* shows him closely concerned with the representation of Shaftesbury and Poole, as well as with the Dorset county members. As a metropolitan politician we see him turning out to support the radical Cooke in Middlesex, and acting on the committee of 'Independent Electors', the anti-government caucus in Westminster.

In the House Dodington was an astute tactitian and an effective debater in a rather old-fashioned style. His speech notes preserved at Harvard display his mastery of procedure, and although his elaborate irony and rather soapy sentiment do not charm us, his speeches extorted tributes from Horace Walpole (who detested him) and Shenstone. But his most important House of Commons asset lay in his long experience of an institution where seniority counted for a great deal, and was marked by Privy Councillorship and membership of White's.

Against all these qualifications for high office had to be set considerable personal handicaps. Always a short, dumpy man, Dodington at 57 was comically fat and ugly, with an absurd up-tilted nose, large mouth, protruding eyes, and pudgy hands. He ate and drank far too much (references to his dinner are the recurring ground bass of the *Diary*) and he was beginning to suffer from gout and other troubles. Nevertheless he had the characteristic physical stamina of a politician. Voltaire paid tribute to this quality, and more than once the *Diary* records long rides, and even walks, under the most difficult conditions, as well as regular journeys by coach lasting from early in the morning until late evening.

Until almost the end of his life, when elevation to the House of Lords made him suddenly catch up with the fashion, Dodington

---

[1] There are frequent references to this numerous Somersetshire tribe in the *Diary*. Their rise to an earldom had been the work of John Poulet (1663–1743) who had briefly been First Lord of the Treasury in 1710–11.

dressed in the style of his youth. The heavy bag wig, full-skirted coat, and elaborate embroidery—'something of la vieille cour' as Hervey said—were no doubt intended to impress country gentlemen with the idea that he was an old-fashioned man like themselves, not a smart London place-man. 'Noll Bluff' was a nickname he particularly valued. During the summer months at Eastbury he was tireless in his cultivation of the local gentry—Sturts, Nappers, and Okedens; he hunted, went to their balls, and, naturally, their political meetings as well.

Balancing this role as the squire's friend at court went that of the patron of arts and letters. Dodington undoubtedly found the writers and artists whom he cultivated useful: the American James Ralph, who was one of his closest familiars, was also, in effect, his private secretary as well as the editor of a succession of journals advertising the views of Dodington and his friends. Fielding had also entered Dodington's life through journalism, and had dedicated *Jonathan Wild* to him at the time when Walpole was going down. Dodington even tried to enlist Samuel Johnson as a journalist. But he was not without a genuine love of literature for its own sake, wrote passable verses himself, read widely, and was an assiduous playgoer. He did much for Thomson and Edward Young, listened patiently to Glover declaiming his vast tragedy *Leonidas*, and dearly loved to read *Tom Jones* aloud to superannuated maids of honour. With Voltaire, whom he had met during the celebrated visit to England in 1727, he was a life-long friend, and the surviving letters show a respect on the part of Voltaire that seems to be genuine. They shared, at any rate, in the defence of Byng.

In the arts he exerted himself, and must have spent large sums on his taste for the splendid. His riverside Hammersmith villa 'La Trappe', which was completed and occupied during the early years of the *Diary*, groaned with statues and was bedizened with gilt leather, tapestries, and peacock's feathers. The principal fireplace was encrusted with sham icicles in stone, for which no doubt Cheere, the leading sculptor of the day, was responsible. The ceilings, supported on two vast porphyry columns polished under Dodington's personal supervision at Ponders End, were by the Italian Servandoni. Through diplomatic friends—Horace Mann, Cardinal Albani the Vatican librarian, Baron Stosch the numismatist and spy—numerous antiques were obtained, and those Dodington did not keep he sold to wealthy acquaintances, among them the Prince of Wales.

Dodington's family circle and closest friends did not correspond to this picture of veteran statesman and patron of the arts which he sought to paint of himself. He was married, but childless.[1] Mrs Dodington (referred to always as 'Mrs D.' to distinguish her from the wife of his cousin, George Dodington of Horsington) was an Irishwoman named Beaghan. She had a trail of Irish relations, one of whom, Edmund Hungate Beaghan, Dodington put into Parliament for Weymouth; another was married to a minor Italian diplomatist named Venturini. But on the whole they seem to have pined for minor promotions in the army, and flit across the scene of the *Diary* with the crowd of other postulants for whom Dodington was expected to provide. There are hints in the *Diary* that Dodington looked for feminine companionship in addition to 'Mrs. D.'; but he does not enlarge on the entry for 20 June 1754, which records that this day 'saw a cruel end to a long and tender friendship'.

On Dodington's side of the family one finds more substantial people, such as George Dodington of Horsington, in the Vale of Blackmore, whose family acres were transmitted to descendants in the late nineteenth century. Other groups of cousins supplied a High Sheriff of Somerset in Samuel Jackson (Dodington himself had been Lord Lieutenant for nearly twenty years until he surrendered the position to Lord Poulet as part of the price of support at Bridgwater in 1741), and Edmund Wyndham, a seedy relation for whom a seat in Parliament and a place at dinner were regularly provided.

Dodington's three closest friends—perhaps cronies would be a more accurate word—were William Breton, a court official who eventually became private secretary to the Princess of Wales and an invaluable listening-post for Dodington; Henry Furnese of New Romney; and Francis Dashwood, baronet of High Wycombe. The last two belonged to mercantile families that had achieved baronetcy under Queen Anne, and Furnese, about whom comparatively little is known, though he was twice Secretary to the Treasury for short periods, seems to have kept up his city connexions. Dashwood, who ultimately inherited the peerage of le Despenser from his remote

---

[1] Mrs. Dodington died in 1756. The date of the marriage is obscure, but probably belongs to the 1730's. It was private until 1742, when Dodington was reconciled with his Temple relations, to whom Eastbury was entailed if Dodington had no heir. It is possible that a long correspondence in Dodington's papers with a certain Mrs. Anne East and her son relate to an illegitimate issue. Dodington clearly took a paternal interest in the young man, whom he introduced to Voltaire, and loaded with Chesterfieldian advice.

INTRODUCTION

relations the Fanes, Earls of Westmorland, is chiefly celebrated as
the organizer of the private Thames-side revels at Medmenham,
popularly, but wrongly, known as the Hellfire Club. The *Diary*
affords strong indications that Dodington was at any rate an
occasional visitor to these preposterous junketings, for when he is
in the neighbourhood of West Wycombe days are significantly
skipped or telescoped. Moreover the only man for whose membership direct documentary evidence exists was a member of the family
with whom Dodington shared political influence in Weymouth;[1] and
Dashwood, as Dodington's executor, laid out the sum he had been left
to erect a monument to their friendship in a hexagonal mausoleum
above the caves where the club is supposed sometimes to have met.

It was Dodington's strength to be in touch with so many worlds;
but it was also his weakness. His closest intimates were for the most
part his inferiors in talent and social status, and he was tortured by
ambition and envy. As a politician he overworked the weapon of
intrigue, which had a fatal attraction for him, and his reputation
suffered accordingly. But there is an amiable, even virtuous, side
to his character which the *Diary* partly delineates. To his nearest
friends he was unswervingly loyal, and to his many dependants
genuinely kind. The *Diary* records many instances of his attempts
to reconcile family quarrels and to console those in difficulties.
Though regarded as politically unreliable ever since he turned
so vigorously against Walpole, he was very generally liked for his
social qualities. But above all he could on occasion display considerable political courage in defending unpopular causes, such as
Byng's, and in an age of brutality was usually to be found on the
humane side of an argument.

The setting of the *Diary* is the political world of the 1750's, of
which a full account has yet to be written. It was the twilight of
the Augustan era in whose morning Dodington had begun his
career. Nothing substantial had been changed since 1715, and
power was in the hands of old men. In 1750 George II was 67, the
Pelham brothers 67 and 65, Hardwicke 60, Argyll 68. 'Old' Scrope,
now over 80, had been managing the Treasury for a quarter of a

---

[1] John Tucker. His letter of 22 March 1766 to Dashwood (Dashwood MSS.
deposited in the Bodleian Library) is not only proof of his membership, but, so far
as we know, the only indubitable proof of there ever having been such a society. See
Old Cause, 253.

century. Largely because of Walpole's jealousy of talent there was a notable lack of established politicians in their fifties—the coming men were in their forties or younger: Pitt was 42, Fox 45, the Prince of Wales 43. George Grenville was 38 and Lord Egmont 39. The Duke of Cumberland was still under 30. These vital facts weighed heavily in Dodington's decision, with which the *Diary* opens, to abandon the comparatively safe but unexciting post of Treasurer of the Navy under the Pelhams, and seek to establish himself as the leading man in the court of the king-to-be. In the year 1750 Dodington was 59—too old to wait, but young enough, perhaps, to see his seniors out before the younger men caught up.

Although a new generation of politicians was on the verge of taking over the reins of power there were as yet only the faintest premonitions of the great new issues of policy that were to be posed in the sixties and seventies as a result of victory in India and America. Such premonitions can be detected in the *Diary*, but they were not yet the subject of political conflict. The issues of the fifties were therefore highly personalized as questions of succession to the crown and to high office. The existence of an active, eligible Prince of Wales, already possessed of considerable political experience, particularly distinguishes the opening years of the period from, say, the successionless world of 1760.

Two deaths, those of the Prince in 1751 and of Pelham in 1754, and one loss of reputation, that of Cumberland in 1757, mark the evolution of this pattern of personal politics. The first sent Dodington back on his painful journey to the old court; the second seriously impeded his progress, and opened the way to Pitt; and the third temporarily halted the advance of Henry Fox, ensured the triumph of Pitt, and left George II a stronger figure at the end of his reign than, perhaps, in any period during its course.

Even before Dodington abandoned the Treasurership of the Navy to take office under the Prince of Wales, his standing with the King had been bad. This was an important factor in his decision to change allegiance. The trouble reached back over seventeen years, to 1731, when Dodington had professed to find it possible to reconcile continued office with cultivation of the newly emergent Prince 'as a private man whom your Royal Highness was pleased to call to your acquaintance'.[1] But the ineradicable bitterness had

---

[1] *Historical Manuscripts Commission, Various Collections*, vol. vi. Dodington to the Prince of Wales, 19 Sept. 1733.

been caused by Dodington's part, fully documented by Dodington himself[1] and by his rival Hervey, in the dispute over increasing the Prince of Wales's allowance from the Civil List in 1737.

This was not a mere family dispute, for the Civil List was far more than a fund at the King's disposal for his own private purposes. It was an indispensable feature of public finance, which, however complex in detail, was thought of on comparatively simple lines. The only major purposes for which Parliament made annual provision were defence and the National Debt (which was generally considered to represent the cost of past wars). All other government expenditure—what would now be called the Civil Estimates— the cost of diplomacy, the civil service, the judiciary, and ministerial salaries, as well as political and secret payments and the direct expenditure of the royal family, was met from the Civil List, voted at the beginning of each reign, and thereafter supposed to remain fixed. Under George II this amount was £800,000 a year, and ministers were accountable for it not to Parliament but to the King alone. The right of the King to choose his own ministers was founded in the fact that he was supposed to pay them out of his own pocket.

The proposal of 1737, that the Prince of Wales's allocation from the Civil List should be raised from £50,000 to £100,000, thus amounted to a demand that one-eighth, instead of one-sixteenth, of the Government's resources for civil expenditure should be placed at the disposal of the leader of the Opposition. Dodington had not felt strong enough to support open parliamentary pressure for this; but he had shown himself willing enough to see it happen by any other means, and the offence, one may be sure, was never forgotten or forgiven by the King. Underlying the whole *Diary*, therefore, is this conflict between a politician who conceived he had a virtual right to office when he wished for it, and a King to whom he was unacceptable.

The years between 1749 and 1751 saw the dynastic opposition in its most perfect and highly developed form. During periods when there was no effective Prince of Wales,[2] opposition politicians had to find the best substitutes they could, as chess players lacking a queen might use some specially marked lesser piece. But a Prince

[1] His account (from the manuscript at Harvard) is printed in the Appendix to the 1784 edition of the *Diary*.
[2] i.e. the early years of George II and the last nine years of his reign; and the first twenty years of George III.

in full possession of his rights and revenues (which at other times reverted to the Crown, and so strengthened 'the possession') made Carlton House a formidable interest, probably the most formidable after the Crown itself.

This expressed itself most obviously in the Prince's entitlement to a household[1] on a scale which was entirely within his discretion (though subject to his financial resources) and was in fact virtually a carbon copy of his father's. This afforded a ready means of attaching and rewarding politicians and their dependants; and was especially attractive to parliamentary place-hunters, since acceptance of an office in the Prince's gift did not involve seeking re-election or any of the other disadvantages attaching to office under the Crown. As a result the professional Opposition in 1749–51 was probably better paid from public funds than it is today. When Dodington accepted the specially created post of Treasurer of the Chamber (and the £2,000 a year that went with it) there were already some 200 posts in the Prince's Household or connected with the Duchy of Cornwall. Twenty-three of these were held by members of parliament, most of them in the Lower House. Out of the eleven senior posts, which constituted the Prince's Council,[2] two were held by peers, and six by members of the House of Commons.

The finance for all this, and for such other political gestures as the purchase of the borough of Old Sarum,[3] and the running of *The Remembrancer*, edited by James Ralph under the assumed name of 'John Cadwallader', came from three sources: the Prince's share of the Civil List, now £100,000 a year; the revenues of the Duchy of Cornwall (mainly tin royalties), the Principality of Wales, and of the Prince's estates in Somerset, Bucks., Surrey, Sussex, Hertfordshire, Lancashire, and Dorset; and borrowing. The borrowing was, of course, on the security of the Civil List the Prince would receive as King, and Dodington significantly records that the loans were underwritten by insurance policies on the Prince's life.

The master and *raison d'être* of the whole complex, Frederick himself, was looked upon, at 43, as a first-class life. Although he had at bottom the stubborn, choleric temper of his family, this was

---

[1] See A. N. Newman's account in *E.H.R.*, 1961.
[2] Technically the Council of the Duchy of Cornwall: actually the Prince's political cabinet.
[3] See *Historical Manuscripts Commission (Dropmore)*, i. 134.

overlaid, as in his grandson's case, by personal theatricality and a desire to be thought a man of taste. He had an inordinate fondness for the drama, and it is hard to believe the number of performances which Dodington records as attended in his company. He made his children act, and even, Dodington tells us, appeared on the stage himself. It is said that Bute first attracted his attention by his talent as an amateur actor.

There can be little doubt that like a number of other princes of his time Frederick Louis had Charles XII of Sweden very much in mind as his model. In his town establishments, Leicester House and Carlton House,[1] he undertook ambitious schemes of redecoration; and at Kew, where each of his children had a plot assigned to cultivate, he had the unpleasant habit of setting his courtiers to work on the landscape. But this pose fitted ill with a fondness for the elaborately trivial. While his practical brother Cumberland was campaigning against that other admirer of Charles XII, Charles Edward, Frederick Louis gave a party at which an iced cake representing the fortifications of Carlisle was demolished by sugar cannon-balls thrown by maids of honour. Indeed, as with his grandson and great-granddaughter, it is possible to detect in Frederick a yearning for continuity with the old dynasty, though of an emotional, not a political kind. He interceded successfully for one of the rebel lords after the Forty-five, gave the frankly Jacobite Earl of Westmorland a place in his entourage, and made Catherine Walkinshaw, sister of Charles Edward's mistress Clementina, a maid of honour to the Princess.

Augusta, Princess of Wales, emerges from the *Diary* as a sensible woman, and quite equal to holding her own in a political conversation; but she was not politically ambitious. Her interests were centred on her family—there were five when the *Diary* begins, and another was to be added—and above all on her eldest son. George, the future king, was 13 in 1749, and a difficult, backward boy. 'Very honest but I wish he were less childish', the anxious mother said to Dodington. But she rightly divined his underlying conative powers —'George', she said, 'will do it'; and she certainly impressed on

---

[1] Both have now disappeared, except for the pillars of the portico of Carlton House, which have been economically incorporated in the National Gallery. Leicester House, which lay on the north side of what is now Leicester Square, was the traditional home of the Princes of Wales from 1718 onwards. Carlton House, which abutted on Dodington's town house in Pall Mall, had been bought by Frederick from the Earl of Burlington's widow in 1732.

him the duty of loyalty to his father's old supporters, to whom
these words refer.

The Prince's affections were centred not on his wife, but on the
slim, sallow, Grace, Countess of Middlesex, who was a Boyle and
something of a blue-stocking. As Mistress of the Robes to the
Princess she drew £500 a year, which was a very acceptable addition
to the £1,000 which her husband drew as the Prince's Master of
the Horse. For the Middlesex family was on bad terms with the
Earl's father, the Duke of Dorset, and Dodington, who had made
or arranged loans for the young couple, worked hard, but in vain,
to reconcile this family quarrel. In the meantime Lady Middlesex
provided Dodington with an invaluable listening-post close to the
Prince.

The Middlesexes, however, did not count for much politically at
Carlton House. The serious leadership belonged to John Perceval,
Earl of Egmont, Charles Calvert, Lord Baltimore, and Dr. George
Lee. Egmont, who was openly grooming himself for the headship
of affairs in the next reign, reappears regularly throughout the
Diary to plague and frustrate Dodington. Baltimore's ambitions
were fortified by marriage to the daughter of one of the biggest
business men of the last generation, Theodore Janssen, and by the
proprietorship of Maryland. But of the three George Lee was the
most interesting. He was an admiralty lawyer with a prosperous
practice, and a House of Commons career going back to 1733.
When the first round of the great challenge to Walpole had been
fought in 1739 over the chairmanship of the Committee of Privileges, he had been the successful opposition candidate, and he had
held minor office under Carteret. He was probably Frederick's
closest adviser, and after the Prince's death the scrutiny of his
political papers was entrusted to this unassuming and confidential
man, who destroyed most of them.

These three, together with such permanent functionaries as
Henry Drax, the Prince's private secretary, and William Breton,
the Princess's, made up what was called 'the family'—i.e. the
courtiers whose regular attendance on their principals was expected.
These personal attendances, as the *Diary* shows, were extremely
time-consuming. Dodington, though he regarded himself as
qualified for membership of 'the family', was never fully accepted
by this inner circle; and with Egmont in particular he had to fight
a duel for influence from which a deep personal enmity developed,

which was to colour the *Diary* down to the opening of the new reign.

Dodington's device for displacing Egmont was an attempt, modelled on Bolingbroke's, to find some sort of political doctrine which the elaborate structure at Carlton House could say that it stood for, in place of the somewhat sordid sense of expectancy which grew with every year that George II added to his seventh decade. This attempt he embodied in his memorandum of 12 October 1749, where he sets out the programme for a respectable and permanent eighteenth-century Opposition. It is, of course, designed to appeal to the independent Members of Parliament whose support would be indispensable for any administration in the next reign: hostility to a foreign policy based on the defence of Hanover and subsidy treaties; colonial and commercial expansion as the only justification for a British war; anti-militarism; and the naturalization of the monarchy.

This was what Dodington meant by 'the disappearance of party'. The notion of a régime which had imposed itself on the native political system, and had to be buttressed with the garrison discipline associated with the word 'whig', was to disappear. For Dodington this programme was expedient only, except for its anti-military content, which he genuinely felt. But the memorandum in which he describes it, and many passages in the *Diary*, have the especial value of displaying how a professional politician used a technical vocabulary in which meanings have undergone complete changes, even though the same words are still in contemporary use. By 'whigs' Dodington unquestionably meant ministerial supporters, and by 'tories' the particular group of country gentlemen whose sympathies, better described as 'legitimist' than Jacobite, still responded more readily to tradition than to argument or the prospect of office. His references to 'people' and 'popular' signify opinion held outside professional politics; while those to 'party' mean rather more than a group depending on a particular patron, which he usually distinguishes as an 'interest'.[1] By 'party' Dodington meant either of two political features: a grouping, usually temporary, publicly committed to like thinking on one issue or set of issues; or the following of a particular chief whose strength lay

---

[1] Even within thirty years of the writing of the *Diary* conventions had changed to the extent of causing the editors of the 1784 edition to substitute 'party' in many places where D. had written 'interest'.

in his parliamentary gifts, rather than in his influence in other ways. Finally, by 'opposition' Dodington always seems to mean a political campaign, not a party grouping, though such groupings might of course form part of the campaign.

All Dodington's plans were frustrated by the sudden death of the Prince; and when the Princess refused to lend herself to carrying on the business of a succession court, the Duke of Cumberland, who detested Dodington, became the only adult member of the royal family to whom discontented politicians could turn. There was no choice but to return to the ministerialist camp, to which he had always kept lines open through such go-betweens as Carey and Hitch Younge. But here he was not only obstructed by the King's inveterate disfavour, but, in rapid succession, received two such damaging set-backs as would have sent most politicians into retirement. The death of Pelham, with whom he had been patiently working towards an accommodation, was followed by ignominious personal defeat at Bridgwater in the general election of 1754 at the hands of his hated rival Egmont. This, the one occasion in the whole *Diary* on which Dodington records his attendance at church, has earned him immortality as the model for the central figure in Hogarth's 'Chairing the Member'.

The sequel to this disagreeable series of rebuffs demonstrates his staying power as a politician. As Hillsborough pointedly observed, Pelham had had the address to play Fox and Pitt off against each other, whereas Newcastle had not. By the late summer of 1755 both the new rivals were wooing Dodington, who came down in favour of Fox, and in December of that year became once more Treasurer of the Navy.[1] He was, accordingly, a member of the celebrated Newcastle–Fox administration which began in disaster the war which Pitt was to carry on so triumphantly.

From the point of view of office he had chosen his associates wisely. But although Pitt was personally repugnant to him—'a ranting buskineer' is his expression for Pitt in the remarkable letter in which he disburdens himself to his crony Dr. Thomson—he was much more in sympathy with Pitt's policy than with Newcastle's. He had stipulated on taking office that he would not support the subsidies to continental troops, and as the Byng affair developed in the summer of 1756 his position became still more difficult. He

---

[1] The correspondence between Fox and D. is in B.M. Add. MS. 38091, and is printed in this edition in supplementation of the *Diary*.

foresaw that his colleagues, knowing their own blameworthiness, would sacrifice Byng; and he was under the strongest personal obligations to defend the unfortunate admiral, both as the professed opponent of military justice and as a family friend.

From this dilemma he was released in the most distasteful possible way, by the collapse of the Newcastle–Fox combination and the refusal of Pitt to continue him as Treasurer, because the place was needed for Grenville. He was able to make his 'bold and pathetic speech' (so Horace Walpole called it) on behalf of Byng, without the restraints of office. But then, to his intense mortification, he found himself excluded, indeed fooled, in the final coalition of 17 April 1757, in which Newcastle and Fox were eventually aligned with Pitt.

The *Diary* from this point to the end of the reign, when it is resumed with glee, becomes the jottings of a disappointed but well-informed politician sourly following the success of his rivals. The full measure of his gall is poured out in the long diatribe addressed to his old friend Lord Talbot in October 1760. It was probably meant for publication as a pamphlet. Three weeks later came the news, by way of Breton, that at last George II was dead.

It has been said, and with truth, that this came too late for Dodington, who was now in his seventieth year: but he, at any rate, did not think so. The *Diary* was taken up again, and a period of furious activity ensued, which can be followed in the correspondence with Bute down to the very last days of his life. His relationship with his new leader was not free from small upsets, but it was a close one, and it brought him the peerage he had coveted for so long, after an interview with the new king recorded in a minute which is one of Dodington's most precious productions. This, too, was the period when he produced his best poem, with its quintessential expression of naïve cynicism—

> Love thy country, wish it well—
> Not with too intense a care;
> 'Tis enough that when it fell,
> Thou its ruin didst not share.

He lived long enough to have Cabinet office, as First Lord of the Admiralty, proposed to him by Bute, and one of his very last letters, written from what proved to be his death-bed, rings with joy at the prospect of high office.

He died at Hammersmith on 28 July 1762, and is buried there. Judged as that of a politician his career was undoubtedly unsuccessful, though it should not be measured entirely by his record in, or in obtaining, office. He regarded himself as a continuing servant of the State, and even when most deeply engaged in opposition intrigues saw nothing inconsistent in assiduous attendance at the Privy Council, of which he was one of the comparatively few commoners to be a member. His historical importance, however, lies in the record he left behind: the day-to-day work of a man whose object and political training it was to be accurate about the affairs that interested him. As a result he succeeded in providing us with one of the best contemporary sources for the political world at the dawn of Britain's great colonial expansion.

The *Diary* originally formed part of a very large political archive, covering the whole of Dodington's career, of which the core is still together at Harvard, though much has been dispersed, and some lost to view altogether.[1] Some of this material has been drawn upon in this edition to supplement the eight folio notebooks comprising the *Diary* itself. The first four of these account for nearly every day from March 1749 to 10 October 1754, when the habit was laid aside, to be taken up again in two notebooks dealing with events from April 1755 to July 1757. These two books to some extent cover the same periods and even duplicate one another at certain points, though at others the entries for the same dates supplement one another. In the present text these parts of the manuscript have been dovetailed to form a continuous narrative, and duplication cut out. A seventh notebook covers, rather sporadically, 1758 and the early months of 1759. The eighth book resumes a detailed narrative with the new reign, and carries it down to 6 February 1761.

Apart from the minimal amount of spatchcocking required to present the fifth and sixth notebooks, we have here reproduced the *Diary* almost exactly as it stands. The contractions usual in eighteenth-century manuscripts have been expanded and most of Dodington's eccentricities of spelling modernized, in the interest of easy reading. His invariably elided 'e' in participles has been allowed to stand as characteristic of the period, and his spelling of proper names has been retained. In items of correspondence we

---

[1] For a full account of this archive, and the whereabouts of such of its contents as can be traced, see *Old Cause*, Appendix II.

have kept to the exact orthography of the originals where these are available.

The editors of 1784 completely disregarded Dodington's punctuation, and restoration of it does much to breathe life back into the document. We have broken down some of his longer paragraphs, and sometimes replaced or varied his favourite stop, the hyphen; and have inserted quotation marks where he reports direct speech. For ease of reference we have adopted a consistent separation into years and months (or groups of months) and divided the whole into four sections.

Annotation has been limited to what seemed necessary for a reader who is reasonably well-informed about the period to follow the narrative comfortably. Biographical information about the many people who figure in the *Diary* has not been given in footnotes, but the Index has been expanded to give summary particulars of identification. We have regarded an adequate Index as among the most important parts of our task.

GENEALOGICAL TABLE: TEMPLES, GRENVILLES, DODINGTONS

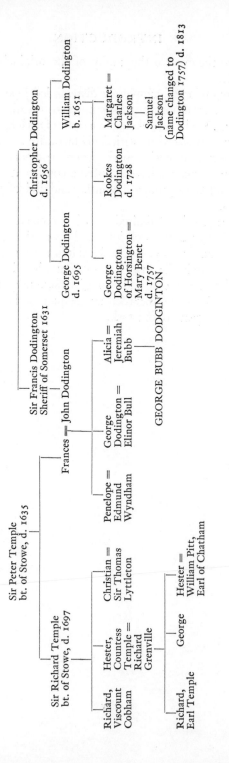

CORRIGENDA

p. xxvi   GEORGE BUBB DODGINTON *should read*
GEORGE BUBB DODINGTON

p. 24, *note* 1   £700,000 *should read* £800,000

PART ONE

THE LEICESTER HOUSE
OPPOSITION

MARCH 1749 TO MAY 1751

1749

MARCH

IN the beginning of this year, I was grievously afflicted with the first fit of the gout I ever had, which, with a fall that strain'd one leg, and wounded the other, confin'd me to my chamber, near three months.

8. During my illness, several kind expressions from the Prince, towards me, were reported to me, and on the 8th of March, H.R.H. order'd the Earl of Middlesex, his Master of the Horse, to send Mr Ralph (whom he had often talk'd to, about me)[1] with a message from H.R.H. to offer me the full return of his favour, and to put the principal direction of his affairs into my hands.

I told Mr Ralph, that I desir'd the two following days to consider of it; and that he should have my answer, at 12 o'clock, on Saturday, the 11th inst.

11. On Saturday the 11th in the morning, I wrote to Mr Pelham, desiring him, as I was not able to go out, to wait upon the King, and in my name, humbly to resign into His Majesty's hands, my office of Treasurer of the Navy.

The same day, I gave Mr Ralph my answer in writing, to the Prince's gracious message, to be deliver'd to the Earl of Middlesex, taking his honour that he would lay it before H.R.H. which Mr Ralph performed, as did also, his Lordship.

Dodington to the Prince 11 *March* 1749

That his Royal Highness may be thoroughly convinced, that Mr Dodington is, in earnest, disposed to be as serviceable to His Royal Highness, and this country, as his circumstances and abilities will

---

[1] See P.W. 484–7 for the note Ralph made at D.'s instance, of what the Prince said —which included the phrase 'we have good subalterns enough, but we want leaders'. Ralph, under the pseudonym of 'George Cadwallader', was at this time living at Gunnersbury (where he provided D. with a *pied-à-terre*) and editing the Prince's organ *The Remembrancer*.

give him leave, he has resigned the office he had the honour to hold under his Majesty.

And having promised this much, he humbly hopes he may be indulged in saying, That, if, by the most gracious offers his Royal Highness is pleased to make, of receiving him to the same degree of favour and protection as he once enjoyed, his Royal Highness means to admit him to the honour of being about his person, at his leisure hours, as a most respectful, most affectionate, and most disinterested attendant, he shall receive that great condescension, with all that reverential duty and respect, that becomes him, to a great and amiable Prince, who is thoroughly capable, by that means, of making the decline of his life much the happiest part of it.

But as to entering into his Royal Highness's public business; to advise or direct the measures which his Royal Highness may think fit to have pursued in Parliament, by his family, and followers, while himself, and his very few most efficient friends, are not in his Royal Highness's service; or presuming to take a lead; or invite, or engage others, to follow his Royal Highness's standard; he humbly hopes it will, in no degree, be expected from him; because he knows, and is convinced, that his rank and fortune must render such an attempt vain and impracticable; nor does he believe, that any body, much his superior in both, could effectually serve his Royal Highness in that way, how necessary so ever it may be, without those additions.[1]

The same morning I receiv'd a very civil letter from Mr Pelham, testifying his concern, and surprise, at my resolution; and desiring that he might see me, before he deliver'd my message to the King; and acquainting me that he would come to me, on Monday the 13th, in the morning, before he went to Court, being then just going into the country.

13. On Monday the 13th, early in the morning, Mr Pelham made me a long visit; with much civility. He seem'd to wish much that this affair might go no further. I told him that I saw the country in so dangerous a condition and found myself so incapable to contribute to its relief, and so unwelcome to attempt it, and that I thought it misbecame me any longer to receive great emoluments from a country whose service I could not, and if I could, I should

---

[1] P.W. 471–2. The aim of all this is, of course, formal appointments for himself and intimates (Dashwood, Furnese) in the Prince's Household. He wrote almost at the same time to Horace Mann disclaiming all intention of entering the Prince's service. (H. Walpole to Mann, 27 Oct. 1749.) His estimate of his resources as a politician, though insincere, was to prove correct.

not be suffer'd to promote; so I beg'd him to execute my commission to the King, upon which we parted.

He came to me again, about eleven o'clock, to let me know that the King accepted my dismission very graciously, but expected that I would continue to act, till he could pitch upon a proper successor. I did so, and was continued in the office till the 3rd of May.

It seems that D. suppressed the missing entries from this point to mid-July himself. The notebook from which the pages appear to have been cut is inscribed in D.'s hand on the cover 'Diary from October 1749 to 14 March 1750' *which suggests he at any rate contemplated suppressing all the compromising entries before his appointment as the Prince's Treasurer of the Chambers in October. The missing entries would give an account of the meeting of 112 opposition parliamentarians which Lord Egmont organized on 1 May, and possibly D.'s views on Bolingbroke's* Idea of a Patriot King, *which was published that Spring. During this interval also, the Prince strengthened his Parliamentary influence by the purchase from Thomas Pitt of the patronage of Old Sarum.* (H.M.C. (Dropmore), i. 134.)

JULY

16. The Prince was extremely good to me, and often admitted me to the honour of supping with him and the Princess. But on Sunday, 16th July, going to Carlton House, to make my compliments, before I went to Eastbury, he order'd me to sup with him, and invited me to spend the day with him, at Kew, on the following Tuesday, being the 18th wanting (as he was pleas'd to say) to talk to me about business.

18. On Tuesday the 18th I arriv'd at Kew, about eleven o'clock. The Prince receiv'd me most kindly, and told me he desir'd me to come into his service upon any terms, and by any title I pleas'd; that he meant to put the principal direction of his affairs into my hands; and what he could not do for me, in his present situation, must be made up to me, in futurity. All this in a manner so noble, and frank, and with expressions so full of affection, and regard, that I ought not to remember them, but as a debt, and to perpetuate my gratitude. This pass'd before dinner.

After dinner; he took me into a private room, and, of himself, began to say, that he thought I might as well be call'd Treasurer of the Chambers as any other name; that the Earl of Scarbrough, his Treasurer, might take it ill, if I stood upon the establishment with higher appointments than he; that H.R.H.'s destination was, that I should have £2,000 pr. An. That he thought it best to put me upon the Establishment at the highest salary only and that he would pay me the rest himself.[1] I humbly desir'd that I might stand upon the establishment without any salary, and that I would take what he now design'd me, when he was King, but nothing before. He said that it became me, to make him that offer, but it did not become him, to accept of it, consistent with his reputation, and therefore, it must be in present. He, then, immediately, added, that we must settle what was to happen, in reversion, and said that he thought a Peerage, with the management of the House of Lords,

---

[1] Cf. Ashford, D., *The Young Visiters*, 42: 'I am the Groom of the Chambers. What Chambers asked Mr Salteena blinking his eyes. These said Edward Procurio, waving a thin arm.' The appointment was, in fact, *ad hoc*, though it involved duties (see below, 3 Jan. 1750). The Earl of Scarbrough's salary was £1,600, and D. eventually accepted the £1,200 here offered, though he noted that he did so under protest. (Below, 16 Sept. 1749; P.W. 486–7; *H.M.C. Var. Coll.* vi. 20.)

and the seals of Secretary of State, of the Southern Province, would be a proper station for me, if I lik'd it. Perceiving me to be under a good deal of confusion at this unexpected offer, and at a loss how to express myself, he stopp'd me, and said, I then promise you, upon the word and honour of a Prince, that, as soon as I come to the crown, I will give you a peerage and the seals of the Southern Province. Upon my endeavouring to thank him, he repeated the same words, and added (putting back his chair) and I give you leave to kiss my hand upon it, now, by way of acceptance, which I did accordingly.

He, then, continu'd to say, that he would provide for my friends, whom he knew, I valued more than myself. That he promised Mr Furnese, the Treasury; Sir Fr. Dashwood, the Treasury of the Navy, or Cofferer; Mr Henley, Solicitor General, and gave me leave to tell them so, adding that he would comfirm it to them, himself: Lord Talbot, I was to settle with, when I saw him in Dorsetshire.[1]

We agreed that he should send for me to Cliefden,[2] when he was settled there, where the warrant should be ordered &c.

Upon the conversation before dinner, I had taken the opportunity to beg the Princess's protection, who answered me in the most obliging manner.

19. On Wednesday the 19th I saw Mr Furnese, and Mr Ralph, at Hammersmith, to whom I related all that had pass'd; and promis'd Mr Ralph that he should be my secretary, if I liv'd to have the seals.

20. Thursday the 20th we set out from Hammersmith to Eastbury, where we arriv'd safe, the same evening, by God's goodness.

23. Sunday Lord Talbot came over. I acquainted him with this whole transaction. He promis'd to support me to the utmost, and do the Prince all possible service. But wou'd accept of no reversion.

31. Monday. Sir Fr. Dashwood and his lady came to Eastbury. I inform'd him, also, of all that had pass'd. He receiv'd, with much pleasure, both what related to himself, and to me. Mr and Mrs Combes, and Miss Hurst din'd with us.

---

[1] D.'s intimate circle. The offer of 'the Treasury' to Furnese presumably means the Secretaryship of the Treasury.

[2] Cliveden Place, near Cookham, Berks., the Prince's rented country house. His occupancy is commemorated by the neighbouring Feathers Inn, though a later set has obscured it.

AUGUST

1. Tuesday. Mr Furnese and Mr Carey[1] came to Eastbury together. Afterwards Mr Kelsal,[2] alone.

2. Wednesday. Lord Talbot return'd.

3. Thursday. The Churchills, with Mr Ansome [*Awnsham Churchill*] and his wife, din'd at Eastbury.

4. Friday. Sir Fr. Dashwood and his lady, Mrs D., and Mrs P. Beaghan, in the coach, and Mr Furnese and I in a chair, din'd at Lord Talbot's, at Melcombe.

5. Saturday. Messrs Furnese and Carey, went to town.

6. Sunday. Lord Talbot went home.

7. Monday. Sir Fr. Dashwood &c went away.

8. Tuesday. Messrs Bance, and Young, came to Eastbury, while we were at dinner, at Mr Drax's.[3]

9. Wednesday. I acquainted Mr Bance with all that had pass'd between the Prince, and me; and offer'd him my endeavours to procure him the reversion of the remittances,[4] or of the Board of Trade, if he had a mind to leave the City. He receiv'd my narrative with much pleasure, and my offers, with great kindness, and affection; protested that he had no wish but to remain, always, my faithful friend and servant, and desir'd, nor would have, nothing. But upon my pressing him, said, that if it must be so, he should choose the remittances,[4] and to have the secret and government of the Bank, as what, he thought, would render him most useful to his friends. To which I agreed, and promis'd to undertake it with the Prince.

11. Friday. Messrs Bance and Young went away.

[1] D.'s contact with the Pelhams.
[2] Henry Kelsal, a chief clerk at the Treasury.
[3] The Prince's private secretary, and also managed the Prince's Dorset property. Originally a Yorkshireman, he is mistakenly described in Namier's account of Wareham (*Structure*, 125) as a local squire.
[4] i.e. of pay to British troops and allies abroad, traditionally the monopoly of the Bank of England. Bance had until recently shared the representation of Westbury with Methuen, but was now out of Parliament.

12. Saturday. We din'd at Mr Churchill's, and when we return'd, found Mr Stanley, at Eastbury.

15. Tuesday. Mr Banks din'd at Eastbury. Lord Barrington came, at night.

16. Wednesday. Lord Anson and Captain Mostyn came, and carried away Lord Barrington to Wilton. We din'd at Mrs Okeden's.

17. Thursday. Mr Wyndham came to Eastbury, Mr and Mrs Pitt of Binfield din'd there.

18. Friday. I told Mr. Wyndham what had pass'd between the Prince, and me, so far as related to myself, only[1]—We din'd at Mr Trenchard's.

20. Sunday. Mr Rd. Tucker came to Eastbury. Lord Talbot and Mr Grove din'd there.

21. Monday. Mr Tucker went away.[2]

22. Tuesday. We din'd at Lord Shaftesbury's.

23. Wednesday. Din'd at Mr Carver's, with the Barbars.

25. Friday. Din'd at Mr Wyndham's, where were Messrs Knatchbull, and Miss Hillman.

26. Saturday. Mr Francis and Henry Fane breakfasted at Eastbury, on their way to Lyme,[3] and our family din'd at Mr Combes's.

27. Sunday. Mr Freke din'd at Eastbury.

28. Monday. Mr Kelsal, Mr Wyndham, and I din'd at Rushmere, at the opening of the hunt. There, Mr Pitt and his brother, Earl of Castlehaven and his brother, Mr Penruddock, Mr Jonathan Pleydell, and parsons etc.

---

[1] As D.'s nearest blood-relation and heir Wyndham was entitled to this degree of confidence.

[2] D. did not at this stage tell his partners in the political control of Weymouth about his new orientation, because Weymouth was still committed to support of the Government, at any rate for this Parliament. (See below, 18 Nov. 1750.)

[3] Sons of the Earl of Westmorland (see 17 March 1750 below) and so cousins of D.'s associate Dashwood, who eventually inherited Westmorland's peerage of le Despencer. Lyme was their family borough (*Structure*, 206–7) at which they provided a seat for Scrope, Secretary of the Treasury. Henry Fane was a Chief Clerk at the Treasury. Francis (who sat for Ilchester) was a Commissioner of Trade 1746–56 and Chairman of Committees in the Commons. He died 1762.

29. Tuesday. Lord Talbot and Parson Crabb din'd at Eastbury.

30. Wednesday. Hunted West Walk. The hunt din'd at Eastbury. They were, Earl of Castlehaven and his brother, Mr Pitt and his brother, Mr Pleydell and his two sons, Mr Jul: Beckford, Mr Penruddock, Mrs Bowers, Mrs Okeden, Parson Franck, Mayor of Shaftesbury,[1] Mr Piggott, Mrs Jones, Mr Jonathan Beaghan[2] came.

31. Thursday. After dinner came to Eastbury, Count Einsidell, and Baron Kreygell, with Messrs Egreland and Williams, their companions.

[1] Shaftesbury was a borough in which D. took much interest. Many references to its Members of Parliament will be found in the following pages.
[2] D.'s brother-in-law.

SEPTEMBER

1. Friday. Count Einsidell, and Mons. Egreland went on, to Dorchester, about 5 in the afternoon.

2. Saturday. Mons de Kreygell, and Mr Williams set out for Portsmouth, about six in the morning.

5. Tuesday. Mr Kelsal went. Mr Wyndham, and I, din'd at Mr Grove's.

6. Wednesday. Captain Beaghan and I, din'd at Mr Bank's.

7. Thursday. I received the Prince's commands by the Earl of Egmont, to attend him at Cliefden.

8. Friday. Mr Wm. Sharpe came to Eastbury.

9. Saturday. Lord Shaftesbury came in the morning. I open'd part of the Prince's scheme to him: he seem'd pleas'd, and willing to assist: and promis'd to try and thought he could answer for Lord Foley. Lord Talbot, and Mr Rogers din'd at Eastbury.

10. Sunday. Mr Sharpe went away.

11. Monday. At half an hour past four, I set out from Eastbury; by the way of Stockbridge, and by the Bye-Post, arriv'd at Gunnersbury, the same day, at a quarter past seven. Mrs D. set out for Bath the same day, in a one-horse chair, with relays.

12, 13. Tuesday and Wednesday. Saw Mr Ralph, and talked with him about Lord Egmont's acquainting Carey with the whole transaction between him and me.[1]

14. Thursday. Went from Gunnersbury to Cliefden. Well receiv'd by all the Family. There was besides, Earl of Bute, and Lord Chief Justice Willes.[2]

---

[1] i.e. Egmont was betraying D.'s new alignment to the Pelhams. This, the first sign of the rivalry between Egmont and D. to lead the Opposition, no doubt precipitated D.'s decision openly to join the Prince's household.

[2] 'Family' is here, as always, used in the technical sense of the Prince's immediate salaried entourage. It is notable that Bute was not yet technically a member of the 'Family', though he had been attached to the Prince since 1747.

15. Friday. Din'd with their Royal Highnesses at Park Place Clief-den. Lord Chief Justice went from thence to Henley.

16. Saturday. Orders to Mr Drax, by Lord Egmont, to make out my warrant. Receiv'd an account that Lord Cobham died on Wednesday the 13th.[1]

17. Sunday. The Prince and Lord Egmont went to town, from Cliefden. The Princess to Kew. They return'd thither about nine. I met them about ten. Lord Bathurst came to Cliefden in the morn-ing, and thence to Kew.

18. Monday. Stayed at Kew. Mr Breton told me of Mrs Evelyn's death.

19. Tuesday. Went with their Hss to Ashley [*Lady Middlesex's country house at Walton on Thames*]. There was Misses Jackson and Rich. Din'd and supp'd there, and return'd to Kew, at three on Wednesday morning.

20. Wednesday. Walk'd in Richmond gardens. Lord Bute left us. Din'd at Kew, and return'd in the evening, to Cliefden.

21. Thursday. Sir William Stanhope came to Cliefden.

22. Friday. Their Hss carry'd me to Windsor, where I left them, and went to Ashley Park, where was Mr Breton.

23. Saturday. At Ashley. Sent an ode to the Princess, with a letter, by her command. [*Letter and ode are lost.*]

24. Sunday. Mr Breton went to Cliefden. I receiv'd an answer from the Princess.

25, 26. Monday and Tuesday. At Ashley.

27. Wednesday. Left Ashley, and went to Gunnersbury. Din'd at Hammersmith.

28. Thursday. Din'd at Hammersmith with Messrs Tucker, and Thomson, and lay at Gunnersbury.

---

[1] D.'s cousin, and next to him in the Eastbury entail. The two had been engaged for the past twenty-five years in litigation concerning the late George Dodington's will, of which Cobham was an executor. In 1743 Cobham had won the last round in the Court of Chancery, but his death abated the suit (though it was later revived by the Grenvilles). The whole is summarized in the Harvard MSS. relating to D.

29. Friday. Din'd at Sir P. Methuen's.[1] Heard the news of Sir Watkin Williams's death, by a fall from his horse.

30. Saturday. Din'd with Mrs Scrope.[2] The Prince and Princess came to town.

[1] D. invariably dined with his political mentor at critical times.
[2] Wife of the Secretary to the Treasury.

OCTOBER

1. Sunday. Kiss'd the Prince, and Princess's hand, as Treasurer of the Chambers. Supped with T.R.H. and Madame de Mirepoix, the French Ambassadress. The Prince pretty eager about Opposition.

2. Monday. Kiss'd the King's hand, at Kensington, was civilly receiv'd.[1] Wrote to Lady Middlesex about what pass'd last night. Sent a servant to Grange, with a letter to Mr Henley. Wrote to Mr Waller. Din'd with Mr Oswald at Wandsworth.

3. Tuesday. Set out from London $\frac{3}{4}$ past eight. Met an answer from Mr Henley, not so full as I expected. Lay at Sutton.

4. Wednesday. Set out before eight, and got to Eastbury before three, where I found Mr and Mrs Dodington.[2] Everybody well, God be praised. Mr Ridout outbid me for Lanston, tho' my agreement was made and the day appointed, for signing.

6. Friday. Mr Drax came—says Lady Middlesex is cunning, and silly—warns me against her. Mr Tynte came.

7. Saturday. Went to Lord Shaftesbury's and left him very well dispos'd. Found General Cholmondely there—at my return found Mr Henley. Show'd him Lord Egmont's letter, and my answer, and the heads I design'd for the Prince. He seem'd to approve, and promis'd to promote every thing, according to my system.

8. Sunday. Mr Henley went away.

9. Monday. Mr and Mrs Dodington, and Mr Tynte went away. Duke and Duchess of Queensberry, Ladies Charlotte and Mary Capel, with two more; Colonel [Archibald] Douglas, Messrs [Andrew] Mitchell and Young, came and breakfasted. They went on to Blandford. Mr Young stayed.

10. Tuesday. The coach set out with Mrs Beaghan, for town. Lord Talbot came. I went with him, as far as Blandford, to see Mr Ridout, who had, very civilly, desisted from his bidding for Lanston Farm.

---

[1] Surprising. Horace Walpole's marginal note says the King laughed in his face. (Copy of *Diary* in possession of Lord Rothschild.)
[2] D.'s first cousin once removed, and M.P. for Melcombe.

12. Thursday. We set out from Eastbury, at 20 minutes after six; and came to Hammersmith at half past nine; without any accident. God be prais'd.

13. Friday. Sent a memorial, with a letter to the Prince. Came to town, at twelve—waited on T.R.H. They lay at Kew, and order'd me to attend them, the next day.

The memorial, submitted with a brief covering letter, is in P.W. 473 ff. It is D.'s most celebrated political essay, and was probably composed in a single day—11 October—when D. was alone in Eastbury. It was only an outline when shown to Henley on 7 October. This fabian document, which was so unwelcome to Egmont and the more eager elements in the Prince's entourage, is as follows:

Sir,

Though I must own I am under but little, perhaps too little constraint, when I converse with your Royal Highness, in the familiarity of private life, which your condescension, often, calls me to: Yet, when I approach you in the light of a great Prince, of admirable endowments, by nature; highly improved by art and observation; a Prince with one foot on the throne of a, once, great and powerful People; called thither by Providence, to prevent, or compleat its ruin: when I approach you in this light, and above all, when I consider, that I am called to offer my serious opinion, relating to a conduct that must determine this awful event; I confess I am too much agitated, between the resolution of doing my duty to my country, and the fear of offending by too full, and plain a discharge of it, to speak to your Royal Highness with that calmness of mind, that full possession of myself, which the greatness of the object, the operation, and the actor require, upon so solemn an occasion.

I have, therefore, chosen this way of memorial as a means to lay my thoughts before your Royal Highness, in a less confused manner, and at the same time, to give you an opportunity of examining them, as your leisure and inclination shall dictate: humbly hoping, only, that you will give them a full and calm consideration, as the settled opinion, after much reflection, of a man bound by duty, and impelled by gratitude and inclination, to prefer your true glory and interest, and the welfare of this country (which are inseparable), to all other, earthly, considerations; and one, who looks upon the faithful discharge of this great duty, as the most important article he is answerable for, to Almighty God, before whom he expects, shortly, to appear.

As nobody has seen this paper;[1] elegance, and accuracy, it may,

---

[1] Henley had seen the outline—see above 7 Oct. 1749.

possibly, want: sincerity, and affection, it, certainly, will not: the head may err; the heart cannot.

I shall begin, Sir, with parliamentary affairs, so far forth only, as they relate to the part your Royal Highness, in your present situation, ought to take in them, by those who are more immediately honoured with your character, and protection.

I choose to begin with this head, because it is most pressing in point of time; because it is what you are, most deeply, engaged in; and because (though perhaps unavoidably at first) it is, now, become the source and cause of all the most considerable difficulties you labour under; and which, each in its turn, may be the subject of different memorials, if you shall please to approve of this method of laying my thoughts before your Royal Highness.

The narrow measure of governing by a party, which has, unfortunately, attended the frequency of Parliaments, (a thing, in itself, most desirable) seems to have been the occasion, that opposition has, too frequently, changed its views, from the redress of grievances, (its ancient, and only justifiable object) to a pursuit of private preferment, or private resentment. Let us take them separately, and see, if a Prince of Wales can appear at the head of either, consistent with his true greatness.

And first, let us consider an opposition carried on for the private preferment of the opposers.—Can a Prince of Wales be preferred?—He must be King; and as he can be nothing else, can such an opposition make him so, one hour before his time? Or if it could, would he not reject it with horror and indignation?

Let us, next, form to ourselves an opposition founded upon resentment; a resolution to pull down, possibly to punish, those that have offended us, without considering consequences.

Will a Prince of Wales appear to act publicly, from resentment, and passion only? And that too, under the disadvantage of appearing to do it, peevishly, personally, ineffectually; when he must, one day, have it in his power to do it, nobly, nationally, and effectually?

Having shewn that the ends, to which oppositions have been, usually, directed, are inconsistent with the interest, and true glory of a Prince of Wales, in your present situation; let us examine, if the methods of opposition, employed to attain those ends, are better calculated for your Royal Highness's great purposes.

In the first case, then, that I have stated, which is that of an opposition founded on self-interest, only: the methods, in short, are a steady and unvariable attention to propose every thing that is specious, but impracticable, or unseasonable: to depreciate and lessen every thing that is blameless, and to exaggerate and inflame every

16

thing that is blameable; in order to make the people desire, and the Crown consent, to the dismission of those in power, and place, to make room for the leaders, and followers of the opposition. But a Prince of your elevation, Sir, cannot act as the head of any Administration; 'tis descending too low: nor can your followers act under any, without ceasing to be so. I humbly think, it is not your interest to drive them from you; and I am sure, it is not theirs, to quit the certain favour of a King, whom they will have contributed to make a great King, for the uncertain, ill-will'd, precarious emoluments, which they may snatch, in the scramble of a new Administration, forced upon the Crown.

The methods of carrying on the second sort of opposition I have mentioned, in which, resentment is the chief motive and ingredient, admit of a very short discussion: they are much the same with the other, only heightened, and inflamed. Proposing things, not only unseasonable, but dangerous, and subversive of government itself: opposing right, and wrong, with equal vehemence: and endeavouring to overturn the whole system, rather than not reach those, who have the supreme direction of it. I presume, you, Sir, who are, by Providence, called to govern, will not contribute to make all government impracticable, or sacrifice to resentment and passion, the welfare and prosperity of the people, in which, your own interest and glory is inseparably implicated, and involved: nor will those, who hope to govern under you, find their account in such a method of opposition.

Be pleased, Sir, to let us make a little stand, here, to see what we have proved; and to consider, what consequences, necessarily, follow from the things proved, that ought to influence your present, and future conduct.

It is proved, I hope beyond all possibility of doubt, that the oppositions we have seen carried on, in this country, hitherto, are neither becoming your Royal Highness, in your present situation, nor advantageous to your followers: that such an opposition never can, either by its means or its ends, establish that point, which, alone, ought to influence the public actions of a Prince: of a Prince like you, Sir, who want only to be seen, as you really are, not as you are misrepresented, (to which misrepresentations, the opposition has, unavoidably, furnished some foundation and pretext) to become the sole object of mankind's expectation, for the redress of all the grievances they feel, and the dispensation of all the future benefits they hope for.

Admitting, then, all this to be proved, what follows from it? Are we to infer, that the opposition, which your Royal Highness countenanced and protected, was improperly and injudiciously entered into, and consequently, that there ought to be no opposition at all?

Are one, or both of these points, the doctrine you would establish?—
Neither the one nor the other.

I am ready to own, that, considering the humiliating situation prepared for your Royal Highness, at your first coming to Britain,
perhaps you had no means of procuring yourself a proper independency, but by having recourse to the unprincely weapon of opposition.
I will, also, willingly admit, that such an independence was necessary
to establish the dignity, and greatness of your representation, and
to shew you, in the proper light of a mediator between the King and
the people: one, from whom they are to hope, and expect every
benefit they wanted, either by your intercession with, or succession
to sovereign power.

But as these concessions are true, and justify your conduct towards
the attainment of that necessary independence, your Royal Highness
must, on the other side, own, that your being obliged to pursue it,
by those means, has forced you to submit to many things, painful to
you, in the execution: improper audiences and applications, con-
descensions and familiarities, that, I humbly apprehend, you feared,
and felt, must lessen that greatness, and public significance, which,
by the independence then struggled for, you were labouring to
advance, and establish.

Your Royal Highness must also allow, that, as this pursuit carried
in its face the full likeness of a private, pecuniary establishment; the
bulk of mankind, not being taught to see it as the foundation of that
independence necessary to make you their advocate, or their defender,
in case they should be aggrieved; the bulk of mankind, I say, not
being taught to see, or rather being taught not to see it in that light,
judged of it in gross, and, as it carried private interest in the face,
concluded (since you went into Court[1] upon gaining your point),
that the private interest was interwoven with the whole, and composed the constituent and essential parts of your intention, and
design.

So that the unavoidable consequences of this method of opposition
became a drawback upon itself, and, in some degree, defeated its own
success. For, though the necessary independency was established,
there was still something wanting, to stamp, and impress upon the
minds of the people, that exalted opinion, that fervent, affectionate
confidence and expectation, which the benevolence of your heart,
and the force and extent of your natural genius (much embellished
and improved) exact from all those, who have the happiness to see
your Royal Highness, in a near and natural light: to find, and to fix
this something, so as it may produce to my country, the full blessings

[1] Used his influence to support Walpole in 1741, to the disappointment of the
Opposition.

18

of your most gracious intentions, and beneficent resolutions, is, under Heaven, the whole object of all my care, pains, ambition, and reward. —Nor do I despair of success.

For I cannot believe, now the end is attained, that your Royal Highness will continue upon yourself those inconveniences, which it might be necessary to submit to, in order to attain it; we, indeed, your servants, by going on in the same eager method, and throwing your great name, and august patronage before us, might gratify our resentments, and possibly, our interests, by forcing ourselves into place under the Ministry. I say possibly might, but I verily believe, that there is not one of us, that harbours so mean a thought; and if anyone differs in opinion with me, upon these great points, I humbly hope your Royal Highness will be persuaded (as I am from the conviction of my conscience), that it proceeds from a different conception of things, only, but from a heart as affectionate and zealous as my own, for your Royal Highness's true interest and glory. But I, still, return to this point, that I do not imagine, that a Prince of your prudence and discernment will continue a pursuit, that cannot, in all human probability, be attended with success: and if it was, could be employed to no desirable end, that falls within the compass of my poor comprehension.

The pursuit I mean, is a majority in Parliament, which I hold, morally impossible to gain; and if it could be gained, I am entirely at a loss to guess, what advantageous use to your Royal Highness could be made of it; on the contrary, I think it the thing, of all others, the least to be wished. For, if we were a sufficient majority to drive out the present Ministry, your Royal Highness would not, I presume, have us take their places; that were to drive us from you, indeed; for, in the present unhappy disposition of the Royal Family, you well know, that to keep the places into which we had intruded, we must act like our predecessors, very dishonourably and disgracefully to ourselves, indeed, but certainly, very offensively to your Royal Highness. Besides, if we were that majority, with all the emoluments and temptations full within reach, and in our power, is your Royal Highness very sure you could stop us, all, and hinder us from rushing in to the plunder?

This great something, then, that is wanting, this necessary point of light, which is not to be found in the present methods, or ends of opposition, must be fixed and ascertained, in order to proportion, and adapt the means to the measure.

Now, according to my understanding, this great and necessary point is, to fix in the minds of mankind, by the dignity, and steadiness of your own behaviour, a strong prepossession of your warm, and beneficent intentions for the welfare of this country, without private view, or resentment: and by such a choice of those, to whom you delegate the principal direction of your affairs, as may create a full confidence, that you are not only thoroughly determined, but also, properly prepared, to carry those intentions into full execution, when you are vested with power to do it.

And now, Sir, I, whom your Royal Highness may, hitherto, have thought an enemy to all opposition, become an humble advocate, in my turn, for an opposition; such an one, as may be productive of this noble purpose, suitable to the greatness of your name, your reputation, and most princely accomplishments: an opposition strongly marked with the public good, where your private views all plainly centre in the public welfare; and those of your followers, are openly, and declaredly, confined to the honour of, one day, carrying your great designs into execution; till that time, to ask for nothing, to accept nothing, but devote themselves to watch over the public, and prevent, as far as they can, any farther encroachments being made upon it, till, by becoming the glorious instruments of your gracious intentions, they can redress all the grievances they have not been able to prevent.

The noble simplicity of this opposition, supported with suitable gravity, steadiness, and dignity, without doors, will awake, and fix the attention of mankind on your Royal Highness, as their proper object of defence, and expectation. And even those personal points, which, though most justly grounded, and ably supported, would now be attempted ineffectually, as the movements of resentment only, and in a sanction, instead of a censure: the prosecution of those very points will, when your power to punish, as well as reward, is equal to your will, be called for by the people, as national justice, and public satisfaction.

To the standard of an opposition thus strongly marked, and characterized with the public good, and the public good only; thus cleared from every cloud, and stain of private interest, and resentment, the honest, the brave, and the impartial, will gather, by degrees, and no slow ones, to increase the dignity, as well as numbers, of your Royal Highness's party. But while they see, or think they see, the least appearance of trifling with the public; or, indeed, till they see the contrary: in my humble opinion, the prospect is so full of misfortune, that I choose to hide it from your Royal Highness, and wish I could hide it from myself.

All which is humbly submitted to your Royal Highness's superior discernment and direction.

G.D.

14. Saturday. Came to Kew at two. Walk'd with the Princess alone, till four. Din'd and supp'd there. Lords Inchiquin and Bute, Ladies Middlesex and Howe, Mr. Breton, and I.

15. Sunday. At Leicester House. The Grenvilles presented for the title of Temple. Supp'd at Carlton House. T.R.H., Ladies Middlesex, Howe, Madame de Mirepoix, Lords Bute and North.

16. Monday. Lord Bute, Mr. Breton, and I set out, about one, for Cliefden; follow'd by T.R.H., Ladies Middlesex and Howe. Lords Inchiquin and Bathurst met us. The Princess talk'd to me, about Lord North for a Governor to Prince George, which I approv'd of.— *Mourning Bride—Arlequin Hulla.*

17. Tuesday. *Tartuffe—Arlequin Sauvage.*

18. Wednesday. Prince shot. We walk'd with the Princess.— *Aurenge Zebe.*

19. Thursday.—*Macbeth.*

20. Friday. We all went to Woborn Fair—Prince George in our Coach.—*Ines de Castro.*

21. Saturday. I was with Prince George.

22. Sunday. Lord Bathurst went to London.—The Princess talk'd much to me, about the Earl of Granville.

23. Monday. Prince George came to me. Lord Bathurst return'd.— *Macbeth.*

24. Tuesday. *Le Distrait Patelin.*

25. Wednesday. *Henry IV.*

26. Thursday. *Les Jolies Amoureuses.—Arlequin poli par l'Amour.*

27. Friday. *Le Grondeur—Les Facheux—Procession des Medecins.*

21

28. Saturday. We left Cliefden. Din'd and supp'd at Kew, and left the Royal children there. We came to town, about one. T.R.H., Ladies Middlesex and Howe,[1] Lord Bute, Mr Breton, and I.

29. Sunday. At Leicester House. Messrs Masham, Bance, and Breton din'd here.

30. Monday. King's Birthday kept. I was at St James's—then at Carlton House—went to dine with Sir Samuel Penant, Lord Mayor, by the Prince's Command. Nobody at the feast, between the Lord Chancellor and me.[2]

31. Tuesday. Their Highnesses went to *The Double Dealer* at Covent Garden. I was there.

[1] Lady Howe, widow of the 2nd Viscount Howe (born 1695), daughter of George I's mistress Charlotte Sophia von Kielmansegge, Countess of Darlington. Some suppose the King was her father. She had a large pension from the King and was a lady-in-waiting to the Princess of Wales. As a piece of court furniture she lived into extreme old age, dying in 1782.

[2] i.e. D.'s position as the Prince's chief adviser was formally recognized by the City.

NOVEMBER

1. Wednesday. Went to Hammersmith after dinner.

2. Thursday. Sent for to be at Carlton House at six. Went to the Academy of Ancient Music, thence to the wax work, thence back to supper. T.R.H., Lady Middlesex, Madame de Munchausen, Mr Breton and I, in Lord Middlesex and my coach.

3. Friday. I went to the Exchequer to settle the sheriffs.[1]

4. Saturday. Din'd and supp'd at Kew. The Prince read me an answer to my memorial written with his own hand. The difference in opinion between us is not considerable. The piece is most astonishingly well-drawn.

5. Sunday. At Leicester House. Lord and Lady Middlesex, Miss Jefferies and Mr Breton din'd here.

6. Monday. Lord Bute, Mr Breton, and I set out from Carlton House, and arriv'd at Cliefden in three hours and twenty minutes. Met by the Earl of Inchiquin, Lord Bathurst, and Mr Masham. Follow'd by T.R.H., Ladies Middlesex and Howe. *The Distrait Mother—Le Fat Puni.*

7. Tuesday. *Les Femmes Savantes—Les Precieuses Ridicules.*

8. Wednesday. *The Recruiting Officer.*

9. Thursday. *Nicomède—Les Plaideurs.*

10. Friday. *L'Irresolu—La Sérénade.*

11. Saturday. Their Highnesses came to town with Lady Middlesex, and Lady Howe, Lord Bute, Lord Inchiquin, Lord Bathurst, Mr Masham, Mr Breton, and I. We supp'd at Carlton House.

12. Sunday. I din'd at Carlton House. The company only the Prince, the Earl of Egmont, and Dr Lee. The business, the immediate steps to be taken, upon the demise of the King; more particularly with regard to the Civil List. H.R.H. said he had had three

---

[1] For Cornwall, as the Prince's official representative.

methods propos'd to him: the first was to let the present Ministry settle it; and then part with them, and the Parliament; the second was to dismiss four, or five of the principal ones, but to vote the Civil List before the Parliament was dissolved; the third (which he was pleas'd to say thought was my opinion) was to dismiss the Parliament immediately, to turn all those out that he did not design to continue, and to throw himself upon the country, for a new Parliament and a provision for himself and Family, which he desir'd should be only a clear annuity of £800,000 per annum, giving back the duties to the publick, with whatever surplus might attend it.[1] The first proposition H.R.H. put out of the question; the second and third he desir'd he might be fully satisfied upon, from a full consideration; because what was there determin'd, he would unalterably stand by, when communicated, and agreed to by the Earl of Carlisle, Lord Baltimore, and Lord Chief Justice Willes. It was discussed, and we were all, at last, of opinion, that the third proposition was the greatest, most popular, and best. H.R.H. came heartily into it, gave us his hand, and made us take hands with each other, to stand by, and support it:—I undertook to find two or three hundred thousand to go on with, till a new Parliament cou'd grant the Civil List.

13. Monday. I kiss'd the Duke's[2] hand. Saw the Earl of Carlisle. He was for the second proposition. Was for keeping the Prince's destination of employments secret, because he was unwilling the Pelhams should know they were desperate with him. Did not see how the House of Lords cou'd be carried on without the Earl of Granville.[3] Sir P. Methuen for the third proposition.

14. Tuesday. Lord Middlesex and Mr Ralph came in the evening. Much talk about bringing the Prince's affairs to some regulation.

[1] Under George II the Civil List, which bore the entire civil expenditure of the central government (not merely the King's personal expenditure) was £700,000 a year for life. It consisted, as in previous reigns, of the hereditary revenues (surrendered to Parliament and revoted) plus certain ear-marked excise duties. Parliament was supposed to make good any deficiency, and the King was entitled to retain any surplus. In practice there was rarely a surplus, and Parliament met deficiencies sporadically and with reluctance. The change in the system here proposed by D. was in fact adopted eleven years later, on the accession of George III, and, as D. had envisaged, it notably strengthened the King's position.

[2] Cumberland.

[3] Carlisle (he controlled two seats—for Morpeth) was making difficulties. He was trying to keep in with both Government and Opposition, his aim being the Garter (attained 1756).

15. Wednesday. Din'd at Carlton House. The Prince, Earls of Carlisle and Egmont, Lord Chief Justice Willes, Lord Baltimore, Sir John Rushout, Messrs Gibbon, Lee, Henley, Nugent, Sir Thomas Bootle, and I. Agreed not to oppose the Address unless there was something very strong in it.[1]

16. Thursday. The Session of Parliament open'd with a very modest Speech. The Address mov'd, and seconded by Mr Charles Townshend, and Sir Danvers Osborne. I thought a very unexceptionable one, and I did not oppose it: Sir John Hynde Cotton did;[2] upon the Peace not being compleat, as is there said. The Earl of Egmont then made a violent, and very injudicious speech against the Address, throwing out every thing he could think, or had heard of, against the Ministry. Lord Baltimore said but little on the same side, and so the matter dropp'd and the Address was voted. I went to the Prince, before I din'd, to give him an account of what had pass'd. He did not seem to make much account of it, one way, or another.

17. Friday. Lady Mary Coke, appear'd at the King's Bench, obtained leave for lawyers, all her relations, and the Earl of Pembroke, to come to her.[3]

Lord Middlesex and Mr Furnese came to me in the evening. Much serious conversation about the behavior, in and out of Parliament, of the Prince's family, and our situation in it. Agreed that it must be altered, or that I could be of no use there, and consequently could not stay. Earl of Middlesex undertook to talk to the Prince about it.

I was presented to the Princess Amelia and kiss'd her hand.

18. Saturday. Din'd with Mr Furnese, Lord Cornbury, Earl of Stafford, and Mr Rollinson. Sent Mr Phillip's letter about the

---

[1] Virtually a meeting of the Prince's 'shadow cabinet' or 'Great Meeting' as it is later formally called (24 Nov. 1749, below). Egmont's subsequent disregard for this formal decision naturally galled the systematic D.

[2] Charles Townshend was making his parliamentary début as a junior minister (Lord of Trade). Cotton was spokesman of the country gentlemen tinged with Jacobitism, with whom D. naturally did not wish to be identified. The distinction between the Prince's followers and Cotton's is clearly drawn below (24 Nov. 1749).

[3] Edward, Viscount Coke, son of the Earl of Leicester, had married a very difficult wife, Mary, the albino daughter of D.'s friend the 2nd Duke of Argyll. She was known as the 'white cat' and her husband kept her virtually a prisoner, until she was produced on a habeas corpus.

Westminster election to the Prince.[1] The Commons presented their Address.

19. Sunday. The Princess's [of Wales] Birthday, but not kept till Wednesday, because Queen Caroline died on the 20th.[2] Din'd at home, Mr Bance only. The Prince order'd me to signify that he wou'd not meddle with the Westminster election.

20. Monday. Din'd at home—Mr Carey. Mr Bodens inform'd me that Mr Douglass, at Lord Robert Bertie's, said that I solicited to come into the Prince's Family, agreeing not to be at the head;—Dr Lee was at the head.

22. Wednesday. The Princess's Birthday was kept. Din'd with me, the following public ministers: Marquis de Mirepoix, Comte de Haslang, Mons. Le General Comte de Lucchesi, Mons. le General Wall, Mons. le Comte de Fleming, Mons. le Comte du Perron, Mons. l'Abbé de Grossa Testa. Messrs. les Chevaliers de Levy, de Laurency, de Tessier. Mons. d'Andrada, Mons. d'Abrieu, Mons. Le Comte d'Einsidell, Mons. le Baron Kreygell, Mons. de Fiorent, Lord Tyrawley, Mr Breton.

22. Tuesday.[3] I went to Lord Middlesex, who had been with me in the morning to tell me that the Prince had sent for him on Sunday, that His Highness seemed much heated having heard from Lord Baltimore that I was in a great Passion at what had pass'd in Parliament last Thursday, and had declar'd that I would have voted against them, if they had divided, upon the Address.—ask'd if such behavior was not intolerable. Lord Middlesex assur'd him that I had talk'd it over with him, in the House, with great calmness, and without the least passion; that Lord Baltimore join'd us, for a very little while, and seem'd to be of our opinion; that he (Lord M) as well as I, thought the Address should have gone without opposition, and that Lord Egmont's speech was very injudicious &c. But the Prince seem'd of the contrary opinion, and the con-

---

[1] Lord Trentham (son of Earl Gower) was defending this seat on appointment as a Lord of the Admiralty. The opposition nominee, Sir George Vandeput, was backed by the caucus 'Independent Electors of Westminster' with which D. had been connected at least since 1744 (see Grego, *Parliamentary Elections*, 107). Mr Phillip may be a connexion of Sir John Phillips, 6th Bt., who was also connected with this caucus, as was George Cooke (see below, 1 Dec. 1749).

[2] Twelve years previously.

[3] The disorder of these entries indicates that D. had departed from his usual practice of writing his journal up daily. Where he did this, the marginal date shows the date the entry was made.

versation ended with directing Lord Middlesex to quiet me) in the evening; and we had much talk. Both he and she [*presumably Lady Middlesex*] were of an opinion that a Party was made against me in the Family, and that it was best to come to an explanation with the Prince.

I supp'd with Their Highnesses at Carlton House. Lords Bute and Inchiquin, Ladies Middlesex and Howe.

23. Thursday. Was to wait upon the Prince who appointed me Friday at twelve o'clock.

Went to Council. Present the King, Dukes of Richmond, Grafton, Bedford, Newcastle, Earls of Pembroke and Halifax, Mr Legge, Sir John Ligonier. 10,000 seamen voted. Earls of Halifax and Broke sworn as Lords Lieutenants of Northamptonshire and Warwickshire. General Huske took the oath as Governor of Jersey. Prize Cause at the Cockpit.

24. Friday. Earl of Middlesex and Mr Ralph were with me to acquaint me that the printer and publisher of *The Remembrancer* was taken up for his paper of last Saturday the 18th inst.[1] But that the Messenger us'd them with uncommon civility, touch'd nothing of their papers, presses or effects and took their words for their surrendering themselves the next morning; my Lord had been with the Prince, who agreed to indemnify them as to the expense: but was very averse that anything should be done to make him at all appear in it: which made them very uneasy.

At half an hour after twelve I went to Carlton House and in a quarter of an hour was call'd in. Sir Tho: Bootle was with the Prince. H.H. took me into a window, told me that he had sent Middlesex to me about the seizing of the printer, and what was to be done?— and then without giving me time to answer, he ran out into reasons why nobody that belong'd to him must appear—I gently let him see that I thought otherwise and insinuated whether, if Mr Ralph should be taken up, it would not be proper that Lord Middlesex and I should bail him. He said, by no means—and therefore Ralph should be spoke to, that he should keep out of the way &c. At last he order'd that he should go to my house at Hammersmith: with which I agreed; thinking that the strongest mark of his protection that we cou'd desire.

[1] This number contained a highly ironical attack on the Pelhams for corruption and manipulating the King, and on Cumberland for his brutal administration of the army.

After much talk about this and some idle accounts about the poll at Covent Garden, he made me set by him, and ran into a long discourse about the Army, and then about the reduction of interest[1] and so let himself into a discourse about the necessity of saying something upon those things in Parliament, to feel pulse, and keep the Party together &c, all which was design'd as an apology (instead of finding fault) to me, for what had pass'd the first day of the Session. I took it up, upon his mentioning talk, and throwing things out to expose &c, and said that I supposed talk might be all right, but people should consider what talk and if they had anything to say. That perpetually throwing out things which one neither understood, nor cou'd prove was, I thought, and always should think, exposing one's self, and not the person aim'd at.— That 'twas for his service, to put little things into his power, to verify beyond contradiction, that he might certainly know what dependence was to be had upon those it came from, when they inform'd him of greater matters. Therefore I would furnish him with one instance. He had heard I was in a great passion about the Earl of Egmont's behavior upon the Address: luckily for me I had never spoken to any body about it but two persons, favourite servants of H.R.H. and particular friends of mine, Lords Middlesex and Baltimore, who join'd us as we were talking of it very calmly; he seem'd to be of our opinion and said he had told Cotton we should not divide with them: I knew that Lord Middlesex had told him how it pass'd, and if he would give me leave to bring Lord Baltimore to him he would tell him that there was not the least heat amongst any of us all. (I knew Baltimore was the author of this dirty piece of cunning). That by this, if he pleas'd, he might see what credit was to be given, for the future, to those who brought him this piece of intelligence. He thank'd me and was very gracious, and talk'd it off, as well as he could, but in the multiplicity of discourse own'd to me that Baltimore had told him, but meant no harm &c.—I told him I had never seen business done in a meeting of a dozen like that on the 15th, day before the Session; that these meetings were always declaratory, though in the shape of deliberation. That the first concoction was always between the Prince and three or four persons at most; that I hop'd to have laid my poor opinions before him in that manner with two or three

---

[1] On the National Debt, for which the Pelham government were making proposals. See below, 28 Nov. 1749.

only, that I hop'd to have found a friend there, especially Lord Middlesex; who, I thought, upon all accounts ought to be in the first digestion: that then we should properly lay our joint thoughts before H.R.H. or, if we differ'd, could reason it out with one another, and he might judge which side to adhere to. But to combat the opinions he adopted, with him separately, was impossible. We could not, or ought not, to dispute with him as we did with one another.

He was a good deal stagger'd at what I said about Lord Middle-sex, and said he ought, no doubt, to be of the Great Meeting: I said of both sure, and added something much in his favour.[1] I then told him, that I found very little disposition to friendship and cordiality with me, in those whom he seem'd principally to confide in &c. He said I must not wonder that there was a little shyness at first, there were so many stories, &c. I replied that I hop'd he did not think I mentioned it by way of complaint, for if it were not with relation to his service, I should never think of desiring the favour and coun-tenance of any one, or all of those gentlemen, as any sort of addition to me; that as he thought it for his service, I already had, though fruitlessly, and would continue to do everything, and go all the way to obtain their good will: that I beg'd he would observe that in consequence of his service, and commands, I would, cheerfully, do this, but separate from his service and commands, it never could have enter'd into my imagination to have made court to those gentlemen, because I never could think nor did I believe anybody else would, that those gentlemen, anywhere, or at any time, could do me any honour by admitting me among them. He then said, that to be sure I was in a situation and upon a foot that I ought not to make court to any man in England, nobody could expect it from me.

Having extorted this expression from him as a mark to remember this part of the conversation by, I left it there.

This is a short recapitulation of a conversation of full two hours: it contains almost every word I said: H.R.H. talk'd all the rest of the time.

Lord Middlesex came after dinner. Messrs Ralph and Furnese din'd with me.

I communicated the whole to them. Lord Middlesex was much

[1] Probably a sarcastic reference to Middlesex's complacency about the open liaison between the Prince and Lady Middlesex.

pleas'd with it: and thinks all will go well in time. I do not, and think there is no prospect of doing any good.

The printer and publisher were set free without bail: only giving their words to appear if sent for, by a Secretary of State.—I sent the Prince word of it, and set out for Hammersmith at half an hour past nine at night.

10,000 seamen voted.

25. Saturday. At Hammersmith——Took physic.

26. Sunday. Mr Stanley came and return'd in the morning. Mr Tucker din'd here.

27. Monday. I went to London: poll'd for Sir George Vandeput, met with a great crowd, but great civility.—Return'd before five.

28. Tuesday. Proposition in Parliament to reduce all the four per cents to three and a half per cent for seven years certain, and then to three per cent redeemable, as before, continuing them for one year: (which they were some of them intitled, for notice) at four per cent.—A debate, and different propositions to me unintelligible, I am sure injudicious, by the Earl of Egmont and others.—Supp'd at Mr Furnese's with the Earl of Stafford, and Mr Ralph.

29. Wednesday. Debate upon the Army. We propos'd but 15,000 men. Din'd with me, Earls of Middlesex and Inchiquin, Lord Baltimore, Mr Furnese, Sir Edward Thomas, and Mr Henley.

30. Thursday. Met the Prince at Lord Middlesex's.—Army estimates reported. Din'd here Messrs Wyndham, Ralph, Probyn, and Thompson.—Went to Council.—Supp'd at Carlton House, T.R.H., Lady Middlesex, and I only.

DECEMBER

1. Friday. We din'd alone.—Mr Cooke came to know of me what assistance from the Prince might be rely'd upon, toward carrying the Westminster election to a scrutiny.[1] I promis'd to lay it before H.R.H.—Supp'd at Mr Furnese's.

2. Saturday. Din'd with Mr Art: Hill, Mr Macartney, and two daughters, Lord and Lady Barrington.—Mr Cooke came. I introduced him to the Prince, who assur'd him the election should be supported.—Supp'd at Carlton House. Lady Middlesex, Lord Bute, and I.

3. Sunday. Din'd alone. Went to Court.

4. Monday. Land Tax 3s in the pound; voted in the Committee.—Much babling—din'd here. Lord Middlesex, Sir Francis Dashwood, Messrs Furnese, Ralph, and Dr Sharpe.[2]

5. Tuesday. Dr Sharpe brought me a map, and a written account of the importance of Nova Scotia. Lord Middlesex, Messrs Ralph, Furnese, and the Doctor came in the evening to consider about bringing a question into Parliament, to defeat any claim, which (as it is reported) the French have made to it. Nothing determined.——

   Supp'd at Carlton House. Ladies Middlesex and Howe, Lords Inchiquin and Bute, and I.

6. Wednesday. At Leicester House, and the Duke of Argyll's. Din'd alone.

7. Thursday. Din'd with us, Lord and Lady Middlesex, Lady Shannon, Lady Charles Edwin, Miss Dyers, Mr Edwin, Colonel Powlett, Mr Trevanion.—Cockpit, on Prizes.—

8. Friday. Receiv'd a letter from Mr Edward Walpole about the Prince's consent to his purchasing a Crown lease in Lancashire.[3]

---

[1] Trentham had won.

[2] Rev. Gregory Sharpe, rector of Birling and brother of William Sharpe. See 8 Sept. 1749 above.

[3] Like any other landed proprietor the King sought his heir's agreement to any transaction affecting the family property. D. is here seen discharging routine duties for the Prince—a demonstration that his appointment was not merely titular. Edward Walpole (Horace's younger brother) was the coiner of the joke in 1741 about D. having gained in weight what he had lost in consequence. (*Toynbee*, i. 154.)

I laid it before H.R.H. and receiv'd his commands.—Westminster poll clos'd.—Scrutiny granted.—to begin the 26th inst.

9. Saturday. I went to Mr [Edward] Walpole, and told him from the Prince, that H.R.H. had great good will for him personally, no objection to his conduct, thought him a good servant of the King's and doubted not, but that he would serve him, as well, when he was King. That as to the thing, H.R.H. disliked the precedent, but besides that he had measures to keep, and might subject himself to the suspicion of having underhand dealings with the Court, by too early compliance with requests of this nature, which was nothing less than giving away, by Act of Parliament, so much of his inheritance.—That therefore, he desir'd a little time, and Mr Walpole should have his final answer before the term for bringing in Private Bills expir'd which is the 18th January.

Mr Walpole confess'd the fact to be as the Prince has stated it, and assur'd me that he had no thoughts of attempting it if H.R.H. refus'd his consent: that Mr Pelham was against it on that account, but importun'd by him declar'd that he could not refuse his father's son, but never would be for another of the same sort, and should move the King in this with much reluctance. This Mr Walpole desir'd I would acquaint the Prince with.

Din'd at Hammersmith.

10. Sunday. Earl of Stafford, Mr Furnese, and Mr Bance din'd with us.

11. Monday. Came to town, saw M.R. [*Master of the Rolls, Sir John Strange, M.P. Totnes*] who still advis'd temporising.

Din'd at the French Ambassador's.

12. Tuesday. Four inspectors of the books of each parish were nam'd at the Sun Tavern Westminster on the part of Sir George Vandeput. Supp'd at Carlton House: Ladies Middlesex and Howe, Lord Bute.

13. Wednesday. Went to Leicester House. Deliver'd Mr Edward Walpole's answer to the Prince, who seem'd in a disposition to grant his consent in proper time.

Messrs Tynte, Roberts,[1] and Tucker din'd with us.

---

[1] John Roberts, Pelham's confidential secretary. Presumably election business at Weymouth and Bridgwater was the subject of discussion.

14. Thursday. Din'd with us, Mrs Drax, Mrs Montagu, Miss Chudleigh, Miss Mostyn, Mrs Clavering, Miss Drax, Mr Drax, Mr Montagu, Mr Elliot, Count Einsidell, Mr Berkeley.[1]—Supp'd at Carlton House, Ladies Middlesex and Howe, General Comte Lucchesi, Lords Baltimore and Tyrawley.

15. Friday. Went to Hammersmith.

16. Saturday. Return'd to town.

17. Sunday. At Leicester House.—At eight o'clock undress'd by order waited upon T.R.H. at Carlton House where came Lords Inchiquin, and Bathurst, and Lady Middlesex, in whose landau, we six, Her R.H. and Lady M., H.R.H. and we three gentlemen went to Mrs Glass's in Tavistock Street, a maker of habits, where we staid till near twelve, and then we hurried in the same manner to Carlton House, where we met Lady Howe and Lord Bute, and supp'd.

18. Monday. Mr Carey din'd with us. Messrs Furnese and Ralph, and Lord Talbot, came in the afternoon. Much talk about the report carried to the Prince that Carey saw the Duke privately: suppos'd to come from Ranby the chirurgeon. Agreed that it must be brought to a full eclaircissement.[2]

19. Tuesday. Din'd with us Lord Southwell, Messrs Macartney, Hill, and G. Hamilton, Mrs Hill, two Misses Macartney, and Mrs Beaghan.

Supp'd with Her R.H., Ladies Middlesex and Howe, and Lord Bute, at Carlton House.

20. Wednesday. Din'd alone. At Leicester House, in the morning. The Parliament adjourned to the ninth January.

21. Thursday. Din'd with us Mrs Henley, Ladies Susan and

[1] A brilliant gathering. Mrs Montagu (later the 'Queen of the blues') was 29. So was the beautiful but stupid Elizabeth Chudleigh (already secretly married to Augustus John Hervey) who was carrying on a flirtation with the King. She and Mary Bridget Mostyn were maids of honour to the Princess of Wales. Miss Drax is probably Susanna, who later married the sixth Earl of Castlehaven (see above, 28 Aug. 1749).

[2] Betrayal. 'The Duke' here is not Cumberland (as surmised by the editor of 1784) but Newcastle, with whom D. was maintaining contact through Carey. The source of this report that the Prince had become aware of his adviser's private contact with the other side is John Ranby, F.R.S., Serjeant Surgeon to the King.

Rebecca Poulet, Mrs Prowse, and Miss Walkingshaw.[1] Messrs
Vere and Anne Poulet,[2] Mr Henley, and Mr Prowse.

Supp'd with H.R.H., Lady Charlotte Edwin, Lady Middlesex
and I only.

22. Friday. Din'd at Mr Stanley's.

23. Saturday. We went to Hammersmith and return'd to dinner
alone.

24. Sunday. At Leicester House. Heard that the Earl of Crawford
died, that morning. Din'd with us, Messrs Rollinson, Bance, and
Tucker.

25. Monday. Din'd with me French Ambassadour, Comtes de
Haslang, Fleming, and du Perron, Chevalier de Levy, Lords Bute
and Tyrawley.—At Leicester House.

26. Tuesday. Went to Kew. T.R.H., Ladies Middlesex and Howe,
Lord Bute, Inchiquin and Bathurst, Messrs Masham, Breton, and
I.—*Lady Jane Grey, Le Mariage Forcé.* Lady M. complain'd of the P.[3]

27. Wednesday. *Sertorius. Le Tuteur.*

28. Thursday. *The Recruiting Officer. Le Bal.* Mr Breton and I went
to Hammersmith, till dinner, Mr Bludworth came.—Lady Middlesex, and I staid together after the company, till half an hour past
two: upon the same subject.

29. Friday. *The Beaux Stratagem. Les Vendanges de Suresne.* Lady
Middlesex and I convers'd an hour upon the same subject after the
company went to bed. Mr Breton and I went to Hammersmith
till dinner.

30. Saturday. We all came to town, after supper. *Le Glorieux.*

31. Sunday. Supp'd at Carlton House. Ladies Middlesex and
Charlotte Edwin, Lord Tyrawley, Mr Breton, and I.—Din'd with
us, Earl Poulet, Messrs Bance, and Breton.

[1] Catherine, sister of Clementina Walkinshaw, mistress to the Young Pretender.
She was an attendant on the Princess of Wales.
[2] D. shared the representation of Bridgwater (for which he sat) with the Pouletts.
There were four brothers, John, 2nd Earl Poulet, the Lord Lieutenant of Somerset;
Peregrine, at this time D.'s colleague for Bridgwater; Vere; and Anne.
[3] He was ill-treating her. She was also pregnant. See 6 Feb. 1750 below.

1750

JANUARY

1. Monday. Waited on the Prince. Din'd, and lay at Hammersmith.

2. Tuesday. Messrs Vere Poulet, and Bastard[1] came over. Din'd alone.

3. Wednesday. At Leicester House. Receiv'd the Prince's commands to acquaint Mr Edward Walpole that he consented to his Bill about Garstang in Lancashire. Return'd to Hammersmith, and din'd alone.

4. Thursday. Din'd with us, Mr Lowe, and Parson Howel. I wrote to Mr Walpole pursuant to H.R.H.'s commands.

5. Friday. Messrs Furnese and Ralph din'd here. Considerations about the Mutiny Bill, and the Public Accounts.

6. Saturday. Din'd with us, Messrs Stanley and Tucker. Came to town at night.

7. Sunday. At Leicester Fields. Din'd at Lord Poulet's, with Messrs Breton, Mildmay, Johnson,[2] Williams, Ellison.
   Supp'd at Carlton House. Ladies Middlesex and Howe, Lords Bute and Baltimore.

8. Monday. Went to Ponders about the lapis lazuli pillars. Din'd at the Ladies Poulets, with Lady Bridget, Bastard, and Mr and Mrs Harris.

[1] William Bastard of Kitley, Devonshire, Earl Poulet's nephew. Later Bastards sat for Devonshire, and the family still flourishes.
[2] Not improbably Samuel Johnson, then launching *The Rambler*, which began 20 Mar. 1750. D. is known to have made contact with the author of *The Rambler* and to have invited him to dinner (Nichols, *Literary Anecdotes*, v. 38) and *Rambler*, 14, is said to be Johnson's repudiation of the connexion.

9. Tuesday. The Parliament met. Din'd with us, Messrs Tucker, Cheere,[1] and Dr Thompson.

10. Wednesday. Leicester House. Din'd alone. Earl of Pembroke died the 9th suddenly.

11. Thursday. Din'd at Mr Furnese's, with Messrs Ralph, Carey, and Dr Sharpe. Went to Leicester House to see *Jane Grey* acted by the Prince's children.

12. Friday. Went to Hammersmith. Thence to the House of Commons, no business. Din'd alone.

13. Saturday. Mr Breton din'd with us.

14. Sunday. Leicester House. Din'd with us, Messrs Furnese, Bance, Glover, and Carey. Supp'd at Carlton House, Ladies Middlesex and Howe, Lord Bute and I.

15. Monday. At the House. It was call'd. Mr Edward Walpole's petition read, and a bill order'd to be brought in. Din'd at Mr Pitt's.

16. Tuesday. At the House. In the Committee on the Mutiny Bill I opposed the filling up the clause that punishes mutiny, and desertion, with word Death, but was not supported.

The speech is among the Harvard MSS., noted by Dodington that 'it was heard with remarkable attention, but no one person either seconded or answered it'. The MS., he says, was written immediately after delivery, 'and therefore I am sure it was spoke in very near the same words'.

I had the misfortune not to be here, last year, when this Bill went through the Committee, and consequently to lose that share of improvement which I might have acquired, by the debates upon it. I am, therefore, likely to fall under the farther misfortune, either of having nobody of my opinion, about this clause; or to report, in a much worse manner, what was enforced, at that time, in a much better.

[1] Henry Cheere (1703–81) the sculptor. See also below, 26 Apr. 1750. He was working on D.'s villa at Hammersmith, and no doubt was concerned with the lapis lazuli pillars just mentioned, which were the wonder of the establishment. There were two of them, seventeen feet high, single stones, specially imported.

But I am, really not satisfied with the whole cast, and intendment of this Bill, in a state of public tranquillity, though I shall say nothing at present, but to the clause before you. My objection is, not to the strictness of the discipline, but to the severity of the punishment, in times of full peace. I am for discipline, and very strict discipline too; in peace, as well as war, but I think the punishment that enforces that discipline, should not, at all times, be equally severe, because the breach of it, is not at all times equally fatal.

You are now upon a consideration of as serious a nature, as any that can come before you: you are, now, proposing, and have filled the most material clause of a Bill for the consent of the House, that is to decide of the lives and liberties of a very respectable body of our fellow-subjects; and the more respectable, because, from that body, you expect the defence of your own, if they should be attacked, from at home, or abroad.

Upon such a subject, any stranger, anybody misinformed, would imagine, that your deliberations must turn, upon what peculiar privileges, what advantages superior to the rest of the community, you should impart to those, who, as you expect, should, more than the rest of the community, devote themselves to the defence of it. But, I fear, this Bill breathes quite another spirit. New crimes, severer punishments, and by more arbitrary and dangerous methods of trial: now, I mean, and unknown to the laws of this country, which, before these Bills broke in upon them, were thought sufficient to punish, and to protect, all denominations of its subjects, in time of peace.

I am not against a Bill of this import. I think we cannot be without one; and am heartily sorry for the necessity I acknowledge we are reduced to, of fostering, and adopting this principle of dissolution, which must, one day, end us.

But, it seems, this body of men are not capable of full liberty:— I am sorry for it, for full liberty is the essence, and spirit of our constitution.—But if that may not be, surely it is prudent to bring them as near to it, as is possible, and to put them as much under the coercion, and protection of the Civil Magistrate, as is consistent with their nature, that they may be a little used to love, and fear, the constitution, which they are either to defend or to destroy.—For they cannot be neutral.

As I see no reasonable prospect of getting free from this necessary evil, I do not deal in Chimaeras, to put an end to it, nor in commonplace, about the danger of it. I really think there is none, to ourselves. I have not the least apprehension of any ill use, likely to be made of it; even though it should pass as it is filled up (which it shall not, if I can help it), by the King, or his successor, and therefore, if I saw

37

any period to it, I should not make trouble myself about it. But though this Bill carries a short duration, in its face, and expires every year, yet 'tis like the fabled giant, contending with that Hercules who was the type of the patron of Liberty, every time it falls to the ground, it rises again, not only with new, but of late with greater force, and becomes more formidable to the constitution it is wrestling with, whenever it appears to be expiring.

If then that be the case, if we are in a time of full tranquillity, if our Princes are as far from desiring any exorbitant powers, as they are from exercising them, when thrust into their hands, necessity surely demands, and the times invite us to practice, that wise maxim, which I have somewhere read, of recurring to first principles of government, and from thence, as from an eminence, to take a survey, in what points we have departed from them, and consider if those deviations have tended to improve, or to impair, the constitution.

In order to apply this maxim to the present case, we must look back a little, and see how our armies were governed, formerly, in times of peace, and by what laws.—Now, by the little that I have been able to pick up, the first Bill of this sort, was passed, just after the Revolution:—the first Mutiny Bill, that ever made its way into a law, to punish Englishmen by Court Martial, within the Realm, was in 1689, occasioned by a sort of rebellion, or mutiny of some Scotch regiments: this was the first Bill of the sort, and before this Bill, there was no martial law for any Englishman, while within the Realm, even in time of foreign war; nor even in domestic commotions, *when peace was restored*; now in the sence of the fundamental constitutional law peace is understood to be restored, when the courts of justice are open, and their course unobstructed: which is a plain indication, that in the sence, and spirit of the constitution the laws of this country, while unrestrained by force, and in their free course, are sufficient to govern, to punish, and protect all their subjects, of what denomination soever. And what confirms me in this, is that there was no power of punishing the fault before us, of mutiny or desertion, within the Realm, even in time of war, by the ancient laws of the land: for they were obliged to pass an act, the 16th, I think, of Henry VI, to make it felony, but at the same time, to be enquired into, and determined, by the Justices of the Peace: and this, and the like Acts, continued down to Queen Elizabeth's time, which, if there had been power to punish by any military law, had been entirely useless, and derogatory to that power.

This Bill then, in 1689 was the first Mutiny Bill, or Bill that subjected Englishmen to Martial law, within the Realm, in time of Peace: but a modest one, compared to those that followed it. It was the beginning of a war, and indeed it punishes with death: but then it reaches none but listed soldiers, and officers in actual pay; it authorises a Court Martial, but then it must be held by a Colonel, and none can vote in it under the degree of a Captain: no Articles of War, no new crimes or punishments: nobody involved, but those listed, and in actual pay, no crime, but mutiny, and desertion.

While the war continued, this Bill continued, always increasing in strength, and encroaching upon the Civil Power, till the Peace of Ryswick; and then, unsettled as that Peace was, in everybody's opinion, and a body of troops kept up during its whole continuance, yet the Parliament would admit of no such Bill. No Mutiny Bill then was, for near three years, to the death of that great Prince; and yet I never read of any complaints for want of discipline, in that army.

The wars began with the Queen's reign; the Mutiny Bill revived, with more power, and extension, and continued to enact, (as this is proposed to do) Death to mutiny, and desertion, till the Peace of Utrecht.—Then, after a short interval, a Mutiny Bill did pass though not with the same powers; and this is the first Bill that ever did establish Martial Courts, and Martial Law in England, at a time of full peace, at home, and abroad.—But then the Preamble sets forth the claim of the constitution, and admits all the doctrine I have laid down, of the abhorrence it has, to all Military Law, in times of peace, and does not punish mutiny and desertion with loss of life, or limb—This was the last year of the Queen's life.

As soon as this Family came over, the Rebellion broke out, and a new Mutiny Bill passed, punishing it with death.—The next year, though the Rebellion was pretty well quelled, yet the Bill passed, with the same severe clause.—And the next, in full and settled peace, was proposed again. Then, there was a very great stand made against it, by a very solemn debate, and it was carried by but very few, I believe not above seven. I remember this thing very well, because it was the first vote I ever gave, in this House, and that, in the same way, I shall give it now. But what is most remarkable, I know not by what fatality, this great point, so strongly, so constitutionally founded, and, then, so ably supported, has never been thought of since, and these Bills have passed, with this sanguinary clause, for above twenty years, as things of course, and nobody has taken the least notice of them till last year, Gentlemen, to their very great honours and reputation, were pleased to look into them, greatly to the advantage of their fellow-subjects, and of their own character.

This detail, which I have gone through in as few words, and with as little parliamentary pedantry, as is possible, is the state of these Bills, and this, their continued progression. Is it not time, then, to apply the Great Maxim I have laid down, and try, at least, to bring this very important body, as near to the complexion, and as much within the power of the ancient laws of the constitution, as we can? And since this gentleman on the Table (the Bill), though he appears to be like a tenant at will, is like to turn out tenant for life, and we shall hardly, ever, be able to eject him, surely it is but reasonable to insert such clauses in his lease, as may make him have some little love and respect for the premises, and prevent him from making waste upon the estate, himself, or suffering others to do it, wantonly.

I am for discipline in an army; I told you so before; I am for punishing, and severely too, the breach of discipline: but I insist upon a proper difference in that punishment, in times of war, and in times of peace: I would bring it to law, and to reason, that is, I would bring it back within the river of Government.

Our Government is composed, I take it, of laws, founded upon reason.—If it is not composed of laws, or those laws are not founded on reason, such a Government is not worth defending. Now my reason tells me, that it is not the action, itself, simply considered, but the consequences of an action, that ought to be the measure of the penalty. It may be always my duty to do a thing, and the not doing it may be always punishable; and yet, at a time when the breach of that duty, neither is, nor can be, in any degree equally dangerous, to what is is, at another time, surely the punishment ought not to be equally severe. When it is war, and in the field, the trenches, or in garrison, I admit that a neglect of discipline so small as, even, sleeping upon his post, may be attended with the most fatal consequences: punish it, therefore, with death, in war, in the field, or in the trenches. I am ready to agree to it: but if five, or six ragamuffins should desert from a company, at Northampton: or two or three companies should mutiny, at Exeter, where is the terrible consequence of it?—Be pleased to consider—you must get them into your power, before you can try them at all—I know you will be so good as to reduce them, and get them into your hands, before you punish them even by this law. So the reducing to your obedience, is equally necessary, by whatsoever law they are tried, afterwards.—If then they have only mutinied, or deserted, does not this Bill leave punishments severe enough, though short of death, to deter them? Are there not left, ay, and exercised too, corporal punishments, that for my part, I should think severer than death itself?—And if in that mutiny (as it frequently happens) they should rob, plunder, or murder, or burn houses, is it not capital, by the laws of the land? Are they not sufficient to punish them? Will they not be hanged? Or are they such favourites of the people, as to be likely to meet with much favour?

Why then separate them from the community? Why deprive them of their birth-right, a trial by a jury, when there is no need of it? I know there will be no ill use made of this power, in the present times, we are safe, ourselves; this then, is our time, as 'tis always our duty, to take care of posterity, to guard and fence them who may be so un-happy as to live in times, to which this reign will be a reproach. You have no right to sport with the life of the meanest of your fellow-subjects, your duty is to defend him as warmly, carefully, as the highest. 'Tis not enough that the lowest amongst us does not com-plain, is not aggrieved. 'Tis your absolute duty to look back, from time to time, and see that he can't complain, that he can't be aggrieved, by suffering no innovation to grow, and encroach by little and little, upon his privileges and security, till they be lost.

Besides, you are doing the most impolitic thing imaginable, by giving an armed body of men separate hopes, and fears, distinct, and incompatible punishments with the known ones of their country, common, once, to themselves, with the rest of their countrymen. How soon will the ignorant place all their hopes, where you place all their fears? When they feel their officer's power of punishing, they will easily infer his power of defending them; and when they find that he can put them to death for disobeying, they will soon believe he can protect them, for obeying: the gradation is natural, and the passage very slippery; and then, where is the constitution?

I really, and sincerely, do not mean the least reflection upon any-body, not the least glance, in what I say, there is no room for it.— The Bill, I know, has been brought in, just as it, now, is these twenty years, the Clause always filled up, as the Honourable Gentleman, now, proposes to fill it, but I think it unnecessary in time of full peace. I know, no ill use will be made of it, by the King; but I appre-hend the precedent; 'tis wantonly sporting away the life, and liberty of your fellow-subjects; for we ought not to deceive ourselves. He that gives the power, gives the thing. He that gives the power of Liberty, gives Liberty, but you have no power, to give it away, which I think you do, if the Clause passes, with this amendement, which it must not do, with my consent.

17. Wednesday. At Leicester House. Lord Rothes presented for the Scotch Grays. At the House—long fribble about printing a Bill.[1] Din'd at Lord Southwell's.

18. Thursday. At the House. Another fribble about receiving a

---

[1] Baltimore and Nugent had pressed an obstructive procedural amendment to a measure governing the terms of discharge from the army, and were defeated (in the first division of the Session) by 192 votes to 99. D. despised such harassing tactics.

petition from the sailors of the *Frederic* privateer. Din'd alone. Supp'd at Carlton House—Ladies Middlesex and Howe, Lord Bute, Mr Breton.

19. Friday. Debate in the Committee upon the Mutiny Bill. Oath of Secrecy subjected to the requisition of the Courts of Justice.

20. Saturday. The Prince's Birthday. The same Ministers and Foreigners din'd here as on the Princess's Birthday.

21. Sunday. At Leicester House. Supp'd at Lord Middlesex's. Prince, the Princess, Lady Torrington, Countess of Inchiquin, Lord Bathurst, Mr Breton, Lady Shannon, Lord and Lady Middlesex, Mrs Rich, Mr Masham, and I.

22. Monday. We din'd alone.

23. Tuesday. Debate upon the revision of sentences by a Court Martial. Carried that they be sent back by the Commanders in Chief: *Once* only.[1]—Din'd alone.

24. Wednesday. At Leicester House. Messrs Dodington, Wyndham, and Tynte presented, who, with Mr Breton and Sir Thomas Robinson din'd with us.

25. Thursday. Went to Hammersmith. Din'd alone.

26. Friday. Din'd alone.

27. Saturday. Mr Tucker din'd with us. The Prince sent for me to supper but I did not go to town. Lord Inchiquin, Messrs Masham, Breton, Teyward, Bance, and Tucker.

28. Sunday. Din'd with us.

29. Monday. Went to the House. Debate upon a turnpike espous'd by the Duke of Bedford. Fullest House and greatest division of any day of the Session. After which the House thinn'd: we insisted upon the Order of the Day, to call the defaulters, which was read, and the call order'd next Monday. The Mutiny Bill was reported, and at the amendment of the Oath, we mov'd to adjourn. Divided and were beaten, by a great majority.[2] I went back, and din'd alone, at Hammersmith.

---

[1] i.e. the power of the Commanders-in-Chief to exert pressure on a court martial by asking it to reconsider its decision was to be limited to one such request.

[2] After being beaten by 72 in a division of 250 they left the House in a body (Walpole to Mann, 31 Jan. 1750). The preceding division, on the celebrated inter-ministerial wrangle over the Bedford Turnpike Bill, had attracted nearly 400 members.

30. Tuesday. Mr Kelsal din'd with us. Came to town. Went to Council. Supp'd at Carlton House. Ladies Middlesex and Howe, Lord Bute and Mr Breton. Mr Drax was there but did not stay supper.

31. Wednesday. At Leicester House. Messrs Cornwall and Bodens din'd with us. Supp'd at Mr Breton's. Ladies Middlesex and Shannon, and Mr Jackson. Lords Middlesex, Inchiquin, and Mr Masham, and Lord Bathurst.

FEBRUARY

1. Thursday. Din'd at Mr Masham's—Lords Middlesex and Inchiquin, Messrs Douglass and Breton. Supp'd at Leicester House, Ladies Shannon and Middlesex, Messrs Breton and Drax. Copy of the Master of the Ordnance's Commission refus'd by the House.[1]

2. Friday. Din'd with us, Messrs Furnese, Ralph, Carey, and Dr Sharpe. At Council.

3. Saturday. Din'd at Mr Furnese's, Lords Stafford and Dillon, Mr Jansen, Count d'Artagnan.

4. Sunday. At Leicester Fields. Din'd with us, Lord Middlesex, Messrs Furnese, Sheriff Jansen, Mr Bance, Ralph, Dr Sharpe. Lord Middlesex, by the Prince's orders show'd me a Motion to be made the next day, for an account of the state of the Port of Dunkirk,[2] and the papers, and offices that had pass'd on that subject. It was agreed that I should wait on the Prince, the next day.

5. Monday. I waited upon the Prince, and told him that I was come to thank him for communicating the Motion to me, which was more than any one of my fellow-servants had condescended to do since I came in his service. He made me a very embarrass'd and perplex'd answer. I then proceeded to say, that I had not been idle, since I came into his service, but had been looking into several things, in order to find something proper to be laid before Parliament.— That I had long had this particular point of Dunkirk under consideration: was determined to be at the expense, to know, and to procure evidence of the present state of it but my acquaintance lay so much out of the mercantile way, that I was at a loss how to go

---

[1] John, 2nd Duke of Montagu, had included this among his many offices until his death in the previous year. Apart from the scent of scandal in the Ordnance—a favourite Leicester House issue—there was the prospect that the job might be given to the Duke of Cumberland (Walpole to Mann, 25 Feb. 1750). In fact the office remained vacant for more than twenty years, and this opposition motion for information about the terms of the late Master-General's appointment was defeated by 151 to 63.

[2] Dunkirk was supposed to be completely demilitarized under the Treaty of Utrecht, and it was a good patriotic point that the Treaty of Aix-la-Chapelle had conceded land defences there, and made no provision for British inspection of the demolition of the sea defences. D.'s dinner party was to discuss this very matter, the important guest being Jansen (Lord Mayor 1755, died 1776), son of the great South Sea magnate Sir Theodore Janssen.

about it: that I had pitch'd upon Mr Sheriff Jansen, being a
trader himself, and much conversant with them, as a proper person
to inform, and assist me: that the great fit of sickness he fell into,
had, till now, disabl'd him from going out, and that yesterday was
the first time I could get him, to dinner. That I suppos'd, that
tho' I was so unfortunate as not be ready H.R.H. was well inform'd
of all things necessary to make out the charge &c.—He said, no,
but to throw it out would make them feel they had *La Corde au Col*,
and it was an opportunity to abuse them &c.—I said, that my idea
had been, to bring something of national weight, which I could fix
by undeniable evidence, upon them, and leave it there. That, if
I could have brought this affair up to that point: then I design'd
to lay it before H.R.H. with this only remark, how far he thought
proper to venture the consequences with France, in the present
condition of this country.—He said the Tories wanted something
to be done, and if he did not do something they immediately
thought he was negotiating.[1]—I told him, also, that I had been for
some time, getting such lights as I could into the affair of Nova
Scotia,[2] that I design'd to lay it before him when I had thought
it to be worthy his consideration: but it was my misfortune to
think that it was necessary to be arm'd with full proof, and conviction of every sort, of the charge we made in the House, before
we brought it there.—Upon that foot I submitted, that in case
upon this question of Dunkirk, it should come out that the port
was left, just in the same condition it remain'd under the Treaty
of Utrecht, without any innovation since the war, the Ministry
not having inforc'd a stricter execution of that Treaty, than ever
was had, would not, I fear'd, make a very strong point against them.
He was pleas'd to say, 'No, to be sure, so long an acquiescence would
greatly diminish the objection'.

Upon these words I left him, and went directly to the House—
In the debate, I argu'd against the inexpediency, and dangers,
(which were the objections set up by the Court, to granting these
papers) that there could be none, because, if it appear'd that there
had been no innovations since the war, and that the port was in the
state it had remain'd under the Treaty of Utrecht,—tho' I did not

---

[1] 'Tories' = Sir John Hinde Cotton's group of country gentlemen (see above, 16
and 24 Nov. 1749). Negotiating of course = negotiating with the Pelhams.
[2] The development of Nova Scotia, confirmed as British by the recent treaty, was
being eagerly hurried by the new first Lord of Trade, Halifax. The town named
after him had been founded in the preceding October.

give it up, but did insist, we had a right to a fuller execution of that Treaty confirm'd by this, therefore I did not give it up—yet, if that appear'd to be the case, no danger or inconveniency could arise from the Motion, because I was sure, I, for one, would not, and I believ'd no gentleman, upon that account, would move anything, that might occasion a rupture with France.—At the end of the debate Lord Egmont, who made the Motion, recapitulated what had been said against it, begun by going out of his way, to say, that he must first, declare that he was sorry to differ from me, but did not agree that it would be sufficient to excuse the Ministry, if it should appear, as I had stated it, that things remain'd at Dunkirk as they were left, before the war &c.—I was much surpris'd at this, considering the expression of H.R.H.'s a few hours before.—We were beat by a very great majority.[1] This night, was publish'd the vilest, and most rancorus [sic] pamphlet against me, that I believe any age or country can show: the author of it, taking by implication, the character of being in the Prince's service.

6. Tuesday. Went to Lord Middlesex's with the words (as near as I could recollect) written down, which I had us'd in the debate, and which he had heard. He agreed to them. I then desir'd him to lay them before the Prince (who was at Kew, and come to see Lady Middlesex, on her miscarriage) and in my name, complain, both of the pamphlet, and the behavior I had met with. Which he undertook.

Din'd alone. Mr Ralph, and Dr Sharpe came after dinner. Much conversation about the pamphlet which, Lord Middlesex told me in the morning, the Prince had told Lady M. (before he went to Kew) was sent him in a letter on Friday night: that he was much incensed at it: that he had immediately sent to Mr Nugent,[2] examined him upon it, and he, absolutely, deny'd it, with detestation and abhorrence; that he had questioned the Earl of Egmont upon it, who had done the same.—Mr Furnese came, who had had a conversation with Lord Baltimore, of his own seeking, when in wine, and renew'd, when sober, in which that Lord declar'd, that there was a combination of the whole Family against me; that they were in a round robin; that I endeavour'd to govern, and supplant them; that they talk'd of me with the utmost inveteracy; that he

[1] By 242 votes to 115.
[2] Robert Nugent, later Earl Nugent, M.P. for St Mawes and at this time Comptroller to the Prince.

was my friend, but however, he would keep his connections &c. We sent Dr Sharpe home, to stay till the Prince went away. Who returned and brought us that very account *which by mistake* I have set down in the page before,[1] as given to me by Lord Middlesex, in the morning, who then only did and could inform me that the Prince had had the pamphlet sent him in a letter, the Friday before, and was much incens'd at it. Lord Middlesex agreed I should see the Prince as soon as might be, after he had seen me in the morning. The Prince as well as we suspected that the pamphlet might come from the Court side, in order to foment, and increase divisions.

7. Wednesday. Went to Leicester House after Lord Middlesex had been with me, who confirm'd last night's account, with the addition that Lord Egmont offer'd his endeavours to find out the author &c.—That the Prince was sorry for what had happened in the House, but as Lord Egmont had differ'd from me, with civility, he did not seem to lay great stress upon it.—It being late, and a public day, I sent in a note to the Prince to know when he would honour me with an hour's conversation. He appointed me the next day, seven o'clock, at Carlton House. Mr Herbert presented as Lord Lieutenant of Wiltshire.

Went to the House. Ryder offer'd to the Mutiny Bill that no Sergeant or Corporal should be reduc'd, but by sentence of Court Martial. Din'd at the Earl of Leicester's. Lord Coke, Messrs Shebrocke and Kelsal.

8. Thursday. Saw Mr Ralph and Mr Furnese: ask'd him if in charging the combination of the Family against me, I might put it in proof, from the conversation between him and Lord Baltimore. I could not persuade him. I sent Mr Ralph to Lord Middlesex to know if I might take notice to the Prince of a circumstance which he told me yesterday morning, and *I have omitted* which was, that the Prince had dropp'd that Lord Baltimore had had a conversation with Mr Furnese, who was very warm. He sent me word he thought it would be improper. At six o'clock the Prince sent me word that he was just return'd from Kew, and found that the Princess had appointed Count Flemming and his lady to be at Carlton House at seven, and therefore fear'd he should not have time to dine, and see me; but desir'd I would come the next day at seven.

We went that night to Hammersmith.

[1] i.e. about the Prince's interviews with Nugent and Egmont.

N.B. Just upon one o'clock this day two very great, and very distinct shocks of an earthquake in Pall Mall at a distance of some seconds.

9. Friday. Went to town in the morning, and to the House: Mr Edward Walpole's Bill pass'd without opposition.—At seven I went to Carlton House.—

—Just as I came, was follow'd in by Dr Lee who brought old Coram[1] with propositions for a vagabond hospital. I was told that the Prince ask'd for me, several times: I was immediately call'd in: I told the Prince, that Dr Lee was there and that I wish'd not to make him wait: he pretended that he had forgot he had been long appointed to bring Coram, on that day, but that he would go out to him, and that they were to go up to the Princess. I saw that he sent for him on purpose, and therefore said, that I had nothing to say to him, but what I should be glad Dr Lee should hear.

He went out to them, and after a little stay, sent them up. He return'd, and began to talk about the earthquake which I continued a little and then ask'd if the Dr was to come down.—He said yes.— When he came, I let the discourse continue general to see if he meant only to give the Dr the opportunity of making a civil visit. But, at last, H.R.H., applying to me, said, he thought I had something to say to him: this, by the Dr's not moving, made it plain, and therefore I begun, by saying, that I should not have presum'd to ask that favour, yet it was a very particular pleasure to me, that he was so good as to admit Dr Lee to be by, and to hear what I had to lay before H.R.H. That I must in the first place return my most humble thanks, for the indignation he had express'd against the vile, and rancorous pamphlet which had been publish'd against me &c.—He said, that as soon as it was sent him, he saw it was design'd to personate Mr Nugent: that he immediately sent for him, who deny'd every part of it, with the utmost abhorrence, that Lord Egmont did the same &c—just as Lord Middlesex related.—I said that I had never thought so basely, of either of them, as to suspect them: that if I had been so injurious to either, yet after so solemn a denial, before the highest Tribunal, their Master, their Prince; near being their King; every trace, or thought of such a suspicion, must be forever, entirely laid out of the question: but that it was evident that the character assum'd was that of one of the

---

[1] The founder of the Foundling Hospital, Bloomsbury.

Family.—Dr Lee said he had never heard of it till last Wednesday, and as he detested all things of that nature, had not yet seen it: and believed he never should.—The Prince said, everybody was infamously abus'd: he, and his father had been often so. That it would do me no hurt, &c. I told him that I was very unfortunate, if I explain'd myself so ill, as to be thought to complain of the pamphlet, further than it hurt his service; that I had, I thought, hitherto, mention'd it only as a ground to return him my most humble thanks, for his most generous interposition, without being applied to: but that I beg'd now, to make another plain, and evident use of it:

That tho' now it was beyond question, that this libel did, no ways, proceed from any of his Family, yet it was as much beyond question, that the behaviour of many of his Family, had given the author grounds to suppose, that the assum'd character, might pass for a real one, and that it was evidently, meant, to fix the charge of my intrusion into the Family, and their detestation of me, to create differences if there were none, and to publish, and inflame them, if there were. That to this fact, thus plainly prov'd by the pamphlet, I would add another, which I thought very unfortunate to myself.—That I knew how disagreeable it was, to bring gentlemen head to head, and that I foresaw, he would not like to admit it; but I could prove it (tho', now I chose to do it, by reason only, and collateral facts) that there was, I did not know what to call it, an opinion, a resolution, amongst the gentlemen, his servants and followers (excepting Dr Lee, whom they nominally excepted) to look upon me, as an improper, and unprofitable servant, and would not unite, or communicate with me, that I knew this to be so, and look'd upon it, as a great misfortune to me, because tho' it did not become me to say, before H.R.H., how I came into his Family, yet, I certainly embrac'd, with the utmost pleasure, the opportunity of belonging, as a servant, to a Prince, whom, of all mankind I should have wish'd to pass my life with, if his misfortune and the misfortune of the public, had plac'd him in a private station.—That the disappointment of so flattering a view was the more sensible, because I was sure, it must arise from some fault, and that no small one, because after what had so lately pass'd, at the other end of the Mall, (meaning St James's) and lively sense H.R.H. had express'd of it, I could not, and did not imagine, that any man, or body of men, would be hardy enough to combine to prescribe to him, who he should employ, to what degree, and in what manner.

This (as I knew it would) fir'd him, and tho' till this he had kept the most profound silence, he interrupted me, and said no body should pretend to do that by him; that he allow'd sometimes, one, sometimes, another to lay their opinions before him but nobody presum'd to direct him, and appeal'd to Dr Lee, if anybody treated him so &c.

I rejoin'd, that, I had said so, and understood it so, and that made this treatment the more sensible, because, I was sure, it must proceed from some fault of mine, which I beg'd to be acquainted with. For it plainly appear'd the dislike to me was real.

That I must, now, proceed to another thing that I once thought, a most certain fact, but had, since, found, was grounded on a mistake: that I had like to have said, that H.R.H. a little contributed to lead me into that mistake, by telling me, when he was most graciously pleas'd to command my services, that all his Family, as well as himself, were desirous of it. That I had heard the same indeed, on all hands, and some of the most considerable, had themselves, long, often, and with great zeal, assur'd me of their warmest desires, and even taken credit, for having earnestly press'd H.R.H. to call me to that honour, which they now thought me so unworthy of. That, therefore, I beg'd they might be ask'd fairly, and openly, what was the reason of so total an alteration, as well as so sudden a one: for I had thought that I perceiv'd a difference even before we came to town, the last time, from Cliefden.—That, as to arrogance, and sufficiency, and design to govern H.R.H. and them, which I suppos'd had been plentifully inculcated: I beg'd (and was glad to do it before the Dr) he would be pleas'd to declare first as to himself, if I had fatigued him with audiences, or laid hold on the many other opportunities I had, to obtrude my own thoughts upon him, or to know his: to complain to him, that he did not communicate what he was doing, to me, and take my opinions, or to presume to expostulate with him, or blame what he had done, without, or for not communicating with me.

—He said, No, indeed that he remember'd but, twice, that I came to him about business. Once was about a paper I had drawn, to lay before him; and the other time, when the publisher of the *Remembrancer* was taken up.—I put him in mind, that, at that time I mentioned to him the alteration I found in his servants; which was so long ago, as last November.—I then ask'd if in the many leisure hours, of private life, he indulg'd me, I ever spoke ill of any one of them, or so much as complain'd or endeavour'd to lessen, or depreciate them, or their performances.—He said No, but to be sure I did not express any partiality to schemes I did not approve of (but did not answer so fully, and fairly upon this head, as the truth is).

I said, the next thing I would now desire H.R.H. to declare, which was, if those gentlemen had treated me with the same fairness, that I was sure he would answer to himself. As to the governing of them, did I ever interfere with them? They form'd their own business, their papers, their own motions, without the least communication with, or complaint from me: that I was sorry for it because they made me a useless servant to him in Parliament; for that it was impossible for me to go thither, and follow their motions at sight, and at hearing, and then to be disowned for my pains.

He laugh'd, and said it was because they had nothing to communicate: they had done nothing, that he knew of. The Mutiny Bill was an agreed point, by all, and they had had nothing else. That as to the Dunkirk Motion, he protested it was a thought of his own, that Dr Lee knew nothing of it, even when he sent it to me by Lord Middlesex.—I reply'd, that, in a conversation where the ground was my misfortune in being render'd useless to a master whose unmerited goodness, and favour was my sole ambition, and reliance, it was impossible that I should take the change so grossly, as to be brought to complain, or to suffer him, one moment, to think that I did complain of him. That I receiv'd the communication he had honour'd me with, as a mark of his favour, and with much respect: that what I spoke of, was the non-communication, and disavowal, of the rest of his servants, both in the Mutiny Bill, and on another occasion.—He said, as to the punishing mutiny, with death, he must, own to me, that he, as well as they, differ'd with me, and had acted so last year: and that Lords Carlisle and Bathurst had differ'd with Lord Bath upon that clause; for which he appeal'd to Dr Lee, who said, he was confin'd by illness (as was I) from coming to the House. As to what happen'd upon the Motion, he was sorry for it but thought it was not of great importance.

—I said, with some warmth, that I thought it was of the highest importance to him. Was it to pass for his sense, was *he* to appear in the light of declaring, that he would, if he were now King, or would force his father, to begin a new broil with France, at this time, in these circumstances of this country, because fifteen months after such a war, ended by such a peace, France had not carried the demolition of Dunkirk farther than it had been carried for thirty-two years last past? Was this a point to be maintained? Was it a doctrine fit for him to pass for its author? I thought it was not, it was imprudent, it could not be supported, and above all most prejudicial to his service, to have it thought he gave ear to such rash councils: besides, that H.R.H. had agreed with me, the last thing he said to me, that very morning; that in the above-mention'd case, if it came out only so, the long acquiescence much lessen'd, if it did not take away the objection. I beg'd pardon for being warm about the consequence of the doctrine, because that was not the use I intended to make of it. What I meant to establish by it, was, to prove a settled resolution to show they would have nothing to do with me and that it prov'd undeniable. Because when Mr Pitt, who answer'd Lord Egmont, came to that part, he press'd his argument thus: 'If it should come out that there is no innovation, as I verily believe the truth is and that it is as it was left by the treaty Utrecht, explained in 1717,[1] will any man say that it is a crime in the Ministry, or a reason to quarrel with France? Will any gentleman say it? Does any one say it?' To this his Lordship made no reply in affirmation of what he had laid down in contradiction to me: which proves, to a demonstration, that he went out of his way in concert with those in conjunction with him, to show all the world, by a public disavowal, that they disclaim'd all concert, and conjunction with me: whether that was for *his* service, he best knew. I beg'd to be understood, that in all I had said, my concern was only with relation to his service; if he was satisfied, I was. I desir'd to govern nobody, to supplant nobody: but that I could not follow them in public in whatever they pleas'd to start; that in things I was not consulted about, where my advice and opinion was neither taken nor even ask'd, I could not go down, and appear to approve, and support: that I was sorry it render'd my services useless to him in the House of Commons, but I could not put myself upon that foot: he said, to be sure it was not to be expected of me, or to that effect. I reply'd, that it was very well, I was perfectly satisfied, if he was.

—I then began to put him in mind, that I had not been idle: that I had thought both of the point of Dunkirk, and of Nova Scotia; and had looked into several things, that might be introductive to

---

[1] By Article iv of the Triple Alliance of 4 Jan. 1717 France reaffirmed the promise to dismantle Dunkirk, as provided in the convention of 1716 negotiated by Townshend and Methuen.

the public accounts; and had, above a month ago hinted something of it, to Dr Lee, and told him I hop'd for his assistance. (This the Doctor readily confirm'd.) That it might go far and affect several families; whether H.R.H. would care to go so far, he would be the best judge. That when I had thought upon any point, where I saw day-light, when I had digested it a little, I chose to lay it before a friend, or two first; if then we lik'd it, and could give it a body, the first of us that had the honour to see him, would lay it before him for his approbation: if it met with that, then, and not till then, I should have thought of communicating it, to those who were, chiefly, to assist in the execution of it. That this might be governing, for aught I knew, but that this was the way of doing business, that I had learnt, and indeed, had never seen any other practis'd.

—They both laugh'd and said to be sure it was not governing, and was the only way of transacting business. I reply'd it was the only way I knew, and it might be governing, but if it was H.R.H. would please to observe that I had not done even that, yet. I then observ'd to him, how extremely hard it was, for a minority, to bring any considerable national abuse into absolute, undeniable proof, all the offices and documents being in the hands of the Court; and desir'd him to look back thro' all the oppositions for forty years past: saying that I could recollect but one, that was brought home and fixed upon the Ministry, which was this very point of Dunkirk: which H.R.H. readily agreed to.

This to the best of my memory was the most if not all material that pass'd. The conversation became general, for a little while, and then H.R.H. call'd for his chair, and left Dr Lee and I together.

When we were alone, I told the Dr that I knew there was a combination against me, that I could prove it, and they knew I could prove it. But that, since I had had an opportunity of explaining myself, fully, to H.R.H. before so good a witness as himself, I was entirely indifferent, as to the event.—The Dr assur'd me, in a seeming friendly, and warm manner, that he should always be glad to act with, and assist me in every thing, that might be for the service of the Prince, and the utility of the country.—I thank'd him properly, and desir'd him to remember, that I had desir'd, and even insisted with the Prince to declare, if ever, or at any time, and in what I had ever attempted to govern him, or complain'd that I did not; adding that possibly I might have had such an idea, might have attempted it, might have miscarried, and been reprimanded for it; and might have grown wiser: but if I had done it, at all, I should hardly have challeng'd the Prince, before him, to declare it:—The next thing I beg'd him to remember, was, that I had fully appriz'd the Prince, that in what I was not consulted about, and advis'd with, I would have nothing to do in Parliament and that I would not go down there upon that foot: and so we parted.

I desir'd Mr Ralph, whom I found at my house, to go to Mr Furnese's immediately, and from there to send to Lord Middlesex's for leave to wait upon him, with an account of this whole transaction, and then I return'd to Hammersmith by eleven.

10. Saturday. Ladies Poulet, Mrs Colebrook, and Stephen Hales, came to see the house.[1] Mr and Mrs Tucker din'd with us.

11. Sunday. Went to town. Saw Lord Middlesex for a moment, before I went to court. He told me that the Prince came to his house, directly from me on Friday night. That he was very thoughtful, all the night, endeavour'd to shake it off, but could not, so that anyone might see that something lay heavy upon his mind, which he could not get rid of. That Mr Ralph had acquainted him with what had pass'd and that last night the Prince, and Princess came to Lady Middlesex who had not been out, since her miscarriage, and stayed late. That, then, it came all out.—That, according to Mr Ralph's relation, the Prince said but little: but according to his, made himself a great speaker:—that he had convinc'd me about the Mutiny Bill.—That I mention'd a combination to govern him, that there was nobody durst enter into such a combination:—that I did not say there was such a thing, or he would not have suffer'd me to go on.—Then what he would do to those who should presume to enter into such a thing!—in short, seem'd to endeavour to laugh it off, and that now all things would go well again, &c.—But again mention'd the conversation between Mr Furnese, and Lord Baltimore, last Tuesday. Lord Baltimore contriv'd to see him as soon as he came from Kew, and before he went to Lord Middlesex's, and represented that conversation, as press'd upon him, by Mr Furnese, at my request, and that he had talk'd very high of me, if not from me, and that I complain'd that he beg'd, and press'd me to come into his service, for that he could not do without me &c—

I ask'd if I might make use of this overture to have this matter

---

[1] Sir Stephen Hales = the savant and incumbent of Teddington; later (1751) chaplain to the Princess of Wales. 'The house', of course, was D.'s riverside villa.

explain'd: he said he was afraid not, it being said in confidence. I then ask'd that in that case Mr Furnese would tell him the whole conversation, if he would relate it to the Prince, fully, and fairly, and fix the lie where it belong'd. He said, he could do that, very well, by telling the Prince, that he was much surpris'd, when he heard him first mention that conversation, but more so, to find that he mention'd it again: and therefore, had contriv'd, in talking together, to draw out of Mr Furnese, the particular account of it, which he would tell him, literally; and beg'd, that, for his farther satisfaction, he would send to Mr Furnese, to give him an account of it, who, he was sure, was a man of honour, and would tell him the whole truth.

I went to Leicester House, was very well receiv'd—Sent to Mr Furnese to see him tomorrow.—Return'd to Hammersmith, to dinner.— Din'd alone.

12. Monday. Mr Furnese came: I read to him what pass'd on Friday, and told what Lord Middlesex had heard from the Prince again, about the turn which Lord Baltimore had given to the conversation between them: which he, again declar'd, to be most false, and that he was ready to declare it to the Prince, if H.R.H. was pleased to send for him.

Intelligence from H.V.[1] of the very great dissensions between the Ministers.—Din'd alone.

13. Tuesday. Came to town. Saw Lord Middlesex. We agreed that he should (as, indeed, was hardly to be avoided) take up this matter again with the Prince, and tell him that I had given him an account of it—that I was most grateful for his grace and condescension, in giving me so full and patient an audience—that I hop'd I had not behav'd myself improperly—that upon the whole, tho' he was my friend, yet he thought the Prince, for his future quiet, should go to the bottom of this affair.—Everybody had their faults—I might be vain—I might be high—and yet wear very well, and be made very useful. He did not mean to push things to extremities—if I had press'd indecently upon H.R.H. or into his affairs, where I was not call'd—tho' it was true I had not intruded into his Family—yet, if I had talk'd impertinently, and vainly, about it, of being beg'd

---

[1] 'Harry Vane, one of the dirtiest of men; a tool and spy of the Pelhams'—Horace Walpole's note in the Rothschild copy of the *Diary*. He was at this time a Lord of the Treasury and later Earl of Darlington. The dissensions were about the Bedfordshire Turnpike—see above, 29 Jan., and below.

and pray'd, and that H.R.H. could not do without me—why it was no heinous fault, but he thought I should be gently made to feel the impropriety of such a behaviour, by a word from H.R.H. or from him in his name.—But it imported H.R.H. to be sure the charge was true, and give me an opportunity of justifying myself, otherwise the party was not equal: H.R.H. having heard but one side. If on the contrary, it should turn out false was it not highly necessary, he should know, what sort of people he had, about him?—That conversation, for instance, which H.R.H. had twice mention'd, and which he had great doubts in his mind was not justly represented to H.R.H., would he give me leave to tell me of it, that I might go to the bottom of it? Or (what would be better) would he send for Mr Furnese, and let him give a full account of it, without ever mentioning to anybody, that he had been question'd, by H.R.H.? This the Prince might keep in his own breast, and not let it go any farther.—His (Lord Middlesex's) intention, not being to go to any extremity; but only that he might know the persons he employ'd; and not reject anybody, for a few faults, that might be useful in many things; nor trust without reserve, anybody, who, tho' useful in some things, and fit to be employ'd, may be dangerous in others, and cautiously to be guarded against. That he should tell him that I complain'd that after having set down quiet under a falsehood which Lord Egmont laid to my charge, of telling Carey what pass'd between H.R.H. and me, at Kew, when he took me into his service (which I could prove, and by Carey himself, was told him by Lord Egmont); after having acquiesced, so long, under that imputation, rather than hurt that Lord, or occasion any, the least, disquiet, in the Family, that I did not expect such a return.

These points Lord Middlesex agrees, are right, and will undertake them.

At the House the Turnpike Bill thro' Bedford, thrown out by 54.[1] Din'd, Messrs Dodington and Younge.

Supp'd at Carlton House. Lady Middlesex, Messrs Masham and Breton, Mr Drax. Went away.

14. Wednesday. At Leicester House, but went away, before the Princess came out. Din'd with us, Messrs Younge and Tucker.

After dinner I went to see Dr Lee, who receiv'd me with much apparent openness. We talk'd much about what the Prince's con-

---

[1] 208 to 154. D. is correct. Walpole (to Mann, 25 Feb. 1750) is wrong.

duct ought to be in case under their present undoubted quarrels, and disunion, either part of the Administration should apply to him, for assistance. This conversation was begun by him: and we both agreed that unless they would restore the King to his Family, by a thorough reconciliation: and to his people, by some popular acts, the Prince should not engage with any of them, and we neither thought them either honest, or able enough to bring about such great events.[1] We agreed in wishing that no such application should be made.

15. Thursday. Carried Mr Warburton[2] to Hammersmith about six o'clock where he lay.

16. Friday. Brought Mr Warburton to London. Council at the Cockpit. Return'd to Hammersmith by eleven.

17. Saturday. Din'd with us, Messrs Harley, Breton, Tucker, and Younge. Supp'd at Carlton House. Lady Middlesex, Lord Bathurst, Mr Breton.

18. Sunday. At Leicester House. Din'd alone.

19. Monday. Din'd alone, at Hammersmith.

20. Tuesday. Din'd with us, Sir Francis Dashwood, Messrs Masham and Breton.

21. Wednesday. Came to town to see Mr Ralph, and in consequence, to put off a meeting. Return'd by eleven o'clock.

22. Thursday. Went to the House.—Motion that the High Bailiff [of Westminster] do attend, tomorrow, to give account of his executing the writ, carried, by 136, to 71.[3] —Cause at the Cockpit. Earl Fitzwalter, and I, differ'd with Mr Baron Clarke, about leading a witness, avowdly interested in a ship taken. We thought he could not be led, against the captor's libel, to anything, but by way of cross-examination, tho' he had been admitted by, and led for him, as an evidence *in Preparatorio*. The Baron thought otherwise—.[4]

---

[1] D. clearly has in mind here a programme of the kind which succeeded so well in 1720, when Walpole and Craggs negotiated the public reconciliation of George and the Prince of Wales and reunited the two wings of the whigs for the great popular measure of redeeming the National Debt.

[2] The herald and antiquary. D. was still showing off his new house.

[3] For a scrutiny following the Westminster election.

[4] This entry is interesting as showing how seriously lay Privy Councillors took their judicial duties.

23. Friday. Went to the House. The High Bailiff examin'd, as to his execution of the precept, and granting a scrutiny. He gave a most reasonable, and decent account of both.—Ask'd the reasons of such an excessive delay—gave very satisfactory ones. The House was much pleas'd with his behaviour, and the Speaker, by their order, told him that he had power to stop all trifling speeches, and impertinent questions, and objections. That the House would support him in it; and recommended to him to sit longer, and use all possible dispatch that was consistent with justice and his duty, which he promis'd, and withdrew:—din'd at Sir Francis Dashwood's. Return'd, at eight, to Hammersmith.

24. Saturday. Din'd with us, Messrs Hampden, Warburton, and Younge. Came to town—finished the cause at the Cockpit—went to supper, at Carlton House, at near twelve o'clock.—Ladies Middlesex and Howe, and Lord Bute.

25. Sunday. Mr Henley was with me: did not think Mr Lascelles's Privy Seal sufficient for a separate point;[1] ask'd me how things went. I told him, but indifferently. That I had no communication with the other gentlemen in our Family, that they were united against me. He treated them very slightly; said indeed that he had had offers enough to be of their Meeting but had declin'd, not thinking himself little enough to follow any body there: that they generally showed him their motions, either in the House, or elsewhere.— I said that did not happen to me; that, therefore, I was determin'd not to meddle with anything, where my opinion was neither ask'd nor taken. That if the Prince lik'd their method of proceeding I was perfectly satisfied, but I would not put myself upon that footing in public. That I would do every thing in my power, spare no expense, no complaisance, or cheerful concurrence in all his pleasures, to make myself an agreeable servant, as long as I had the honour to belong to him, but that in his public business, I would never intrude myself, but that it was impossible for me to follow those gentlemen, tho' I did not, in the least, desire to govern them. This, as well as I can remember was all material that I said.

He said much more of them, blaming them without reserve for their sufficiency, &c.—that they were inform'd of nothing at bottom, but dealt only in invectives, and that not very well:

---

[1] See below 2 July. There was a possible opposition issue in the clearance of the Ordnance accounts by prerogative writ, and not by audit.

perpetual imputation, and suspicion, without being able to make out any thing, which would, if encourag'd, make all government impracticable. Displeas'd with Dr Lee, for not telling him, that he was to have the seals, as our Chancellor,[1] if Sir T. Bootle had died. I said, that Lord Baltimore forc'd him to ask the Prince for it: who told him he most sincerely wished to oblige him, but that he had promised Dr Lee, in case of accidents, to give him the seals, and that Lord Baltimore was by, when the promise was made:—which usage he took very ill (and I think justly) of Baltimore, who, he said when he press'd him to ask, assured him that he knew that the Prince would gladly grant it to him:—with much more of this sort.

I went to Leicester House,—where was Mr Henley. Lord Egmont came, and immediately took Mr Henley into a private room, where they had a conversation of near an hour.—This surprised me much. —In the afternoon, I met their Royal Highnesses by order at Lady Middlesex's, where came Madame de Munchausen, and Mr Breton. We went in our own coaches to a fortune-teller's which was young Des Noyers, disguis'd, and instructed to surprise Madame de Munchausen, which he did sufficiently.[2]—Had some talk with Lady Middlesex,—very dejected and full of complaints at the encouragement the party met with that was united against us.—From the fortune-teller's we went to supper at Carlton House.

26. Monday. Lords Bute, Inchiquin, Bathurst, Messrs Masham, Breton, and I, follow'd their Royal Highnesses, Ladies Middlesex and Howe, to dinner at Kew. Mr Bludworth was with us. *Arminius. Damon and Phillida.*

27. Tuesday. Work'd in the new Walk [at Kew]. *L'Avare. The Lottery.*

28. Wednesday. All of us, men, women, and children worked at the same place—cold dinner. *Macbeth.*

---

[1] i.e. of the Duchy of Cornwall.
[2] She was a celebrated frump, wife of the Hanoverian minister-resident.

MARCH

1. Thursday. *Le Malade Imaginaire. Monsieur de Pourceaugnac.*

2. Friday. Went to Hammersmith—came back time enough to breakfast with T.R.H. *The Chaplet First. The Stratagem.*

3. Saturday. *The Funeral. Devil of a Wife.*

4. Sunday. Came to town by one o'clock. Went to Leicester House. Din'd at Lord Bathurst's. Went to meet Sir Francis Dashwood, and Lord Middlesex, and Mr Furnese, at Mr Ralph's: we went thro' several points of business, and determin'd to proceed.[1]

5. Monday. Went to the House. Din'd with us Lord Inchiquin, Sir Francis Dashwood, Messrs Masham, Breton, Bludworth, and Oakington.

6. Tuesday. Went to the House. Din'd at Sir Francis Dashwood's. Went to Council, on a prize cause.

7. Wednesday. At Leicester Fields. Din'd there, with the Bedchamber woman. Lord Egmont mov'd for papers relating to Nova Scotia—refus'd by 139 to 69. I was not at the House.—

8. Thursday. The election for the County of Middlesex. Sir Francis Dashwood, Messrs Furnese, Breton, and I went in Sir Francis's coach at eight o'clock, to Mr Cooke's in Lincolns-Inn Fields—a great meeting there. We set out with him, about nine (my coach following) thro' Knights-bridge, Kensenton, by the gravel pits, to Acton, and thence to Stanwell Heath, which was the general rendezvous. From thence to Brentford Butts, which was the place of poll.

It began about one. I poll'd early, and got to my coach, which was so wedg'd in, that, after much delay, I found it impossible to make use of it: so that Mr Breton, and I, were forc'd to take two of my servants' horses, with livery housings, and ride, without boots, ten miles, to Lord Middlesex's at Walton, to meet T.R.H. at dinner.

We got thither by five o'clock, and found them attended by Lord Inchiquin, and Mr Bludworth in the Park.—Din'd at six.—My

---

[1] i.e. with public support of Cooke's candidature for Middlesex—see entry for 7 Mar., below.

coach did not get thither till nine.—T.R.H. lay at Kew.—We all came away between ten and eleven. Mr Breton, and I in my coach. Got to town between twelve and one.

Poll for Mr Cooke	1617
for Mr Honywood	1201
We carried it by	416

N.B. This day at three quarters past five in the morning exactly was a violent shock of an earthquake.

9. Friday. Went to the House. It was agreed to augment the Master of the Rolls salary. Went away when the House went into a Committee of Supply, upon the Hanaper Office—where it was resolv'd that the augmentation to the Rolls should be £1,200 per annum.

Din'd at Mr Heath's with the Earl of Stafford, and Mr Furnese. Mrs Heath was too ill to appear.

10. Saturday. Din'd at Lord Carlisle's. Sir Paul Methuen, Dr Lee, Mr Breton. Went to *Othello*, for Mr Barry's benefit.

11. Sunday. At Leicester House. Din'd at Hammersmith. Messrs Bance and Tucker.

12. Monday. In the morning went to the Duke of Argyll's. From thence to town, and to the House—nothing of consequence. Return'd to Hammersmith. Din'd alone.

13. Tuesday. Din'd alone. Came to town after dinner.

14. Wednesday. At Leicester House.—To meet Lady Middlesex early on Sunday morning. Return'd to Hammersmith. Din'd alone.

15. Thursday. Went to the House about the Fishery.[1] Came back to Hammersmith: din'd alone. Return'd to supper at Carlton House. Came back after supper. Lady Faulconberg and Mr and Mrs Breton.

16. Friday. Din'd with us, Lord Carlisle, Sir Paul Methuen, and Dr Lee.—Committee of Supply clos'd.

17. Saturday. Din'd with us, Earls of Westmorland and Litchfield, Sir Francis Dashwood, and Mr Furnese. Came to town.

18. Sunday. Had much talk with Lady Middlesex. Agree in opinion

---

[1] The Herring Fishery, in which D. had a financial interest. See below, 19 Sept. 1750.

as to the disagreableness, and impropriety of our situation, but that we must go on this summer as well as we could.—At Leicester House. Lady Bolingbroke dy'd this morning. Din'd with us, Mr Glover.

19. Monday. Set out for Kew with Lord Bute, and Mr Breton: there went with us, Lord Inchiquin, Messrs Masham, Bludworth, and Lord Bathurst. Ladies Howe and Middlesex. *Andromache. Hobb.*

20. Tuesday. Lord Inchiquin went to town and return'd to dinner. *Julius Caesar.*

21. Wednesday. T.R.H. went to their drawing room, and return'd by five to dinner.—Mr Breton and I to Hammersmith. *The Busy Body. Beggar's Wedding. Ill.*

22. Thursday. *Le Bourgeois Gentilhomme.*

23. Friday. *Beggar's Opera.*

24. Saturday. *Recruiting Officer.*

25. Sunday. Came to London. T.R.H., Mr Breton, Lords Bute and Bathurst, the two ladies, and I went into their countries. Lord Inchiquin, Messrs Masham, and Bludworth, din'd at Hammersmith.

26. Monday. I went to the House. Return'd to dinner with Mr Carey. Found Mr Kelsal at home. They both lay there.

27. Tuesday. Mr Stanley came, and return'd. Din'd with us, Messrs Dodington, Tucker, and Carver.

28. Wednesday. Went to Leicester House. Lord Vere Beauclerk kiss'd hands as Baron Hanworth. Return'd and din'd alone.

29. Thursday. Went to Council, at St James's. Sworn of the Council, Earl of Hyndford, Lord Anson, Sir Thomas Robinson. Return'd, with Mr Breton, who din'd with us. Sent for to supper with T.R.H. —Lady Middlesex and Mr Breton.

30. Friday. Return'd, before eleven. Din'd alone.

31. Saturday. Din'd alone. Came to town. Supp'd at Mr Furnese's. —Lord Middlesex, Sir Francis Dashwood, Messrs Ralph, Carey, Dr Sharpe.

APRIL

1. Sunday. At Leicester House. Din'd with us, Comte d'Artagnan, General Ligonier, Sir Francis Dashwood, Messrs Furnese, Booth, and Stanley.

2. Monday. Attended T.R.H. to Kew. Lord Bute, Messrs Masham, Breton, and I.—Found there Lords Inchiquin and Bathurst, and Mr Bludworth. Ladies Middlesex and Howe came with the Princess. *Firidate. The Beggar's Wedding.*

3. Tuesday. *All For Love.*

4. Wednesday. *Le Menteur.*

5. Thursday. *The Provok'd Wife.*

6. Friday. We went to course on Epsom Downs. The ladies in a landau. We din'd at H.R.H.'s hare-warren—*Le Chevalier à la Mode.*

7. Saturday. *Theodosius.*

8. Sunday. We all came to town with T.R.H. I din'd with Sir Francis Dashwood, Lord Middlesex, Messrs Furnese, Ralph, and Carey. Return'd to Hammersmith and found Mr Bance, who lay there.

9. Monday. Mr Bance went away. Din'd with us, Mr Gage, Sir Thomas Gordon, and General Oglethorpe.

10. Tuesday. Din'd with us, Earl Poulet, his brother, and Mr Mildmay. We came to town at night.

11. Wednesday. Council at St James's. King present. Regency nam'd.[1] We all kiss'd his hand, and then took leave. Went to Leicester House: thence to Hammersmith to dinner. Din'd alone.

12. Thursday. Went to the House of Lords. The King spoke and prorogued the Parliament. Return'd, and din'd alone.

13. Friday. Mr Hampden, and Mr Breton (who stayed all night) din'd with us.

---

[1] Against his annual holiday in Hanover. See below, 16 Apr.

14. Saturday. Messrs Fane and Breton din'd with us. We lay in town.

15. Sunday. Easter Day. No court. Din'd alone.

16. Monday. The King went to Harwich. The wind chang'd to N.E. Din'd with Sir Francis Dashwood, Messrs Vyner and Furnese there. Lay at Hammersmith.

17. Tuesday. Din'd alone. Dr Thomson lay here.

18. Wednesday. Dr Thomson went away. Din'd with us, Mr and Mrs Masters, and Miss Montagu, and Lord North.[1]

19. Thursday. Din'd alone. Sent for to supper, to Carlton House. T.R.H., Ladies Middlesex and Faulconbridge, Messrs Masham and Breton. Return'd, after supper.

20. Friday. Din'd with us, Messrs Poulet and their sisters, Sir Charles and Lady Tynte, Messrs Bastard and Breton.

21. Saturday. Din'd with us, Mr Macartney, and Ralph. We lay in town.

22. Sunday. Mr Drax, who was ill of the gout, sent to desire to see me. I went, and he told me, that petitions had been obtain'd from the miners in Cornwall, for the holding a Tin Parliament. That they were referr'd to the Prince's Privy Council, who had rejected them under a persuasion that there was a job at bottom. That the Prince was so far in it, that notwithstanding the disapprobation of his council, he had order'd a Privy Seal to be made out, to the Lord Warden of the Stanneries, to call, and hold a parliament on, or before the second of November.

That the nature of the Prince's revenue upon tin, was as follows viz:—All tin that is raised, throughout the Duchy of Cornwall, must be brought to the Prince's smelting house, and when smelted pays four shillings per hundred weight (which is 120 lbs). Thence, when made into pigs, it goes to the coinage, which is only a stamp, with the Prince's arms; and then, and not before, it is marketable.

Besides this duty of four shillings per hundred weight throughout the Duchy, no tin can be dispos'd of, till the Duke has taken the quantity he pleases.

[1] Father of the Prime Minister.

This is called the preemption.

This preemption has never been exercis'd by Princes, and seldom leas'd out. Once it was undertaken by Queen Anne, and Lord Treasurer Godolphin, and Mr Boscawen (afterward Lord Viscount Falmouth) on the other part: by which, for the present exigence, the Crown got the power in several boroughs, tho' they lost by the undertaking (which was occasion'd by the war). This lease was again renew'd by the succeeding administration, but I believe not carried into execution. The lease must be granted by an Act of the Parliament of the Tinners; which Parliament is called, and held, by a Privy Seal to the Lord Warden, for that purpose.

The Duchy is divided into four districts, each of which sends six members: the voters must be freeholders. They choose a Speaker, &c.

The quantity of tin raised annually, at an average of many years past, is 2,200 tons: the market price to the exporter from $4^l.5^s.$to $4^l.10^s.$ per hundred weight; so that the Prince's revenue upon that head, amounts to about $8,800^l.$ per ann. clear of all deductions; for there are other small duties that defray the charge of officers, collection, &c. N.B. The consumption is much less, and the freight dearer in war; but then, as the commodity is necessary, the vent is proportionally increased, the first years of peace.

Last year, the two companies of Mine Adventurers, and Mine Battery, both, petition'd the Prince for the lease of this preemption. The petitions were referr'd to his Privy Council and rejected. They offer'd his Royal Highness an advance on his revenue of $1,200^l.$ per ann. and a loan of $10,000^l.$ at 5 per cent. without insuring his life which he is oblig'd to do, at 5 per cent. additional, on all he borrows.

This not succeeding, a petition has lately been obtain'd from the Tinners, praying for a Parliament, which was, as I have said, rejected by the Council, supposing it was meant to procure a lease, for the advantage of those who were at the bottom of the former offers, which were so very disproportionate, that nothing but gross imposition can be expected from that quarter. These persons Mr Drax takes to be Mr Thomas Pitt and Dr Ayscough.

To show the impropriety of the proceeding, and the danger of the job, Mr Drax observ'd that this Parliament, tho' it could do no Act without the Prince's assent, yet might come to several resolutions that might be disagreeable to submit to, and yet inconvenient to break thro' and then proceeded to state the advantages of the lease of preemption: which from what has been offer'd he apprehends the Prince is not properly appriz'd of.

The offer, last year, he states at an advance of 1,700¹. per ann.— 1,200¹. annually, and the loan of 10,000¹. at 5 per cent. at 500¹. per ann. because he must pay 5 per cent. additional, elsewhere, for insuring his life.

He says that he is well assur'd, that the Tinners are ready to agree and contractors to engage, to take all the tin that shall be coin'd at 3¹.5ˢ. per hundred weight, and to avoid the clamour of a monopoly, they will oblige themselves to sell it at 4¹.5ˢ. which is below the market price. The gross gain, then, of 1¹. per hundred weight, upon 2,200 tons, is, per ann.   .   .   .   £44,000 0 0

The money to be employ'd for 2,200 tons, at 3¹.5ˢ. per ton, is 143,000¹. Supposing half this sum always employ'd at credit, deduct for interest   .   .   2,860 0 0
Charges of management, freight, &c.   .   .   3,000 0 0
                                                    5,860

Remains against risk and accidents net gain, per ann. 38,140 0 0

These calculations, he says are right. He does not know what is at the bottom of this; nor what offers have, or will be made, but by what is pass'd, he is very suspicious; and earnestly desir'd me to dissuade H.R.H. from it, if possible; he knew it would be very difficult, because he was sure they lur'd him to it by showing him new acquisitions in the Cornish elections.

Went to Leicester House. Return'd to dinner. Monsieur Servandoni,¹ Dr Thomson and Mr Tucker din'd with us.

23. Monday. I went to Turnham Green. We din'd alone.

24. Tuesday. Mr Warburton came. We went to Ranelagh, to see the preparations for the Masquerade. He din'd with us.

25. Wednesday. Went to Leicester House. Din'd with the Speaker. Lord Feversham, Sir P. Warren, Messrs Vyner, Furnese, and

¹ Giovanni Geronimo Servandoni (1695–1766), the Italian artist and designer. He was working on D.'s gorgeous villa at Hammersmith for which he designed the principal ceilings and the sculpture gallery, 85 feet long. D. also introduced him to the Prince of Wales, and he appears to have drawn up a scheme for Kew. See below, 13 June.

Hampden. Supp'd at Carlton House. Ladies Middlesex and Berkeley, and Mr Breton.

26. Thursday. Mr Cheere din'd with us. Went to the concert at the Crown and Anchor, with Lord and Lady Middlesex, and return'd at night.

27. Friday. Mr Warburton came: we rode to the Duke of Argyll's, who was not at home. Din'd with us, Messrs Warburton and Breton. Dr Thomson came, at night, and lay here.

28. Saturday. We stay'd at Hammersmith. Din'd with us, Messrs Furnese, Fielding,[1] and Carey. N.B. The King arriv'd at Hanover Sunday the 22nd.

29. Sunday. Mr Bance, and I din'd at Whitton with the Duke of Argyll. We came to town in the evening, and lay there. I supp'd at Carlton House—Ladies Middlesex and Howe. Lord Bute, Messrs Masham and Breton.

30. Monday. We came to Kew, for all the week. T.R.H., Ladies Middlesex and Howe, Lords Bute and Inchiquin, Messrs Masham, Breton, and I. *Theodosius.*

---

[1] The novelist, by this time J.P. for Westminster and Chairman of Middlesex Quarter Sessions. *Tom Jones* had been published in the previous year, and he was now working on *Amelia.* Fielding had been patronized by D. (*Jonathan Wild* is dedicated to him) as a political writer against Walpole, along with Ralph and Whitehead.

MAY

1. Tuesday. *Oroonokoo.* Music. Lord Bathurst came.

2. Wednesday. The Prince and Princess and ladies, went to the Drawing Room at Leicester Fields.—I went to Hammersmith. We all return'd to dinner. *Le Misanthrope.* Music.

3. Thursday. Lady Middlesex, Mr Breton, and I pass'd the morning at Hammersmith. Return'd to dinner. *The Committee.* Music.

4. Friday. Lord Baltimore came, and din'd with us in the garden, and return'd. We went upon the water. *Macbeth.*

5. Saturday. Sir Thomas Bootle came and lay here. We went to see Sion House. *The Fop's Fortune.*

6. Sunday. T.R.H. return'd to town, and I, to Hammersmith. Mr Ralph din'd with us.

7. Monday. Monsieur Servandoni came to Hammersmith to direct the finishing the gallery &c. I went to London, and return'd, to dinner alone. Dr Thomson came.

8. Tuesday. Dr Thomson went away. Sir Francis Dashwood carried me to the foot-ferry. Din'd, and supp'd at Kew. Ladies Middlesex and Howe. Lords Middlesex, Bute, Inchiquin, and Bathurst: Mr Breton, and I—lay in town.

9. Wednesday. At Leicester House. Din'd at Mr Furnese's. Went to Council. Return'd to Hammersmith.

10. Thursday. Thomson went away. Din'd here, Lord and Lady Berkeley: Mr and Mrs Drax.

11. Friday. Monsieur Servandoni, and I went to Gunnersbury. Din'd with us, Messrs Furnese, 2 Sharpes, Carey, Ralph, Tucker.

12. Saturday. Din'd with us, Mr Bance, who lay there. We came to town in the evening.

13. Sunday. About eleven o'clock, the Prince sent to me to come to Leicester House, as soon as I could. I got thither by half

after eleven. I found the groom-in-waiting, and the Bishop of Oxford.[1] The Prince came soon to us, and said the Princess had been ill, since three in the morning: by this time Duke of Chandos, and Lords Egmont and North, Messrs Cust, and Breton were come.[2] We went into the bed-chamber, at three quarters past eleven. The groom withdrew. We found in the bedchamber, Ladies Middlesex, Berkeley, Irwin, and Howe, Lady Bayly, Mrs Cornewall, and Payne. The midwife upon the bed with the Princess, and Dr Wilmot standing by. Just at half past twelve she was delivered of a Prince,[3] without once complaining or groaning the whole time. Then the Prince, the ladies, and some of us sat down to breakfast, in the next room. Then prayers below stairs. The Prince wrote to the King. The Duke of Bedford came for the letter. A numerous Drawing Room. There, appear'd all the Ministers, and persons in the chief employments. N.B. the Ministers were not sent for to the labour.[4] The Prince put off the public dinner, and servants in waiting, and order'd me to dine with him, in private at Carlton House. There was nobody din'd there but Lady Middlesex and her Lord, Mr Drax, Breton, and I.

14. Monday. Call'd at Leicester Fields. Din'd at Cranford, Lord Berkeley. Return'd to Hammersmith. Visconti[5] came.

15. Tuesday. The Duke of Dorset came—Lady Stapylton—din'd with us the Duke of Argyll, Sir H. Bellendine, Sir Francis Dashwood, Messrs Fletcher Maul, Dr Stuart, Furnese, Kelsal, Breton, Oswald.

16. Wednesday. The Prince's public table (which lasts about ten days, on account of the Princess's lying-in) began on Monday: when I was invited, but put it off, till today, when I din'd there. We were fifteen. Five ladies, all of the Family, six men of the Family, three that were not, and the Prince. The three not of the Family were the Duke of Kingston, the Marquis of Granby, and Dr Lee.[6] Return'd to Hammersmith after dinner.

[1] Thomas Secker, later Archbishop of Canterbury.
[2] All of the Prince's Household. Chandos was Groom of the Stole. North a gentleman of the Bed-chamber. Cust (also M.P. for Grantham) Clerk of the Household.
[3] Prince Frederick William. He did not survive childhood.
[4] Showing the continued alienation of the Prince from his father's advisers. D.'s private dinner with the Prince afterwards was a signal favour, especially as his enemies Egmont and Baltimore were not asked.
[5] Giovanni Baptista Antonio Visconti, the antiquary.
[6] Although Lee was in fact the Prince's most intimate adviser, Dodington carefully excludes him from 'the Family' because he held no paid office.

17. Thursday. Din'd here. Sir Francis and Lady Dashwood, and Miss Wheat, and Mr Furnese.

18. Friday. Din'd alone.

19. Saturday. Din'd alone. Went to town. Supp'd at Sir Francis Dashwood's.   [A day omitted]

21. Monday. Went to Leicester House to enquire. Carey din'd with us. Return'd at night, to Hammersmith.

22. Tuesday. Din'd alone.

23. Wednesday. Went to town. Met Mr Furnese, and Drake at the Earl of Middlesex's. Spent three hours examining the tin affair, which appears to be a scandalous job—resolv'd to go to the bottom of it. Din'd at Leicester House. Ladies Berkeley, Irwin, Bayly, Misses Chudleigh, and Neville. Lord Egmont in waiting. Lords Middlesex, Baltimore, Charles Hay, Sir John Cust, Lord Chief Justice Willes, Messrs Charles Stanhope,[1] Boone and Evelyn. Went to the Duke of Dorset, about Prince Henry's bathing in the sea at Walmer Castle.[2] Return'd at night.

24. Thursday. Din'd alone.

25. Friday. Went to town—settled with the Duke of Dorset that Prince Henry should not go to Walmer as 'twas a garrison, and the King's leave to be ask'd. Return'd to Hammersmith. Din'd with us, Messrs Ralph and Dr Thomson.

26. Saturday. Din'd alone. The Prince sent for Servandoni to attend him, at Kew on Monday. Came to town.

27. Sunday. Went to Leicester House. Mr Bance din'd and Mr Carey supp'd with us.

28. Monday. Saw Mr Drake about the tin. Din'd alone. Return'd to Hammersmith.

[1] Brother of the first Earl of Harrington and cousin of Earl Stanhope, he had been Secretary of the Treasury at the time of the South Sea Bubble, from which he made a large fortune and ruined his political career. He died in 1760.
[2] Frederick's second son William Henry, later Duke of Gloucester, then aged 7. Walmer was Dorset's official residence as Warden of the Cinque Ports.

29. Tuesday. Din'd alone. Signor de Grossa Testa, Lord and Lady Powerscourt came in the afternoon.

30. Wednesday. Came to town. Went to Leicester House. Lords Archbishop and Chancellor sent for, to settle the christening of the young Prince: the King having sent no orders from Hanover, tho' applied to. Lord Middlesex, Messrs Furnese, Bance, and Drake, met at my house, to consult farther about the tin affair. I din'd at Mr Furnese's.

31. Thursday. Came to Hammersmith. Din'd there. Messrs d'Andrade, d'Abrieu, de Grossa Testa, Breton, and Thomson.

JUNE

1. Friday. Messrs Kelsal, and Lovel din'd with us. Lovel says the miner brings what is call'd black tin to the smelting house, and delivers it by weight, to receive so much white tin at the Coinage, (which is quarterly) and take a tin bill for it, (if he be poor) which is marketable. Promis'd to inform himself farther. Le General Comte de Lucchesi, and the Minister of France came in the afternoon.

2. Saturday. Went to see Mr Oswald, at Wandsor.[1] Din'd alone. Came to town.

3. Sunday. Went to Leicester House. Din'd alone.

4. Monday. I went from town to dine with the Duke of Argyll. Call'd at Hammersmith, and found there Lord, and Lady Middlesex, and Lady Shannon. Return'd to town at night.

5. Tuesday. Went to Hammersmith with Mr Macartney: return'd, and din'd with him.

6. Wednesday. Din'd with the Prince, at his public dinner, 16 in company. All of the Family, except Lord Tyrawley, and Sir W. Stanhope.

7. Thursday. Went to Hammersmith with Mr Vere Poulet. Din'd at Carlton House with the Prince. Lord and Lady Middlesex, and Mr Breton.

8. Friday. Din'd alone. The Princess saw company, from 7, till 9 o'clock, for the first time, and once only. The Family went in, before any of the company were admitted. Return'd to Hammersmith in the evening.

9. Saturday. Mr and Mrs Oswald, and Mr Bance din'd with us. Mr Bance lay here.

10. Sunday. Went to Leicester House. Din'd alone. Mr Ralph came in the afternoon.

11. Monday. Came to town. Din'd with Mr Furnese. Sir Francis Dashwood came.

[1] Wandsworth.

12. Tuesday. Din'd with Sir Francis Dashwood. Return'd to Hammersmith.

13. Wednesday. Went to Kew to dinner, and carried Monsieur Servandoni. T.R.H. approv'd his plan. The Prince order'd me to stay with him till he went to London. Nobody then, but Lady Middlesex and Mr Breton.

14. Thursday. Mr Aldsworth came from the Duke of Bedford, with dispatches that came from Hanover signifying the King's approbation that Prince George, Lady Augusta, and brother of the Princess should be sponsors for the young Prince. Bishop of Oxford sent for. City order'd to compliment her on Wednesday.[1] Lord Bathurst came. We went to see Chiswick. Lady Howe, and Lord Bute, order'd to meet us, tomorrow at Lord Middlesex's.

15. Friday. The Prince, Lord Bathurst, and I rode out. Met the ladies, and Prince George, at Askley, where we din'd. After dinner went to Weybridge, Lord Portmore's. Return'd to Kew.

16. Saturday. Walk'd in Richmond Gardens. Lords Bathurst, and Bute, return'd to town.

17. Sunday. The Prince, and Mr Breton came to town in an open chair, about 1 o'clock: and I in another. The Princess, the royal children, and the ladies, came about three. I went to Leicester house.
   Din'd alone, and new dress'd for the christening. Went to Leicester House, at 8 o'clock. The child was christen'd, between 9 and 10 by the Bishop of Oxford—the sponsors as above—the Lord in Waiting (Lord North) represented the Princess's brother. Prince George gave the name: which was Frederic William. Nobody, of either sex, was admitted into the [christening] but the actual servants, except the Lord Chief Justice Willes, and Sir Luke Schaub.[2] Mr Furnese supp'd here.

18. Monday. Lord Middlesex, and Mr Drake were with me. Much talk about the Prince's tin, and the scandalous transaction about it, encourag'd by some of his servants. Drake thinks a vast profit

[1] 'The City ordered' = 'The City Corporation ordered congratulations to be delivered'.
[2] The Swiss-born diplomatist, who was now nearing the end of his long career of confidential service to George I and George II. He died in 1758.

may arise from farming it, both to the Prince, and the farmer: who would give him 200,000[1], by way of fine, for the farm.—I think little, or nothing can be given or got. But to get rid of him, and please Lady Middlesex, who seem'd to lean a little towards him, I left it thus.—That if any creditable man, or body of men, will take the best lease the Prince can give of his tin, reserving to H.R.H. his 4^s per hundredweight (which is 120) to be rais'd, and collected with the same dignity, and Royal Prerogative, as it now is: oblige themselves to pay to the miner, or owner (whom I put in the place of his tenants) 3[1] 5^s per cwt (of 112 lbs): bind themselves never to raise the price of tin, above 3^s per cwt higher than the market price shall be, at the time of signing the lease: and to deliver all that is rais'd at, or below that price. If for a 7 years lease, containing these conditions, they will pay H.R.H. else, by way of fine, 100,000[1] sterling without any reprizes, or deduction, he will make them such a lease, as shall be a sufficient security for them to undertake upon.

19. Tuesday. Went to dinner to Kew. Lord and Lady Middlesex, Lord Bathurst, Mr Breton, and I. T.R.H. and all of us, came to town, after supper.

20. Wednesday. Went to Leicester House—Lord Mayor, and Aldermen came to compliment the Princess upon her lying-in. Letter from Hanover with orders that those Knights of the Garter that did not walk shou'd choose their own proxies. The Prince designs Lord Inchiquin for Prince George's proxy.[1] Messrs Wyndham, and Breton din'd with us.

21. Thursday. We din'd alone. Went to Ranelagh with Lord and Lady Middlesex, Miss Jackson, Mrs Dodington, and Mr Breton.

22. Friday. Went to Kew with Lord and Lady Middlesex and Mr Breton. Lord Bathurst came; and we all went to Weybridge to dine with the Earl of Portmore, where was Lord Charles Hay. After dinner, we went upon the water, and then return'd to supper at Kew.

23. Saturday. We went with T.R.H. by water in the morning. Saw Lord Cholmondeley's house. Din'd in Merlin's Cave[2], where

---

[1] At the annual Garter Ceremony.
[2] An eating house in Clerkenwell, commemorated today by Merlin St.

Mr Bludworth came. Supp'd at Kew, whence T.R.H., and the rest of the company return'd to town, and I to Hammersmith.

24. Sunday. Din'd with us, Messrs Macartney, Breton, Bance, Kelsal, and Lovel.

25. Monday. I met Mr Vaneck junior, by appointment, at Lord Middlesex's about the Prince's tin. We had two hours conversation, the result of which is amongst the papers relating to that matter.— But upon the whole, to have all that is raised, and a liberty to advance the price 5 per cent. he could give no more than 66 shillings per cwt. so that supposing the tinners would be contented to bind themselves to the present market price of 64 (which I think they would not) the whole gain to the Prince would be 2 shillings per cwt. or 2[1] per ton, which upon 2,500 tons (the quantity suppos'd to be annually rais'd) amounts to 5,000[1] per annum.—

26. Tuesday. Went to Kew with Lord and Lady Middlesex, and Mr Breton, where we found Lord Bathurst: Lord Bute and Lady Howe came. We din'd, and supp'd there, and return'd to town at night.

27. Wednesday. Went to Leicester House. Lord, and Lady Middlesex, Miss Jackson, and Breton din'd with us, at Hammersmith. We all return'd to town at night.

28. Thursday. Lady Middlesex, Lord Bathurst, Mr Breton, and I waited on T.H.R. to Spittal Fields to see the manufactures of silk, and to Mr Carr's shop, in the morning. In the afternoon, the same company, with Lady Torrington in waiting, went in private coaches to Norwood Forest to see a settlement of gypsies. We return'd, and went to Bettesworth the conjuror's, in hackney coaches—not finding him we went in search of the little Dutchman, but were disappointed: and concluded by supping with Mrs Cannon, the Princess's midwife.[1]

29. Friday. Saw Mr Furnese, Mr Carey, and Mr Ralph, and had much conversation with him about the prosecution intended against

[1] Mrs. Sidney Cannon, or Kennan, celebrated as a collector of curios as well as in her profession, attending Lady Middlesex in her miscarriage as well as the Princess of Wales. When she died in 1754 Horace Walpole bought her collection of 'Brobdingnag combs, old broken pots, pans and pipkins, a lantern of scraped oyster-shells, scimitars, Turkish pipes, Chinese baskets' for Strawberry Hill. (Toynbee, iii. 397, and Arthur Young, *Autobiography*, 10–12.)

his paper. Din'd at Monsieur d'Abrieu's with the ministers of Portugal, Venice, and Modena, and Messrs Camisfort and Breton. T.R.H. went to Kew, and Lord Bathurst din'd there.

30. Saturday. Went to Council to confirm the sentence of a Swedish capture, which had been depending since 12 November 1745. From thence, call'd at Hammersmith, and carried Signor Servandoni, with the Prince's plans, to Kew: where I found Lord, and Lady Middlesex, Lord Bathurst, and Mr Breton. Sir Thomas Bootle came. We din'd, and supp'd there, and return'd to town, with T.H.R., at night.

JULY

1. Sunday. Went to Leicester House. At dinner receiv'd orders to have a post-chaise ready, at seven. We met at Carlton House T.R.H., Lady Middlesex, Lord Bathurst, Mr Breton, and I. We went with Lady Middlesex's coach, and my post-chaise, to Bethnall-Green to see Mr Murrie's collection of curiosities. From thence we return'd to London, and supp'd at the Temple with Sir Thomas Bootle, the Prince's Chancellor, where we met Lady Howe, Lord Bute, and Mr Masham. We parted at two, and I return'd to Hammersmith.

2. Monday. Mr Furnese, Mr Ralph, and I din'd with Mr Oswald, at Wandsworth. We had much talk about the public.—Resolv'd at my return to meet, and prepare for Parliament Enquiry such points as should appear most liable [to] censure: particularly to look into the grounds of Mr Lascelles' Quietus by Privy Seal; the expenditure during the war; the management of the Ordnance office; the affair of Nova Scotia; the Canada expedition &c. Mr Oswald thoroughly dispos'd to assist us. Return'd to town.[1]

3. Tuesday. Din'd at Lord Talbot's, with Lord Eglinton, Sir Francis, and Lady Dashwood, and Miss Wheat. Lord Talbot inform'd me of the many lies that were told of me to the Prince, and the unalterable inveteracy of the Family against me. God forgive them, I have not deserv'd it of them. Went to Hammersmith at night.

4. Wednesday. Went by water to town. Call'd at Lord Bolingbroke's. Return'd to dinner. Din'd alone.

5. Thursday. Din'd at Mr Furnese's. Return'd, and did not go to bed.—Offer'd Dr Thomson a room in my house, and £50 per annum, which he accepted.

6. Friday. At $\frac{3}{4}$ past one o'clock set out in my post-chaise from

---

[1] Edward Lascelles was Chief Engineer and Surveyor-General of the Ordnance. His accounts for war-time expenditure had been cleared by exercise of the prerogative instead of by submission to the audit of the Exchequer. Oswald was an old political ally of D., and this approach marks the climax of several attempts to draw him into D.'s system (see 2 Oct. 1749, 15 May and 2 June 1750).

Hammersmith to Eastbury. Got thither by $\frac{3}{4}$ past four in the afternoon, the same day, extremely well, and without the least accident: and found all things in very good order—God be prais'd.

7. Saturday. Mr Okeden came in the morning. Mr Carver din'd with us.

8. Sunday. Din'd with us, Mr and Mrs Okeden, Mrs and Miss Jicke, Mrs Farris, Messrs Carver and Gould. In the afternoon we went to see the course. Met Mr and Mrs Drax, coming to us.

9. Monday. Din'd alone.

10. Tuesday. Din'd at the ordinary, at Blandford. Went to the races. Lord Craven's horse won the £50 plate, by the two first heats. Return'd to the ball at Blandford. Got home by twelve.

11. Wednesday. Din'd at the same ordinary. Cudgel-playing in the afternoon. Return'd by nine.

12. Thursday. Din'd at the same ordinary. Went to the races—Messrs Sturt, Frampton, Napper, and Carver's horses started—the two last distanc'd the first heat. Mr Frampton's ran from the starting post the second heat. Mr Sturt's won. Return'd to the ball, and thence home by twelve. Installatn[?].

13. Friday. Din'd alone.

14. Saturday. Din'd alone.

15. Sunday. Din'd alone.

16. Monday. Went to Mr Drax's. Din'd alone.

17. Tuesday. Din'd alone.

18. Wednesday. Mr Crabb din'd with us.

19. Thursday. Mr and Mrs, and Miss Fanny and Molly Drax, and Messrs Banks and Earl din'd with us.

20. Friday. Mr Dodington came. Mr Blake din'd with us.

21. Saturday. Mr Dodington went away. Mr Thomas Churchill din'd with us.

22. Sunday. Din'd alone. Mr and Mrs Bower came in the afternoon.

23. Monday. Din'd alone.

24. Tuesday. Mr and Mrs Dodington came.

25. Wednesday. Messrs Trenchard and Bromfield, Mrs Trenchard and Bromfield din'd with us. [Wrote to] Cardinal Albani.

26. Thursday. Went to see Mr Sturt's water. Din'd alone.

27. Friday. Din'd alone.

28. Saturday. Din'd alone.

29. Sunday. Din'd alone.

30. Monday. Messrs Tucker and Younge came, and Mr Carver din'd with us.

31. Tuesday. Din'd alone.

AUGUST

1. Wednesday. Din'd alone. Sent to Mr Ralph, by Whitehead, a scheme of opposition to be communicated to Lords Middlesex and Talbot, Sir Francis Dashwood, Messrs Furnese, and Oswald.[1]

2. Thursday. Din'd alone.

3. Friday. Mr Richard Tucker went away in the morning. We all din'd at Mr Carver's.

4. Saturday. Messrs Dodington, Tucker, and their wives went away.—Mr Younge went to dinner with Mr Beckford. [Wrote to] Mr Slabrendorf.

5. Sunday. Went to see Messrs Beckford, and Ryves. Din'd alone.

6. Monday. Mr Carver din'd with us.

7. Tuesday. Messrs Beckford, Bower, and Carver din'd with us.

8. Wednesday. I din'd at Mr Pleydell's. Mr Younge went away.

9. Thursday. Din'd alone.

10. Friday. Din'd alone.

11. Saturday. Din'd at Mr Drax's. News of the Duke of Richmond's death on the Wednesday before.

12. Sunday. Din'd alone.

13. Monday. Din'd at Lord Arundell's.

14. Tuesday. Din'd at Mr Trenchard's.

15. Wednesday. Messrs Ryves, and Williams din'd with us.

16. Thursday. Went to see Miss Sturt. Din'd alone.

17. Friday. Din'd at Mr Banks's.

18. Saturday. Mr Wyndham came. Lord and two Ladies Shaftesbury, Mrs [?], and Miss Sturt. Messrs Sturt, Carver, and Crabb din'd with us. [Wrote to] Lady Middlesex.

---

[1] Clearly the fruit of country reflection. The paper is lost. Whitehead was the steward and organizer of Dashwood's Medmenham revels.

19. Sunday. Mr Grove din'd with us.

20. Monday. Went to Mr Giles. Din'd alone.

21. Tuesday. Din'd alone.

22. Wednesday. Messrs Okeden, and Jones of Ireland din'd with us. Mr Breton came from Bath, at night.

23. Thursday. Din'd alone.

24. Friday. Mr Breton, and I din'd at Mr Drax's.

25. Saturday. Mr Breton went away. Din'd alone.

26. Sunday. Din'd alone.

27. Monday. Mrs Churchill, and Miss Churchill of Henbury. Mr and Mrs Churchill of Kent. Mr and Mrs Thomas Damer din'd here.

28. Tuesday. Went to Mr Bower's. Din'd alone. Mr Douglas came.

29. Wednesday. Din'd alone.

30. Thursday. Lord and Lady Arundell, Lady Gifford, and Monsieur de Laval din'd with us.

31. Friday. Mr Douglas went away. Messrs Thomas Trenchard and Picard, and Miss Trenchard came in the morning. We din'd at Lord Shaftesbury's.

SEPTEMBER

1. Saturday. Mr Drax, and family, Mr and Mrs Barbar, Mr Carver, and Mr Younge, din'd with us.

2. Sunday. Din'd alone.

3. Monday. Mr Younge went away. We din'd alone.

4. Tuesday. Mr Furnese came in the morning from Dorchester. Mr Blake din'd with us.

5. Wednesday. Mr Furnese went away. I went to see Sir William Napper. Din'd alone.

6. Thursday. Mr Wyndham went to Horsington. Mr Tucker came, din'd, and went on to Salisbury, in order to meet us at Mr Bance's.

7. Friday. Mrs Dodington, and I set out from Eastbury, between 4 and 5 o'clock. Went to Mr Younge's, whose horses carried us to Everleigh—where we found our own, which brought us to Ramsbury. There we met Mr Bance, and his chaise, in which we arriv'd at his house, at Challow, about 4 o'clock.

8. Saturday. At Mr Bance's.

9. Sunday. Lord Barrington came over to see me, but did not stay dinner.

10. Monday. Left Mr Bance's between 4 and 5 o'clock. Got to Sir Francis Dashwood's between 10 and 11.[1]

11. Tuesday. At Wycombe. Sir Francis told me, what he had learn'd from Mr Boone viz: That they were satisfied that my design

---

[1] The first chance of consulting about the 'scheme of opposition'. Ralph had already reported to D. on 23 August (*H.M.C. Var. Coll.* vi. 21) Waller's dislike of it as likely to appeal to only part of the Prince's court, and his preference for 'a sensible opposition, grounded on such facts as might serve to expose the administration to the bottom'—to which he added significantly that 'embarking H.R.H. on such an opposition is the strongest security for his future conduct'. Dashwood thought D.'s proposals too vague but 'did not consider himself qualified to supply what was wanting'.

when I came into the Family, was to turn them all out even to the women, &c—that the Prince told him (Boone) that I forc'd myself into his services, and that he could not help taking me &c. That Lord Egmont said he knew that the Prince never advis'd with, or communicated anything to me &c.—That Lord Egmont defray'd the Prince's expenses at Bath &c.

12. Wednesday. Went to Cliefden—met Lord Bathurst going away. Very kindly receiv'd—Lord North, Messrs Boone, Cust, and Scott, and Lady Howe were there. Went with T.R.H. to Windsor. Return'd, and was order'd to stay another day. Din'd with T.R.H. at Desnoyer's.

[13.]¹

14. Friday. Sir Francis, and I return'd to Wycombe, by ten in the morning.

15. Saturday. I came from Wycombe to Hammersmith.

16. Sunday. Messrs Furnese, and Ralph came to me.—We had much conversation.—We agreed that the Prince should, as soon as possible, be brought to some eclaircissement, and inform'd, with proof, of the lyes that have been told him of me, by Lords Egmont, and Baltimore, &c.—That otherwise, I could not act in public with them &c. This is to be done by Lord Middlesex.

17. Monday. Went to town to see Sir Paul Methuen, and return'd to Hammersmith, to dinner. Mr Breton call'd here. [Wrote to] Mr Stanley.

18. Tuesday. Mr Breton call'd here. About 12 o'clock I went to Kew. There was Ladies Middlesex, and Howe, Lords Middlesex, and Bute, Mr Breton.—They played at Bumbase.² We din'd, and supp'd, and I chose to come home.

19. Wednesday. Went to a meeting at the King's Arms tavern, 'Change Alley, at 11 o'clock, about the Herring Fishery—Propos'd

¹ The omission of this day—the 13th, of all possible dates—coupled with the visit of Whitehead mentioned earlier and the neighbourhood of Wycombe, strongly suggests a meeting of the Medmenham brotherhood. D. almost never omits a day altogether.
² A childish card-game.

to choose the Governor, &c by lists.—Much oppos'd by the Scotch interest.—I argu'd for it, from the authority of the Act of Parliament which at last prevail'd, by 19, against 7.[1] Brought Carey back to Hammersmith, who lay there.

20. Thursday. Went to town. Saw Mr Ralph, after much talk agreed to go to Mr Waller's, on Tuesday. Return'd to Hammersmith, and din'd alone.

21. Friday. Mr Breton din'd here.

22. Saturday. Went to town—return'd, and din'd alone.

23. Sunday. Din'd with us, Sir Paul Methuen, Mr Furnese, Mr Jeffreys, Mr Ralph, and Mr Carey.

24. Monday. Went to town.—Return'd, and din'd alone. [Wrote to] Monsieur Servandoni.

25. Tuesday. Carried Mr Ralph with me to Mr Waller's, in three hours. Much debate about the means of forming an opposition, and its end: at last he promised to act heartily with me, and we agreed to begin with the Ordnance.

26. Wednesday. I return'd to Hammersmith. Din'd alone.

27. Thursday. Carried Dr Thomson to Ashley [Lord Middlesex's] in two hours. Much talk with my Lord that day, and the next morning. Agreed that the country was in a deplorable state: and that the safety of the Prince's succession was in great danger from the maxims he had adopted, and was encourag'd in by those he most hearken'd to at present, of continuing to embroil this country, on account of Lower Saxony: and of not paying off any taxes. Agreed also that Lord Middlesex should procure some explanation: or that both of us should neither meddle with, nor appear in the business of the House.

28. Friday. Return'd, and din'd alone.

29. Saturday. Went to Cheere's. Return'd, and din'd alone.

[1] Having achieved all this he found he had no right to be present, his namesake cousin of Horsington being the shareholder. (See *Correspondence, &c., of James Oswald*, p. 482.)

30. Sunday. Went to town. At Leicester House. Lord Bute kiss'd hands for the Bed-chamber—Colonel Robinson, as Equerry. N.B., This gentleman, as well as Lord North, are to remain under the title of servants to the Prince, but are to attend the Princes George, and Edward, as Governor, and Equerry. Din'd with Lady Middlesex. Saw Sir Francis Dashwood in the evening. Supp'd at Carlton House, Ladies Shannon and Middlesex, Mr Breton and I. Order'd to attend T.R.H. next day, to Kew, and stay till Wednesday. Return'd to Hammersmith at one o'clock.

OCTOBER

1. Monday. Came to Pall Mall. At two the Princess with Ladies Middlesex and Howe went to Kew. Lord Bute and I call'd upon the Prince at Kensington. Went on to Kew. Mr Breton came with the Prince. Play'd at lanterlu.[1]

2. Tuesday. Walk'd all the morning. Lord Bute and Lady Howe stay'd at home. Went to the play, and return'd to supper. Lady Howe did not go: Lord Bute went to town, but neither went to the play, nor return'd.

3. Wednesday. Play'd at cricket. Lady Berkeley came. Din'd at six. About nine T.R.H., Lady Berkeley, and Mr Breton, set out for Cliefden.—Ladies Middlesex and Howe for town, and I for Hammersmith.

4. Thursday. Went to town. To Council at the Cockpit. Petition to free the cargo, consisting of wool, chiefly, of two ships that came from Santa Cruiz, and Saffia, with foul bills of health. Order'd that the cargo should be air'd before they were freed. Din'd alone, and return'd. [Wrote to] Messrs Stanley and Mann.

5. Friday. Went to town. Return'd, and din'd alone.

6. Saturday. The same.

7. Sunday. Din'd here, Sir Francis Dashwood, Dr Thomson, and Mr Kelsal, who lay here.

8. Monday. Went to town by 8 o'clock—waited upon Lady Middlesex, [and] to the Portuguese chapel to hear the funeral service perform'd for the late King of Portugal. It lasted 5 hours. There were three private, and one High Mass celebrated. Also a funeral service. —All in Latin.—Return'd, and din'd alone.

9. Tuesday. Went to town. Return'd, and din'd alone.

10. Wednesday. Went to town, return'd and din'd alone.

11. Thursday. Din'd alone. [Wrote to] Cardinal Albani.

12. Friday. Went to town, return'd.—Din'd alone.

[1] i.e. loo, the card game.

13. Saturday. The same.

14. Sunday. Went to see Mr Oswald, at Wandsworth. He is in Warwickshire. Mr Breton din'd with us.

15. Monday. Went to town. Return'd and din'd alone.

16. Tuesday. Din'd here, Messrs Ralph and Younge.

17. Wednesday. Din'd alone.

18. Thursday. Came to town. Went to Council. Present Archbishop, Lord Chancellor, Lord Privy Seal, Duke of Bedford, Mr Pelham, Lord Chief Justice, Mr Speaker, Master of the Rolls, Sir Thomas Robinson. Parliament prorogued to 22 November. Lay in town.

19. Friday. Din'd with us, Messrs Solicitor General, Breton, and Furnese.

20. Saturday. Din'd alone. Went to *The Provok'd Wife*.

21. Sunday. T.R.H. came to town for a few hours, in the afternoon, and return'd to Kew. Mr Breton din'd with us.

22. Monday. Went to Lady Middlesex's at one. She and Lady Howe in one coach: Lord Bute, Messrs Masham, Breton, and I in another, set out for Kew Ferry: where T.R.H. join'd us, and Prince William came into our coach. We arriv'd at Cliefden about 5. Found there Lord Bathurst and Mr Bludworth. *The Royal Convert*.

23. Tuesday. *Le Mari Gargon. Crispin Précepteur.*

24. Wednesday. *Alcibiade.* Oratorio.

25. Thursday. The Prince went to London to receive the patent of Governor of the Herring Fishery. Took with him Lords Bute and Bathurst, and Mr Masham—was to dine at Carlton House, lie at Kew, come hither by dinner. Messrs Bludworth, Breton, and I stayed with the Princess. Din'd, had music, played at faro and supp'd with her.

26. Friday. The Prince return'd between 3 and 4. *Beggar's Opera.*

27. Saturday. T.R.H. and Lady Howe went as far as Kew with Lady Middlesex who went to town to Lady Caroline Colyeare's

wedding with Mr Curzon. T.R.H. return'd at 7 o'clock. We din'd, and play'd at cards.

28. Sunday. Prayers.—Afternoon, Faro.

29. Monday. *The Indian Emperor.*—A French scene, by the Prince, alone.

30. Tuesday. *Le Joueur. Hobb.*

31. Wednesday. *The Relapse.*

NOVEMBER

1. Thursday. Went to Wooburn Fair. *Tamerlane.*

2. Friday. *The Relapse. Crispin Précepteur.*

3. Saturday. Lord Bathurst went to Gloucestershire, Mr Bludworth to Hampshire. T.R.H., Ladies Middlesex and Howe, Lord Bute, Messrs Masham, and I, to Windsor. Saw Mr Topham's drawings at Eton. Din'd at Mr Masham's. Left him there, and came to Carlton House to supper.

4. Sunday. Went to Leicester House. Din'd alone. The King landed about 12 o'clock, at Harwich, and came to St James's between ten, and eleven.

5. Monday. Went to St James's. Kiss'd the King's hand. Din'd alone.

6. Tuesday. Lord Poulet, and Mr Breton din'd here. Went to Mr Scrope's.

7. Wednesday. Mr Breton din'd here. Went to Dr Lee's, and Mr Bodens.

8. Thursday. Messrs Carey, Ralph, and Probyn din'd here. I went to *Macbeth.* Supp'd at Carlton House. Lady Middlesex, Lord Bute, and I only. Gave Mr R[alph] 34 guineas.

9. Friday. Took physic. Din'd alone.

10. Saturday. Lords Poulet and Bute, Messrs Breton and Fane din'd with us, and Mr Tucker came in. Supp'd at Carlton House. Lady Middlesex, Mr Breton, and I.

12. Monday. Din'd alone. Went to Mr Scrope's. Mr Chamberlayne paid me £40 from Colonel Younge, due at midsummer.

13. Tuesday. Mr Carey din'd here.

14. Wednesday. The King's birthday was kept. Din'd alone. Went to Sir Paul Methuen's.

15. Thursday. Din'd, no company but Dr Thomson.

16. Friday. Sir Miles Stapylton din'd here. Went to Mr Drax's.

17. Saturday. Din'd alone. Went to Mr Scrope's. Supp'd at Carlton House. Lady Middlesex, Mr Breton.

18. Sunday. Westminster Bridge open'd. Mr Tucker and I went to Mr Scrope's, to desire him to acquaint Mr Pelham that as we suppos'd that when he engag'd for the charter of Weymouth, he understood he was to have two friends there, during this Parliament, tho' no such conditions were actually express'd, yet if Mr Plumer[1] should die (who was that day cut for the stone) we were too nice upon points of honour to take the advantage, of what might be imply'd tho' not specify'd, and therefore would choose any unexceptionable gentleman he should name. Any other, or one who by his relations, or situation might seem to be put there with a view to make a separate interest, we would not choose. And the insisting upon such an one should look on as a premeditated design to make war, which, when we were in the right, we were ready to begin, as soon as they pleas'd. Mr Tucker din'd here. Went to Sir Paul Methuen's.

19. Monday. The Princess's birthday. Went to Leicester Fields. Din'd there MM le Marquis de Mirepoix, General Wall, Comte du Perron, Baron Hop, Businella, l'Abbé de Grossa Testa, Baron de Munchausen, Marquis d'Ayé, Comte de Lascaris, Comte de la Marmora, de Lausandière, Baron de St Fiorent, Duke of Queensberry, Earl of Middlesex, Earl of Bute, Earl of Bath, Mr Breton. Went to Sir Paul Methuen's. Call'd at Mr Drax's.

20. Tuesday. Din'd alone. Went to Council. Supp'd at Mr Furnese's who came to town that day.

21. Wednesday. Went to the King's Lever. Heard there that the Earl of Burlington was struck with an apoplexy last night, but about 12 this morning a message was brought that he was come to himself, and was a little better. The King came to Council. Proclamation order'd to prorogue the Parliament till the 17th January then to

---

[1] Richard Plumer (1685–1750) did die. His chequered parliamentary career of twenty-eight years and four different seats had included St Mawes (1734–41) and shows him to have been a ministerialist. The meaning of the following words is that while Pelham had been entitled to nominate Plumer for that Parliament, the formal bargain did not extend to his nominating for a casual vacancy.

meet and do business. Order'd 8,000 seamen. Went to Leicester House. Din'd alone. Went to the Duke of Argyll's, and Mr Scrope's.

22. Thursday. Din'd alone. Supp'd at Carlton House. Ladies Middlesex and Howe. Duke of Queensberry, and Bathurst.

23. Friday. Din'd here the Duke of Argyll, Messrs Fletcher, Vaughan, and Lynn. Mr Breton supp'd here.

24. Saturday. Din'd at Mr Henley's. Went to Mr Drax's.

25. Sunday. Went to Leicester House. Heard there, that the King, at his Lever, said he had receiv'd news of the death of the Maréchal de Saxe. Din'd alone. Went to Mr Breton's, Sir Paul Methuen's, and Mr Scrope's. Supp'd at Carlton House. T.R.H., Lady Middlesex, and I only.

26. Monday. Din'd at the French Ambassador's. Went to Mr Drax's.

27. Tuesday. Din'd here Lord Robert Bertie, Sir William Irby, Envoys of Portugal and Venice, Marquis d'Ayé, Comte de la Marmora. Went to Lord Bolingbroke's, and the Speaker's.

28. Wednesday. Went to Leicester House. In the evening we went to Hammersmith.

29. Thursday. Din'd alone. Came to town. Went to the play of *Henry V*. Supp'd at Carlton House. T.R.H., Lady Middlesex, and I only.

30. Friday. Messrs La Rocke, Kelsal, and Tucker din'd with us.

DECEMBER

1. Saturday. Din'd alone. Came to Pall Mall. Went to Mr Scrope's.

2. Sunday. Mr Bance din'd with us. Went to Lord Bolingbroke's, and Sir Paul Methuen's. Supp'd at Carlton House. Lady Middlesex, Mr Masham, and I.

3. Monday. Din'd here, Earls of Middlesex, and Stafford, and Mr Ralph.

4. Tuesday. Dr Thomson din'd here.

5. Wednesday. Din'd alone.

6. Thursday. Went to Council, Sheriffs prick'd. Duke of Dorset declar'd Lord Lieutenant of Ireland in Council. Din'd alone. Went to the *Merry Wives of Windsor*. Supp'd at Carlton House. Ladies Howe, Middlesex, Lady Charlotte Edwin, Lord North. Lay at Hammersmith. [Wrote to] Messrs Mann and Nicolini.

7. Friday. Mr Hampden came in the morning. Din'd alone.

8. Saturday. Din'd alone. Came to town. Went to Mr Scrope's.

9. Sunday. Went to Leicester House. Duke of Dorset kiss'd hands. Din'd with us, Duke of Queensbury, Lords Bute and Hillsborough, Messrs Masham, Macky, and Colonel Lyttelton. Went to supper at Carlton House. Ladies Middlesex and Howe, Mr Masham. Went to Hammersmith.

10. Monday. Din'd alone. Receiv'd orders to attend the Prince at Kew on Tuesday, and lie there.

11. Tuesday. Came to town, and Mr Tucker and I went to Mr Pelham at Mr Scrope's, by appointment; we settled the Weymouth re-election, according to the agreement made on obtaining the new charter, and he recommended Lord George Cavendish. Lord and Lady Middlesex, and I went to Kew, and Mr Masham.

12. Wednesday. T.R.H., and we, came to town. Messrs Rocke, and Tucker din'd with us. Went to Mr Scrope's.

13. Thursday. Din'd alone. Went to Council.

14. Friday. Din'd at Colonel Lyttelton's—went to Mr Scrope's, Drax's, Duke of Argyll's, and Lord Bolingbroke's.

15. Saturday. Din'd here, Drs Thomson, and Sharpe, Ralph and Carey.

16. Sunday. Went to Leicester House. Din'd here, French Ambassador, Spanish and Bavarian Ministers, Messrs de Lausandière, and d'Abrieu, the Duke of Dorset, the Earl of Bath. Supp'd at Carlton House. Ladies Middlesex and Howe. Earl of Bute.

17. Monday. Went from Hammersmith (where I arriv'd last night from supper at Carlton House to dine with the French Ambassador). Return'd to Hammersmith. [Wrote to] Cardinal Albani: given into the hands of the French Ambassador.

18. Tuesday. Din'd and lay at Kew. Lady Middlesex, Lord Bathurst, Mr Bludworth.

19. Wednesday. Came to town with T.R.H.—went to Leicester Fields. Din'd with us, Dr Sharpe, Messrs Saxby, Ralph, and Carey. Return'd to Hammersmith.

20. Thursday. Earl of Uxbridge and Sir William Irby breakfasted here. Din'd alone.

21. Friday. Din'd alone.

22. Saturday. Came to town. Din'd at the Duke of Queensberry's. Call'd upon Mr Furnese. Supp'd at Carlton House. Ladies Middlesex and Howe, Lord Bathurst.

23. Sunday. Went to Leicester House. Paid Mr Bance £400, part of 1,700 Roman Crowns, by him remitted to Rome, to pay for statues. Din'd at Sir William Irby's. Call'd upon Mr Furnese.

24. Monday. Din'd alone. Went to Sir Paul Methuen's. [Wrote to] Messrs Stanley and Servandoni.

25. Tuesday. Mr Younge din'd with us. Pass'd the evening, and supp'd at Lord Middlesex's with T.R.H., and all the children but Prince William. Ladies Shannon, Howe, Miss Rich, Lords Bute, Bathurst, Messrs Masham, Sir Thomas Bootle, Bludworth.

26. Wednesday. Went to Leicester House. From thence to Hammersmith to dinner. Din'd alone.

27. Thursday. Din'd alone. Sent for to supper at Carlton House. Lady Middlesex, Mr Bludworth, and I. Set out to Hammersmith, at one o'clock. Reason to suspect there were highwaymen on the road.

28. Friday. Din'd alone.

29. Saturday. Came to town. Din'd at the Earl of Carlisle's,— and supp'd at Mr Furnese's.

30. Sunday. Din'd with us, Envoys of Portugal, and of Sardinia, Monsieur de Munchausen, Duke of Queensberry, Lord Drumlanrig, Lord Charles Douglas, Lord North. Supp'd at Carlton House. Messrs Masham, Breton (who went away), Lady Middlesex, and I.

31. Monday. Din'd at Mr Masham's. Had a long, and I hope useful, and productive consultation, all the morning, with Messrs Oswald, Furnese, and Ralph. Went to Mr Scrope's in the evening.

1751

JANUARY

1. Tuesday. Went to Leicester House. About 4 o'clock Ladies Middlesex and Howe, Lord Bathurst, Messrs Masham, Breton, and Bludworth, Sir Thomas Bootle, and I, set out from Carlton House for Kew, where we din'd. *Cinna.*

2. Wednesday. *La Comtesse d'Orgueil.*

3. Thursday. 2nd *Part of Henry the Fourth.*

4. Friday. *The Silent Woman.*

5. Saturday. *The Suspicious Husband.* Return'd from Kew with T.R.H., after supper.

6. Sunday. Went to Leicester House. Din'd alone. Lady Gage.

7. Monday. Renewal of the consultation of last Monday with Messrs Furnese, Oswald, and Ralph. Some progress made.—Sir Paul Methuen, Earl of Carlisle, Sir Miles Stapylton, Dr Lee, and Sir Thomas Bootle, din'd with us.—Supp'd at Lady Middlesex's. It being Twelfth Night she went 75 and I 125 guineas with the Prince, who sent us word we had lost 8 guineas between us two.

8. Tuesday. We all return'd to dinner at Kew, viz: T.R.H., Ladies Middlesex and Howe, Lord Bathurst, Messrs Masham, Bludworth, Breton, Bootle, and I. *Les Horaces.*

9. Wednesday. T.R.H. went to London to their drawing-room, and return'd to their dinner.—*Plain Dealer.*

10. Thursday. *Merry Wives of Windsor.*

11. Friday. *First Part of Henry the Fourth.*

12. Saturday. T.R.H. and all of us, but Mr Bludworth, came to town.

13. Sunday. Din'd with us, Dr Lee, Messrs Masham, Douglas, and Cambridge. Was at Leicester House—the evening at Mr Furnese's.

14. Monday. Messrs Furnese, Oswald, Ralph, and Lord Talbot met at my house and made further progress in business. Din'd alone. Mr Waller's.

15. Tuesday. At one o'clock receiv'd orders to come and dine, and lie, at Kew. Ladies Middlesex and Torrington, Mr Masham, and I, went together. Play'd at faro. Lord Bathurst came on horseback.

16. Wednesday. Came to town to the Drawing Room. Din'd at Carlton House. The Prince, Lords Granby, Middlesex, Egmont, Limerick, Sir John Rushout, Sir Thomas Bootle, Dr Lee, Messrs Bathurst, Henley, Nugent, Gibbon, and I.

17. Thursday. The session open'd.—Long debate upon the Address. Division: 74 to 203—Mighty simple—Lady Middlesex.

18. Friday. Lord Westmorland¹ was here. I propos'd a cooperation, with a small number of peers: which he seem'd to approve of, and promis'd to endeavour to make it practicable. Went to Council in the evening.

19. Saturday. Lord Talbot, Sir Francis Dashwood, Messrs Furnese, Waller, Oswald, and Ralph, spent the morning in further prosecution of business. Sir Francis din'd with us. Mr Scrope's, and Lady Middlesex.—

20. Sunday. Went to Leicester House.—Din'd at Devonshire House. —The Duke [of Devonshire], Lords Frederick and George, Marquis of Hartington, Mr Pelham, Lord ——, Mr Ellis, Mr Tucker.²—At nine went in private coaches to Mr Glass's (where we sent for a conjuror) with T.R.H., Ladies Middlesex and Howe, Lord Inchiquin, Sir Thomas Bootle.—Supp'd at Carlton House.

21. Monday. The Prince's birthday kept. Din'd with me, Marquis de Mirepoix, General Wall, M. d'Abrieu, Comte du Perron. Abbé de Grossa Testa, M. de Lausandière, Marquis d'Ayé, Comte de la

¹ One of the few remaining Jacobites. In the previous October he had been Charles Edward's host on the Prince's clandestine visit to London, and had decided the Stuart cause was hopeless.
² Settling Weymouth. Lord George Cavendish was the Pelham nominee (see 11 Dec. above). Contrast the entry for 14 Jan. above for D.'s activity in organizing the opposition.

Marmora, and de Lascaris, Baron de St Fiorent, Comte de Haslang, Duke of Queensberry, Lord Talbot, Sir Francis Dashwood, Mr Breton.

22. Tuesday. Debate upon some queries about the army, that were dispers'd.—Agree with Lords to burn them.[1] I was not at the House.—Had a defluxion on my jaw, and a sore throat. Din'd at the King's Head with Lords Halifax, and Talbot, and Sir Francis Dashwood. Came home much worse.

23. Wednesday. Continued in violent pain. Din'd here, Sir Francis Dashwood, Messrs Ralph, Carey, and Dr Thomson.

24. Thursday. Took physic.—Still remain'd in continual pain.—
—Din'd alone.—Worse at night.

25. Friday. Much worse.—The pain fix'd upon a tooth.—Neither ate nor drank. A bad night. Din'd here, Messrs Ralph and Cary.

26. Saturday. Had a tooth drawn by [not clear in manuscript] with infinite pain.—Was easier. Din'd alone, grew worse at night, and slept ill.

27. Sunday. Not well.—Din'd here, Messrs Furnese and Carey.

28. Monday. Continued ill.—Din'd alone, took physic.

29. Tuesday. Was better.—Went for the air to Hammersmith.—Return'd with a fit of the colic. Din'd here, Messrs Ralph and Carey. I could not dine, nor sup. A bad night.

30. Wednesday. Worse of the colic, neither ate nor drank.—Took a glyster which gave some ease.—Ate at night—but an indifferent one.

31. Thursday. Less complaint, but very slow recovery.—Very weak, and low-spirited.—Din'd alone.—A better night, but not a good one.

[1] i.e. the 'queries' or seditious pamphlets.

FEBRUARY

1. Friday. Ill, and a bad night.

2. Saturday. Din'd at Dr Lee's.

3. Sunday. Worse. A bad night.

4. Monday. Went to the House.—Army voted. 240 to 117.

5. Tuesday. Took physic. Paid Mr Mann £100 for his brother.[1]

6. Wednesday. Went to the House to hear the charge against Mr Murray, brother to Lord Elibank, for words spoken against the High Baily, the day of his making the return for Westminster (15 of May last). After the trial was over, and first question mov'd, I left the House and came to Hammersmith.—Never saw an accusation worse supported—by anything but numbers. Paid Mr Selwyn £120.

7. Thursday. Din'd alone.

8. Friday. Went to town to wait upon Mr Waller's motion which did not come on. Return'd to dinner. Din'd alone.

9. Saturday. Came to town, din'd here les Marquis Doria, d'Ayé, and Marmora and Mr Stanley.—At Mr Ralph's.

10. Sunday. Evening at Mr Scrope's. Supp'd at Carlton House. Lady Middlesex, Earl of Inchiquin, and I. Servandoni came.

11. Monday. Amongst others Mr Oswald was here, who treated me in the most affectionate, and friendly manner. Told me all his views and the offers that had been made him: and concluded by saying that he wish'd always to act with me: and that he would accept of the Prince's service, if he might come into it, as my friend, and by, and thro' my hands, but that he would not come in, by any other hands, or canal.—Lady Middlesex call'd upon me in the evening.

12. Tuesday. Went to wait on H.R.H. at Kew. Propos'd to him the securing Mr Oswald, by my weight with him. The Prince hesitated a little, as having made a trial some time ago, by another hand,

---

[1] i.e. Horace Mann—for antiques.

without success.—At last allow'd the importance of the acquistion, and order'd me to sound Mr Oswald's disposition toward it.— H.R.H. order'd me to dine and lie there.

13. Wednesday. Came to town. Mr Oswald din'd with us,—and agreed to come to Hammersmith, the next morning, to settle what report I should make to the Prince.—Went to Council, and thence, to Hammersmith.

14. Thursday. Mr Oswald did not come. Din'd alone.

15. Friday. Mr Oswald came and was pleas'd to put himself entirely into my hands, and to rely upon my friendship—but being both desirous to hear the disposition of the money for the services of the year, he carried me to the House, and agreed to come to Hammersmith on Monday next to fix my report, with relations to him.— Voted 3ˢ per £ on the land, which with the malt, and £40,000 out of the Sinking Fund, makes the Supply. Return'd to Hammersmith. Din'd alone.

16. Saturday. Din'd alone. Went to town. Dr Lee came to me.— I talk'd over to him at large the points of the Spanish Treaty.—Mr Lascelles's Privy Seal—and ordnance contract—and the expedition. He seem'd to approve of them. I gave him several papers to look over at home.—He told me very frankly that whatever I propos'd he would cheerfully support with all his power in the debate, but as he was enjoin'd secrecy, and would keep it, he could not be the mover, or seconder, because that would look like breaking short with Lord Egmont, and those he had acted with.

17. Sunday. Went to Leicester House. Din'd at Mr Waller's. Earl of Carlisle, Sir Paul Methuen, Sir Miles Stapylton, Sir Thomas Bootle, Dr Lee, who gave me my papers, thought the Treaty would not be a point strong enough, but approv'd of the others. Supp'd at Carlton House. Ladies Middlesex and Howe, Messrs Masham and Breton. The Prince left us before supper, with the head ache. After supper, I return'd to Hammersmith.

18. Monday. Mr Oswald came, and we agreed upon the method of my report to the Prince. Din'd alone. [Wrote to] Cardinal Albani and Mr Mann.

19. Tuesday. Went to Kew at three o'clock in my own coach. Found there T.R.H., Earl of Bute, Lord Bathurst, Messrs Masham, Bludworth, and Breton. *Britannicus*.

20. Wednesday. *Man of the Mode*.

21. Thursday. Lords Bute and Bathurst went early to town. The Prince went at twelve, attended by the Earl of Inchiquin and Mr Bludworth. Messrs Masham, Breton, and I went to Hammersmith. Return'd at four. The Prince half an hour after. *Venice Preserv'd*.

22. Friday. *Harry the VIII*.

23. Saturday. I began by telling the Prince, that on the Monday Mr Oswald was with me, to acquaint me that he had receiv'd positive offers from Court: he was surprised, and ask'd me what they were: I told him that tho', to be sure as I ow'd my first duty to him, I was to conceal no thing from him that related to his service; but that there were also other duties that I held sacred, and if I discover'd the secret of a friend to him, I hop'd H.R.H. would be pleas'd to promise me that it should go no farther, which he did, I then told him that Mr Oswald had been offer'd to be made Comptroller of the Navy, with promise that he should have the assistance of all Mr Pelham's power to reform the abuses of it; and full liberty to follow his own opinion in parliament &c. and that he came to ask my opinion upon it. The Prince concluding he would accept of it, said he was glad he should find so honest a man in business. I told him that from the many reasons I had given him, he declar'd to me that as he saw no reformation could be thoroughly effectual, but by the concurrence of the Crown, which was not to be hop'd for in our present situation, he had much rather attach himself to H.R.H. from whence only we could hope for that concurrence: but that as he was no Courtier, and had no connections of that kind, he must be contented to do his best in the station that was offer'd him.—That I bid him seriously consider whether, in case I would venture to sound H.R.H.'s disposition towards him, he would impower me to say that he would refuse all offers of the Court in case the Prince were inclin'd to admit him into his service.—That he told me that I positively might, upon which I promis'd to undertake it. After a good deal of talk, the Prince

thank'd me, and order'd me to send Mr Oswald to him to Leicester House between seven and eight o'clock on Thursday next. *Rehearsal*. We return'd to town after supper.

24. Sunday. Went to Leicester House. Din'd here, Mr Bance, Earl of Inchiquin, Mr Breton.—At Sir Paul Methuen's.

25. Monday. Mr Oswald din'd here—told me, he was much embarrass'd at what had pass'd, since he saw me: of which he gave me the following account. Sunday the seventeenth, Sir Henry Erskine[1] was introduc'd to the Prince, for the first time: Monday the eighteenth, Mr Oswald was with me to settle the report I was to make to the Prince—on Tuesday the nineteenth in the House Sir Henry asks him—'Have you receiv'd any message from the Prince?' 'What do you mean?' 'Has the Earl of Egmont deliver'd you no message?'— 'I don't know the Earl of Egmont'. 'He will then, for I was introduc'd to the Prince, last Sunday, and he ask'd me if I knew you—I said, yes, intimately: ask'd how you were dispos'd towards him I replied that I thought you had the highest regard for him &c. He said, I must send to him, by Dr Lee, or Lord Egmont, for what comes from them, is the same as if it came from me.' This seem'd strange to us, but I think I guess the drift. Mr Ralph.[2]

26. Tuesday. Went to the Earl of Shaftesbury's. Much talk with him about separating the Tories from the Jacobites on the quarrel between them about the late University election,[3] which was to be done by bringing them to a declaration of few heads, which he said he had made use of, and hoped he should succeed. Mr Stanley din'd here. Duke of Argyll's.

27. Wednesday. Went to Leicester House. Mr Breton din'd here. Went to the Oratorio together. Sir Francis Dashwood's.

---

[1] See below, 1 Mar. 1751.

[2] i.e. D. had been once again out-manœuvred by Egmont, who did not intend to let D. have the credit of acquiring Oswald for the Prince's entourage. The most significant part of the interview between D. and Oswald had been that Oswald would come in as D.'s friend.

[3] In the by-election for a succeesor to Lord Cornbury (see 18 Nov. 1749 above) as member for Oxford University there had been three candidates—Sir Roger Newdigate, who was elected, Sir Edward Turner, and Edward Harley, son of the 3rd Earl of Oxford, who was supported by the Ministry. Although Newdigate got in, the fight between him and Turner (here characterized as Jacobite and Tory) was perilous and bitter: an illustration of the impact of University politics over a wider field. (See Ward, *Georgian Oxford*, 188–91.)

28. Thursday. At ten Mr Oswald came to me from the Prince whom he found at Carlton House and who kept him till that time. Receiv'd him very generously, and talk'd to him of many subjects, and many persons, but never nam'd my name.—They agreed that he was to have the Green Cloth,[1] and to kiss hands at lady-day. [Wrote to] Mr Mann.

[1] i.e. in the Prince's court.

MARCH

1. Friday. Went to the House. Mr Townshend advis'd with me about General Anstruther's affair.[1] I beg'd him to be very sure of his proofs, before he began a charge in Parliament.—He ask'd to come to me tomorrow, and show me his papers, which I agreed to, but desired him to consult wiser persons than I. Din'd alone. Mr Ralph's.

2. Saturday. Mr Townshend came, and I fairly show'd him that calling for the reports in Council would lead him to embarrass the Ministry, who in this case of Anstruther had delay'd justice: that I should be glad it should come forward, but not from him, without approving him when his motion would end, since he asked my advice, as a friend, &c. He thank'd me much, and it being late, desir'd to come again tomorrow morning. I din'd at Lord Barrington's—Mr Scrope's. Supp'd at Carlton House. Ladies Middlesex and Howe. Lord Bute went away before supper—Mr Breton.

3. Sunday. Went to Leicester House, but just as I was going, Mr Townshend came, and to my infinite surprise, told me that he had been with the Earl of Egmont, who had given him a question which comprehended the civil and military behaviour of General Anstruther, which he would read me. He did so, and ask'd my opinion. I was astonish'd at his ignorance,[2] and said, I had nothing to object to it. Mr and Mrs Breton din'd here. Mr Ralph.

4. Monday. Motion by Mr Townshend seconded by Colonel Haldane, for copies of all courts martial held by Anstruther, while he commanded in Minorca; and of all complaints against him in Council, and the proceedings thereupon. Agreed, without division,

[1] Lieutenant-General Sir Philip Anstruther (1678–1760), when Governor of Minorca in 1742, had court-martialled and cashiered Sir Henry Erskine, then serving as a subaltern there, for 'dark and intricate crimes'. The attempt to arraign him for abuse of power arose partly from personal pique on Erskine's part, partly from propagandist anti-militarism, and partly from Scottish ill-feeling. Erskine, moreover, was an adherent of Egmont—See above 25 Feb. The Townshend here concerned is George Townshend, Charles Townshend's elder brother, later Marquess Townshend.
[2] i.e. of the non-alignment of D. and Egmont.

103

to drop the courts martial till some particular facts were alleged, but to let the Council papers come. Din'd alone.

5. Tuesday. Mr Furnese din'd here. Sir Paul Methuen's.

6. Wednesday. Went to Leicester House. The Prince told me he caught cold the day before, at Kew—was blooded.[1] Din'd at M. Munchausen's. At Mr Scrope's.

7. Thursday. Went to the House for Mr Waller's Turnpike. Delaval's play.[2] Prince and Princess not there.

8. Friday. Prince not recover'd. Our passing next week at Kew put off. Din'd alone. At Mr Ralph's. Paid him 39 [guineas].

9. Saturday. Din'd alone.—The Speaker's.—The Prince better.—Supp'd at Leicester House. Ladies Middlesex and Howe. Mr Masham.

10. Sunday. Went to Leicester House. The Prince saw company.—Mr Breton din'd with us.—At Lady Middlesex's, Mr Ralph, and Mr Scrope's. Lay at Hammersmith.

11. Monday. Went to the House.—Papers relating to General Anstruther call'd for. Return'd at night. Din'd alone.

12. Tuesday. Went to Mr Waller's Committee. King pass'd the Malt Bill. Prince there.

13. Wednesday. Went to the Linen Committee[3]—then to Leicester House.—The Prince did not appear, having a return of a pain in his side. He supp'd on Tuesday at Carlton House.—I return'd.

14. Thursday. Went to Leicester House.—The Prince asleep—twice blooded, and a blister to his back—as also to both legs that night.—Din'd at Sir Francis Dashwood's, and return'd to Hammersmith.

---

[1] Pneumonia supervening on influenza seems a more probable cause of the Prince's fatal illness than the commonly accepted chill after a walk in damp clothes (Walpole to Mann, 21 Mar. 1751). The headache on 17 February is significant, and so is D.'s bad bout in that month.

[2] The great amateur performance of *Othello* by the Delavals (see Askham, F., *The Gay Delavals*, 56). The House of Commons adjourned early for members to attend, but the newspaper reports that the Prince presided are incorrect.

[3] D. was a tireless advocate of protection for Irish linen.

15. Friday. Went to Leicester House—Prince had a plentiful evacuation, and was out of all danger.—Went to the House, and from thence carried Mr Tucker back to dinner.

16. Saturday. Din'd alone.—We came to town in the evening.— Went to Leicester House.—Prince without pain or fever. Mr Ralph's and Mr Scrope's.

17. Sunday. Went twice to Leicester House. Prince had a bad night, till one this morning, then was better, and continued so.—Din'd at Sir Charles Tynte's.—Lady Middlesex's, Sir Paul Methuen's.

18. Monday. Went to the House. General Anstruther put in his answer. Lady R. Poulet, and Miss Wyndham din'd here. Lady Middlesex's and Leicester House. Prince better, and sat up half an hour.

19. Tuesday. Went to the Linen Committee. Mr Oswald din'd with us. Settled the questions about General Anstruther, and sent them to Mr Townshend. At Mr Ralph's. Lay at Hammersmith.

20. Wednesday. Went to Leicester House, thence to the House of Commons, thence back to Hammersmith. Was told at Leicester House, at three o'clock that he was much better, and had slept eight hours the night before: which I suppose was the forming the mortification, for he died that evening, a quarter before ten, as I found by a letter from Mr Breton at six o'clock.

21. Thursday morning. I came immediately to town, and found by Mr Breton, who was at Leicester House when he died, that for half an hour before, he was very cheerful, ask'd to see some of his friends, ate some bread and butter, and drank coffee: he had spit for some days, and was at once seiz'd with a fit of coughing, and spitting, which last was so violent, that it suffocated him. Lord North was sent to the King.[1]—This morning the King order'd him to be opened.—An abscess was found in his side, the breaking of which suffocated him. N.B. His physicians, Wilmot, and Lee, knew nothing of his distemper; as they declar'd, half an hour before he died, that his pulse were like a man's in perfect health. They either would not see or did not know the consequences of the black thrush, which

---

[1] Who said, 'Why, they told me he was better.'

appear'd in his mouth, and quite down his throat. Their ignorance, or their knowledge of his distemper render them equally inexcusable for not calling in more assistance.

N.B. From Tuesday the 12th, that he supp'd at Carlton House, and relaps'd before he went to bed, the Princess never suffer'd any English man or woman, above the degree of a Valet de Chambre &c. to see him: nor did she vouchsafe to see anyone, man, or lady of the Family: not even the Lady in waiting, till Sunday last, when it was absolutely necessary that somebody should appear, to receive compliments; and then Lady Scarbrough was order'd, instead of a Lord, who she apprehended, I suppose, would have expected to see the Prince. She saw Dr Lee, one day before the death, and just after it, she had a long conference, till past twelve, with him, and the Earl of Egmont.[1] This morning Lady Middlesex got to see her, but was not sent for. Lord Middlesex sent in, and was admitted. She sent in for the Duke of Chandos, and also for the Earl of Scarbrough at night. At Mr Ralph's and Lady Middlesex's.

When this unfortunate event happen'd I had set on foot, by means of the Earl of Shaftesbury, a project for union between the independent Whigs, and Tories, by a writing, renouncing all tincture of Jacobitism, and affirming short, but strong constitutional and revolutional principles. I gave his Lordship the paper. His good heart, and understanding made him indefatigable, and so far successful, that there was good grounds to hope for a happy issue: these, so united, were to lay this paper, containing these principles, before the Prince; offering to appear as his party, now, and upon those principles, to undertake the administration when he was King, in the subordination and rank among themselves, that he should please to appoint.—Father of mercy, thy hand that wounds alone, can save!

22. Friday. Several, in much distress, here. The Earl of Shaftesbury, and Mr William Beckford[2] here, by their own appointment. They said they came to ask directions what to do under this fatal change of situation: I said that it appeared to me that if the Pelham party did not, instantly, drive out the Bedford party,[3] they must be drove

---

[1] During which all the Prince's private papers were destroyed (Walpole to Mann, 1 Apr. 1751). According to Walpole, Egmont held a meeting of the Prince's supporters the day after the death, to which D. was, of course, not invited.

[2] Father of the author of *Vathek* and then M.P. for Shaftesbury (1709–70).

[3] Comparison of the 1784 text and the manuscript shows that the 1784 editor altered 'party' to 'interest', throughout this entry, no doubt feeling that 'party' had

out by them, tho' now the weakest, but would become the strongest, having the King's favourite, and now, only son, at their head,
and at the head of the army: that he would, by their party, small
as it might be, and the military, force the Regency, and then where
are the Pelhams? That this necessity enforced the necessity of the
projected union.—That being collected, and publicly purg'd from
Jacobitism, they became a respectable body. That if they were
applied to for assistance, they might then give it upon such conditions, and for such share of power as they thought safe and honourable for themselves, and their country: secondly, if they were not
applied to, and the court took a right turn, they might, like honest
and disinterested men, support it without coming into it. And
lastly, what was most to be fear'd, if they were not applied to, and
the Court took either a dangerous turn, or continued in the same
consuming way they would be ready to do, what it was their duty
to do—*viz*. oppose to the utmost, and declare that they mean to
wrest the administration out of those hands, to take it into their
own, and apply it to better purposes. That despair, which was
blameable before, was now become criminal.

They went away, much satisfied, and determined to act accordingly.

Went to Leicester House.—Princess afflicted, but well.[1]—Went
to Council at night, vastly full. Common prayer altered: but Prince
George left as he now stands.[2] The physicians made a report, and
deliver'd a paper being an account of the body when open'd—I
have a copy.— Order'd the bowells to be put in a box covered
with red velvet, and carried in one of his coaches, by such atten-
dents as his Groom of the Stole should appoint, and buried in
Henry the VIIth's chapel. Order'd a committee to meet when sum-
mon'd to settle the ceremonial of the funeral.—Lady Middlesex's.

23. Saturday. Went to the Earl of Westmorland's—Lord Guernsey
there—held conversation much to the same purpose.—He said he
heard that Sir John Hynde Cotton had propos'd sending for gentlemen up, acquainting them at the same time that nothing was to

---

come to mean something different. In the preceding entry he inserted the word
'party' to describe the 'Independent Whigs and Jacobites' there referred to, though
D. does not use the word there.
    [1] She was seven months pregnant; and D. was counting on her as the keystone
of his new political system.
    [2] i.e. not made Prince of Wales.

be propos'd to them, but to sit still and wait Court.[1] I modestly doubted of that measure, from experience, of the disposition of those gentlemen, who I thought would neither come, if nothing was propos'd, nor stay, if there was nothing to do: but yet would implicitly follow a few of their Lordships in one or the other: from which I thought it follow'd that their Lordships should form a set of propositions for the centre of union and then call them together, to own them, and act upon them, either taking places (if they were to be had upon honourable terms) or without places.

I was in every part most warmly supported by Lord Guernsey, and by Sir Edward Deering who came in. I left them together, and thought by the very affectionate manner of Lord Westmorland, when I left the room, that I had never before made so much impression upon him. Went to Leicester House—the Princess continues well. Din'd here, Mr Furnese, and Mr Carey. Sir Paul Methuen's.

24. Sunday. Went to the Duke of Dorset's—much talk.—Thinks of the state of the nation, of the Pelhams, just as we do; as also of the danger from [the Duke of Cumberland]. Mr Cooke came—recommended [Disp][2] to him.—Din'd here, Messrs Bance and Glover. At the Speaker's, he also in the same way of thinking—stay'd till past one—examin'd the settlements, creations, and regencies of the Royal Family &c. At Leicester House.—Princess well.

25. Monday. Much talk with Lord Limerick. He in the same way of thinking—but both agree that the Pelhams have not enough resolution to do any thing great. At Leicester House—Princess well—din'd alone—Sir Paul Methuen's and Mr Scrope's.

26. Tuesday. Went to Leicester House—Princess well.—Paid Dr Thomson to Lady Day. Receiv'd £400 from Mr Spareman, an old debt from Mr Walter. Lady Middlesex's and Mr Ralph's.

27. Wednesday. Mr Warburton and I went to Hammersmith. He din'd with us. Went to Leicester House—Princess well—Went to Council,—Orders to the Lord Steward and Chamberlain, to issue warrants for black cloth, wax lights, &c. for the room at Westminster where the body shall be laid, &c: to the Groom of the Stole, and Master of the Horse to his late Royal Highness to regulate the march of the servants, &c. Orders to the Earl Marshall,

---

[1] i.e. see what the Government did.   [2] Not clear in manuscript.

to direct the Heralds to prepare for the consideration of the Council, a ceremonial for the funeral of H.R.H. upon the plan of those of the Duke of Gloucester and of Prince George of Denmark, which were formed upon the plan of the funeral of Charles the second. Mr Ralph's.

28. Thursday. Sir Francis Dashwood from the Earl of Westmorland desir'd to know, if I thought it prudent to make an overture to Mr Pelham, as a party to join him, if he would engage to fix the land tax next year at two shillings in the pound, and reduce the army. I sent my duty to the Earl and beg'd to know if they[1] were united enough to make overtures, as a party; and if so, what the party was to do, in return, in case Mr Pelham complied.

N.B. These conditions are nugatory, and yet the last, of all others, the most difficult to obtain. If they are united, they should now demand great, and national conditions for the safety of the whole; which will be obtain'd as easily, at last, as the reduction of the army at present; which reduction, except in view of economy is trifling. Any army may be equally ruinous, and yet some must be kept, till the nation can be arm'd by a proper regulation of the militia.

Mr Cope, Furnese, and Carey din'd here. Went to Leicester House—Princess well—Lady Middlesex's and Sir Paul Methuen's.

29. Friday. Went to Leicester House. Princess well. Din'd at Sir Thomas Robinson's.—At the Duke of Argyll's, and the Speaker's, where we turn'd over precedents with relation to the grants of the Duchy of Cornwall, and of the Government, during minorities.[2]

30. Saturday. Went to Leicester House. Princess well.—Messrs Furnese, and Carey din'd here—Lady Middlesex's.

31. Sunday. Went abroad, and was taken ill: continued visiting.— Saw Mr Prowse, and found him well dispos'd to the main system. Went to dinner to Sir Francis Dashwood's, but could not eat. Got home, and continued very ill.—This night died the Earl of Orford:[3] King at Leicester House.

[1] The 1784 text gives 'we' for 'they' throughout this passage, thus conveying that D. regarded himself as acting with the Westmorland Tory clique. On the contrary, he was acting as an external manipulator.

[2] With the future of Cornish patronage—the heir's chief asset—in mind. Under Queen Anne the Crown had been much strengthened by the possession of the Duchy of Cornwall, and the same was to be true now until George III's reign was well advanced. D. made a habit of using the Speaker's library for references on constitutional points.

[3] Setting his countess free to marry Sewallis Shirley.

APRIL

1. Monday. I took physic, which did me a great deal of good.—Thanks to my ever gracious God!

2. Tuesday. Went to Leicester House—Princess well—At Sir Paul Methuen's.

3. Wednesday. At Leicester House—the Princess well.—Din'd at Sir Francis Dashwood's. At Council, about the funeral. Ceremonial from the Heralds read.—Their orders were to form it on the plan of the Duke of Gloucester's, and Prince George of Denmark.—But had different orders privately: which I did not know. I thought there was very little ceremony, and therefore said, that I suppos'd that they had complied with the orders which their Lordships gave, about the plans this funeral was to be formed upon. Lords said, 'To be sure': and none seem'd to have any doubts, or concern'd themselves about it, so I said no more: tho' I am satisfied it is far short of any funeral of any son of a King.—After the Council was up, I ask'd the Lord Chancellor about it, who said that he suppos'd the Heralds had complied with their orders, but that he knew nothing of it, and had never seen any of the plans. I told him that I mention'd it, because, if it should appear that any mark of respect to the deceas'd shown in the funeral was omitted in this it would certainly give great distaste.—I think they must alter it.

4. Thursday. Went to Leicester House—Princess well.—Din'd here, Messrs Sharpe.—King at Leicester House.—At Lady Middlesex's.

5. Friday. Went to Hammersmith.—Return'd to dinner. Messrs Breton, and Cope din'd here.—At Leicester House, Princess well.—At Sir Paul Methuen's.

6. Saturday. Went to Leicester House.—Princess well.—Din'd alone.—At Mr Scrope's.

7. Sunday. Saw the Earl of Westmorland but his Lady being present, could not talk fully with him.—Mr Glover din'd here.—Earl of Shaftesbury came in the afternoon, and agreed to drive it to a short point, with the Earls of Westmorland and Oxford, either to form

a regular Party, immediately, or to give it entirely up. If a party then to fix the subscription for a paper by Mr Ralph, supported by about twenty of us at 10 guineas each, and what else we can get.

8. Monday. Went to Leicester House—Princess well.—Mr Stanley din'd with us.—Came to Hammersmith at night.

[A day omitted]

10. Wednesday. Went on horseback to Mr Oswald's.—From thence over Westminster Bridge, to the Earl of Westmorland's. Had a long conversation with the Earl Stanhope, and him, and left them persuaded of the necessity of forming a Party, united by constitutional principles reduc'd into writing, and sign'd by all the party.—Much talk of those principles, of which I mention'd such as occurred to me, which they approv'd of.—I told them that I had once drawn such a Political Creed for the last opposition, but the gentlemen did not care to sign it. That, now I thought that the younger part of our friends were very much in earnest, and wanted only proper leaders, and proper points to unite heartily. The Lords agreed that something should be digested immediately. I told them, that to make a beginning, if they pleas'd I would send them the paper mention'd, where possibly some hints might be of use: they seemed very desirous to see it: I went home, and sent it directly, to the Earl of Westmorland. I have done enough, and henceforth shall live to myself, the years which God in his mercy may grant me, unless call'd upon to assist.

9. Tuesday. Went to see Mr Ralph in the morning. Din'd alone.

[A day omitted]

11. Thursday. Took physic. Mr Oswald came to [see] me. Much talk about the state of affairs, in which we agreed. I told him the steps I had taken towards a union of parties: that I thought I ow'd it to our friendship to acquaint him that if that great plan could be effected, I must take my share in it. He approv'd the greatness, and honesty of the design: at the same time told me that Mr Pelham had renew'd his offers since the Prince's death, to which he had given a very general, cool answer and said he hop'd, from the renewing that offer, to find that Mr Pelham had found resolution enough to have enter'd into engagements with some more of us, and have avail'd himself of the present dispositions of the people: to put himself upon his

country, and get rid of his open enemies and false friends, which was, now, most practicable, and necessary to prevent his own being undone by both.—He, and Mr Okeden, din'd with us.

12. Friday. Mr Tucker din'd with us.—Return'd to town at night.

13. Saturday. Lord Limerick came to consult about walking at the funeral. By the Earl Marshall's order, publish'd in the common newspaper of the day, (which with the ceremonial, not publish'd till ten o'clock, I keep by me) neither he as an Irish Peer nor I as a Privy Councillor, could walk. He expressed a strong resolution to pay his last duty to his Royal friend, if practicable. I beg'd him to stay till we could get the ceremonial: he did and we there found, in a note, that we might walk. Which note, publish'd seven, or eight hours before the attendance requir'd, was all the notice that Lords, their sons, and Privy Councillors had (except those appointed to particular function) that they would be admitted to walk.

At seven o'clock, I went, according to the order, to the House of Lords. The many slights the poor remains of a much-lov'd master and friend had met with, and were preparing the last trouble he could give them, sunk me so low, that, for the first hour, I was incapable of making any observation.—The procession began, and except the Lords appointed (as I have said before) to hold the pall, and attend the chief mourner, and those of his own domestics when they were called in their ranks, there was not one English Lord, not one Bishop, and there was but one Irish Lord (Viscount Limerick), two sons of Dukes (Earl of Drumnalrig and Lord Robert Bertie), one Baron's son (Mr Edgecumbe) and two Privy Councillors (Sir John Rushout and myself), out of their great bodies, to make a show of duty to a Prince so great in rank, and expectation.

While we were in the House of Lords, it rain'd very hard, as it has done all the season; when we came into Palace Yard the way to the Abbey was lined with soldiers, but the [managers] had not afforded a covering of rough deals overhead; by good luck while we were from under cover, it held up. We went in at the S.E. door, and turned short into Henry the VIIth's chapel. The service was perform'd without either anthem or organ. So ended the sad day— Quem, Semper, acerbum—Semper honoratum.

N.B. The corps, and bowels were remov'd last night to the Prince's lodgings, at the House of Lords. The whole Bed-chamber were ordered to attend it, from ten in the morning, till the enterrement. They had not the attention to order the Green Cloth to provide them a bit of bread; and these gentlemen, of the first rank and distinction, in discharge of their last sad duty to a lov'd, and loving master, were forc'd to bespeak a great cold dinner from a common tavern in the neighbourhood.—At three, indeed, they vouchsaf'd to think of it and order'd them a dinner—but the disgrace was compleat, the tavern dinner was paid for, and given to the poor.

N.B. The Duke of Somerset was chief mourner, notwithstanding the flourishing state of the Royal Family.

14. Sunday. Went to Leicester House—Princess well.—Messrs Bance and Bodens din'd with us. Sir Paul Methuen's, and Sir Francis Dashwood's.

15. Monday. Lord Shaftesbury came to acquaint me that the project of union went on very successfully. I advis'd him to appoint a meeting for tomorrow of the Earls of Westmorland, Oxford, and Stanhope, to settle the points, in writing that are to be the centre of that union. Din'd at Sir Francis Dashwood's, where Earl Stanhope read us the draught of a preamble to such points, which extremely good.—Mr Scrope's.

16. Tuesday. Went to the House.—The motion to put off the third reading of the naturalization [bill], for two months, was carried by 129 against 116. Mr Furnese din'd with us. The report of the demission of the Duke of Bedford, and Earl of Sandwich yesterday, and the introduction of the Earl of Holderness, and Lord Anson into their places, is not true: but good reason to think it will. —If so, surely they design to curtail the Southern Province. Return'd to Hammersmith.

17. Wednesday. Mr Ralph din'd here.

18. Thursday. Went to the House. Mr George Townshend open'd General Anstruther's affair, and mov'd a question concerted with the Court; which was that his Majesty should be addressed to inforce his orders in consequence of the report of his council to oblige Lieutenant General Anstruther to make some satisfaction to those of Minorca whom he had oppress'd—which must be very unsatisfactory and insufficient.

Mr Townshend, who of his own accord engag'd in this affair, who of his own accord on very slight acquaintance, desir'd my advice, whom I treated with great generosity, as he acknowledg'd to me and others, who, imprudently, went from me, to the Earl of Egmont, and brought from that Lord, a long, inflammatory question, which he desir'd me to correct: but I declin'd it; who receiv'd from me the proper question in writing, concluding with one to establish a civil government in Minorca; this gentleman, without giving me the least intimation, contents himself with moving this same court question; and that Lord, the other day, so violent, who drew a question so very different, thought fit even to absent himself.—Such wonders has the poor Prince's death already produced! Return'd to Hammersmith.

19. Friday. Din'd here, Drs Sharpe and Thomson, and Mr Ralph.

20. Saturday. Din'd alone.—Came to town.—Sir Paul Methuen's.

21. Sunday. Din'd at Lord Middlesex's—was told that Mr Montagu, as her Auditor, Mr Douglas, (and Mr Boone, in the room of Sir John Cust) as Clerks of her Green Cloth, Mr Bludworth as her Commissioner of the Horse, Messrs Leslie, Scott, and Robinson, as her Equerries, kiss'd the Princess's hand today.

22. Monday. Came to the House. Hearing of the Sugar Colonies put off, till next year. Messrs Furnese, and Carey din'd with us. Went to Hammersmith.

23. Tuesday. Din'd at Sir Francis Dashwood's—Find by Lord Talbot that we are not likely to come in a union. For now the terms they propose to sign, are of a sort, that imply an exclusion of coming into office. Now as no good can be done to this country, but by good men getting into office, 'tis all over, and I give up all thoughts of ever being any farther useful to mankind.—

24. Wednesday. Came to town. Went to the House—Erskine's accusation against Anstruther—baffled by the Court thro' the act of Grace.—Return'd to Hammersmith.

25. Thursday. Went to town to consult my constant friend Mr Bance about retrieving if possible the captainship of the *Dodington* Indiaman, which Mr Tucker imprudently, and unkindly, opposes me in, and by being concern'd (tho' not equally with me) and having

the management of my affairs, has led the rest of the proprietors (though I believe without any such intention) to think I was engag'd, and so to engage themselves to the person he espouses, which disappoints me in serving the person recommended to me, by the Princess of Wales.

Mr Bance has just brought Mr Tucker to me, who desists from his engagement: but I am persuaded it is now too late.—This at Hammersmith since I return'd.[1]

26. Friday. Went to town about this ship, but did no good. Went to the House. A message from the Crown to the Lords—then a message to the Commons from the Lords, by Masters in Chancery, to continue sitting some time—then a message from the Crown to the Commons, by the Chancellor of the Exchequer, recommending the Princess of Wales for Regent, with such limitations as the Houses shall think fit—then a message from the Lords by the Chief Justice of the Common Pleas and the Chief Baron, with an address of thanks, agreed to nem. con.—I return'd.

27. Saturday. Din'd with us, Mr Berkeley, Mr Breton, Mr Ralph, Drs Thomson, and Sharpe. We came to town.

28. Sunday. I din'd at Gunnersbury.

29. Monday. Mrs Dodington din'd with us.

30. Tuesday. Went to the Lever.—Then to Council.—Lord Holderness came over—for the seals I suppose.—Earl Harcourt sworn in.—Earl of Egmont sworn as Lord Lieutenant of Cumberland.—Din'd alone. Lady Middlesex and Lord Talbot.

---

[1] Maddening, just at the moment when he wished to secure the Princess's goodwill. It must have been almost a satisfaction when the *Dodington*, on her next voyage, was lost. The entry is interesting as showing Tucker as D.'s business partner, as well as political colleague.

MAY

1. Wednesday. Went to the House.—Lancashire check linen.—Din'd with us, Messrs Furnese, Carey, Younge, Dr Sharpe. Mr Scrope's.

2. Thursday. Mr Kelsal din'd with us.

3. Friday. Went to the House. Resolutions to pave Pall Mall, by a pound rate—Sir Francis Dashwood, Lord Trentham, General Oglethorpe, and I, order'd to prepare a Bill. Sense of the House taken, if the young Prince of Wales's new servants should be re-elected: it was agreed, not. The Act was read: but those who seem'd to favour a re-election, forgot to call for the warrants that appoint them servants to the Prince: by whom are they sign'd, if by the King, the case would not have admitted a word of dispute. The persons concern'd were, Lord Downe, Gentleman of the Bedchamber, Mr Selwyn, senior, Treasurer, and Mr Stone, Sub-Governor. Mr Stanley din'd with us.

4. Saturday. Din'd at Mr Prowse's.

5. Sunday. Rode out. Din'd alone. At Lord Trentham's about the pavement.

6. Monday. Saw several of my neighbours about the pavement, and sent them away, pretty well satisfy'd.—Went to the House.—Lord Trentham, Sir Francis Dashwood, and General Oglethorpe din'd with us. We spent the whole evening about the pavement.

7. Tuesday. Went to the House of Lords. The Regency Bill brought in,[1] and open'd by the Duke of Newcastle.—Second reading tomorrow. Nothing said but by the Bishop of Worcester who mov'd that it might be printed, and that Lords might have time to consider it between the second reading, and committal. Duke of Newcastle agreed to the printing, and it pass'd, upon the question put. In less than ten minutes after the question, the Duke got up, and said he was told by Lords that it was very improper to print

[1] It provided for the Princess Dowager of Wales to act as Regent if the King died before Prince George was 21. This was not enough for D., since the Bill also provided for a Council to assist the Princess, and the prolongation of Parliament: in other words the Bill made sure that the Pelhams would retain the strings of power on a demise of the Crown in the immediate future.

the Bill, upon which they resolv'd not to print it, and the Bishop being supported by no one Lord, very decently offer'd to withdraw his motion.—Sure it was too late after it became a question, voted, and agreed to. Din'd at General Oglethorpe's.—Sir Paul Methuen's.

8. Wednesday. Went to the House of Lords. Regency Bill read a second time, and committed for Friday: not a word said against it. Din'd at Sir Francis Dashwood's.

9. Thursday. Had intelligence that upon a message from the Earl of Bath the Princess had signified her thorough approbation of his Bill.—Had much consultation about what was to be done, considering how much fruitless pains, (as it now appear'd) I had taken to write, and form a party, and yet no sort of concert was thought upon, even in these great points.—The opinion seem'd that I should not go down.—Din'd alone.—Lay at Hammersmith.

10. Friday. Went to the House of Lords—they went into a committee upon the Regency Bill. The clause for erecting the council was oppos'd by Earl Stanhope alone, who said that such a council was a novelty, and he was against erecting it, because he thought it unnecessary; till he heard better reasons for it, than he had, as yet, heard.—Nobody answer'd or supported him, and he gave no farther reasons—so the clause was carried by a division of 92 to 12.—When they came to the clause of prolonging the Parliament, Lord Talbot stood up, and show'd the weakness of the Chancellor's arguments that were drawn from history: and then said the prolonging of the Parliament was an invasion of the people's rights, that it was means to perpetuate a corrupt one, and was one of the things that the whole legislature could not do, because they could have no real power to do it.—Lord Granville spoke warmly for it, as the best part of the Bill, all of which he approv'd of—and no one lord seconded or supported Lord Talbot—so they divided and I return'd to Hammersmith.

11. Saturday. Mr Ralph din'd with us to whom I communicated my present resolution of meddling no more with public affairs, till some party worth appearing with, shall unite, in the service of the country.

12. Sunday. Din'd with us Sir Francis Dashwood, Messrs Solicitor General, Hoskins, Beckford, Carey, Breton, Furnese.

PART TWO

OUT OF PLACE

MAY 1751 TO APRIL 1754

1751

MAY

13. Monday. Went to town, to dine with Sir Francis Dashwood, and the gentlemen about the Paving Bill. Did not go to the House, where the Regency Bill was read the first time, for reasons given to Ralph, last Saturday. Sir Francis came home, and acquainted me that nobody but Mr Thomas Pitt and he spoke against the Bill—Tories totally silent—Court for it, Dr Lee and Nugent speaking for it, all the Princess's, and late Prince's Court for it—I return'd at night.

14. Tuesday. Mr Tucker taken ill yesterday—Mr Ralph and Dr Thomson din'd here.

15. Wednesday. Went to town. Din'd with Lord Trentham about the paving—return'd.

16. Thursday. Mr Ralph din'd with us—Committee of the Regency Bill. Clause establishing the council, debated: oppos'd by the Speaker in a very fine speech. Mr William Pitt, and Mr Fox had strong words, tho' both for the Bill: Mr Fox for them also, but defending the Duke:[1] Mr Pitt for the restrictions, lest the next Regent should claim full powers, if the Princess should die, aiming at the Duke: reply'd upon each other two or three times: but Mr Fox did not vote at last—Mr Pitt, and the Grenvilles in place, voted for the Bill, but Lord Cobham spoke, and voted against it.—Thus it was reported to me, but I was not there.

17. Friday. I went to meet about the Paving Bill, at Lord Trentham's—return'd, and din'd alone—They went today, in the House, upon the clause for the prolongation of the Parliament—what they did, I don't yet know.

[1] Cumberland.

18. Saturday. Dr Sharpe and Mr Ralph din'd here. The doctor lay here. Mr Hampden din'd here.

19. Sunday. Messrs Bance and Breton din'd here—The Committee upon the prolonging Clause sat late. No concert between any five people—nor any performance as I am told.

20. Monday. Mrs Dodington and I went to town, over the new bridge.[1] Return'd to dinner where we found Mr Dodington who lay there—Regency Bill pass'd.

21. Tuesday. Went to town to get the Paving Bill read, but could not. Return'd and found Mr Younge, who din'd with us.

22. Wednesday. Went to town. Was to wait on the Duke of Newcastle to thank him for getting me leave to drive thro' St James's Park, while the King is at Kensington—we parted very civilly.[2] Got the Paving Bill read the first time. Paid Lord Middlesex £140 for a set of seven of the Prince's horses. Din'd at Sir Walter Blacket's. —Return'd at night.

23. Thursday. Went to Kensington and kiss'd the young Prince of Wales's hand: but did not see the King. Return'd, and din'd alone.

24. Friday. Messrs Breton and Cheere din'd with me.

25. Saturday. Din'd with us, Sir Francis Dashwood, Sir Charles Tynte, Sir Charles Mordaunt, Misses Benett and Murray[3]—came to town.

26. Sunday. Mr Glover and Mr Dodington din'd with us. Sir Paul Methuen and Lady Middlesex.

27. Monday. Din'd alone. Went to Hammersmith at night.

28. Tuesday. Went to town, to go up the water with the Spanish and Sardinian ministers, Messrs Lascaris and St Fiorent, and Lord Barrington—We landed at Hammersmith, where we were met by the Marquis de Mirepoix, French Ambassador, M. d'Abrieu, and Lord Ashburnham—we all din'd there.

[1] Westminster Bridge.
[2] As usual one begins with small gestures. It was not merely injured pride that had caused D.'s ostentatious absence from the debates on the Regency Bill and his equally ostentatious interest in a non-controversial private measure.
[3] Probably Fanny Murray, the courtesan and actress.

29. Wednesday. Rode to Colonel Lyttelton's—found Mrs Dodington at my return, who lies here.

30. Thursday. Din'd here Lady Tynte, Miss Sturt, Sir Charles Tynte, Messrs Breton and Evans. We went to Ranelagh.

31. Friday. Went to the House about the Paving Bill, which was read the second time and committed to a private committee. I return'd, and din'd at the French Ambassador's, at Hammersmith—Mrs Dodington went to London.

JUNE

1. Saturday. The French Ambassadress came unexpectedly, and breakfasted with us. Din'd here, Mr and Mrs Prowse, Mrs Mildmay and Mr Dean of Wells, Mr Francis Fane, and young Mr Prowse.

2. Sunday. Din'd here, Sir Miles[1] and Lady Stapylton, Sir Hugh Dalrymple, Mr Macky, Messrs Breton and Glover.

3. Monday. Din'd alone.

4. Tuesday. Went to the House. Was in the chair of the committee upon the Paving Bill, went thro' it, and am to report it to the House next Friday.—Din'd with Sir Francis Dashwood—Return'd.

5. Wednesday. Waited upon Madame de Mirepoix.—Din'd alone—came to town.

6. Thursday. Went to Sir Paul Methuen's and Mr Scrope's.

7. Friday. Went to the House. Reported the Paving Bill—Council,[2] and much debate against it.—Carried to go on with the amendments, but forc'd to adjourn at the first amendment, because there were but 35 members. Din'd with us Sir Francis Dashwood, Mr Younge, and Carey.

8. Saturday. Went to the House, got the Bill reported, and order'd to be engross'd. Mr Breton din'd and went to Hammersmith with us.

9. Sunday. Took physic. Mr Bance din'd with us. French Ambassador came in the morning.

10. Monday. Took physic. Din'd alone.

11. Tuesday. Din'd with us Lords George Cavendish,[3] Trentham, and Duncannon, Sir Francis Dashwood, Messrs Ellis,[3] Breton, and Tucker.

---

[1] A Medmenham Franciscan.
[2] i.e. Counsel were heard for the opponents to the Bill.
[3] Treasury nominees accommodated at Weymouth—see above 11 December 1750.

12. Wednesday. Din'd with us Lord and Lady Berkeley, Mr, Mrs, and Miss Harriet Drax. We came to town.—That evening Lord Sandwich receiv'd his letter of dismission.

13. Thursday. Went to Sir Paul Methuen's. Supp'd at Whites.[1]

14. Din'd at Mr. Scrope's.—Went to Lady Middlesex's. Brought Dr Sharpe to Hammersmith with us.—Heard that the Duke of Bedford resigns the seals of Secretary this morning at Kensington.

15. Saturday. Din'd here, Messrs William Sharpe, Forrester, and Ralph. Lord Trentham resign'd the Admiralty.

16. Sunday. Din'd alone.

17. Monday. I went to Council at Kensington. Earl Granville sworn in as President: Earl of Coventry took the oath as Lord Lieutenant of Worcestershire. Mr Breton came to dinner, and to stay all night.

18. Tuesday. Went to Mr Southcote's with Lord and Lady Berkeley. Din'd at their house at Cranford—from thence came to town.—Heard that Lord Holdnerness receiv'd the seal of Secretary this morning.

19. Wednesday. Lord Hartington introduc'd into the House of Lords—made Master of the Horse.—I din'd at Lord Middlesex's. Return'd to Hammersmith at night.

20. Thursday. Din'd with us Mr and Misses Macartney, Sir Francis Dashwood, and Mr Furnese.

21. Friday. I went to Council, at Kensington. Earl of Holderness sworn, first as councillor, then as Secretary of State. Duke of Bedford and Lord Burleigh took the oath of office as Lords Lieutenants of Devonshire and Rutland. Din'd with us Earl Poulet, Messrs Poulet, Breton, and Creed. Came to town at night.

22. Saturday. Went to Ponders End to see my lapis lazuli pillars. Paid the maker £50 on account. Din'd with Mr Furnese. At Sir Paul Methuen's.

---

[1] D. had been a member since it was founded, but appears not to have visited it since his resignation in 1748. This is all of a piece with the noticeable change in his visiting list (from opposition to ministerialist) since the Prince's death. He also wanted to pick up what he could about the extrusion of the Bedfords.

23. Sunday. Went to Dr Lee's—settled about the statues &c.[1] Din'd at Mr Breton's. At Sir Paul Methuen's.

24. Monday. Return'd to Hammersmith. Din'd there. Mrs and Miss Churchill, and Bolt. Messrs William and Joseph Churchill, Leslie, Ralph, Carey, and Breton, who staid. [Wrote to] M. Servandoni.

25. Tuesday. Mr Breton and I went to town. I waited on the Princess to take my leave. She receiv'd me in a very obliging manner. The Parliament rose.

26. Wednesday. Din'd here Dr Sharpe and Mr Ralph.

27. Thursday. Din'd here Mr Breton and Colonel Mills.[2] This morning, I wrote to the Duke of Newcastle, inclosing Colonel Mills's memorial, who is in the Emperor's service as Duke of Tuscany. The memorial set forth that the Ostend Company bought two settlements, Banquibazar and Corelon of the Mogul:—a rebel seizes the province of Bengal in 1744, and takes Banquibazar from the Emperor's governor. He desires the King to assist him either to retake the province, with consent of, and for the Mogul; or in making war upon the usurper, who took and retains his forts without recompense. He submits to the King entirely the share and disposition of the gains, and plan of the expedition. N.B. This plan was attempted five or six years ago and cost the Emperor £15,000, and we prevented it at the instigation of the East India Company.

Mr Mills assures me that the province of Bengal is the richest in the known world.—That he knows where to lay his hands on £50 millions sterling.—That he can make himself master of it with 1500 men, and designs to carry no more, which the Emperor will furnish, and all he asks of us is shipping, and stores &c., enough to carry them, to be added to the three ships which the Emperor has, and bought for this expedition, before, when we disappointed it.

[1] Which D. had sold, or helped to sell, to the Prince. This shows Lee as completely in control of winding up the Prince's affairs.
[2] An adventurer. He is referred to in the correspondence between Horace Walpole and Mann (Toynbee, ii. 284, 289, 302) as allegedly in the Imperial service, and it is possible that Mann, who seems to have been impressed by him, introduced him to D. For the fate of the Ostend Company's establishments in Bengal, see *Cambridge History of the British Empire*, iv. 115–16. Colonel Mills was right, but Clive was already in India. The memorial is not among the Newcastle MSS.

28. Friday. Set out from Hammersmith at half past three, and arrived at Eastbury at half an hour past six in the evening, without any accident, God be prais'd.

29. Saturday. Din'd alone.

30. Sunday. Mr Okeden din'd with us.

JULY

1. Monday. Mr Shirley, and Lady Orford din'd with us.[1]

2. Tuesday. Our races began.—I rode to Blandford, din'd at the ordinary.—Thence to the course.—Three horses started.—Mr Martindale, a Londoner's, horse won the two first heats (and consequently the plate) against Mr Sturt and Captain Norris.—Return'd to Blandford to the ball—thence home.—Very wet till five o'clock.

3. Wednesday. Went in the coach to Blandford. Din'd at Captain Okeden's—very wet morning—went to the course in the coach—three horses started. Mr Sturt's and Captain Norris's, and Mr Withers's, from Windsor.—Mr Sturt's won the two first heats.—There was an assembly at Blandford, but we return'd home from the course.

Soon after our return came a message from Lord and Lady Falmouth, to beg a lodging, not being able to get a bed in all Blandford, the town was so full.—They got hither, by nine o'clock, and lay here.

4. Thursday. The weather was so bad that it hindered me from going to dine with the gentlemen, at Blandford.—

—There was but one horse enter'd (which was Mr Martindale's) so he drew £10, and the plate was not run for. We went to the ball at night, and return'd.

5. Friday. Din'd alone.

6. Saturday. Din'd alone.

7. Sunday. Din'd here Duke Hamilton and Mr Sturt.

8. Monday. Din'd alone.

9. Tuesday. Rode out with design to go to Mr Sturt's, but was prevented. Din'd with us, Lord, and Ladies Shaftesbury.

---

[1] Sewallis Shirley was the fourteenth son of the first Earl Ferrers and was at this time M.P. for Brackley. He had been Lady Orford's lover since 1746, and was now shortly to marry her (her husband, the 2nd Earl, had died in April).

10. Wednesday. Rode to Mr Sturt's. Met Duke Hamilton and the gentlemen going to Mr Bathurst's.—Return'd, and din'd alone.

11. Thursday. Mr and Mrs Shirley,[1] and Mr Sturt din'd with us, and Mr Blake.

12. Friday. We din'd alone.

13. Saturday. Mr Crabb din'd here. Wednesday evening the Princess walk'd in Carlton Gardens, supp'd, and went to bed very well, was taken ill about six o'clock on Thursday the 11th, and about 8 deliver'd of a Princess.—Both very well.—This morning died the Duke of St Albans at London.[2]

14. Sunday. We din'd alone.

15. Monday. We din'd alone.

16. Tuesday. Lord and Lady Arundell, and Miss Gage din'd here.

17. Wednesday. Mr and Mrs Bower came in the afternoon.

18. Thursday. Mr and Mrs Beckford din'd here.

19. Friday. We din'd at Mr Trenchard's.

20. Saturday. We din'd at Lady Shaftesbury's. Dr Sharpe came in the afternoon.

21. Sunday. Din'd alone. The weather this week past has been remarkably wet, and foggy. Mr and Mrs Ryves came in the afternoon.

22. Monday. We din'd alone. The same, till

28. Sunday. Mr and Mrs Okeden din'd, as did Dr Thomson from Salisbury.

29. Monday. Mr Younge came.

30. Tuesday. Messrs Tucker and Gollop came. We rode out, and Messrs Carver and Bodens din'd here.

31. Wednesday. Din'd alone. The western mail robb'd near Blackwater by one man, about one o'clock on Monday morning.

---

[1] See above, 1 July. They were now married.
[2] Crabb, a clergyman, had been at Oxford with D. Here D.'s clerical news service is seen at work.

AUGUST

1. Thursday. Din'd alone. Messrs Tucker and Gollop went away.

2. Friday. Din'd alone.

3. Saturday. Din'd at Mr William Churchill's. Mrs D, and her sister, Mr Younge, and Dr Sharpe in the coach. Dr Thomson and I in a chair. Coming from thence about 6 o'clock in Mr Churchill's meadow, from a causeway too narrow, call'd their private road, the coach was overturn'd in a wet ditch: the company, particularly the gentlemen, very much wetted, and if there had been a foot more of water must have been suffocated.—We were oblig'd to go back, and play at cards, till daylight. By God's goodness, there was no mischief.—I came home with them in Dr Sharpe's place, in Mr Churchill's coach. We got safe home on Sunday, about six in the morning. Drs Sharpe and Thomson came home, in the chair in the evening.

4. Sunday. We din'd alone.

5. Monday. We din'd alone. Dr Thomson went away.

6. Tuesday. Mr and Mrs Fielding din'd with us.

7. Wednesday. Dr Sharpe went to Dr Wright's. We din'd at Mr Arundell's.

8. Thursday. Mr Younge went away. We din'd alone.

9. Friday. Din'd alone.

10. Saturday. Din'd here Messrs Carver and Bodens.

11. Sunday. Took physic. Din'd alone.

12. Monday. Din'd alone. [Wrote to] Mr Mann, Cardinal Albani, Signor Niccolini.

13. Tuesday. Dr Sharpe return'd to dinner and brought Dr Wright with him.

14. Wednesday. Dr Wright went away. We din'd alone.

15. Thursday. Came Dr Taylor,[1] Mr Burroughs, Mrs and Mr Thomas Allen.

16. Friday. Mr Crabb din'd with us.

17. Saturday. We din'd alone.

18. Sunday. Went to church. Dr Sharpe preach'd. Went to Mr Beckford's in the afternoon, carried Mr Okeden, who din'd with us.

19. Monday. Din'd with us, Lord Sandys. his son, and Dr Barton.

20. Tuesday. We din'd alone.

21. Wednesday. We din'd alone. Mr Breton came.

22. Thursday. Mr William Churchill, and Miss Bolt, Messrs Salter.

23. Friday. We din'd alone.

24. Saturday. We went to Mr Drax's and return'd to dinner.

25. Sunday. Din'd alone.

26. Monday. Din'd alone, and went to see Mr Portman's gardens.

27. Tuesday. Din'd alone. Went to see Mr Kingston's nursery, and to Mr Bowers.

28. Wednesday. Mr, Mrs, and two Misses Drax came hither in the morning. We din'd alone.

29. Thursday. Din'd alone.

30. Friday. Din'd alone. Messrs Tucker came.

31. Saturday. Din'd alone.

---

[1] Probably Dr Robert Taylor (1710–62), President of the Royal Society and physician to George II.

SEPTEMBER

1. Sunday. Din'd alone.

2. Monday. Din'd alone.

3. Tuesday. Messrs Breton, Taylor, and Mrs Allen went away.—Din'd alone.

4. Wednesday. Set out from Eastbury at four in the morning. Got to Hammersmith without any accident, God be prais'd at three quarters past five, the same evening.

5. Thursday. Din'd alone.

6. Friday. Went to town to see Lady Middlesex. Return'd to dinner.—Din'd here Sir Thomas Robinson, Messrs Furnese and Carey.

7. Saturday. Din'd alone.

8. Sunday. Went to town: return'd to dinner. Found Mr Kelsal, who lay here. News of the birth of a Duke of Burgundy. M. de Mirepoix made a Duke, and peer of France.

9. Monday. Went to town. Return'd to dinner: Mr Cheere din'd here.—Went to the French ambassador's.

10. Tuesday. Din'd here Lord Middlesex, Messrs Furnese and and Ralph, Drs Sharpe and Thomson.

11. Wednesday. Rode to Sir Richard Hoare's. From thence to Mr Furnese's, where I din'd.

12. Thursday. I went to town, return'd to dinner. All the Poulet family din'd here.

13. Friday. We went to town. I din'd at Mr Macartney's. We return'd in the evening.

14. Saturday. Messrs Fielding and Ralph din'd with us.

15. Sunday. I went to Court at Kensington.[1] Messrs Poulets, Furnese, Kelsal, Ralph, and Carey din'd here.

16. Monday. Din'd alone.

17. Tuesday. Mrs D., Dr Thomson, and I went to Sir Francis Dashwood's at West Wycombe,[2] where we arriv'd at four o'clock, where we found Earl Stanhope and his lady and son, just arriv'd.— The Dr and I rode from Garrad's Cross.

18. Wednesday. At Wycombe.

19. Thursday. Set out from Wycombe at half past ten: arriv'd at Hammersmith at half past three.—Mr Kelsal came to lie here.

20. Friday. Went to town to fetch Mrs Beaghan. Return'd to dinner.

21. Saturday. Din'd alone.

22. Sunday. Mr Hampden din'd here.

23. Monday. The French Ambassador came. Mr Ralph din'd here.

24. Tuesday. The Bishop of London[3] came. Din'd alone.

25. Wednesday. Went to London. Din'd at Lord Middlesex's. Return'd at night.

26. Thursday. Mr Kelsal went away. Colonel Mills and Mr Ralph din'd here.

27. Friday. Din'd alone.

28. Saturday. Comte de Richecourt, the Emperor's Minister, and Colonel Mill[s] came here in the morning to talk about the expedition to Bengal. I immediately wrote an account of it to the Duke of Newcastle.—Lord and Lady Middlesex also came. We din'd alone.

---

[1] For what George II said about this and subsequent regular visits, see 5 May 1752 below.
[2] This entry, one of the very few recording an actual visit to West Wycombe, throws doubt on the existence of orgies at this date. Mrs. D. was of the party.
[3] Thomas Sherlock.

29. Sunday. Went to Kensington. Mr Fielding din'd here.

30. Monday. L'Abbé de Grossa Testa and General Guise[1] din'd here. [Wrote to] Mr Mann.

[1] Lieutenant-General John Guise (d. 1765) was a veteran of Marlborough's war and a connoisseur of pictures. He was also a kinsman of Mann's. Grossa Testa, the Modanese envoy, was no doubt also concerned in the picture business.

OCTOBER

1. Tuesday. Went to town. Din'd at Mr Scrope's. Went to Lord Middlesex's. Lay in town. Receiv'd a very civil letter from the Duke of Newcastle, about the expedition to Bengal.

2. Wednesday. Waited upon the Duke of Newcastle, was very friendly receiv'd. He told me all that had pass'd about Bengal, and put the event upon the consent and concurrence of the East India Company.—Call'd upon Dr Lee, who told me that the gentlemen accus'd of a secret treaty with the late Prince, had put it in issue with the King, that the Prince applied to them, and that they refus'd, and referr'd the King to the Princess for the truth of their assertion to be false.[1]—Saw Sir Paul Methuen.—Return'd, and Mr Kelsal din'd here.

3. Thursday. Lord Chief Baron Bowes,[2] Messrs Furnese, Hoskins, and Carey din'd here.

4. Friday. Went to wait on the Comte de Richecourt, and the Bishop of London. Colonel Mills came, to whom I deliver'd the Duke of Newcastle's directions, that if he would consent that Mr Drake, and Alderman Baker of the East India Company, should ask leave of the Court of Directors to receive proposals from him, they were ready to ask it, and if obtain'd, to enter into matter with him. Din'd alone.

5. Saturday. Din'd alone.

6. Sunday. Went to Kensington. Din'd at the Spanish ambassador's with the Comtes du Perron, Lascaris, and St Fiorent, Marquis d'Abrieu, Comte de Bolannos, Dr Augustine, and the Abbé de Grossa Testa. Went to Mr Scrope's, and return'd at night.

7. Monday. Went to town—saw Mr Lee. Went to Lady Middlesex's. Return'd to dinner. Din'd alone. [Wrote to] Cardinal Albani.

[1] This had been in 1747 (see Add. MS. 35870, ff. 129–31, and *Bedford Correspondence*, i. 320–3). The Prince, advised by Talbot, Baltimore. Lee and Dashwood had proposed a formal opposition with a programme framed to appeal to country gentlemen. The group of Tories approached had returned a cautious answer, and the plan had come to nothing.

[2] Chief Baron of the Exchequer, later Lord Chancellor, in Ireland. One of D.'s regular Irish correspondents.

9. Wednesday. Went to town to dine with Sir Francis Dashwood who went into Lincolnshire the next day. Return'd with Mr Ralph who lay here.

8. Tuesday. Mrs D. and I went to Mr Kelsal and from thence, to see Osterly Park, which is a very fine place. Mr Kelsal and we return'd here to dinner.

10. Thursday. Went to town. At Lady Middlesex's. Din'd here Lord and Lady Middlesex, Ladies Shannon and Howe.

11. Friday. Went to town. Return'd, and Mr Carey din'd and lay here.

12. Saturday. Din'd at home. Went to the play. Lay in town.

13. Sunday. Din'd at the Comte du Perron's with the French and Spanish ambassadors, Messrs de Munchausen, Grossa-Testa, and d'Abrieu. News of the death of the Prince of Orange.[1]—Went to Mr Scrope's.

14. Monday. Waited on the Princess. Receiv'd most graciously. She was pleas'd to send for the Prince of Wales, Prince Edward, and Augusta in. Return'd to Hammersmith. Din'd alone.

15. Tuesday. Went to town. Din'd at Gunnersbury. Return'd to Hammersmith.

16. Wednesday. Went to town. Return'd to dinner. Din'd with us Messrs Sharpe and Blair.

17. Thursday. Went to town and din'd alone.

18. Friday. Went to town. Return'd and din'd alone.

19. Saturday. Din'd in town alone, and lay there. Went to Lady Middlesex's, Sir Paul Methuen's, and Mr Scrope's.

20. Sunday. Messrs Churchill din'd with us. Saw Mr Scrope. Lay in town.

21. Monday. Return'd to Hammersmith to dinner.—Din'd alone.

---

[1] William V, the first hereditary Stadtholder of Holland. He was married to Anne, eldest daughter of George II. An instance of the rapid intelligence available to D. through his diplomatic contacts. Horace Walpole did not hear until at least two days later. (To Chute, 17 Oct. 1751: *Toynbee*, iii. 75.)

22. Tuesday. Went to town. Din'd at Mr Macartney's. Went to Council. Return'd at night.

23. Wednesday. Went to town. Return'd to dinner. Din'd alone.

24. Thursday. Went to town. Saw Mr Dawkins's drawings of the antiquities he saw in the East:[1] which are very fine and curious. Return'd, and din'd alone.

25. Friday. Went to town—brought Mr Ralph back to dinner, to meet Mr Furnese, and Mr Carey, who lay here.

26. Saturday. Went to town with Mrs D. Din'd alone. We went to the play, at Covent Garden, with the Ladies Poulet.

27. Sunday. Din'd alone. Went to Mr Scrope's.

28. Monday. Din'd alone. Went to Lady Middlesex's. The King came to St James's.

29. Tuesday. Lord Chancellor, Lord President, and I went from the Cockpit to dine with the Lord Mayor. There were none of the Council but us there. Lord Granville, and I went together. Return'd to Hammersmith at night.[2]

30. Wednesday. Went to town. King's Birthday. Drawing-room in weepers. I did not go, but return'd to dinner. Mr Ralph din'd here. The Tobacco Trade had [entry uncompleted].

31. Thursday. Went to town. Council at St James's. 10,000 seamen order'd. Din'd in town. Return'd at night.

---

[1] James Dawkins (1722–57), the archaeologist and Jacobite. He had already measured the Parthenon, and these drawings were the result of his expedition to Palmyra and Baalbec, which he was the first modern archaeologist to visit. His next trip was to Paris, on behalf of the Pretender.
[2] Straws in the wind of D.'s evolution towards the Pelhams: the visit to Methuen (19), the regular visits to Scrope, the conference with Furnese, Ralph, and Carey (25) and the appearance at the Lord Mayor's banquet in company with a leading member of the Government. The Mansion House was, of course, opposition territory.

NOVEMBER

1. Friday. Din'd alone. Mr Lee came in the evening, and return'd.

2. Saturday. Din'd alone. Came to town in the evening. Lay in town.

3. Sunday. Messrs Bance and Brewer din'd here.

4. Monday. Went to the Exchequer Chambers, where the Sheriffs were appointed. Mr Carey din'd with us. Return'd to Hammersmith in the evening.

5. Tuesday. Went to town, and carried Mr Tucker. Din'd at Lord Middlesex's. Went to Council after dinner. From thence return'd to Hammersmith.

6. Wednesday. Din'd alone.

7. Thursday. Mr Furnese din'd here.

8. Friday. Din'd at Gunnersbury.

9. Saturday. Din'd alone.

10. Sunday. Din'd in town. Return'd at night.

11. Monday. Din'd alone.

12. Tuesday. Din'd alone.

13. Wednesday. Din'd alone.

14. Thursday. Went to town, and lay there. Call'd at Sir Paul Methuen's, Duke of Argyll's, and Mr Scrope's. Parliament open'd. Lord Downe and Sir William Beauchamp Proctor mov'd and seconded the Address. No opposition to it. Din'd, and supp'd at Lord Middlesex's.

15. Friday. Return'd to Hammersmith with Mr Ralph, who din'd there.

16. Saturday. We remov'd to Pall Mall—Din'd alone—Went to Sir Paul Methuen.

17. Sunday. Din'd alone. Saw Mr Vaughan to little purpose.

18. Monday. Din'd alone. The account Carey brought me, I think, puts an end to the Bengal expedition. At Sir Paul Methuen's and the Duke of Argyll's.[1]

19. Tuesday. Messrs Oswald, Mills, Ralph, and Carey din'd here. Went to Council.

20. Wednesday. Went to the House. Order to commit Mr Murray to Newgate renew'd.[2] Din'd alone. At the Duke of Argyll's and Sir Paul Methuen's.

21. Thursday. Din'd alone. Went to Council—and Mr Furnese's. Saturday the Duke [of Cumberland] had a bad fall from his horse hunting at Windsor. Took no care of it, till Wednesday.

22. Friday. Din'd alone. Went to the Duke of Argyll's and the Speaker's.

23. Saturday. Din'd alone. Went to Messrs Scrope's and Furnese's.

24. Sunday. Din'd with us Sir Charles Mordaunt, and Tynte, Messrs Poulets, Berkeley, and Bond, and Prowse.[3]

25. Monday. Din'd alone. Went to Sir Paul Methuen's and Lady Middlesex's.

26. Tuesday. Went to Council at St James's, where proclamation with £500 reward was made for apprehending Mr Murray: in consequence of a resolution of the House. Din'd alone. Went to Council at the Cockpit.

27. Wednesday. Mr Tucker din'd here—went to the Duke of Argyll's, and Mr Scrope's. Army voted: 180 to 45.

28. Thursday. Din'd alone. Council at night. Went to Mr Furnese's, and the Speaker's.

29. Friday. Din'd at the Duke de Mirepoix.

30. Saturday. Din'd alone. Supp'd at Lady Middlesex's.

[1] An example of Carey's activity as go-between for D. and the Government. D. now waits on two of his closest political friends to pass the news on to them. The visits are repeated after the conference with Mills and Carey next day.

[2] Alexander Murray, a Jacobite who had been a prominent supporter of the candidature of Sir George Vandeput at the Westminster election (as D. had been—see above 6 Feb. 1751). As a result he had been committed for contempt of the House of Commons.

[3] A notable gathering of leading West Country and Midland M.P.s.

DECEMBER

1. Sunday. Din'd here Messrs Trenchard, Cambridge, Churchill, Kelsal, Carver. Went to Mr Scrope's.[1]

2. Monday. Din'd alone—went to the play. The King there.

3. Tuesday. Din'd at Mr Furnese's. Went to Council.

4. Wednesday. Din'd here Messrs Furnese, and Carey.

5. Thursday. Mr Ralph din'd here. Went to Council. [Wrote to] Messrs Selwyn.

6. Friday. Mr William Sharpe din'd here.

7. Saturday. Din'd alone. Went to Messrs Furnese's, and Scrope's. Supp'd at Lord Middlesex's.

8. Sunday. Din'd here Messrs Furnese, Hoskins, Carey, Bance. Supp'd at Lord Middlesex's.

9. Monday. Din'd at Mr Churchill's. Went to Sir Paul Methuen's.

10. Tuesday. Din'd alone. Went to Council.

11. Wednesday. Din'd alone. Went to Mr Scrope's, and the Speaker's.

12. Thursday. Din'd at Mr Vane's.

13. Friday. Din'd alone. Went to Sir Paul Methuen's. Supp'd at Lady Middlesex's.

14. Saturday. Din'd alone. Last Thursday dyed Lord Bolingbroke.

15. Sunday. Din'd here Messrs Poulet and Mr Glover, Ladies Susan and Rebecca Poulet, and Miss Sturt. I went to Mr Scrope's.

16. Monday. Din'd alone. Went to the Duke of Argyll's, and the Speaker's.

17. Tuesday. Messrs Tucker din'd here. Went to Council.

[1] Here the gathering is of Dorset notables: again reported to the Treasury.

18. Wednesday. Went to Hammersmith. Mr Cooke din'd here.

19. Thursday. Went to Hammersmith.—Went to Council where the Trustees for Georgia agree'd to surrender their charter to the King, absolutely and unconditionally.

20. Friday. Din'd here, Messrs Vane, Mr Solicitor General, Messrs Furnese and Carey. Went to Council. News of the Queen of Denmark's death.

21. Saturday. Was to wait upon the Princess of Wales.—Receiv'd in a manner most remarkably kind[1] by her, and all the royal children. Din'd here, Mr and Mrs Dodington.

22. Sunday. Mr Bance din'd here. At night we came to Hammersmith.

23. Monday. Mr Bance came, and Mr Tucker din'd here.

24. Tuesday. Mr Bance went to town. I din'd alone. Mr Bance and Mrs Beaghan came.

25. Wednesday. Mr Bance went away in the evening.

26. Thursday. Messrs Bance and Furnese came. Din'd here Lords Bath and Montfort,[2] Mesdames Bristowe and Roane.

27. Friday. Mr Carey came—no strangers.

28. Saturday. Went to town. Return'd to dinner. Din'd here, Sir Thomas Robinson, and Mr Duncombe.

29. Sunday. Mr Kelsal came, and din'd here.

30. Monday. Mr Ralph came, and din'd here.

31. Tuesday. Mr Ralph went away. I went to London.—To Mr Scrope's—supp'd at Lord Middlesex's.

[1] Considering the inumerable contacts with the Pelhams he was now conducting through Scrope, the Speaker, and the Solicitor-General. In the past three weeks he had reviewed his whole political force.
[2] The gambler. In 1755, ruined, he made his will, asked the lawyer if it would stand good if he shot himself, walked into the next room, and did so. (Toynbee's *Letters of Horace Walpole*, ii. 279–80.)

1752

JANUARY

1. Wednesday. Waited upon the Princess—most kindly receiv'd. Return'd, with Mr Furnese, to dinner. Colonel Vane din'd here.

2. Thursday. Mr Furnese went away. We din'd alone.

3. Friday. Mr Lee din'd here.

4. Saturday. Mr Bance came.

5. Sunday. Din'd alone.

6. Monday. Mr Lee din'd here. Mr Bance went to town. The King plaid.

7. Tuesday. Went to town. Return'd to dinner.

8. Wednesday. Din'd alone.

9. Thursday. Mr Lee din'd here. Begun the pavement.[1] [Wrote to] Cardinal Albani, Messrs Mann and Sharpe.

10. Friday. Din'd alone.

11. Saturday. Mr Bance came. Messrs Tucker din'd here.

12. Sunday. Din'd alone.

13. Monday. Din'd alone. Mr Bance went.

14. Tuesday. Came to town. Went to Council at St James's— Sheriff's prick'd. At a Committee at the Cockpit in the evening. Supp'd with Lady Middlesex.

15. Wednesday. Return'd to Hammersmith, and din'd alone.

[1] Of Pall Mall.

16. Thursday. Mr Stanley came. Din'd alone.

17. Friday. Mr Stanley went away. Messrs Roberts, and Tucker, din'd here.

18. Saturday. We came to town. Din'd alone. Went to Sir P. Methuen's, and Mr Waller's.

19. Sunday. Mr Wyndham din'd here. Sir P. Methuen's and Mr Waller's.

20. Monday. Mr Furnese din'd here. At the Duke of Argyll's.

21. Tuesday. Messrs Furnese and Tucker din'd here. At the Cockpit—and supp'd with Lady Middlesex.

22. Wednesday. Mr and Mrs Fielding din'd here. At Messrs Waller's, Drax's, and Scrope's.

23. Thursday. Din'd with Mr Furnese. Went to Council.

24. Friday. Din'd alone. At Mr Scrope's.

25. Saturday. Went to Hammersmith. Return'd. Messrs Vaughan and Carey din'd here. At the Speaker's.

26. Sunday. Solicitor General, and Messrs Furnese and Jeffreys din'd here. On a malicious report that I had forc'd myself on the late Prince of Wales, and into his service, I explain'd that whole transaction, to the Solicitor General, and produc'd to him, all the proper vouchers that verified it, step, by step.[1]

27. Monday. Din'd alone. At Mr Scrope's.

28. Tuesday. Duke of Bedford attacked the Subsidiary Treaty with Saxony ALONE.[2] Din'd here Duke Hamilton, Lord Eglinton, Lord Talbot, Lord Litchfield, Messrs Macky and Stanley.

29. Wednesday. Din'd at Lord Montfort's.

[1] e.g. Ralph's minute, and perhaps extracts from the *Diary*.
[2] The attendance at the debate on the Subsidy Treaty with Saxony in the Commons had also been singularly thin. Egmont had gout, Pitt absented himself, Cobham went away. (Horace Walpole the Elder to the Duke of Bedford, 22 Jan. 1752; *Bedford Correspondence*, ii. 107.)

30. Thursday. Messrs Furnese and Carey din'd here. Went to Council, where Lord Granville, very imprudently, drew in question the validity of the French treaty of commerce, making enemies on French bottoms free from capture. This was, however, left undecided.

31. Friday. Din'd at Mr Furnese's. At Mr Scrope's.

FEBRUARY

1. Saturday. Went to Mr Ralph's, and to Hammersmith. Return'd to dinner alone. At Sir Paul Methuen's.

2. Sunday. Mr Furnese din'd here, and gave me an account of what pass'd between him and the Solicitor-General Mr Murray about a message to Mr Tucker, by Mr Ellis, from Mr Pelham, to know what was to be done on a new election at Weymouth:[1] pretending that the chusing two at his nomination, was to last always. The Solicitor enter'd into a detail of my affairs, with much affection, and warmth: said he knew there was not the least indisposition towards me, in the Ministry; was afraid that the King had been strongly prejudic'd against me personally. That he would take it upon him to bring the matter to a proper issue, one way, or another: for it was by no means, fitting that I should offer, or ask anything that I was not sure of being well receiv'd. He behav'd nobly, and like a friend.—The event is with God—. Supp'd with Lady Middlesex.

3. Monday. Went to Hammersmith: return'd to dinner alone.

4. Tuesday. Din'd alone. Went to Council. Gave the Solicitor General an account in writing of the whole proceeding of the late Prince of Wales, in the demand of £100,000 per annum in Parliament.[2]

5. Wednesday. Din'd at Lord Bath's.

6. Thursday. Messrs Poulet and Warburton din'd here. Went to the Cockpit to a Prize Cause: which turn'd upon the authenticity of the treaty of commerce with France concluded. Several Lords (of which the Lord President was one) doubted of its being in force. I did not; and it was decided at last, by virtue of that treaty.
    [Wrote to] Dr Sharpe.

---

[1] See above—11 Dec. 1750 and 20 Jan. 1751. Ellis was one of the Pelham nominees for Weymouth, and Lord George Cavendish the other. The 'new election' refers to the prospective general election of 1754. For D.'s exercise of influence at Weymouth see 20 Sept. below.
[2] Printed in the Appendix to Penruddock Wyndham's edition of the *Diary*. This narrative of the Crisis of 1737, transmitted to the Ministry, represented D.'s pledge to become once more a faithful ministerialist.

7. Friday. Din'd alone. At Mr Scrope's.

8. Saturday. Went to the Cockpit in the morning. Ended that long dispute of General Anstruther and Minorca, by referring the costs and damages he is to pay to the Master of the Rolls and General Bland.

9. Sunday. Din'd Glover with me.

Mr. Furnese call'd who had seen the Solicitor-General, and was inform'd that there was not the least indisposition in the Pelhams, but on the contrary a willingness to live well with me. That they said it would not be impossible to remove the ill impressions made upon the King, but there must be a little time, &c. If they remov'd the Pitts, &c. then it might be easy &c.

10. Monday. Mr. Ellis was here,—introduc'd the talk of his election for a new Parliament. I told him that I thought my behaviour public and private, even in opposition, never had given just cause of offence to the Pelhams, or show'd any indisposition to live personally well with them: that as I was, now, entirely free from engagements, I was sincerely desirous of Mr. Pelham's favour and friendship; if he would accept of my friendship and attachment. If then, he car'd to accept of my services, he might, *upon proper conditions*, command my interest, and in that case nobody would be more welcome to me at Weymouth, than he, Mr. Ellis. That this was in Mr. Pelham's breast, who best knew his own disposition, but that mine was entirely inclin'd to be his friend and servant, *upon proper conditions*. This of proper conditions, was frequently repeated, and Mr. Ellis desir'd to observe, that there was neither promise nor engagement. Din'd alone. Supp'd with Lady Middlesex. [Wrote to] Messrs Selwyn, and Servandoni.

11. Tuesday. Din'd here, Messrs Furnese, Sharpe, and Kelsal. Went to the Cockpit.

12. Wednesday. Din'd here, Lord Litchfield, Sir Francis Dashwood, Messrs Furnese and Shirley.

13. Thursday. Went to Council at St James's. Lord Berkeley of · Stratton, and Sir G. Lee sworn in. Cockpit, at night.

14. Friday. Went to Hammersmith—return'd to dinner. At Mr Scrope's.

15. Saturday. Saw the Solicitor-General, by appointment. Found his report much less favourable than Mr Furnese understood it.— That the Pelhams were very well dispos'd to me, but that the King was so much prejudic'd by former misrepresentations, that he fear'd they could answer for nothing &c.—So we parted:—I taking it for a thing entirely broke off: (as I do). He saying that he did not yet, see it in that light.

16. Sunday. Din'd at Sir Francis Dashwood's—went to Sir P. Methuen's.

17. Monday. Din'd at Sir Francis Dashwood's.

18. Tuesday. Din'd alone. At Council at night.

19. Wednesday. Din'd at Lord Litchfield's.

20. Thursday. Mr and Mrs Dodington, Messrs Breton and Wyndham, din'd here. At the Cockpit at night.

21. Friday. Went to the Oratorio.[1] Waited on the Princess, and was very graciously receiv'd yesterday.

22. Saturday. Din'd at Mr Harvey's—Went to the little theatre in the Haymarket.

23. Sunday. Din'd at Hammersmith. Mr and Mrs Dodington, Mr and Mrs Tucker, Messrs Fremantle, Thomson, Lisle, and Lee. Return'd at night.

24. Monday. Supp'd at Lady Middlesex's. [Wrote to] Mr Mann.

25. Tuesday. At the Cockpit.

26. Wednesday. Messrs Breton, Furnese, and Carey.—at Sir P. Methuen's.

27. Thursday. Went to the Cockpit.

28. Friday. Came to Hammersmith.

29. Saturday. Mr Warburton, and Mrs Dodington came.

---

[1] Probably Handel's last Oratorio, *Jephthah*.

MARCH

1. Sunday. Mr Warburton and I din'd at the Duke of Argyll's.

2. Monday. Mr Warburton went away. I call'd upon Mr Ralph.

3. Tuesday. The King's birthday kept. I was at it, and return'd to Hammersmith.

4. Wednesday. Din'd alone. The Doctor [Thomson] came.

5. Thursday. Went to Council after dinner, and return'd at night. Messrs Dodington, Tucker, and Kelsal, din'd here.

6. Friday. Din'd alone.

7. Saturday. Mr and Mrs Dodington went away. Lord and Lady Berkeley, and Mr Wright, and Mr Breton din'd here.

8. Sunday. Mr Stanley came. Mr Fielding din'd here.

9. Monday. Din'd alone. Mr Stanley went.

10. Tuesday. Din'd alone. Messrs Fielding and Thomson came and din'd. They, and Mr Breton, went away.

11. Wednesday. Din'd alone.

12. Thursday. Din'd alone. Went to Council. Lay in town. [Wrote to] Mr Mann.

13. Friday. I was to wait on the Princess—chapter of the Garter. Chosen, Prince Edward, the Stadtholder, the Earls of Lincoln, Winchelsea, and Cardigan. The Stadtholder and Lord Cardigan, by proxy. Return'd to Hammersmith, to dinner.

14. Saturday. Took physic. Din'd alone.

15. Sunday. Din'd here, two Messrs Harvey, two Messrs Poulet, Messrs Fielding, and Lee.

16. Monday. Din'd alone.

17. Tuesday. Took physic. Din'd alone.

18. Wednesday. Din'd alone. Came to town to Council, on the particular cause of a prize taken from the Spaniards by Admiral Knowles the 3ʳᵈ September 1748 in America. It turn'd upon the interpretation of the terms for hostilities ceasing in those parts, which were fix'd by the Preliminaries of Aix la Chapelle (which refers to the Treaty of Suspension, between us, and France, 1712) and the proclamations here, and other acts of state, there. I deliver'd my opinion at large, for restitution, the Lords took a further day to give judgement, but the majority seem to be with me, and think it must be so decided. Lay in town.

19. Thursday. Din'd at Sir Francis Dashwood's. Went to Council. A cause on a capture by Admiral Griffin in the East Indies: commonly call'd the Lascar's Cause.[1] The claim against them appear'd to be a manifest forgery, and was rejected: and the prize must be adjudg'd to them, when we meet next.

20. Friday. Return'd to Hammersmith—din'd alone.

21. Saturday. Din'd alone.

22. Sunday. Mr Fielding din'd here.

23. Monday. I came to town in the morning. Din'd at Sir Francis Dashwood's. Went to Mr Scrope's, and the Speaker's. Mrs Dodington came, and din'd in town.

24. Tuesday. Din'd Mr Shirley's. Sir P. Methuen.

25. Wednesday. Din'd alone. Lady Middlesex.

26. Thursday. Din'd alone. Went to Council.

27. Friday. Mr and Mrs Dodington din'd here. I went to Sir P. Methuen's.

28. Saturday. Mr Carey din'd here. I supp'd at Lord Talbot's.

[1] This case concerned the right of certain Indian seamen, locally recruited by Anson for his cruise in the East Indies, to share in prize money. The decision in their favour speaks well for the uprightness of the Prize Court. (*Gentleman's Magazine*, xxi. 327.)

29. Sunday. Din'd alone. Mr Speaker's and Mr Scrope's.

30. Monday. Went to Council at St James's. The King declar'd the Regency, as usual, and the Councillors took leave, and kiss'd his hand. Din'd here, Sir William Stanhope, Sir Francis Dashwood, Sir Harry Bellendine, Messrs Shirley, Madden, and Furnese.

31. Tuesday. The King set out, about four this morning, for Harwich. Din'd at Mr Shirley's. Sir P. Methuen.

APRIL

1. Wednesday. Din'd alone. At the Duke of Argyll's.

2. Thursday. Din'd at home. At the Speaker's.

3. Friday. Din'd at Lord Barrington's. At Mr Scrope's.

4. Saturday. Din'd alone.

5. Sunday. Mr Glover din'd here. Lady Middlesex came to me, in the evening.

6. Monday. Went to Hammersmith. Din'd at Gunnersbury. Supp'd with Lady Middlesex.

7. Tuesday. Din'd alone. Went to Council. Yesterday the King sail'd about two. I return'd to Hammersmith.

8. Wednesday. Din'd alone.

9. Thursday. Mr Shirley, and Lady Orford din'd here. This morning my old acquaintance Mr Scrope died at 84. I went to Council, and return'd at night. [Wrote to] Messrs Mann and Niccolini.

10. Friday. Mr Sharpe din'd here.

11. Saturday. I went to town. Christen'd Mr Forth's son. Colonel Caulfield the other godfather. Din'd at Lord Carlisle's. Return'd at night.

12. Sunday. Went to Mr Ralph's. Messrs Bance and Tucker din'd here.

13. Monday. Din'd alone.

14. Tuesday. Went to town after dinner—and lay there. At the Speaker's and Lady Middlesex's.

15. Wednesday. Went with Lady Shannon, Lady Middlesex, Messrs Dodington and Jeffreys, Lord Middlesex and Mr Breton, to see my lapis lazuli pillars, at Ponders End.[1] Din'd at the White Hart at Tottenham. Return'd at night.

---

[1] Imported from Italy and to be erected at the entrance to the sculpture gallery in D.'s villa at Hammersmith. (See 22 June 1751 above.)

16. Thursday. Went to town in the morning to consult the Speaker about Dr Thomson's privilege.[1] Return'd to dinner, and brought Mr Carey with me. After dinner carried him back, and went to Council. Return'd at night.

17. Friday. Went to town to attend Dr Thomson's action of defamation against Saxon, the apothecary, at the King's Bench. Began at 6, ended past 9. Evidences speaking to the Doctor's skill and reputation. Duke of Roxburgh, Earl of Middlesex, Mr Levison, Sir Francis Dashwood, Sir Francis Eyles, Mr Drax, and myself. He carried his cause, and the jury gave £20 damages. After the trial I din'd at Lord Middlesex's, and return'd at night.

18. Saturday. Messrs Breton and Bance din'd here, the last return'd.

19. Sunday. Went to Lord Hillsborough. Din'd alone.

20. Monday. Went to town. Din'd at Earl Poulet's.

21. Tuesday. Mrs D and Mr Breton went to town. I din'd at Mr Furnese's. Went to Council. The Solicitor-General told me he had spoke to Mr Pelham, as from himself.—That there was a real good will, and desire to take me with them.—But fears to engage me, lest they on their part, should not be able to fulfil their engagement. —Were afraid of the King, and of the Party: that is the old Walpolians, nicknamed the Black-Tan &c[2]—but advis'd me, by all means to see him. That I should meet with a friendly, confidential reception &c.—This is nothing,—but obliges me to see him.

22. Wednesday. I went to see Sir P. Methuen.[3] Return'd to dinner where I found Messrs Dodington and Tucker, and their wives, and Mr Freke.

[1] Thomson was now involved in litigation (see following entry) resulting from his comments on the professional skill of the Prince of Wales's doctors and for debt. The question of privilege arose from his employment by D. (a Member of Parliament) as personal physician, and the 'disagreable affair'—presumably the possibility of his arrest for debt—referred to on 8 May below.

[2] The earlier printed texts at this point read '. . . of the party (the old Walpolians) nicknamed the Black-tan'. D.'s actual punctuation and capitalization suggest that even as early as this it was common usage for a politician to refer to 'the Party' without qualification, as today. See also entry for 27 May 1755, where Newcastle is again recorded as speaking of 'the Party'. 'Black-Tan' presumably refers to the terrier-like qualities of the old Walpolians.

[3] Inevitably, after a political invitation such as he had just received. Nevertheless D.'s reliance on Methuen, which the full diary alone brings out, is sufficiently remarkable in an experienced politician of past fifty.

23. Thursday. Bishop of Exeter with his wife and daughter, and Messrs Furnese, Jeffreys, and Carey din'd here. I went to the Cockpit,—and return'd.

24. Friday. Lord and Lady Carlisle, Sir P. Methuen, Sir G. Lee, and Mr Breton din'd here.

25. Saturday. I went to town to talk with Sir John Ligonier about Lee, the surgeon.[1] Din'd at Lady Middlesex's, and return'd.

26. Sunday. Mr. Breton came.

27. Monday. Ladies Shannon and Middlesex, Mr and Mrs and Miss, Mr and Mrs Edward, Drax, din'd here. Lady Middlesex's birthday.

28. Tuesday. Went to the Cockpit and return'd. Mr Breton went away.

29. Wednesday. Mr Crowle din'd here.

30. Thursday. Went to the Cockpit. Return'd at night. [Wrote to] Messrs Mann and Selwyn.

[1] One of the late Prince's doctors. The object of the talk was to get Lee a post in the army medical service, which he was given (see 6 Dec. 1752 below).

MAY

1. Friday. Din'd alone.

2. Saturday. Went to town about Dr Thomson. Council at night. Return'd.

3. Sunday. Mr and Mrs Henley, Messrs and Mrs Talkingham din'd with us.

4. Monday. Came to town. Din'd at Sir Francis Dashwood's. Lay in town.

5. Tuesday. Saw Mr. Pelham in Arlington Street, by appointment. Begun by telling him that the application I had receiv'd from Mr Ellis about his election at Weymouth, I look'd upon only as giving me handle to wait upon him: for I was come to offer him not only that, but all the services in my power, and that I was authoriz'd to say the same from all my friends. He said he should willingly embrace it, were it not for fear, that he should not be able to fulfil what he wish'd on his part.—I ask'd if he would admit of a confidential conversation—He said he would have no reason to wish any other—that what Ellis had said was from him, and meant to produce such a conversation.

I then ask'd him, if there was any real inclination in the Duke of Newcastle and him to accept of us into their friendship, and protection, if objections could be remov'd; for that I knew the different facility of removing them, when there was a little good-will at the bottom, and when it was the work of importance only—he would observe that I did not arrogate importance; but if I had it, I would accept of nothing that was only owing to that—That at my time of life, nothing could tempt me to come into any Court, upon the foot of force, and intrusion—That I said this to explain to him that I desired to live with him, and his, as their attach'd friend and servant, that I desired no rank that could justly create envy in my equals, or any sort of power that might occasion suspicion in my superiors.—Reserving only that if he gave me a musket, and order'd me to a post, I would certainly fire—That if clouds should arise, I was not afraid to meet the great geniuses now on the stage.

He said there was real good wishes, and good-will, and for
nobody more: but how to put it in execution was what hinder'd
him from saying all he wish'd—That there were difficulties, and
great ones, with the King, on account of my quitting his service for
the Prince's, &c.—I replied that I was aware of a prejudice of that
kind, but that I believ'd when it was represented to the King, and
by him, as his opinion, that I could be of some utility to his service,
by my own, and my friends' weight, particularly, in chusing several
members, it would be means to remove those prejudices. For that
tho' I knew that no pains had been spar'd to make him believe the
contrary: yet I did assure him as a gentleman, and his servant, that
the interest of Weymouth was wholly in Mr. Tucker and me; that
in the country it was impossible to chuse one member against us,
at least, without the utmost violence: that, indeed, he could give,
a great deal of trouble there, and I own'd, could chuse any four he
pleas'd at Westminster. But that I knew it was not in his temper,
and could not think it could be for his interest to have recourse to
flagrant acts of violence to chuse two members (which was the
most that was pretended,) where he might have all four, and me too,
without any violence at all.

He did not pretend to set up any right of the Court, or that they
design'd to make use of any against me but said—To be sure what
I had hinted must be the way that he must talk it to the King: and
that he would tell me truly all that he knew about the King's
prejudice to me. That he was angry at my quitting, but receiv'd
it better than he expected, as he told me, to which he referr'd &c.,—
but at my coming into the Prince's service afterwards, he broke out,
and said, to him 'Here is a fine end of civilities; here is Dodington,
you made me give him a great employment, the other day, and,
now, he has thrown it at your head, and is gone over to my son:
and what is more remarkable, a nominal place is made for him, to
give him a pretence of putting himself at the head of his measures,'
and more to this purpose. After this, upon my coming to Kensington, on a Sunday,[1] some time after the Prince's death, the King said
to him, 'I see Dodington here, sometimes, what does he come for?'
To which he reply'd, that indeed he did not know, that he did not
believe that I had any particular views, because he had never heard
the least hint of any; which if I had formed any, he believ'd he
should sooner than another, from the long acquaintance between

[1] See 15 Sept. 1751 above.

us: that he was sure, my coming was to show my duty, and that I desir'd to live in his favour: and he suppos'd I might wish for his protection and desire to come into his service, but that was guess only: the King said, 'No, there has been too much of that already', and that the conversation did not end well.

That he would tell me the bottom of all his politicks, and his brother's too, for they must in the end be the same, and that was to chuse a new Parliament that should be all of a piece, such a one as might serve the King if he liv'd: and be steady to put the young King in the right way, if the old one dy'd—That he meant a thorough Whig Parliament: for when there were factions, though a wise man was obliged to avail himself of them, as well as he could, that was never desirable, nor what he meant, but he wish'd to have a thorough Whig Parliament all of a piece.—I replied that I approv'd of what he said, and thought that the offer I made him from myself, and friends, might contribute to facilitate that end.—He said, that it was for that end that he told it me.—That they were, now, without competition as well with the King as they could possibly hope; but that he was not so weak as to imagine that it depended upon any thing but the ease they procur'd him in carrying on his service: that his temper was to be observ'd and complied with, &c.—That in this thing, he himself was most sincere, and desirous to effect it, and would do his best, and was sure his brother would do so too, and he would write to him in conformity—That as to borough matters, when he was press'd about Weymouth (as to be sure both of us must expect) he thought the best language he could hold was, that he and I liv'd very well together, and that he had no reason to think that anything would be done there that was disagreeable or disserviceable to him: and that I should deal in the same general terms, &c.

I said that as to quitting the King's service, I did not do it by any compact with the Prince, that it was full four months after, before his Royal Highness made me any offers, and then did it in such a manner that left me no room to refuse, without offending him for ever. That Mr. Solicitor-General Murray knew this, and I had living and written evidence to prove it uncontestably. Since I came into the service, I could appeal to him, whether my behaviour was not entirely calculated to soften, rather than inflame: even to the loss of my favour; whether, when the little incendiary system prevail'd, by which alone many of those about his Royal Highness

could ever be of any significance, since I could not stop it I did not
absent myself from the House, rather than take part, or countenance
it.[1] But however, I desir'd the King should know that I would not
justify with my King, and my master, and submitted myself to think
I was to blame, since he was displeas'd and therefore begg'd his
pardon, which was all in my power to do except by my future
services to show him that I deserv'd it. That this with the interest
I could, and was willing to center towards his service, I thought
might be sufficient to remove objections, that had really no foundation: especially, when convey'd through so able, so powerful, and
I trusted, so friendly a canal. That, upon the whole, he might see,
and I meant he should, that I was very desirous this event should
take place, from a sincere wish to attach myself to him, and to
end my life with those with whom I began it. That I was desirous
to serve my country, and I chose to do it with the good liking of
the King—but if his Majesty shut up that way, I must endeavour
to do it by such ways as should offer themselves in the course of
things.

He renew'd the assurances of his sincere wishes and endeavours,
in a very decent manner, and added that he was restrain'd from
saying what he wish'd out of the regard he ow'd me not to say any
thing he was not sure to perform, and concluded by inviting himself, in a most gentlemanlike and obliging manner to Hammersmith.

6. Wednesday. Return'd to Hammersmith. Din'd alone.

7. Thursday. Went to Council in the morning—return'd to dinner
—Mr and Mrs Freke, Mr Gould, Mrs Harris, Sir Francis Eyles,
Messrs Kelsal and Falconer din'd with us. Went back to the Cock-
pit. Lay in town.

8. Friday. Went to the Speaker's in Surrey with Mr Chamberlayne,
about Dr Thomson's most disagreable affair. Return'd to town,
and thence to Hammersmith.

9. Saturday. Earl Poulet, Messrs Poulet, Kelsal, and Breton, din'd
with us. The two last lay here.

[1] A significant variation here from the Penruddock Wyndham text, which makes
D. allege he tried to stop 'the little incendiary system'.

10. Sunday. Mr and Mrs Cornwall, and Colonel Powlett din'd with us.

11. Monday. Sir Francis and Lady Dashwood, Miss Wheat, and Mr Furnese din'd here. I communicated to Sir Francis what had pass'd between Mr Pelham, and me: and offer'd him to be of the party, when he din'd at Hammersmith—which Sir Francis declin'd.

12. Tuesday. Din'd at Mr Furnese's. Went to the Cockpit. Told the Solicitor General the whole conversation with Mr Pelham. Lay in town.

13. Wednesday. Din'd at Mr Mildmay's. Mrs D and I supp'd at Lady Middlesex's.

14. Thursday. Din'd at Sir William Stanhope's, at Twickenham. Mrs Beaghan came to Hammersmith.

15. Friday. Din'd here Sir Thomas Robinson, Mr Duncombe, Mr Younge, Mr and Mrs Dodington, who lay here.

16. Saturday. They went away. Din'd at the Duke of Argyll's.

17. Sunday. Din'd here Sir Charles Tynte, Messrs Mildmay, Bond, and Bance. Mrs Mildmay, Busby, Miss Mildmay, and Lady Tynte.

18. Monday. Din'd alone.

19. Tuesday. Lord and Lady Litchfield din'd here.

20. Wednesday. Din'd at Sir Harry Bellendine's.

21. Thursday. Went to see Lord Radnor's with Mrs D and Mr Breton, who came with me from Sir Harry Bellendine's, and return'd today.

22. Friday. I went to see Lady Middlesex. Return'd and found Mr Ralph at dinner.

23. Saturday. Din'd with us, the Ladies, and Mr Vere Poulet, Mr and Mrs Harris.

24. Sunday. Prince of Wales' birthday.—I went to St James's. Great Court, but not in new clothes. Return'd to dinner, found Messrs Hampden and Bance.

25. Monday. Din'd here, Lord Lincoln, Messrs Pelham, Vane, and his son, Solicitor-General, and Furnese. Much wine, and as much good humour as I ever met with: both lasted till almost eleven o'clock.

26. Tuesday.[1] I din'd in town. Went to the Cockpit. Return'd at night.

27. Wednesday. Din'd here, the Portugal Minister, and Mr Breton.

28. Thursday. Went to Council. Din'd at the Duke of Argyll's. Council again in the evening. Return'd at night.

29. Friday. Din'd at Gunnersbury.

30. Saturday. Din'd here, Lord Barrington, Messrs Masham, Stanley, Breton, who lay here.

31. Sunday. Din'd at Lord Lincoln's, with Mr Pelham &c. Staid late, but return'd.

[1] See the letter of the Primate of Ireland to D. of this date (*H.M.C. Stopford-Sackville* i. 182).

JUNE

1. Monday. Mr Breton went away, and Mr Younge din'd here.

2. Tuesday. At the Cockpit after dinner. Return'd.

3. Wednesday. Alone.

4. Thursday. Went to town to see Sir Paul Methuen. Return'd to dinner with Mr Breton. Dr Thomson and Mr Lee din'd with us. After dinner Mr Breton, and I went to Ashley to see Lady Middlesex. Lord Middlesex gone to town. Lady Shannon ill of gout.

5. Friday. At Ashley.

6. Saturday. Came from Ashley at noon. Met Lord Middlesex at Twickenham. Din'd at Hammersmith.

7. Sunday. Mr Breton went away. Din'd at Mr Pelham's at Esher. Much drink, and good humour.

8. Monday. Din'd alone.

9. Tuesday. Came to town to see Mr Bance. Went to the Cockpit. Lay in town.

10. Wednesday. Din'd with Mr Sharpe at Brock Hill. Lay in town.

11. Thursday. Din'd with Lord and Lady Middlesex. At Mr Breton's. At the Cockpit. Return'd.

12. Friday. Sir Francis Dashwood and Mr Ralph din'd here.

13. Saturday. Mrs D. and I went to Mr Cambridge's by water. Mr Breton lay here.

14. Sunday. Din'd with Mr Pelham at Gunnersbury. Much drink.[1]

15. Monday. I din'd en famille with Lord and Lady Lincoln at Mr Vane's. Return'd at night, and Mr Breton went to town.

[1] This further convivial interview, the fourth since 5 May, is omitted by Wyndham.

16. Tuesday. Alone. Went to Council and return'd.

17. Wednesday. Din'd with Mr Vane. Return'd.

18. Thursday. Went to the Cockpit after dinner. Complaint by Mr Webb against Mr William Sharpe[1] for taking exorbitant fees. To be heard next Tuesday.

19. Friday. Din'd here, Messrs William and Philip Sharpe, Dr Thomson, Messrs Comyns, Vane, Carey, Tucker, Pommeroy, Collard, and Chamberlayne, Mrs Comyns and Sharpe.

20. Saturday. Went to attend Dr Thomson's cause. The Court would not enter into proofs whether he was or was not my servant.[2] Mr Breton came.

21. Sunday. Mr Breton went to Ashley. I went to Mr Oswald's who express'd much affection, and attachment for me.

22. Monday. Mr Ralph din'd here.

23. Tuesday. Din'd in town. Went to the Cockpit. Mr Webb's accusation of Mr William Sharpe for taking 3 guineas as a Council fee in every Prize Cause, of the gainer only, heard—and judg'd to be false, groundless, scandalous, and malicious. Return'd.

24. Wednesday. Din'd here Messrs Breton, Furnese, Williams, Carey, Verschaffelts.

25. Thursday. Went to the Cockpit. Return'd.

26. Friday. Went to see Mr Kelsal, and he came, and lay here.

27. Saturday. Mr Verschaffelts din'd here—and I paid him £100 in part for his statue.

28. Sunday. Mr Breton came. We went to see Mr Furnese.

29. Monday. Mr Kelsal went. We din'd alone.

30. Tuesday. I came to town before dinner. Mrs D and Mr Breton in the evening. Went to the Cockpit. Lay in town.[3]

---

[1] One of the Clerks to the Privy Council, and a familiar of D.'s. Philip Sharpe (see next entry) also a Clerk of the Privy Council, and the Rev. Gregory Sharpe, D.'s private clergyman, were his relations.
[2] And so entitled to privilege.
[3] And replied to the Primate of Ireland (*H.M.C. Stopford-Sackville*, i. 184).

JULY

1. Wednesday. Din'd with Mr Arthur. Lady Lincoln brought to bed of a son.[1]

2. Thursday. Alone. Went to the Cockpit.

3. Friday. We return'd to Hammersmith.[2]

4. Saturday. Messrs Ralph and Breton din'd here. The last staid.

5. Sunday. Mr Tucker din'd here, and we went to Colonel Lyttelton's.

6. Monday. Went to town to meet Lord Middlesex and Counsellor Forrester. Lord Middlesex gave me full power to make his submissions, and endeavour to reconcile him to his father.[3] Carried Mr Breton. We din'd at Mr Furnese's. Owen try'd, and acquitted for publishing Mr Murray's case—N.B. the third great case where the juries have insisted on judging the matter of law, as well as fact. The two [others] are Bushell the Quaker reported by Lord Chief Justice Vaughan, and the Bishops, in James II.[4]

7. Tuesday. Went to town to see the Duke of Dorset. I chose to put the question to him hypothetically. If his son should throw himself at his feet, and declare an unreserv'd submission, and sorrow for what is past—What would he do?—He was much mov'd—I desir'd he would not answer me then, as I had no such commission—but consider of it. Because as the family was to come to me, at Eastbury, if I should happen to receive such a commission, I should think it my duty to both him and his son to lay it plainly before him, if it was full, and ample, as it ought to be.

8. Wednesday. Mr Verschaffelts din'd here.

[1] Noted as the ultimate heir to the Newcastle dukedom.
[2] And received a long letter on theological matters from Dr. Gregory Sharpe (*Seward Anecdotes*, ii).
[3] The Duke of Dorset: see below 7 July.
[4] See above, 6 Feb. and 26 Nov. 1751. The Hon. Alexander Murray had been condemned for breach of privilege of the House of Commons by interfering, on behalf of the 'Independent Electors' in the Westminster by-election. W. Owen had been printer of the Prince of Wales's organ edited by Ralph, *The Remembrancer*.

9. Thursday. Din'd here the Ladies, and Mr V. Poulet. We went to Ranelagh. [Wrote to] Messrs Selwyn and Mann.

10. Friday. Din'd here, Duke of Devonshire, Marquis of Hartington, Lord George Cavendish, Earls of Lincoln, Ashburnham, and Waldegrave, Messrs Furnese and Breton.

11. Saturday. I went to town, and return'd to dinner. We went to Vauxhall.

12. Sunday. Din'd here Mr Fielding, and Breton. We lay in town.

13. Monday. We return'd at night.

14. Tuesday. Went to the Cockpit. Return'd.

15. Wednesday. I went early to town to take my leave of Mr Pelham, and found him. After a little general conversation, I rose to go away, and said that the Solicitor General had told me that it was not only his own, but his [Mr. Pelham's] opinion that nothing of our affair should be broke to the King, till his return: so that I ask'd him no news. He said it was their opinion.—That he had treated me with the utmost sincerity and would do so.—That he sincerely wish'd the thing, and would do everything in his power to bring it about.—That all reasons were for it.—That he had told me the peculiarity of temper, the prejudices &c., that made things disagreeable: but he would do his best.

I replied that considering the name he bore, I could have no doubt of his sincerity, and, therefore, must wait the event.—But that I thought, when through a canal so favourable, the King was informed that when I quitted his service, it was not by a bargain, to enter into the Prince's.—That I never made him any proposition at all.—That it was above four months after my quitting that the Prince made me any.—When his Majesty is desir'd to reflect when I came into that service, how much I endeavour'd to bring a little temper, and moderation into it; and when I could not succeed in that, would not support the incendiary part, and did not come to the House:—That the Princess, the Solicitor General, and other living witnesses which I could produce, knew the first; and that I could appeal to him [Mr. P.] for the truth of the last. But that setting all this aside, when his Majesty should be inform'd that I would not justify against my King, and my master.—That, since he was displeas'd, I was willing to think myself to blame, and humbly to beg his pardon, assuring him that my future services should deserve it.—Here I desir'd him to observe, that when a gentleman asks pardon, with us, he is entitled to it, and it was what I would not do, to any subject in the world, or to any Prince, but himself when I was in the right. When he was assur'd that I was capable of facilitating his affairs, and that his chief servants were desirous to receive me. If all this, represented by those he did, and ought chiefly to rely upon, would not do, I hop'd he Mr Pelham would think that I had discharg'd my humble duty to his Majesty and shew'd how desirous I was of passing the rest of my life with him, and under his protection: for I thought I had said and done as much as any man of honour could do, or say, and gone as far as was possible.

He said that he understood me perfectly well—wish'd the thing cordially, and would do all imaginable justice, and leave nothing in his power unattempted to persuade the King—That, in short, he had told to me the bottom of his politicks—That he had a great regard for all Europe, but did not trouble himself much about it—That his concern was to keep things upon a right foot at home—That if the King was willing to *arrondir* his affairs, and let them get together as many as they could of those who could best contribute to it, in order to go on as he was bred up, and endeavour to choose a thorough Whig Parliament, which would make the remains of his Majesty's life easy, and would settle the young Prince upon the throne, so as to secure him a prospect of a prosperous reign.—if they would let him do this, he was at their service; if not, he could be contented to be a private man as well as another.— Not that he complain'd of the King, &c.—In short, here, he spoke a little Pelham, but intelligible enough to those who know the language. So we parted very kindly. I return'd, and found Messrs Ralph, Kelsal, and Chamberlayne, who din'd with us.

16. Thursday. By the Princess's commands I went to pass the day with her at Kew. I got thither about eleven, in the morning, and we pass'd two, or three, hours together alone in the gardens.

I inform'd her by her order of the state of the Irish affairs, which had made so much noise.—She ask'd me about a report she had heard about a reconciliation between the Duke of Dorset, and Lord Middlesex. I said it would be impracticable unless Lord

Middlesex would entirely submit to his father, and even then his behaviour had made the wound so deep that I could not be answerable what the Duke would do. She seem'd desirous of it, and wish'd I would try.—I told her that as they were to be with me in the country I would see what Lord Middlesex could be brought to, for from thence only it must move, if at all. I open'd myself no farther to her.

We came in an hour before dinner. I dined at the Bed-chamber woman's table, where was Mr. Cresset, who behav'd very courteously to me, and is a very knowing man. After dinner, her Royal Highness sent for me. We walked round Richmond Gardens. She was attended by the Ladies Augusta and Elizabeth, Messrs Cresset and Bludworth.

When we return'd, she order'd me to come in with her. We sat down, and she turn'd the discourse upon the Ministry. I perceiv'd she had heard something of the late correspondence between Mr Pelham and me. I therefore thought fit to tell her, that from an opportunity which had arisen from them, I had lately renew'd my correspondence with them; and had taken occasion to tell them, that I was desirous of ending my life in quiet, with those with whom I had begun it and whom I most esteem'd, &c.—That they receiv'd my offers of friendship very civilly, and seem'd desirous to receive me. But apprehended the prejudices of the King to me from the honour I had of belonging to the Prince, &c.—That the answer I made was that my inclinations were sincere: as I supposed their kind acceptance was also—that for the rest I must leave it to them.—I then put her in mind that I never ask'd anything of his Royal Highness.—That he never propos'd anything to me till four months after I had quitted my employment; that I then testified my surprise to her, and acquainted her with all that pass'd, before dinner. She said she remembered it perfectly well.—I then reminded her, how from my appearance as a servant at Cliefden, I form'd a plan of temper and moderation: that knowing her right way of thinking, I ventur'd to communicate it to her, and beg'd her protection in the execution of it, even before we came to town— that I always persisted in it, and never would enter into any other.— She said it was very true, she was a very good witness of it, and would always say it, &c.—I ask'd leave to wait on her at Kew if she should be there at my return, which she gave me, in a very obliging manner, and then got home by ten at night.

17. Friday. Din'd with us Messrs Furnese and Ralph.

18. Saturday. Din'd alone.

19. Sunday. Din'd alone, and neither Mrs D. nor I went to bed.

20. Monday. At half past three, Mrs D. and I set out in our post-chaise for Eastbury, where we arriv'd at six the same day, without any accident: thanks to goodness.

21. Tuesday. Alone.

22. Wednesday. Mr Okeden breakfasted here. Din'd alone.

23. Thursday. Alone.

24. Friday. Alone.

25. Saturday. Mr Blake din'd here.

26. Sunday. Alone.

27. Monday. Alone.

28. Tuesday. Messrs Trenchard and Bromfield din'd here.

29. Wednesday. In the evening came Lord and Ladies Middlesex and Shannon, and Dr Thomson.

30. Thursday. The family only.

31. Friday. The same.

AUGUST

1. Saturday. The same. We drove out.

2. Sunday. The same.—Went to Mr Banks's.

3. Monday. Lord and Lady Shaftesbury, and Mrs Noel, and Mr William and J. Beckford din'd here.

4. Tuesday. We went to see Lord Shaftesbury's. Mr Banks din'd here.

5. Wednesday. We rode to the Lodge, and thence to see Mr Gottmans, and [by] Blandford home.

6. Thursday. At home. Mr Breton came.

7. Friday. Din'd at Mr Banks's.

8. Saturday. At home.

9. Sunday. Went to see Mr Drax's.

10. Monday.
11. Tuesday. } At home. Mr Ralph came.

12. Wednesday. Mr Shirley and Lady Orford breakfasted and lay here. Mr and Mrs Beckford din'd here.

13. Thursday. Mr Shirley and Lady Orford went away.

14. Friday. At home.

15. Saturday. At home. Dr Lidderdale came.

16. Sunday. Lord and Lady Middlesex &c went away. Mrs D., Breton, Ralph, and I went with them to Wilton. Din'd there, and return'd.

17. Monday. Alone.

18. Tuesday. Messrs Churchill, Mrs Lynch, and Bolt din'd here.

19. Wednesday. Alone.

20. Thursday. Mr Yorke din'd and lay here.

21. Friday. Mr Yorke went away. We din'd at Mr Beckford's. Mr and Mrs Dodington came.

22. Saturday. The family alone.

23. Sunday. Mr and Mrs Tucker came.

24. Monday. Alone.

25. Tuesday. Mr and Mrs Tucker went to Weymouth.

26. Wednesday. Dr Lidderdale went away.

27. Thursday. We went to see Mr Portman's, and return'd by Blandford.

28. Friday. The family only.

29. Saturday. The family only.

30. Sunday. Dr Taylor, Mrs Allen, and her two sons came. News of Mr Poulet's death,[1] on Wednesday. I sent a servant to Lord Poulet with a letter, to endeavour a reconciliation in his family. Mr Breton went away.

31. Monday. Lord and Lady Arundel, and Lady Harriet Ratcliffe din'd here. Mr and Mrs Dodington went away.

[1] Peregrine Poulet, who shared the representation of Bridgwater with D. The quarrel in the Poulet family was between the two elder brothers (the Earl and Peregrine), and the two younger (Vere and Anne). D. wished Vere to succeed to the seat, see below 4 Oct.

SEPTEMBER

1. Tuesday. Took physic. Messrs Tudor and Blackman din'd here.

2. Wednesday. Din'd with the hunt, at Sir William Napier's. Dr Taylor &c went. Roy came.

N.S.[1]

14. Thursday. The hunt din'd here, consisting of Messrs Pitt, John Pitt, Pleydell, Jonathan Pleydell, Vansittart, Harcourt, Chafin, William Chafin, Penruddock, Okeden, Jones. Mrs Dodington return'd.

15. Friday. Mrs Dodington, Mr Ralph, and I set out for Poole: we arriv'd in my coach in 3 hours and a half. On our side Silver was put up against Jolyffe for sheriff and Hyde against Masters for Mayor. We were, exclusive of the out-burgesses votes (which we offer'd, but were refus'd), 33 to 44 for sheriff, and 35 to 48 for Mayor, so we lost both, and I think Mr Trenchard's election in danger.[2] N.B. They poll'd several minors, but I fear not so many as their majority. We set out at 4, got home at 5, bringing Mr Wyndham with us. Mr Roy went away.

16. Saturday. Mrs Dodington went away. Mr Younge came to dinner.

17. Sunday. The family only. Mr Breton came at night.

18. Monday. Mrs D and I din'd at Lord Arundell's.

19. Tuesday. Family only.

20. Wednesday. Mrs D, Messrs Wyndham, Ralph, and I set out at 11 for Weymouth. We got to Mr William Pitt's at Kingston Hall, a little after 3, when we din'd. Went thence before 6, and got to Mr Tucker's before 9. Mr Breton staid at Eastbury. Mr Younge went home. We went to see the Mayor before supper.

---

[1] Lord Chesterfield's Act, omitting eleven days, now came into force.
[2] George Trenchard, one of the M.P.s for Poole. This loss of a friendly returning officer was indeed fatal to him at the election of 1754 and marks the end of Dodington's power in the borough once (1741) described as his 'washpot'.

21. Thursday. Waited on the Mayor to a new election. Mr Swaffield chosen without opposition. Din'd with the old Mayor at the Crown. Very wet weather.

22. Friday. Set out from Weymouth about 11. Order'd a dinner at Lord Orford's at Piddletown, they being in France. Return'd to Eastbury by 8. Mr Breton left Eastbury the day before, having receiv'd an account that his mother was struck with an apoplexy, at Bath.

23. Saturday. Mr Trenchard, and his son, and Mr Fleet and his wife din'd here. Mr Wyndham went home with Mr Trenchard.

24. Sunday. The family only.

25. Monday. Mrs Okeden din'd here.

26. Tuesday. Mrs Dodington and I set out from Eastbury at 20 minutes past 3 in the morning: and arriv'd here at Hammersmith at 5 minutes past six in the evening, without any accident. God be prais'd.

27. Wednesday. Mr Furnese, and Carey din'd here. Dr Thomson came, and return'd.

28. Thursday. I went to town in Mr Furnese's chaise.—Call'd at Mr Pelham's: found him. He gave me an account of Earl Poulet's correspondence with him, about the vacancy at Bridgewater. I mention'd what I had wrote to his Lordship to make it a means of reconciling the family. He seem'd much indispos'd to Mr Vere [Poulet]. There was company so we could not talk fully.

I design'd to talk to him again at Council, but I came too late; they were up, having nothing to do but prorogue the Parliament, and issue a proclamation for a Scotch peer, on the death of the Duke of Gordon. I went to see Lady Middlesex, and Sir P. Methuen, but found neither. Return'd to dinner. Mr Lee came.

29. Friday. Mrs Dodington, and I din'd alone.

30. Saturday. We din'd at Gunnersbury.

OCTOBER

1. Sunday. Messrs Furnese and Hoskins din'd here.

2. Monday. Went to town to meet the Duke of Dorset. I made his son's submissions to him, and endeavour'd to procure a full reconciliation. We had a long conference. He alleged the many, almost unpardonable provocations which I know to be true.— Did not absolutely refuse to forgive him.—Boggled much at the freeing him from his debts, and said, that nothing but his distresses drove him to think of his duty, and expected some actions, to convince him of his sincerity. To this I said that as to enumerating provocations, I thought our most rational point was to look for reasons to forgive, instead of materials to continue the quarrel. That as to paying his debts I wish'd it were come to that, for I could make that very practicable. As to the motives of his repentance, I allow'd it, but he must allow that they were, too often, the same, with those of us all, to our common Father, to whom we were more oblig'd than we could be to our natural ones.—That he accepted our repentance, tho' grounded on distress. Should we refuse it when offered to us? As to actions, what should they be?—would he please to prescribe? This was matter of some difficulty, and as the conversation had been very long, we agreed to meet again, to consider if any temperament can be found. I much doubt it: but if Lord Middlesex would help himself—as I think he will not—it might succeed. I return'd to dinner.

3. Tuesday. Din'd here Messrs Cooke and Ralph.

4. Wednesday. I went to town to see Mr Pelham.—Laid before him the utility of his taking the occasion of Mr P. Poulet's death to make up the quarrel between the Earl and his brothers, by choosing Mr Vere Poulet in his place.—He would not enter into it—Mr Vere had left them unhandsomely, had treated him ill, personally, wherever he might be heard.—That for the union of the family he was for that,—but would have nothing to do with Mr Vere from his personal behaviour, tho' he could very well live and treat with those who oppos'd, and even oppos'd him personally. —Which, considering those he has about him, was, I thought,

saying in effect that he would take a blow from a strong man, but would not from a weak one.

—Said that they knew nothing positive as to the King's coming, but should know by the next courier if he design'd to go again [to Hanover] next year. For that he had wrote to his brother, to beg to know of his Majesty if he would have the Parliament meet before, or after Christmas. If he had any necessary reasons to have it rise early in the Spring, it must meet before: if not, people would like it better after Christmas.

We touched upon the subsidies attending the election of a King of the Romans. His face fell and he grew very uneasy upon it.— Express'd much dislike at the way it was conducted.—Said he was always against these subsidies; that his idea was that if the dissenting electors would give in the ultimatum of their demands and perform the conditions before they receiv'd the reward, then, indeed, when we were sure of our bargain, it might be worth considering if it were prudent to pay the price; but to be buying one elector after another was what he could not come into. It must have an end.—He had said so in Parliament. That as I was not there, he would tell me what he said, for he found he had been misrepresented.—I told him that I had from many quarters heard how he was understood; that tho' I was satisfied that he said nothing but what was proper, yet whatever was the general acceptation was worth attending to:—that it was allow'd on all hands, that he declar'd against these subsidies in general. But that he was for the present demand, as it was to be the last, and as he had good reason to think that it would certainly attain the end:—that it was, by somebody, fasten'd upon him, who rejecting all that others had said, declar'd he gave his consent singly on the assurances given by him [Pelham]. He ask'd 'Who? Pitt?'—I said 'No, I thought I was told it was Mr Fox'—He repeated in a low voice, 'Oh, Fox', with great signs of uneasiness, and discomposure, and so I left him.

Mr Ralph din'd here.

5. Thursday. We din'd alone.

6. Friday. Mr Ralph din'd here. Mr Kelsal came. Dr Sharpe came in the afternoon.

7. Saturday. Mr Kelsal went. We din'd alone. Dr Thomson came from Ashley and went to town.

8. Sunday. Dr Thomson came and carried Dr Sharpe to Ashley after dinner. I wrote to Mr Cresset to know when he thought the properest day for me to wait upon the Princess. He wrote for answer that as soon as he could see her he would acquaint me.

9. Monday. Receiv'd a letter from Mr Cresset that H.R.H. would see me this morning. I made haste to dress, and got to Kew by half after eleven.—Saw H.R.H. very soon. She, the Ladies Augusta, Elizabeth, and I went out, just at twelve. We walk'd without setting down, 'till ¾ past two.—Much talk upon all manner of private subjects, serious and ludicrous. Her behaviour open, friendly, and unaffected.—She commanded me to dine there, and pass the afternoon with her. When we came in, we met Lady Middlesex, who had sent me word she was to be there. We din'd, and after dinner the Princess sent for me, and she and Lady Middlesex and I walk'd as long as it was light. As we came in she said that she had a petition from the Prince, that we would play at comet with him, which he was very fond of. The party was, the Princess and Prince of Wales, Prince Edward, the Ladies Augusta and Elizabeth, Ladies Middlesex and Charlotte Edwin, and myself. Lady Middlesex soon return'd to Ashley where she had left Lady Shannon very ill of the gout. I staid till near ten. The Princess was pleas'd to command me to pass the day with her next Saturday.
    Found Drs Sharpe and Thomson, return'd from Ashley.

10. Tuesday. We din'd alone.

11. Wednesday. Went to town in the morning. Receiv'd an account from Bridgewater, that at the mayor's feast, the 7th, Mr Balch, being present, was declar'd candidate to succeed Mr P. Poulet.—I sent an abstract of the letter with one of my own, to Mr Pelham, immediately, and then return'd to Hammersmith to dinner.

12. Thursday. Din'd here Messrs Fane, Ralph, and Lord Dupplin. Miss Griselda Pelham married to Mr Watson.

13. Friday. Went to town.—Talk'd to Mr Pelham about this sudden event at Bridgewater. He agreed that it was wholly Earl Poulet's fault in not determining, and recommending somebody sooner. He seem'd to be well enough satisfied with the character I had given him of Mr Balch. When the post came in I found

another letter from Dr Taylor,[1] which I sent him immediately from hence.

14. Saturday. Din'd alone. Receiv'd a letter from Mr Pelham about Bridgewater, which I answered.

15. Sunday. The Princess having sent to desire me to pass this day with her, instead of yesterday, I waited on her accordingly, between eleven and twelve. I saw her, immediately, and her Royal Highness, the children, and Lady Charlotte Edwin went a-walking till two, and then returned to prayers. Thence to dinner: as soon as it was over, she sent for me and we sat down to comet: Their Royal Highnesses, the Princess, Ladies Augusta and Elizabeth, the Prince of Wales, Prince Edward, Ladies Charlotte Edwin and Howe, and I. After we rose from play about nine, the royal children retir'd, the Princess call'd me to the farther end of the room, and the two ladies who were to sup with her, remain'd at the other end.

She began by saying that she lik'd the Prince should, now and then, amuse himself at small play, but that Princes should never play deep, both for the example, and because it did not become them to win great sums. From thence, she told me that it was highly improper, the manner in which the Princess Amalie behav'd at the Bath; that she play'd publicly all the evening, very deep. I asked with whom? She said the Duke and Duchess of Bedford: that it was prodigious the work she made with Lord Chesterfield: that when he was in Court, she would hardly speak to him; at least as little as was possible to a man of his rank; but that now, she sent to enquire of his coming before he arriv'd; when he came sent her compliments and that she expected he should be of all her parties at play; that he should sit by her always in the public rooms, that he might be sure of a warm place, &c.

—I asked her how these demonstrations with him and the Bedfords were to be represented to the King. She said, she did not understand it: that when the Duke of Bedford, went out, he treated the Duke of Newcastle very ill to the King, not only as to public but as to private matters with relation to Lord Gower. But that, some time afterwards in the summer, he relented, and ask'd an audience, when he unsaid great part of what he had said (and on which account the King had been very angry with the Duke of

---

[1] D.'s spy at Bridgwater.

Newcastle) and laid it upon misinformation. I asked her if that was so. She said she was sure of it, and knew it to be so. I observ'd to her, that after all this, in the winter, his Grace made a formal attack, and a very strong one too, in the House of Lords, upon the Saxon subsidy. She said it was true, and that then the King was again very angry, and told her that he did not know his own mind. And that she had no opinion of his judgment, but that he was govern'd by Lord Sandwich, whom she did not think very well of; who made him resign, and that they were both very much combin'd, and in intimate correspondence with the Duke of Cumberland. How they managed with the King she did not know, but she thought they did not mean to act, or at least to any purpose now: that their views were upon the minority.[1]

I said in that light, it seemed highly imprudent for the Duke of Bedford to resign his office, which gave him a settled place in the council of Regency. She said it was true, it was Lord Sandwich's doing, but she was satisfy'd the minority was their point of action.

I said that it was necessary for her Royal Highness to look about her a little, and to secure friends that she could trust, to see that justice was done her, in that event, not only from that quarter, but from all quarters, for she must have observ'd that the Government had taken the best care they could to secure themselves. She said, 'Yes, good folks! they had not neglected themselves;' and she should do as I had hinted not only for her own sake, but the sake of her son, and of the nation.

I said, that not knowing what party her Royal Highness would take in the Regency Bill, I had prepared myself to oppose it; that I should have oppos'd it in a very different manner than those who meddled with it, either did, or knew; that I would have oppos'd it upon principles that should have made the King himself weary of the Bill; not as an opposition to the King, and his Ministers; but as a measure of his Ministers to secure their own power at the expense, and in diminution of the power of the Crown; and I did believe, that with the assistance I was sure of, I could have hung on the Bill so long, and show'd it in such lights, that at last the King should have been out of humour with it, before it pass'd, as I had reason to believe he was, since. That, however, when I found that she took the party of acquiescence, which, upon con-sideration (tho' I thought I should hardly have had the prudence to

[1] i.e. of the future George III.

advise it) I was thoroughly convinc'd was much the most wise, and adviseable that could be taken, she knew I dropp'd all shew of opposition, and went no more to the House, that I might furnish no handle to render me obnoxious; that with the same view in the late transaction between Mr Pelham, and me, I had made ten steps to their one, so that if nothing came of it, nobody could say that I was desirous to continue, and propagate resentments, &c.—That I thought the persons in power, extremely proper for her to go on with, in case of a minority, and all I meant by mentioning the Regency Bill, was to show that as they had taken all proper precautions for their own security, it might not be unreasonable that her Royal Highness should keep a look out, and secure such friends, that, tho' they acted with the government, might see that she had her due share of it, for that there was such a thing as being great and inconsiderable; that we might be born the one, but must owe our considerableness to ourselves. That, however, to be sure there was nothing to be done at present, but sit still, and watch events: that all was very well, that the King was very kind to the royal children, and very respectful to her, &c.

She said that in general she had no objection to the Ministry, she saw very little of them; that indeed she had seen the Duke of Newcastle before he went, but what she could not excuse or forgive them for, was their not doing something for the Prince's servants: that after so long a time, and so many vacancies that happened, taking notice of no one of them look'd as if they had a studied design to keep old prejudices, and resentments alive: that she was sure they could do it if they would. They might have prevail'd upon the King before now, if they had set about it willingly: could they pretend they could not prevail with him for persons who must be indifferent to him after what they had made him do for Pitt? I said that I agreed to all she said, with relation to their influence with the King, when reason was so evidently with them, and was the more flattered with it, because it was so much my own way of thinking, that, if nothing should come of what was in agitation between us, and they should continue to hold up the King's personal indisposition towards me, I should impute it wholly to their want of inclination. She said, that notwithstanding what I had said of the King's kindness to the children and civility &c to her, that did not impose upon her: these were things she could not get over: she wish'd he were less civil, and put less of their money into his pocket:

that he got full 30,000*l. per ann.* by the poor Prince's death: if he would but have given them the Duchy of Cornwall, to have paid his debts, [it would have been something]. Should resentments be carried beyond the grave? Should the innocent suffer? Was it becoming so great a King to leave his son's debts unpaid? and such inconsiderable ones?

I ask'd her, what she took them to be. She said she had endeavour'd to know as near as a person could properly enquire, who not having it in their power, could not pretend to pay them, and she thought that to the tradesmen and servants, they did not amount to 90,000*l.*; that there was some money owing to the Earl of Scarbrough; and that there was abroad, a debt of about 70,000*l.* That it hurt her extremely, tho' she did not shew it.

I said that it was impossible to new-make people—the King would not, now, be alter'd and that there was nothing added to the prudence of her conduct in taking no notice of it. She said she could not bear it, nor help sometimes giving the King to understand it, in the strongest and most disagreeable light: she had done it more than once, and would tell me how it happen'd the last time.

'You know', says she, 'the Crown has a power of resumption of Carlton House, and gardens, for a certain sum: the King had not long since, a mind to see them: he came to make me a visit there: we walk'd in the gardens and he seem'd mightily pleased with them, commended them much, and told me that he was extreme glad that I had got so very pretty a place: I said that it was a pretty place, but that the prettiness of a place was an objection to it, when one was not sure to keep it. He reply'd that, indeed, there was a power of resumption in the Crown for 4000*l.*, but sure I could not imagine that it could ever be made use of against me, how could such a thought come into my head? I said, no, it was not that, which I was afraid of, but I was afraid there were those who had a better right to it, than the Crown or I either: He said, "Oh, no, no. I do not understand that. That cannot be." I reply'd, I did not pretend to understand those things, but I was afraid there were such people. He said, "Oh, I know nothing of that, I do not understand it"—and immediately turned the discourse'.

I was pleas'd with the ingenuity of the attack, but could not help smiling at the defence, nor she neither when she told it. I said that I thought she had done all that could be expected; that prudence required letting that, and several other matters sleep; that

I was convinc'd that the high, and just opinion people had of her, made them wait with patience.

She said they were very good to her; that George had no other way of thinking, and would certainly do it; but yet, she durst not let anybody have the comfort of knowing it; that would put everything into a flame: upon which, she observ'd to me the delicacy, and ticklishness of her situation.

I then took the liberty to ask her what she took the real disposition of the Prince to be. She said that I knew him almost as well as she did: if he was very honest, she wish'd he were a little more forward, and less childish, at his age; that she hop'd they would improve him. I beg'd to know what methods they took; what they read to him, or made him read; and if he took much to any of the people about him. She said she really did not well know what they taught him, but to speak freely, she was afraid not much: that they were in the country, and followed their diversions, and not much else that she could find out. That we must hope it would be better when we came to town.

I said that I did not much regard books, that what I wish'd the most was that his Royal Highness should begin to learn the usages, and knowledge of the world: be inform'd of the general frame, and nature of this government, and constitution, and of the general course, and manner of business, without descending into minutias. She said she thought so too, and that Stone[1] told her that when he talk'd to him upon those subjects he seem'd to give a proper attention, and made pertinent remarks: that Stone was a sensible man, and capable of instructing in things, as well as books: that Lord Harcourt and the Prince agreed very well, but she thought he could not learn much from my Lord: that Scott, she believ'd was a very good preceptor: that for the good Bishop, he might be and she supposed he was, a mighty learned and able man: but he did not seem to her very proper to convey knowledge to children; he had not that clearness she thought necessary: she did not very well comprehend him herself, his thoughts seem'd to be too many for his words: that she did not see that the Prince took very particularly to anybody about him but his brother Edward, and she was very glad of it, for the young people of quality were so ill educated, and so very vicious, that they frighten'd her. I told her I thought it

[1] The Prince's tutors were at this time Lord Harcourt, the Bishop of Norwich, Andrew Stone, and George Lewis Scott. For the scandal concerning Stone see December 1752 below.

a great happiness that he shew'd no disposition to any great excesses, and beg'd to know what were his affections and passions. She said that he was a very honest boy, and that his chief passion seem'd to be Edward.

I said if, as her Royal Highness had mentioned, the negative that the Ministry seem'd to continue upon the Prince's friends, I presum'd to ask her about [the young Prince's] affections towards his father's memory; because he was now, bred in a manner, and in hands, so totally unacquainted with the [late] Prince, and those that were about him, that at his age he might very easily be brought to forget them; which I fear'd at the first setting out in life would give a very disadvantageous, if not a dangerous impression of him: that trifles are of consequence, in the first outset (particularly those that relate to the heart) to Princes whose lightest actions engage the attention, and whose elevation exposes them to the continual inspection of mankind: that many good things lose their gloss at least by untoward impressions: that a great deal of power might be requir'd to do things where affection and confidence were wanted which a very little might bring about, where they were once established, by favourable first impressions. That for these reasons I should be extremely sorry that his Royal Highness should entirely forget those that had been faithfully attached to his royal father, as that attachment was the only reason that could be given to justify the proscription they now lay under.

She said that she agreed with me, that nothing could be more disadvantageous, and hurtful to him: that it would hurt her very sensibly: that she had no reason to apprehend it: that he seem'd to have a very tender affection for the memory of his father:[1] that she encourag'd it as much as she could: that when they behav'd wrong, or idly (as children will do) to any that belong'd to the Prince, and are now about her, she always ask'd them how they think their father would have lik'd to see them behave so to anybody that belong'd to him, and that he valued: and that they ought to have more kindness for them, because they had lost their friend, and protector, who was theirs also, and she found that it made a great impression upon them.

I humbly beg'd that she would cultivate, and improve the personal influence that her many virtues, as well as natural affection gave her over the Princes: that I was sure that from that influence,

---

[1] D. writes marginally 'N.B.'.

and the settled opinion of her prudence with all mankind, all the disinterested and sensible amongst us hop'd for a happy settlement of the new reign: that I did not mean authoritatively, and during a legal minority, but during the very young part of the King's life, and till time and inclination had brought him thoroughly to weigh, and understand what the government of a great country was. She express'd herself civilly for the regard I testify'd for her, and said she could have nothing so much at heart as to see him do well, and make the nation happy.

N.B. I forgot something very particular, *viz.* In expressing her dislike to the Princess Amelia and the Duke [of Cumberland], she said, that tho' she did not value those things, nor seem to see them, she could not but wonder at the very little regard that the Duke was pleas'd to shew her: that she had been at Kew the whole summer, and he had never vouchsaf'd to favour her with a visit: that she had been ill for three weeks, not much indeed, but so that the town reports were that she was dying; but his Royal Highness never thought her worth sending after once to know how she did. She said she was very indifferent to these matters, but could not help wondering what views they had in it.

I got home between ten and eleven, and have been the more particular in this conversation, because it carries an air of friendship, and openness, which I, no way, expected from a great lady, who had establish'd a character for prudence in not opening herself much to anybody, and of great caution to whom she opens herself at all.

16. Monday. Mr Furnese came—we din'd alone.

17. Tuesday. Mrs D. and I went to town to see Lady Shannon who came yesterday. I saw Lord Middlesex, and had much talk with him, in presence of Lady Middlesex. We return'd and din'd alone. In the evening I sent Lord Middlesex a draught of a letter from him to the Duke of Dorset—which he will not send, nor I believe do anything for himself—if so, he will render it impossible for me to do anything for him.

18. Wednesday. ⎫
                 ⎬ Din'd alone.
19. Thursday.   ⎭

20. Friday. Messrs Ralph and Carey din'd here. The last staid.

21. Saturday. Lord Hillsborough call'd here. Sir John Ligonier breakfasted here. Mr Carey went away. Din'd alone.

22. Sunday. I went to town with design to go to the Prince's drawing room: as I did, in black, being in mourning for the Countess Temple.[1] After a little time, the Earl of Hyndford was so obliging as to come to me, and tell me that he believ'd I had forgot that they did not appear in mourning that day, it being the Coronation. —So I was forc'd to slip away.

I spoke to the Solicitor General to consider how I was to open the transaction between Mr Pelham and I to the Duke of Newcastle. Return'd, and din'd alone.

23. Monday. I went to see Lord Hillsborough and the Bishop of London. Din'd alone.

24. Tuesday. Mr Ralph din'd here.

25. Wednesday. Sir Francis Dashwood and Mr Furnese din'd here.

26. Thursday. Mrs D., and I went to town.—Council at the Cockpit. Parliament prorogued to the 11th January. Three ships of 50, and 60 guns order'd to be built, on a new model. Receiv'd my draught with a letter, in a good degree conformable to it, from the Earl of Middlesex to the Duke of Dorset.—Sent him a draught of one to his mother. Din'd with Lady Middlesex. We return'd, at night.

27. Friday. Mrs D. was so ill as made me very uneasy.—Din'd alone.

28. Saturday. Mrs D., and I went to town. Return'd to dinner. Din'd alone.

29. Sunday. I went to St James's—Princess Amelia at Bath—the Duke not there. Return'd after dinner.

30. Monday. Dr Sharpe came. We din'd alone.

31. Tuesday. Earl of Strafford came here for the first time. Din'd here Drs Sharpe and Thomson, Messrs Ralph and Lee.

[1] His first cousin once removed, daughter of Sir Francis Temple, Dodington's uncle's uncle. He valued his Grenville relations even though he was on bad terms with them and it here led to a grotesque social and political gaffe.

NOVEMBER

1. Wednesday. Din'd alone. Dr Sharpe went away.

2. Thursday. Din'd alone

3. Friday. Mr Bance call'd here, we carried him on his way to Cranford. Return'd, and din'd alone.

4. Saturday. Mrs Dodington, and I went to Town. Young Messrs Allen, and Harvey from Bridgwater din'd with us. Lay in town.

5. Sunday. We went to court. Din'd with Lady Shannon, and lay in town.

6. Monday. We brought Dr Sharpe with us in the morning to Hammersmith.—Din'd there. Lord and Lady Strafford, and Lady Aston.

7. Tuesday. We went to the Duke of Argyll's. Din'd alone. Dr Thomson came.

8. Wednesday. Dr Sharpe went away. We din'd alone.

9. Thursday. I din'd with the Lord Mayor. No councillors, but those of the law, except the Speaker, and myself. Return'd to Hammersmith, at night.

10. Friday. Din'd alone. Dr Thomson, and Mr Cary lay here.

11. Saturday. Mrs Dodington was bled.—Dr Thomson and Cary went away. Din'd alone.

12. Sunday. Din'd alone.

13. Monday. We came to town. I went to the Exchequer Chamber.

14. Tuesday. I went to the Duke of Dorset. Deliver'd a letter to him, and one to the Duchess, from Lord Middlesex.—Much conversation to induce a relation, could not obtain a declaration of the condition on which he would be reconcil'd—objected much to the

usage he had receiv'd, in which he was too well grounded. Next the incapacity he was under of paying his son's debts.—I told him we were not come to that, yet—I wish'd we were, I could point out means, then, very easily, to show that these debts were not so formidable &c.—I hinted some.—Then we were broke in upon. This is again, to be broken up.

Went to the Cockpit at night.

15. Wednesday. Mr Poulet din'd here.

16. Thursday. Din'd alone. Went to the Cockpit, in the evening.

17. Friday. Din'd here Colonel Scot, and Messrs Sharpe.

18. Saturday. Went to Hammersmith with Mr Stanley. Return'd to dinner. Din'd here, Messrs Stanley, Furnese, William and Dr Sharpe. THE KING came to town about 5 o'clock.

19. Sunday. Mr Glover din'd here. Went to the Speaker's. Propos'd, upon supposition he was in the chair of the new Parliament, Dr Sharpe for his chaplain.—General answers of regard for me, and esteem for him. I think I find he will be Speaker, and hope he will get some reversion for his son, as his inducement.

20. Monday. Lord Dupplin, Messrs Fane, Messrs Tudor and Vanderdussen, din'd here. Messrs Munchausen and Schullenberg, came in the afternoon.—I went to Sir Paul Methuen's.—Duke of Newcastle arriv'd, about ten this morning.

21. Tuesday. Went to the Duke of Newcastle's, who receiv'd me with very much kindness.—Kiss'd the King's hand.—Went to Council at night.

22. Wednesday. Was to wait on the Princess. Gave her a full account of the transaction about a reconciliation in the Dorset family.—She receiv'd it with great goodness, and treated me with much condescension. Din'd alone.

23. Thursday. Went to Hammersmith. Din'd alone. Council at night.

24. Friday. Mr Ralph din'd here.

25. Saturday. Captain Beaghan din'd here. I went to the play.

26. Sunday. Mons. Lamberti, the French agent, came here. Insisted that the King must go to Hanover early next spring—that the election of a King of the Romans was the thing next his heart—that, by the Golden Bull, absolute unanimity of the Electoral College, as also of that of the Princes, was requir'd—that upon those conditions, and satisfaction to her allies, (the Palatine and Prussia) France would not oppose it; but would, without that satisfaction.— That the pecuniary satisfaction of 1,200,000 florins, and the barony to the Palatine, was settled, but the expectation of Ortenaw was not.—That when Bavaria left France for the House of Austria, the recompense was fix'd by the treaty of Fussen; that we engag'd for the performance—that a private treaty was since sign'd, by the Duke of Newcastle, Messrs. Munchausen and Haslang, by which we further engag'd to make it good that the Bavarian subsidy was to be augmented—That of Cologne to be settled.

I ask'd why all these things might not be negotiated here, as well as at Hanover. He said because the Ministers that treated those affairs there, did not come here. That there were another sort of men. Men of business, and abilities, wholly bred to it, and not for characters and show. That the German Princes also sent thither their confidants and Ministers of their states, which never came thither, as resident Ministers.—That nothing farther, of effect, could be done here, this winter, in that matter, and that all the negotiations would be with France about the limits in America, and as for that, they had cart loads of memorials to exchange with us, whenever we pleased; and the other part of the negotiation would be with Spain. Mr Beaghan and his sister din'd here. Went to Sir P. Methuen's.

27. Monday. King's birth-day kept. At Court. Lord Hillsborough began a conversation with me.—He thought there must be some disturbance arise from the Pitt party: that tho' they were so well plac'd they were uneasy: that they neither were lik'd nor lik'd.— I said I could not conceive that they would stir.—He said yes; for that Pitt's passion was ambition, not avarice. That he was at a full stop as things were, and could have no hopes of going farther: he was once popular: if he could again make a disturbance, and get the country of his side, he might have hopes: now, and on this system, he could have none.

I said I thought they could not part with what they had, &c.

—He said, they had the Temple pocket: that to his knowledge, they were all, as one, and would stand and fall with Pitt, as their head: and he, Hillsborough wonder'd they did not break out. He expected it. I said, that in all likelihood, if such a thing was on foot, he would know it, as soon as any body: for he must be sensible that it was impossible for them to attempt it without holding out a hand to people to extend and fortify their own connections, &c.

He said to be sure, but not to him, that they knew his opinions too well: that when they broke from me, *he follow'd me*: that he never was more than commonly acquainted with Pitt—that Pitt had once din'd at his house, and they visited perhaps once, in a winter.— That he lov'd George Grenville personally, but no ways espous'd his politics. That for himself, indeed, his alliance with Lord Kildare naturally led him to Mr Fox: that he was much more likely to succeed than Pitt—that they could not be quiet, but had been dabbling with the Prince, and prevented by his death, as, to be sure, I knew, and Mr Pelham knew, and therefore must be disagreeable to each other, and they could have no hopes of rising by him. That Mr Fox had something very frank, and open about him, and that he resolv'd to push for his turn:—not by opposition, for he said he had a family, and could not afford to part with his emoluments; but if accident should happen, he pretended to succeed: that, indeed Mr Pelham's life was as good as his: and he would not oppose him; but that he should endeavour and look'd upon himself as next.

I ask'd if he held out his hand, &c. He said yes,—to all the world: that it was prodigious how much he had together.—He had got the Duke [of Cumberland], the Dukes of Marlborough, and Bedford, Lord Sandwich, and the Duke of Richmond of course. That he was very well with Lord Halifax, who seemed to trim as near as he could, between Mr Pelham and him: and that now he was endeavouring to get Lord Hartington. That, if Pelham were out of the way, he thought that the Duke of Newcastle did not like Fox personally, nor did the Chancellor. As to Pitt, the King himself would be against him.—'But', says he, 'I think you are not acquainted with Fox'. I said that I had always known him and always lik'd him very well, but had not convers'd much with him of late. He said he wonder'd at it, and what should be the reason of it. I said I fancied it was occasioned from the other side: and that tho' I lik'd Mr Fox very well, I imagin'd he might not much like me. He said he could not think that. I said I fancied some lies might be told him, but that as I was sure I never had deserv'd ill of him and, if it was so, his opinion of me must be, and ought to be extremely indifferent to me. He said he had never heard any thing drop from him of that kind, and if he had any dislike, it must be from my pushing Sir Robert Walpole, for he really lov'd him.

I said that surely my breaking with Sir Robert Walpole was nothing personal to him: I did it publicly, at the expense of a considerable employment, what Mr Fox thought of it was what never did, nor ever could give me the least concern.—Then the conversation became general, which, before, I thought very singular.

28. Tuesday. Went to the Duke of Dorset's. Obtain'd that he would willingly see Lord Middlesex, on condition that from thence he would form no pretension to have his debts paid, to a seat in Parliament, or a place.—I took this down in writing. I doubt Lord Middlesex will not go: if he does, and resolves to continue and use all his advantages, he will succeed. But it must be the work of time, perseverance, and insinuation.—Went to the Cockpit at night.

29. Wednesday. Mr Furnese din'd here.

30. Thursday. Princess's birthday.—Lord Middlesex, and Dr Sharpe din'd here. I deliver'd the Duke of Dorset's message, gave him an account of the conversation, and said what I thought was proper. I do not know his resolution as to going.

DECEMBER

1. Friday. Sir Thomas Robinson and I went to Hammersmith and return'd to dinner. Mr William Sharpe din'd here. Went to the Cockpit.

2. Saturday. Mr Bodens din'd here. Went to the Speaker's.

3. Sunday. Din'd here Messrs Clairant, Rollinson, Furnese, Stanley, Poulet, Jeffreys.

4. Monday. Din'd alone. Went to the play at Drury Lane.

5. Tuesday. Din'd at Lord Middlesex's. Lord Harcourt resign'd being Governor to the Prince. He offer'd to do so unless Mr Stone, (put as Sub-Governor by the Ministers) Mr Scott, Tutor in the Prince's time (but recommended by Lord Bolingbroke) and Mr Cresset, made Treasurer by the Princess's recommendation, were remov'd.—The King desir'd him to consider of it, but he continuing in the same resolution the Archbishop and Lord Chancellor were sent to him, to know the particulars of his complaints against those gentlemen: he said the particulars were fit only to be communicated to the King, and accordingly waited on his Majesty, which ended in his resignation.—The Bishop of Norwich sent his resignation by the same prelate and lord. His reasons, (if he gave any) I should have known, if a gentleman who was going to tell me had not been interrupted by company.

6. Wednesday. Duke of Dorset was here to tell me that Lord Middlesex had wrote to the Duchess for leave to wait on her: and that she had appointed tomorrow morning.—I hope all will in time go well. Mr Beaghan din'd here. Lord Barrington was here and promis'd me that Mr Lee's affair should he settl'd tomorrow at £100 per annum: 5s per truss for the men in actual service abroad and 2gns per head for those whom he shall cure at their return.[1]

7. Thursday. Mr Kelsal din'd here. I went to the Cockpit—and Sir Paul Methuen's.

[1] See 25 May 1752 above.

8. Friday. Lord Middlesex was here to tell me that he had seen the Duke and Duchess of Dorset. That he was very coldly receiv'd by the Duchess; and not much better by them both together. This I think very injudicious in them, and shall endeavour to persuade my Lord to persevere.—Captain Beaghan and Mr Tucker din'd here. I went to see Dr George Lee.

9. Saturday. Lord and Lady Middlesex din'd here. We went to the theatre in the Haymarket.

10. Sunday. Mrs D and I went to Hammersmith, and din'd at Mr Tucker's. I sup'd at Mr Furnese's.

11. Monday. Din'd alone. Went to Sir Paul Methuen's.

12. Tuesday. Mr Pelham sent for Cary the surgeon on pretence of the Westminister Election; but in effect to question him about a letter he had wrote to Mr Vane, which Mr Vane sent him up and he interpreted to insinuate that I was out of humour that nothing was settled, or said to me. Said I must know how much this squabble with Lord Harcourt had engross'd their whole time, and thoughts, in a disagreeable manner. That they could not be *throwing at* the King, every day—said that he had the greatest kindness, and esteem for me &c and that a proper person should speak to me, shortly &c.—Din'd alone. Went to the Cockpit.

13. Wednesday. Mr Stanley din'd here, and we went to *The Rehearsal*.

14. Thursday. Messrs Furnese, Kelsal, and Bodens din'd here. I went to the Cockpit, and afterward to the Duke of Argyll's. [Wrote to] Cardinal Albani, by Lord Bolingbroke.

15. Friday. Din'd alone. Went to Sir Paul Methuen's.

16. Saturday. Din'd at Mrs Fane's.

17. Sunday. Went to the Duke of Dorset's.—Think I left him dispos'd to receive his son kindly. I saw Lord Middlesex, who, I hope, will make a proper use of all opportunities. Din'd here, Lord Halifax, Lord Montfort, Messrs Vane Junior, Draper, Furnese, and Jeffreys.

18. Monday. Din'd at Lord Barrington's. Went to Lady Middlesex. Lord Waldegrave declar'd Governor to the Prince.

19. Tuesday. Mr Furnese din'd here. Went to Lady Middlesex's.

20. Wednesday. Went to Council at St James's. Seamen declar'd. Earl of Waldegrave sworn of the Council. Din'd alone. Went to Lady Middlesex's.

21. Thursday. Din'd alone. Went to the Cockpit.

22. Friday. Was with the Duke of Dorset. We talk'd over the affair of the Prince's family[1] and agreed that there must be a counter story of the Court side, or the resigners would run away with the public.—Left him well dispos'd to his son. Din'd alone. Went to Lady Middlesex's.

23. Saturday. We went to Hammersmith. Return'd to dinner.

24. Sunday. Mr Bance din'd here.

25. Monday. Christmas Day. I took physic.

26. Tuesday. Sir Thomas Robinson and Mr Hampden din'd here. Went to Lady Middlesex's.

27. Wednesday. Went to wait on the Princess, who was abroad. Evening at Sir Paul Methuen's.

28. Thursday. Went again to wait on the Princess. She was again taking the air. I staid till she return'd. She was pleas'd to send the royal children to prayers, and stay with me. I resolv'd to avoid mentioning all public affairs, on account of the disturbances, now fresh in the Prince of Wales's family, and therefore, began by acquainting her with what had pass'd, relating to the reconciliation, in the Dorset family, since I saw her Royal Highness.

She said she was afraid that it would be hard to complete it, so as to answer Lord Middlesex's ends entirely; and seem'd to be of opinion, that tho' Lady Middlesex was no ways in fault, and tho' neither the Duke nor Duchess had dropp'd the least word about

[1] i.e. the scandal resulting from the resignation of Lord Harcourt and his allegations of Jacobitism.

her; and though Lord George [Sackville] had been with Lady
Middlesex twice, in the same house with her, and never once, saw,
and ask'd after her (for which she blam'd him very much) yet she
inclin'd to think that Lady Middlesex should go to wait upon the
Duchess.

I was glad to have her opinion, for I wanted to know it. I reply'd
that there were oddnesses about them that were peculiar to that
family, and I had often told them so. She said there was something
very odd among them, and laughing, added, that she knew but
one family that was more odd, and she would not name that family
for the world. I said, it did not become me to guess at her Royal
Highness, but if it did, I was sure I could not guess it, in a hundred
years.

She laugh'd and said, '*A propos*, there has been fine doings in our
family, a very fine bustle indeed. I am glad we are rid of them.' I
said it had, indeed occasion'd a great deal of talk. She said she was
quite weary of hearing it—that there was such an outcry at two
people leaving them, as if they were the most considerable men
in the nation; who occasion'd as much wonder, and outcry, two
years ago, when they came to them, on account of their being too
unknown to come there. That she knew nothing of the Jacobitism,
the arbitrary principles, the dangerous notions of those that were
accus'd, or any such attempted to be instilled into the children:
that she could not conceive what they meant: that the Bishop,
indeed was teaching them logic, which she was told was a very odd
study for children of their age, not to say, of their condition.

I said that whatever they meant, to be sure before things came to
these extremities, they both must, often, have apply'd to her Royal
Highness and laid before her some ostensible reasons, at least, as
a ground for their resolution to resign when the King returned.
She said, never: that she knew nothing of their intention till Lord
Harcourt had been with the King. That the Bishop had several
times given her an account of the progress they made.—That he
behav'd in the most flattering and servile manner, in the accounts
he gave, and then, he often insinuated, that there were those about
the Prince, who set his Royal Highness against him, &c.—That
she told him, (as the truth was) that she was entirely innocent of
any such practices, herself, and did not know of anybody that could
be accus'd of it; particularly, could not perceive by the children,
when they were with her, that any ill offices had been done him.—

That the last time he had been with her, he complain'd more strongly of being disregarded, beg'd her protection, showing the great necessity of a preceptor's being respected, and supported, &c. Upon which she told him, that she always inculcated to the children to show him great respect, and was very far from endeavouring, or even wishing, it should be lessen'd: 'And this,' says she, 'not for love of you, my Lord, but because it is fitting, and necessary; for if they are suffer'd to want respect that is due to one degree, they will go on to want it, to another, till at last, it would come up to me, and I should have taught them to disregard me.' This, she said, was the last conversation she had with the Bishop.

I ask'd her if she could remember when it was: she said she thought about the end of September, or soon in October. That as to Lord Harcourt, he never took the least notice of her; that she had hardly seen him, three times, the whole summer, tho' they lived so near together at Kew: that when he came for the Prince, so far from sending in to her, that would stay in the hall, and tho' press'd to it, by the servants, would not come into the picture room, where we always sat, when she was above, till she came to us, or sent for us up. I ask'd, if he always fetch'd the Prince home: she said, 'Yes, at a certain hour.' I said I had heard so, and did indeed, a little wonder, in myself that I had never seen him, when I had the honour to play at cards with his Royal Highness in private; for as the game could not be up to a moment, I thought it natural his Lordship should let his Royal Highness know that he was below, and I presum'd she would, as naturally, send for him up.

She said to be sure she should, and I might well wonder. But so far from that, he never came near her: that he had been twice this year in Oxfordshire, and that she never knew when he went, or when he return'd. I then said, that I could not conceive, however, according to the common form of things, that tho' his resolution might be taken it was impossible but that he must have waited upon her, to lay some reasons before her, by way of expostulation or apology, before the King came home. She said, 'Never, nothing like it:' that, since his return from Oxfordshire the last time, the very first time she saw him, was at the foot of the stairs, at St. James's, the night the King came (Nov. 18); that the next time was the birth-day [27th] in the private rooms, that he endeavour'd to avoid her, but she got between the door, and him, and took him by the coat, and said he was very fine. He said, 'Madam, it is all the manufacture of Spitalfields,' and so got off. That the Tuesday before he had been with the King, to represent that her children were in way of imbibing dangerous notions, &c. That he had no authority and could do no good unless Stone and Cresset, and Scott were dismissed.—That they were Jacobites, &c. and had been bred so, they and their families.

I said that this charge upon their families and education made me smile. For that, tho' I had a personal regard for Lord Harcourt, and did stedfastly believe that he was as faithful a servant, and subject, as any this family had anywhere; yet I was sorry to say that I remember'd his predecessor, following the Oxford circuit, a very poor but reckon'd a very shrewd lawyer; which shrewdness in the poor professor, as he rose had justice done it and was called genius and abilities as it really was; for he was very able, very skilful, and more eminent by his talents and capacity than by his post. But till the last years of his life always reckon'd a thorough Jacobite: stands impeach'd upon these principles, and tho' not proceeded against, excepted in several acts of grace. That I was sure Lord Harcourt abhorr'd these principles and would with cheerfulness risk everything for this royal family, but thought it strange that people should not allow conversion to be as natural and sincere in other families as we had happily experienced it in his; and that upon the whole I could not conceive what they meant by this whole transaction, as to the matter and yet less as to the manner.

She said that however it was, the King was very well pleas'd with them; but that she could easily guess what they meant. I said that now I was serious in assuring her Royal Highness that I really could not guess. She said that one might guess by their falling upon Mr Cresset who had no more to do with the Prince's education, than I had.—That they had a design to get his place for another, and she thought it was for Lord Talbot's brother: but as the King took her recommendation, now Cresset was to be brought into the quarrel.—That these gentlemen were leagued with some greater people, that she need not name to me, to get the Prince to their side, and then, by their behaviour, to throw her off from her temper and so make their complaint to the King stronger and make her disoblige him, in defending the accus'd; not doubting if they could have force'd her into any indiscreet warmth to have made so plausible a story to the King as might have compass'd their ends, which was to have carried the Prince into those other hands, at last, by taking him from the people now about him and by degrees, consequently, from her. This failing, the next step, says she, was the Bishop. 'He comes to take his leave of me and with abundance of fawning and flattery, thanks me for all my goodness to him, and all the regard I had been pleased to shew him, &c. when he was in the family; hoping that I would believe, that he left it like an honest man. I replied,' says she, 'that, for the regard I had show'd him or any service I had done him, he ow'd me no obligation, it was no more than was his due and what I should always pay to any-body that the King was pleas'd to put about my children, in the same station.—That as to the motives of leaving the family, as I did not know them, I could say nothing to them. Then,' continues she, 'comes my Lord of Harcourt: and he in a drier way than the Bishop takes his leave by thanking me for the favours and support he had received from me, while he was in the family: and in return, I thank'd his Lordship for the constant care and attention he had bestow'd upon my sons.'

I said that I was surpris'd at the whole before, and by what I had heard from the public whither I would or not; but that, now I was astonished.—She said she thought she had some little reason to take it ill, that such grievous complaints should be made of management about her son, without giving her the least previous information of it: that Lord Harcourt complain'd strongly to the King of dangerous notions, arbitrary principles to be instilled to the Prince and that he could be of no use, unless the instillers of them, Stone, Cresset, and Scott, were dismissed &c. That as he nam'd no particulars, the King had sent the Archbishop and the Chancellor to command him to acquaint them with the particulars in his name [they did not go to the Bishop.]—That his answer was that the particulars were fit only to be communicated to the King, and that he would wait on his Majesty with them. (All this I knew before.) That he did so, and that she had since talk'd with the King about it, and that he told her that he had only run over the same general topics again without entering into any particulars at all. That the King had assur'd her of this and she believ'd, he told her the truth. But, she said, they had miss'd their ends, for the King was in very good humour with her and the children, and imputed nothing to them in this whole transaction.

I said that I was extremely pleas'd that her Royal Highness had not been thrown off her temper by this behaviour, considering how offensive it was, how deep it was laid, and who were at the bottom of it. For that I, particularly, and I believed all good men, plac'd their chief hopes in the Prince's continuing, chiefly in her hands, and direction, and in her preserving this influence over him, which was justly due to her, from her prudence, as well as from nature. She said they would not find it easy to make her lose her temper.

I told her of an anonymous letter, sent to Dr Newton, a popular preacher at St George's, setting forth the dangerous way the Prince's education was left in, then touching on the Doctor's popularity, and concluding by putting it to him, as a duty, to take notice of it in the pulpit. She had not heard of it, and seem'd at a loss to guess what it meant. I said the only meaning I could put to it was, indeed I thought too much refinement, and that was that they had, or would write anonymous letters to the same purpose, to forty or fifty of the London clergy in hopes that amongst so many, one hot-headed fellow might be found, who would take fire at it and endeavour to distinguish himself by trying to raise a flame about it.

But I did not think proper to tell her Royal Highness of another anonymous letter, that was sent to General Hawley, on Wednesday the 20th inst. which, when it was open'd, contain'd nothing to him, but was a sort of a representation or remonstrance to the King from the Whig nobility and gentry; setting forth their great concern and apprehensions for the Prince's education from the hands that he was now in; their dissatisfaction at the manner, in which the power of the crown was lodg'd; that, indeed, some of those, who by their offices were called Ministers and ought to be so, were sometimes tumbled and toss'd about, but that there was a permanence of power plac'd in three men, that they look'd upon to be dangerous and that these men entirely trusted, and were govern'd by two others, one of whom had the absolute direction of the Prince and was of a Tory family and bred in arbitrary principles; and the other bred a profess'd Jacobite of a profess'd Jacobite family, and his brother, now, at Rome, a favourite of the Pretender and his Secretary of State. In short, the corollary was that Murray, Solicitor General, and, Stone, govern'd this country. This letter was sent to General Hawley with an intent no doubt, that he should carry it immediately to the Duke [of Cumberland] that his Royal Highness might lay it before the King, and make what first impressions he pleas'd. Whether the General did so first or not, I don't know, but I do not suspect him of so much finesse, but what is certain, is that he sent it, or carried it to the Secretary of State who laid it before the King. What was the effect, I can't tell but I know they were very much intrigu'd, to find out whence it came and who was the author.[1]—Went to Lady Middlesex's in the evening.

29. Friday. Mr Carey din'd here. I went to see Dr Sharpe in the evening.

30. Saturday. ⎫
            ⎬ At home.
31. Sunday ⎭

[1] This memorial, of which Horace Walpole was the author (see his annotation in his copy of the *Diary* in possession of Lord Rothschild) is printed on pp. 488–91 of the second, and later editions of the *Diary*. The object was to inflate Harcourt's resignation into a political/historical issue, foreshadowing the opposition propaganda of the next three decades. Hawley was the recipient as an officer close to Cumberland, whose colleague he had been at Culloden.

1753

JANUARY

1. Monday. Din'd alone. Went to Dr Sharpe's.

2. Tuesday. Din'd alone.

3. Wednesday. Mr Furnese was here who from talking to the Solicitor General brings me new proofs of the King's indisposition towards me.—Din'd here, Lord Drumlanerick [Drumlanrig], Colonel Stuart, Mr Stanley, Count de Linden, General Elliot, Colonel Elliot.

4. Thursday. Din'd alone.—Went to the play.

5. Friday. Went to Hammersmith. Walk'd back to White's. Mr Bodens din'd here.

6. Saturday. Din'd alone. Went to the Speaker's.

7. Sunday. Mr Beaghan din'd here.

8. Monday. Din'd alone. To Sir Paul Methuen.

9. Tuesday. Dr Thomson and I went to Hammersmith. Return'd to dinner. Din'd here Messrs Breton, Furnese, Carey. St John. Bishop of Peterborough was made Preceptor to P.W. [Prince of Wales].

10. Wednesday. Mrs D and I went to Hammersmith. Return'd to dinner. Din'd here Messrs Breton, Tucker, and Beaghan.

11. Thursday. Parliament met. Mr Beaghan din'd here.

12. Friday. Mr Breton, Mrs D, and I went to Hammersmith, and return'd to dinner.

13. Saturday. Din'd alone.—I went to the play at Drury Lane.

14. Sunday. Mrs D and I went to Mr Ralph's at Hammersmith. Din'd here Colonel Vanderdussen, and Mrs Beaghan.

15. Monday. Din'd alone.

16. Tuesday. Messrs Furnese, Ralph, and Carey din'd here.

17. Wednesday. Lords Halifax, Hillsborough, Hobart, Barrington, Messrs Berkeley, Breton, Stanley, and Barrington, din'd here.

18. Thursday. Din'd at Lord Hillsborough. Went to the Cockpit.

19. Friday. Mr Tudor and I went to Hammersmith. Din'd alone. Mrs D and I went to Lady Middlesex's.

20. Saturday. I had much talk with Mr Vane about our negotiations with the Court who seem'd to think it much in their interest to agree with us. He express'd much fear of the Duke [of Cumberland], and his party. Din'd at Mr Stanley's.

21. Sunday. Mrs D, Dr Sharpe, and I went to Mr Ralph's at Hammersmith and din'd at Pall Mall.

22. Monday. Mr Breton din'd here. We went to the play.

23. Tuesday. Din'd alone. Went to the Cockpit.

24. Wednesday. Mrs D and I went to Hammersmith. Return'd to dinner.—I din'd with Mr Berkeley.

25. Thursday. The Princess sent for me to come to her into the Garden.—I found her with the Ladies Augusta and Elizabeth. We began talking of the reconciliation in the Dorset family: from that, she spoke of the Prussian memorial,[1] of which I gave her my sentiments: which were, that it was, and no doubt was meant to be very offensive, not only in matter but in manner, for that thro' the whole, there is no mention made of the King, but the representation is made to the nation and to the Ministry, which I thought indecent. —She said she thought it perplex'd them very much.—I reply'd that it must do, from the difficulty of finding a way to resent the

[1] Prussia had given notice of a cessation of interest on the Silesian Loan until a dispute about shipping had been settled.

affront. She said if we did that Hanover was open, and he [the King of Prussia] could do what he pleas'd with it as easily as I could come into the garden where we were, from my terrace. I said he had taken an imprudent occasion to insult the King because this quarrel was on a point purely English, without the least mixture of German, and could not be resented on the Electorate without alarming every Prince in Germany. That he must know that the House of Austria watched with impatience to recover Silesia; that he was less a match for Vienna than Hanover was for him; that I knew he wanted a war because he felt his country sinking under the number of troops which he kept in it, in time of peace; that I did not think France was in a condition, or a disposition, to enter into a war immediately, and if he was not very sure she would, I thought he played very deep and very dangerously indeed.

This, as well as the rest of this conversation, which was long, being carried on walking in the cold, the Princess muffled up, and mostly speaking low that the children might not hear, and but confusedly. I shall choose to throw the principal parts together as shortly, and as clearly as I can tho' not exactly in the order it was spoken, but as much in the words as I can recollect.

The Duchess of Devonshire's assembly, of last Monday, was mentioned; from thence Mr James Pelham's of last night, which was professedly for hazard, and for the Ministry and Court. She express'd great dislike at their playing publickly at forbidden games, spoke reasonably, and warmly, of the ill example and encouragement it gave to all sorts of dissipation, &c. I agreed to this and mention'd the precautions Lord Treasurer Godolphin us'd to conceal his passion for play, tho' he practis'd it to the last.

I added (to change the discourse) that it was but once a year at a relation's house; that they had little to do, for all Parliament opposition was over; no body attended, and therefore it was natural that they should amuse themselves a little. She said yes, all seemed to be quiet now, but how long would it last so? They never were in so ticklish a situation, as at present; that they were frighten'd three years ago, but with very little or no reason, but now they had reason; that they must know it and feel it, and she was amaz'd they did not look out for assistance and friends that they could depend upon, but that their cowardice would be their ruin. &c.[1]

---

[1] Considering D. was actually in negotiation with the Pelhams for precisely this purpose, the Princess was skilfully flattering him just as much as he flattered her.

I said that I wonder'd at it too, that their own real friends and dependants were very much narrow'd; but at the same time she would please to consider that it was not easy for them to make new connexions, for people of rank and real efficiency, that were unengaged and truly neuters were but few, and against almost every one of those few, either from false representations or caprice, the King had taken prejudices, which they did not care, or did not dare to combat, which I suppos'd hinder'd their strengthening themselves. She said with much warmth that when they talk'd to her of the King, she lost all patience, that she knew it was nothing; that in their great points, she reckon'd the King no more than one of the trees we walk'd by, (or something more inconsiderable, which she named); that it was the pusillanimity which would make an end of them &c.

I said that it was, indeed, surprising, and if they really were willing to accept of assistance (which I thought they really wanted) I was very sorry for it. Because, to be sure, in great things the King must comply with what was reasonable. 'Indeed,' says I, 'Madam, to put a Lady of your Bedchamber, or a Groom of the Stole, about your Royal Highness, with whom you must live, or your Private Treasurer, who must enter into all your little domestick, personal details, I ought to consult your inclinations, nay, even your caprice: but to recommend one of your Receivers, in Cornwall, your interest and the facility of your service ought only to be considered; and you ought not to be indulg'd in rejecting him, from having taken unfavourable impressions of him because it would render your service impracticable, and all, so rejected, must believe that I ly'd and never meant to serve them, or that I had no interest with you, and should not, long, be able to support myself.' She said it was most certainly so, the King was nothing in these things, and everybody would drop from them one by one by their own cowardice.

I told her that surely, she had a right to insist upon their acting, considering the great support she had given them in the late ticklish, family transaction.[1] She said she had done them service, but it signified nothing, if they did not help themselves. I said, it was great pleasure to me to find that her Royal Highness favour'd those gentlemen because I really lik'd and esteem'd them, much more than any, that were now endeavouring to succeed them, and was desirous to live with, and support them: that I knew nothing

[1] i.e. the question of the tutors.

of particulars, but that I spoke the language of the town, in saying that she had very greatly and usefully espous'd them and therefore ought to have great weight with them. She said she was afraid the town said more of it than she desir'd; that the truth of it was that to be sure it was her's, and her family's business, to keep well with the King, and consequently to countenance the Ministers he employ'd, and she had done so; but she did not understand that she was bound to them so as to be in their hands. I said that there was the difficulty, that it was hard to avoid falling into the hands of one side or the other; that it was a very ticklish situation, and here I stop'd.

She said she had help'd them and was astonish'd at their cowardice in not making new friends. What ground did they stand upon? Could they doubt but that her good brother, and sister were all day long, doing them all imaginable mischief at St. James's, lessening every favourable thing, heightening and exaggerating every unfavourable one? The Duke of Bedford stirring Heaven and Earth in the country, and opening his house and courting every body in town? What would become of them? Every body would leave them by degrees, and all from their pusillanimity.

I said I was very sorry for their inaction, for that Her Royal Highness would be pleas'd to observe that, to people, who by their situation, are thrown into politicks, action, in that case, is what life is to the body. We cannot cease to live for a time, and then, take up life again: so in politicks we must act, in some way, or another, and we can't cease action, for a time, and then take it up again. That I wish'd the present Ministry unfeignedly well, and was desirous to employ all my credit, and friends in their service; that besides my friends, and their interest, I would undertake to chuse five members for them, without putting them to a shilling expence, or desiring them to make a tide-waiter: that I thought much, if not their all, depended on a new Parliament, and I was willing to give them my poor assistance as her Royal Highness had espous'd them, and as I was, in my opinion, and inclination, much more prepossess'd in their favour than for any body, that was in any likelihood to succeed them.

Here ended all that was material. I am at a loss to guess why this great lady presses conversation of this kind upon me. I neither attempt, nor desire[1] her confidence, nor am I so low as to be fond of

---

[1] P.W. prints 'deserve', a clear misreading, typical of his prejudice. If D. was not being quite straightforward in this passage, he was incapable of saying, even to himself, that he did not deserve the confidence of royalty.

half confidences. I think she must become nothing, either siding with the Ministry or the Duke. A third party of her own, is her only resource, in case of a minority, but where she will find that party, may be difficult, and where she will find resolution to attempt it, or to support it, may be more difficult. It may possibly be her wisest party, and possibly the party she has, or will shortly take, very shortly, and very privately (instigated by the pusillanimity of the Ministers) to take hands with the Duke [of Cumberland], agree together to repeal the Regency Bill, be sole regent in appearance, and he in effect. This I think certain, that if they do not take away the army from the Duke immediately and with éclat, he will overcome both her and the Ministry, who will think of struggling when it is too late, but I think will not dare to strike when it would be easy and decisive.

26. Friday. Din'd alone. Went to Sir Thomas Robinson's assembly.

27. Saturday. At home with Dr Sharpe.

28. Sunday. Din'd at Sir George Lyttelton's. Went to Sir Paul Methuen's, and the Speaker's.

29. Monday. Mr F. Fane, and I introduc'd Mr Balch[1] here. Lord Dupplin, Messrs Francis Fane, Thomas Fane, Breton, Balch, Dr Sharpe, Tudor, Sealy, Harvey, Allan.

30 Tuesday. Din'd at Lord Feversham's. Went to the Speaker's.

31. Wednesday. Mrs D, Mr Wyndham, and I went to Hammersmith. Return'd to dinner. Mrs D went with me to Lady Middlesex's.

---

[1] D.'s intended running mate in the approaching contest at Bridgwater. He was a local man, as yet unknown to politics—see 11 and 13 October 1752 above.

FEBRUARY

1. Thursday. Went to the House to vote for the liberty to import champagne in bottles. Lord Hillsborough mov'd it: Mr Fox seconded it. We lost it—Ayes 74, Noes 141. Din'd at Lord Halifax's. Went to Sir P. Methuen's.

2. Friday. Mr Beaghan din'd here.

3. Saturday. Din'd at the Earl of Westmorland's.

4. Sunday. Messrs Balch and Glover din'd here.

5. Monday. The Comte de Linden, Messrs Stanley, Clairant, and I went to Hammersmith and return'd to Pall Mall to dinner with Lord Barrington, Lord Strange, Sir George Lyttelton, and Mrs Lyttelton.

6. Tuesday. Din'd at Sir Henry Bellendine's. Went to the Speaker's.

7. Wednesday. Went to the Council. The Sheriffs appointed. Din'd here Messrs Bance, Furnese, Beaghan, and Ralph.

8. Thursday. I went to wait on the Princess. Saw her alone. Entertain'd her with town talk, and pleasantries that had pass'd where I din'd. She began at once by saying she had good news to tell me: that they were very happy in their family; that the new Bishop[1] gave great satisfaction; that he seem'd to take great care, and in a proper manner: that the children took to him, and seemed mightily pleas'd. I said I was very glad that all their Royal Highnesses were pleas'd with the Bishop, who I did not know by sight, but that she would give me leave to hope that they were all very well pleas'd with the new Governor[2] also, who was my very good friend and for whom I had a very great regard.

She said, 'Yes, indeed'; that she was but little acquainted with him but from all she saw she had a very good opinion of him, that he was very well bred, very complaisant, and attentive, &c. and the children liked him extremely. 'But,' says she, 'I look upon a Governor as a sort of pageant, a man of quality for show, &c. I

---

[1] Peterborough.   [2] Lord Waldegrave.

stick to the learning as the chief point. You know how backward they were when we were together and I am sure you don't think they are much improv'd since. May be it is not too late yet to acquire a competence, and that is what I am most solicitous about, and if this man, by his manner, should hit upon the means of giving them that, I shall be mightily pleas'd. The Bishop of Norwich was so confus'd, that one could never tell what he meant, and the children were not at all pleas'd with him.' I said that the whole transaction was a very odd thing, that, to be sure there must be some bottom to it which we at a distance did not know.

She said she thought so; that the stories about the History of the Père d'Orléans was false; the only little dispute between the Bishop and Prince Edward was about le Père Péréfixe's[1] history of Henry IV, and that was nothing at all to produce such an event. That there must be politicks at the bottom; that there was a story that the Bishop had said that Murray the Solicitor General when he was first appointed, told him that Lord Harcourt was only a cipher; that as he had parts and abilities, he might easily get the whole into his own hands, and advis'd him not to omit so fair an opportunity. That she believ'd it was a lie, but if it was true the Bishop was a bad man to betray the private advice of a friend.

I said that I was most confident it was false; that Mr Murray had too much sense to meddle at all with what did not belong to him; but if he had done it (which I could never believe) I was sure it could only be in favour of his friend Stone with whom he was very much concern'd. That I look'd upon Mr Murray to be a very eminent man and much the most able, and efficient, if not the only one, that was openly and honourably attach'd to the Ministry. She said, that it was very likely; she thought they had very few and wondered at their not getting more friends, that it was their cowardice only which hindered them. That if they talked of the King, she was out of patience; 'twas as if they should tell her that her little Harry, below, would not do what was proper for him; that just so the King would sputter and make a bustle, but when they told him that it must be done from the necessity of his service, he must do it, as little Harry must when she came down.

I said I was sincerely sorry, not for the present, but that I apprehended this want of real, attach'd, and declar'd friends might produce ugly consequences and contests in case of a demise. She

[1] Pères d'Orléans and Péréfixe were historians of the French Wars of Religion.

said it was to be apprehended but she could not help it. I said that they ought, for her sake, and from what they ow'd her, to think of those consequences. She said they ow'd her nothing; that for the last disturbance in the family she protested she knew no more than she had told me; that she never conceiv'd it would come to an open rupture, and again protested that when she heard that Lord Harcourt had been with the King, on his arrival to lay down, she was as ignorant of it, and as much surprised at it as I could be, at best. That what had been done since, in the replacing them, was done in the puzzled way, that I knew, in which she had very little or no share; and that for the Ministers, she never had seen them in her life.

'Madam,' says I, 'your Royal Highness will forgive me but if I had not caught myself, I was just going to say, "Lord, Madam! what do you mean?"' 'I mean', says she, 'just as I say. The only way I could see them, in the Prince's time, I don't call seeing them, and since that I never have seen the Duke of Newcastle, what I should call more than once, but as I am speaking to you with great exactness, it was twice; Mr Pelham I have never seen at all, no, not once. The Duke was once here, with the Archbishop and the Chancellor, upon some formality; and last year, when the King was out of the way, he stole over to Kew to take his leave, but has never been here since his return, tho' every body has, Lady Yarmouth, Munchausen, Lord Anson, &c. Mr Pelham has behav'd better, and always very civilly: he had not the same reasons; he might indeed, at first, before our money-matters were settled, have taken that occasion to come, but as he did not do it, he has had no call, and fears, I suppose, the King's jealousies and suspicions, who is never without them. When the Duke was with me, indeed, I gave it him, testified very strongly my surprise to him, that he should neglect such a body of the late Prince's Servants; that tho' they had wish'd me, and my part of the family, better than any party, yet, as that was over, and they were willing to come under him, surely some of them were worth accepting. If they were not to be rewarded for their attachment, sure it was strange they were to have an exclusion put upon them for it. He shuffled about continuous; he said to be sure it should be thought of, and brought about. I said, indeed it was surprising, for that those gentlemen, instead of having acquired any merit by their services were not allow'd even the fair play that they would have had if they had never entered into the service of the Royal family: I thought it very disadvantageous because, in case of a demise, that would be all to be done, which might have been long settled, and ready to act in case of accidents.'

She said that the Duke durst not come near her for fear of her sister Amely. I ask'd her if she thought he could be ignorant of her dislike to him, even to inveteracy. She said, no; but still he was afraid of her. That he had, once, since he came, got leave to see her but on condition that somebody should be in the room: but that upon the case I mention'd, she should soon enough have him trotting upon all fours to her; that she had nothing to do with them; could they believe, if the time ever came, she should forget those that she had mention'd to them? That she should forget what she ought, most, to remember, from duty, from interest, and from gratitude? She could not help it, it must be *alors, comme alors*. Maybe the fewer engagements she was under the better. Thus ended this other very singular conversation.

9. Friday. Din'd at Lord Hobart's. Went to Sir Paul Methuen's.

10. Saturday. Din'd at Lord Carlisle's.

11. Sunday. Lord Middlesex: Messrs Harley and Glover: (who read his tragedy of *Medea*) din'd here.

12. Monday. Mr Beaghan din'd here.

13. Tuesday. Din'd at Lord Barrington's. Duke of Bedford mov'd for Nova Scotia papers, ably. Yesterday, wrote Marquis Niccolini, for wine.

14. Wednesday. Din'd here Dr Sharpe, Messrs Ralph and Carey.

15. Thursday. Din'd here Messrs Breton and Kelsal.—The Cabinet met, and sat late on the strange imputation of Bishop Johnson [of Gloucester], of Messrs Stone and Murray being Jacobites and having drunk the Pretender's health at Vernon's, the linen-draper's, above twenty years ago.—They got but half through, and sit again tomorrow.

16. Wednesday. Din'd here Lords Licthfield and Talbot, Sir Francis and Mr Dashwood, and Mr Macky.

17. Saturday. Din'd at Lord Strange's.

18. Sunday. Din'd here Messrs Balch, Fremantle, Lee, Sealy, and Lisle.

19. Monday. Took physic.—Din'd alone.

20. Tuesday. Din'd with several people of quality at an entertainment given by the Comte de Linden; at the Brawn's Head.

21. Wednesday. Took physic. Din'd alone.

22. Thursday. Din'd alone. Went to Lady Middlesex's.

23. Friday. Went to Hammersmith to open the glasses and tapestry. Din'd with Mr Tucker. Ended Lord Ravensworth's extraordinary Committee, which began Thursday the 15th and sat seven nights.[1]

24. Saturday. Mrs Dodington, Mr Breton, and I went to Hammersmith. Din'd at Lord Barrington's. Went to Sir Paul Methuen's.

25. Sunday. Mr Rollinson din'd here. Went to the Speaker's.

26. Monday. Din'd alone.—Went to Lord Hobart's concert, which is extreme good and perfectly well understood.
    The Cabinet met to settle the report to be made for the King upon Messrs Stone and Murray's affair of which more hereafter.

27. Tuesday. Din'd here Sir Francis Dashwood and Dr Sharpe.

28. Wednesday. Din'd here, Lord Bute, Messrs Breton and Ralph. Went to Lady Middlesex's.

[1] i.e. on Bishop Johnson's allegations.

MARCH

1. Thursday. Din'd at Mr Furnese's.

2. Friday. Din'd alone. Went to Lady Grace Vane's assembly, and to see Lady Shannon.

3. Saturday. Din'd alone and went to the new play of the Earl of Essex.

In the morning went to wait upon the Princess, who was pleas'd to tell me that Mr Stone was determin'd to prosecute Mr Fosset for defamation; that his counsel was the Attorney General, Mr Hume Campbell, Mr Ford, and Sir Richard Lloyd. I said, tho' I was in no connection with Mr Stone that entitl'd me to call him friend, yet I had long known and observ'd him; that I had a real esteem for him, and thought him both very honest, and very able, and was convinc'd that the King had not a more faithful subject nor one more truly affectionate to every branch of the Royal family; that upon that foot, I was not without apprehensions of bringing such a thing into a Court of Justice. Failure in the least circumstance of proof; tampering with evidence, or juries, &c. made me a little uneasy. She said she was so too, but they would have it so: that Stone had behav'd very well to her, and to the children; that, tho' it would be treason if it were known, yet he always spoke of the late Prince with great respect, and with great civility of all those that he knew the Prince had a real value for. That Lord Harcourt behav'd very differently; that he not only behav'd very ill to her, but always spoke to the children of their father, and his actions, in so disrespectful a manner, as to send them to her almost ready to cry, and did all he could, to alienate them from her; in so much they themselves were sensible of it since he left them, and that George had mentioned to her once, that he was afraid he had not behav'd to her so well as he ought, sometimes and wonder'd he could be so misled. That she said, no, but that, now and then, not with quite so much complaisance, as a young gentleman should use to a lady.

I said I flatter'd myself that she could find a very different behaviour in Lord Waldegrave. She said, yes indeed, that she very well lik'd all she saw of him. I said that this whole thing seem'd much deeper laid than Murray and Stone, and struck at the Pelhams. She said, most certainly—they must be blind if they did not see it, and the greatest cowards alive, if they did not resent it: that now was the time, and they were undone, if they did not make else of it; that the King took the thing highly in their favour, talk'd of it as the most unworthy attack, told her that Stone had serv'd him faithfully these twenty years, that he knew all that he himself knew; that if he were a peer, every body would think him proper to be Secretary; that he had been with her for an hour and held this sort of conversation.

I said I was very glad he had taken so favourable an impression; that I hop'd, and believ'd it would last, but however it should be made use of, while it was so strong, because it was possible it might cool, considering, as her Royal Highness herself had been pleased to observe to me, who were always about him at St. James's, and that the Ministry had nobody there. She said, to be sure they must strike while the iron was hot, or be ruined: that she had told Stone so, who said they had promis'd to do what was proper &c.: that she had replied, 'Mr Stone, it is action, now, and not words that must be expected.' That she had seen her great, great fat friend (the Duke)[1] who talk'd to her about it, and ask'd her if she did not think it a very disagreeable thing: that she said, yes, but did not regard it. He ask'd her if she was not very sorry that it happen'd; that she replied, 'Not at all, if the Ministers made a proper use of it'. She told me that Murray had behaved with spirit, and made an exceeding good speech, of which she gave me a detail as far as she remember'd, and particularly took notice that he mark'd strongly that it was not he, and Stone that were principally struck at, and that he laid it home to the Ministry.

4. Sunday. I took physic.

5. Monday. Went to the House, and presented a petition against a turnpike for the Earl of Thanet.[2] Din'd alone. Went to Lord Hobart's concert.

6. Tuesday. Mr Breton and Dr Sharpe din'd here. I went to a cause,

[1] Cumberland.
[2] D. had political affiliations with the Thanets and had himself once (1741) been returned for Appleby on their interest.

at Council; the Solicitor, who was for the appellant, left the reply to the Attorney, during which we had a conversation, in which he acquainted me with his behaviour: only that Stone was principally meant and nam'd by Lord Ravensworth who from what Fosset had said to him, in private conversation, came up, and insisted that Stone should be dismiss'd, and that so peremptorily to the Duke of Newcastle, that he was oblig'd to lay it before the King, who slighted it; but Stone insisted with him to have it examin'd into, which gave occasion to the bringing it before the cabinet council. When he (Murray) heard of this, he sent a message to the King humbly to acquaint his Majesty that if he were called before such a committee, on so scandalous and injurious an account, he would resign his office, and would refuse to answer. That the King highly approv'd of it: that when it was over, and Stone had been heard, he thought proper to demand an audience, and made a speech, most of which he repeated to me. It was full of spirit and charg'd the matter home, as a combination deep laid against the Ministry, &c.

I said everybody saw it so and thought that if they did not act they were undone: that the King was now in the most favourable disposition; how long it would last, might be doubted, considering who was nearest to him,[1] and nobody to parry for the Ministers: that I had some reasons to think the Princess was much alarm'd at their inactivity; that unless they could show they had strength of friends to second her, how could she support them? That I had it from coffee houses, that the design was to end in repealing the Regency Act, and making the Duke regent; that, if they did not represent strongly to the King that if he lik'd the absolute tranquillity of the two houses, he must leave it to them to make use of such instruments as they thought proper to continue it, [they were ruined]. He approv'd of all I said, step by step, in very strong terms; seem'd much alarm'd at the repeal of the Regency Bill; said that all I said was true, that they must act or be undone: they knew it, and he thought they certainly would: and particularly approv'd of what I propos'd to say to the King.

7. Wednesday. Went to Council at St James's. Mrs Dodington, Dr Sharpe and I din'd, and lay at Hammersmith.

8. Thursday. Mrs Dodington, Dr Sharpe, and I went to see the manufacture of tapestry from France, new set up at Fulham by the

[1] i.e. Cumberland.

Duke. The work, both of the Gobelins and of Chaillot, call'd savonnerie, is very fine, but very dear. Mr Ralph din'd here.

9. Friday. Mr Hampden din'd here.

10. Saturday. Sir F. Dashwood, Messrs Furnese and Tucker din'd here.

11. Sunday. Dr Sharpe and I went to dine with Sir Francis Dashwood, and return'd at night.

12. Monday. Rode to Gunnersbury. Din'd alone.

13. Tuesday. Mr Ralph din'd here.

14. Wednesday. We din'd in town. Went to Lady Middlesex's.

15. Thursday. Went to the House to attend the Earl of Thanet's petition against a turnpike. Was beat by 37 to 19—.

16. Friday. Mr Pelham, Mr Vane, Mr Furnese, and I din'd together by appointment at Mr Vane's. The offer of our thorough attachment, and return for his thorough friendship and protection, in bringing us into court, was renew'd, and my views of meaning to support their power, and not share it as a Minister, was explain'd. Mr Pelham, in a very frank, and honourable manner declar'd his thorough desire, and inclination to accept our friendship, and return his own:—That if his friendship was sufficient to effect the whole, he would with pleasure engage for the whole—But that he could not answer for the King, whose prejudices were very strong against me, and most so, for my having quitted him for his son &c. —but that every thing in his power he would do, to remove them, to make way for a measure so truly agreeable to him.

I then enter'd into a detail (which I offer'd to prove) of the injustice, and unreasonableness of these prejudices: and then said, that from this long account, he might naturally expect a request to enter into a justification, either by myself, or by him: but that I did not desire to justify, with the King: that all I desir'd him to say to the King was, that tho' it never was in intention to offend him, it was sufficient that he was displeas'd for me to think myself to blame without pretending to justify myself, and that to induce him to forget it, I humbly offer'd him my services, and all the interest I had in the House, and out of it, for the rest of my life. I added that I thought this submission, and this offer of five members at least, should be sufficient to wipe out imperfections, even if I had been a declar'd Jacobite.

He said, it was all that could be said, and all should be made of it, that his credit could make. But that should it be practicable, and I were in any station, and the King should not be brought to behave to me as I might justly expect, I should grow uneasy, and be dissatisfied, as in the case of Pitt, to whom they could never prevail on him to be commonly civil. I told him no, not in the least. He said yes, I might fancy so, but he believ'd I should. I said that I answer'd with certainty because I had consider'd and made up my mind about that. That all I wish'd of the King was to make me over to him (Pelham) to let him dispose of me, as he thought fit, and suffer him to receive my friendship, attachment, and services; that I desir'd by no means to encroach upon his Majesty's time or thoughts, or behaviour provided he gave him (Pelham) leave to employ me for his Majesty's services in the way that was most agreeable to him. That I would give him my reasons with the utmost freedom; which were that, indeed if I were a New Man, and in any station, I should in paying my court expect that sort of civil return that was my due: but after such unworthy prejudices taken, so void of all foundation, tho' I would not justify, yet I never desir'd any conversation or intercourse with his Majesty, more than a distant, but profound respect, on my side, and that as seldom as was consistent with the duty of a most faithful, and respectful subject.

Upon the whole he behav'd in so open, and noble a manner, as to chuse to make it plain, ten times, (tho' he did not make use of the expression exactly) that I should rather see that he wanted power, than have any doubt of his sincerity, if it did not succeed; and that the doubt of his strength and power alone, hinder'd him from promising positively to effect it, and therefore, (if I judge this right) I am oblig'd to him, and will be his friend, whether it succeeds or not.

17. Saturday. Din'd alone. Lady Middlesex, Mrs Dodington, and I went to Barry's benefit.

18. Sunday. Din'd alone.

19. Monday. Din'd here, the Duke of Queensberry, Lords Drumlanerich, Douglas, and Talbot, Messrs John Stuart, Sir Francis Dashwood, Sir Hugh Dalrymple, and Macky.

20. Tuesday. Din'd at Sir H. Bellendine's.

21. Wednesday. Went to Hammersmith with Mrs Dodington.

22. Thursday. Came to the House of Lords. The Duke of Bedford open'd the affair of Fosset's report against the Bishop of Gloucester, Stone, and Murray, and appeal'd to Lord Ravensworth, who open'd the whole transaction, in a long narrative. Then the Duke, in a long speech, founded his question upon that narrative which, in substance, was to address the King for the whole proceeding before the Council. The Chancellor and Duke of Newcastle answer'd him, and to make this question (which was foreseen, and I think need not have been so timorously apprehended) the more unnecessary, they had obtain'd of the King to dispense with the oath of those Lords of the Council upon this occasion, and to acquaint the House with the whole proceeding, which those two Lords did, pretty much at large. The debate was very long and low; the Duke of Bedford's performance moderate enough. He divided the House, but they were not told, for these went below the Bar with him, the Earl Harcourt, Lord Townshend, the Bishop of Worcester and Lord Talbot only. The Bishop of Norwich and Lord Harcourt both spoke, not to much purpose, but neither in the least supported the Duke's question.

Upon the whole, it was the worst judg'd, the worst executed, and the worst supported point that I ever saw, of so much expectation. I return'd to Hammersmith that night.

And I think I will shortly set down the exact truth of this strange, important trifle.

Mr Fosset, Messrs Murray, and Stone, were much acquainted, if not school-fellows, in early life. Their fortune led them different ways. His to be a country lawyer, and Recorder of Newcastle. Johnson, now Bishop of Gloucester, was one of their associates. The day the King's birthday was kept they din'd at the Dean of Durham's, in Durham. This Fosset, Lord Ravensworth, Major Davison, and one or two more, who retir'd after dinner into another room, the conversation turning upon the late Bishop of Gloucester's preferments it was asked who was to have his Prebend of Durham: the Dean said that the last news from London was that Dr Johnson was to have it: Fosset said he was glad that Johnson got off so well, for that he remember'd he was a Jacobite several years ago; and us'd to be with a relation of his who was very disaffected, one Vernon, a mercer, where the Pretender's health was frequently drunk. This passing among a few familiar acquaintance, was thought no more of. This spread, however, so much in the north (how, I never heard accounted for) and reached Town in such a manner, that Mr Pelham thought it necessary to desire Mr Vane, who was a friend to Fosset, and employ'd him in his business, to write to him, to know if he had said this, of Johnson, and if he had, if it was true. This letter was wrote on the 9th of January; it came to Newcastle the Friday following.

Fosset was much surpris'd, but the post going out in a few hours after its arrival, he immediately answer'd the letter by a long, but not very explicit one. This Friday happen'd to be the club-day of the neighbouring gentlemen to Newcastle: as soon as, among the rest, Lord Ravensworth, who was a patron and employer of his came into the town, Fosset acquaints him with the extraordinary letter he has receiv'd: and being asked to see the copy says he kept none; but desires Lord R to recollect if he held such a conversation at the Deanery of Durham, the day appointed for the birthday. Ravensworth can remember nothing at all of it. They go to the club. R goes the next morning to see his mother in the neighbourhood, and stays till Monday, but this thing of such consequence, lying upon his thoughts, he returns by Newcastle. He and Fosset have another conversation, and in endeavouring to refresh each other's memory about this dreadful delinquency of Johnson, Fosset said he could not recollect positively, at such a distance of time, if Johnson drank those healths, or had been present at the drinking them; but that Murray and Stone had done both, several times. Ravensworth was excessively alarm'd at this, with relation to Stone, on account of his office about the Prince; and thus the affair of Johnson was quite forgot, and the episode became the principal object.

There were many more conferences between R and Fosset upon this subject in which he persisted that Stone, and Murray were present at the drinking, and drank their healths. It may be observ'd here that when he was examined upon oath, he swore to the years 1731, or 1732 at latest. Fosset comes up, as usual, about his law business, is examin'd by Messrs Pelham and Vane, who never had heard of Murray or Stone being nam'd, and is ask'd, and answers, only with relation to Johnson, never mentioning either of the others.

But the love of his King, his country, and posterity, burn'd so strongly in Ravensworth's bosom that he could have no rest, till he had discovered this enormity. Accordingly when he came to town, he acquainted the ministry, and almost all his great acquaintance with it, and insisted upon Stone's being remov'd. The ministry would have slighted it, as it deserv'd, but as he persisted, and had told so many of it, they could not help laying it before the King, who tho' he slighted it, was advis'd to examine it; which examination produc'd this most injudicious proceeding in Parliament. The Duke of Devonshire was the only one of the committee absent from the House.

The ministers, and indeed everybody else, did imagine, and I believe, still do, that this whole affair is combin'd with the resignation, and that there was a set of pretended friends to the Pelhams, ready to take advantage of it; and I know Mr Pelham did think that this motion would give great lights into it. How far their expectations are answer'd, I can't say: mine were entirely disappointed; for the whole was so ill conducted and supported, that I should be almost tempted to believe that the grounds which carried our conjectures almost into certainties, had no foundation at all. As I came from Hammersmith I call'd on Mr Pelham, and the Duke of Dorset, and return'd as soon as the House was up.

23. Friday. I came to town to Mr Stanley's private Committee, and return'd to dinner with Dr Sharpe.

24. Saturday. Dr Sharpe, Mrs D, and I din'd in town. We two went to Mrs Drax's rout, and return'd at night all three.

25. Sunday. Dr Sharpe, and I, came to town. I went to court. We din'd at Mr Fremantle's and after dinner I christen'd Mr Lee's son. Mrs D and I return'd.

26. Monday. Mr Younge and Mr Tucker din'd with us. Mr Younge lay here.

27. Tuesday. We all came to town. I went to Mr Stanley's Committee. Din'd alone. Went to the Cockpit.

28. Wednesday. Din'd at Lord Middlesex's. Went to Mrs Prowse's rout.

29. Thursday. Was to wait on the Princess. She seem'd much pleas'd that the affair had ended so well in the House of Lords, and said that it was owing to the King's steadiness, and resolution, that it went no farther. That he took it with good sense, and proper firmness, without which not all the Lords of the Cabinet would have behav'd as they did.

N.B. This is the first time that I ever heard her speak favourably of the King.

In mentioning my reasons for having an opinion of Mr Stone without any friendship with him, I said that from thence, I was glad when I heard he was put about the Prince. She said she was not: on the contrary, she was very sorry, and much frighted at it. I was surpris'd, and ask'd her why. She said, 'Because the Prince had always taught her to believe that he was a Jacobite, and that she firmly did believe it'. That the Prince was convinc'd of it, and when things went ill abroad, us'd to say to her in passion, how could better be expected, when such a Jacobite as Stone was trusted &c.

At Lady Tynte's rout. Din'd here Mr Kelsal, and Lovel.

30. Friday. Din'd here Messrs Breton, Younge, and Ralph. Lady's S. and R. Poulet's rout.

31. Saturday. Din'd alone. Lady Chesterfield's rout. Went to La Trappe.[1]

[1] From now on it is 'La Trappe', not 'Hammersmith'. The villa was almost complete. The name may be no more than an innocent irony about the purpose of the villa being conversation. It could be a reminiscence of Medmenham.

APRIL

1. Sunday. Din'd at the Duke of Queensberry's. Return'd at night.

2. Monday. Din'd alone.

3. Tuesday. We din'd alone, and went to town after dinner. I went to Council.

4. Wednesday. Din'd alone. Went to Sir Paul Methuen's.

5. Thursday. Din'd at Mr Vane's. Staid till 12, then went to La Trappe.

6. Friday. Took physic. Din'd alone.

7. Saturday. Lady Middlesex, Mrs Dodington, Lord Middlesex, Drs Sharpe and Thomson, Mr Breton, and I went to Ponders End to see the lapis lazuli pillars. They are finish'd and very fine. Mrs D. and I went from La Trappe, and took them up, at London. All din'd at Tottenham: and she and I return'd to La Trappe at night, with Dr Sharpe.

8. Sunday. Messrs Stanley and Breton din'd here.

9. Monday. Dr Sharpe went to town. Din'd alone.

10. Tuesday. Din'd in town.—Went to the Cockpit.—Brought Dr Sharpe back.

11. Wednesday. Messrs Rich and Thornhill din'd here.

12. Thursday. I din'd at Lord Middlesex's, and return'd.

13. Friday. Din'd alone.

14. Saturday. Mrs Dodington came. Mr Tucker din'd here.

15. Sunday. Mr and Mrs Tucker din'd here. Mr Tucker carried Mrs Dodington to town.

16. Monday. Mrs Dodington, and I went to town.—We din'd alone.—I supp'd at Mr Furnese's.

17. Tuesday. I din'd at Lord Talbot's. Went to Lady Bath's assembly, and return'd to La Trappe, afterwards.

18. Wednesday. Din'd alone.

19. Thursday. Went to town to see Mr Pelham: thence to Council: thence to Lady Middlesex's. Din'd at Sir Francis Dashwood's. Return'd at night.

20. Friday. Mr Bance and Shipway breakfasted here. Mrs D. and I carried them to Cranford bridge, and return'd to dinner.

21. Saturday. Ladies Shannon and Middlesex breakfasted here, and Mr Tucker din'd with us.

22. Sunday. I rode to, and din'd at, the Duke of Argyll's. Mrs D. fetch'd me home in the coach.

23. Monday. Din'd alone.

24. Tuesday. Din'd at Mr Furnese's, at Gunnersbury.

25. Wednesday. Mrs D. and I, went to town, and return'd to dinner.

26. Thursday. Mrs D. and I din'd at Mr Kelsal's, at Norwood.

27. Friday. Din'd alone. News of Lord Barnard's death.[1]

28. Saturday. The same.

29. Sunday. Din'd here Lords Bath and Montfort, Messrs Herbert, Furnese, Solicitor General.

30. Monday. Din'd alone. We lay in town.

[1] The new peer was to be Henry Vane, the Pelhamite go-between.

MAY

1. Tuesday. Din'd at Lady Middlesex's.

2. Wednesday. Lord Middlesex, and Mr Forrester were with me to suggest a plan for laying a state of his [Middlesex's] debts before the Duke of Dorset: they amount, it seems, to £15,000. We agreed to settle it on Sunday, the 13th, at Hammersmith.—We came thither to dinner, and brought Mr Kelsal with us.

3. Thursday. Din'd alone.

4. Friday. Mrs D. went in the chaise, Mr Kelsal and I rode. We return'd to dinner. [Wrote to] Verschaffelts.

5. Saturday. Mr Kelsal went home. Lord Dupplin and Mr Fane din'd here.

6. Sunday. Din'd here Lord Talbot, Messrs Stanley and Harvey.

7. Monday. Mr Ralph din'd here. He gave me account that Mr William Beckford was with him last Saturday: told him that they had a body formed (not a large one) which would act together; that they found it necessary to employ the press; that they thought him the ablest person, &c. That they propos'd setting forth a paper. He desir'd to know who (besides Mr. Beckford) he was to be engag'd with—was answered, with the Duke of Bedford. Ask'd if the Duke of Cumberland protected them. Answer'd 'He could not tell'. Ask'd, if he, Ralph was, with his instruments, to be secur'd and protected against all law prosecutions—what establishment for himself—and if he was to lay down his own plan, and write in conformity to it, or if it was expected that he should be confin'd. Answered, to the first, that he should be thoroughly protected, and by those who would own him in both Houses. To the second—that his allowance should be handsome, but could not take upon him then to name the sum. To the third, that he was to be at entire liberty. Upon which, being press'd to go to the Duke of Bedford, who desir'd to see him soon, he promis'd Mr Beckford to take an early opportunity of waiting upon his Grace.[1]

[1] So *The Protester* was born. Rigby sent a copy of it to Bedford in June. The Beckfords were eagerly putting themselves at the disposal of Bedford (*Bedford Correspondence*, ii. 127-8).

8. Tuesday. Carried Mr Ralph to town, he designing to go to the Duke of Bedford's tomorrow. Lord Barnard call'd upon me: I talked very strongly to him. Told him of the open manner of inlisting all sorts of people against the Pelhams, mentioned Ralph's resolution. Put him in mind, that I had offered his services as my friend, bade him recollect in how improper a manner Mr Pelham refus'd him; told him, that I had reason to expect that he should have given up his resentments to him, on my account; but that certainly prudence should have made him do it, for his own sake, when he might have plac'd to my account, tho' he might not think me worth it; and thereby seem'd the man, and pretended to persist in his resentment. Lord Barnard said he was sorry for it, and himself, should immediately have taken Ralph as belonging to me. That he thought writing also of great consequence tho' Mr Pelham did not. I said Mr P mistook himself; he and I knew that no man was more susceptible of the effects of it, no man was more easily hurt by it: was there a stronger proof of it, than the present case? What was this irreconcileableness against Ralph occasioned by, but the impression of a pamphlet, which after all, the man did not write? That I was sure, he would repent it very soon, and I no way farther interfer'd in it; yet I desir'd he should know this, and more particularly, that as I had given him the offer of a most useful, honest, and able man, and upon rejecting it, had, some time since, given him fair warning, by him, Lord Barnard, of what would happen, I must have no complaints, or insinuations, or even thoughts, that I was in any way, art or part, in anything that might come out: it was language I would not hear, and insinuations I would not suffer. I was sorry for the step, because I knew how naturally people were misled when they were hurt. Who knew what a man that had been Secretary of State, might furnish? and how galling it might be rendered by the ablest pen in England? That I was griev'd to see so little spirit oppos'd to so much vehemence, and virulence as their declar'd enemies acted with; that their efficient enemies, 'twas true, were but few in number, but yet they were the King's son, and daughter, and a Duke of Bedford: that I thought they had not three such efficient friends, in or out of St James's: that my fears suggested, and reason confirm'd it, that if they did not exert themselves, and give proof of their power to the world, by their protection to their friends, the numbers would gradually drop from them: that their all depended upon the new Parliament: that I hoped they were active about it:

that I had some little influence, as well as positive interest, in that election, but that I knew no more what they were about, and how to apply that influence, than if I had never known their names: that, however, he was to understand that these were the fears, not the complaints; that I had nothing to complain of: that I meant, and ask'd, the Pelhams' friendship, and good-will, and in return offer'd my services and attachment: that Mr Pelham was pleas'd to accept of this offer, and promise his friendship and countenance in return: that I never ask'd him for any emolument, at any time, or in any manner: that his Lordship knew I had been wish'd to do so, but never would, resolving to leave it wholly to Mr Pelham how he thought proper to make use of my personal services; those, that were in my power, in my present situation, I had promis'd, and he should have them; nothing but words had, yet, pass'd between us, but he should see that I would act. In my present state, all I could give him, was my country interest, and influence in the elections. He should have them. I would certainly chuse any two he pleas'd at Weymouth, and tho' I knew nothing of his measures, all my influence should go in the way that I could guess he most wish'd: that I did and should leave the rest, entirely to him, as it was to fulfil his own part. If he thought I could be of no other and further use, I could not help it; if he thought I might, he would produce me in the way that he thought would best enable me to perform it: that this was wholly his affair—it did not depend upon me: what depended upon me, I should certainly perform. That therefore, tho' I desir'd he should know all this, clearly, and explicitly, yet I expected he would understand it as it really was, only the naked sentiments, and apprehensions of a friend without any mixture of complaint, or having the least intention to complain.

I have forgotten to insert in its place an instance of their timidity towards their friends, which I mention'd and is too striking to be omitted. I ask'd how he thought our friend Murray felt, to find that his friends in power suffer'd a most offensive, and hurtful calumny, meant at them too, to be fix'd on him, and made matter of examination, instead of being rejected with indignation, by a Court the most unprecedented, through the whole proceeding, that ever met: 'I suppose', says I, 'you will tell me that there were reasons that made it unavoidable: I know it, the Cavendishes would not stand it, but lean'd the other way. Stop here a moment. Is not that saying, "Let it hurt who it will, let it be never so inconvenient and lessening to you, we will not forfeit, nay not venture one atom of our credit with the herd." To return, Murray condescends to defend himself; treats calumny and clamour with the noble contempt they deserve; but artfully winds in an apology to them: they are satisfied—that is, after having been the subject of an illegal enquiry into an impertinent, disgraceful, imputation, those gentlemen, when not the least speck appears upon him, are satisfied. To be sure, he thinks himself much oblig'd to them. After all this, and when the same scandal was brought into the most publick assembly, with the impotence of proof, in order to spread it through the nation, what do his friends in power do? they say, he was effectually justified, without doing one act to show their resentment of the persecution he had suffered, either by disgracing the abettors, or punishing the authors of it. How must a most able, active, openly attach'd friend, think you, feel such tameness?'

He said, he thought (and I believe he did think) as I did.

We had a Council at night about the regulations of Minorca. Mr Pelham came to me and told me that he had seen Lord Barnard, that he thought himself extremely oblig'd to me for what had pass'd between us; was highly sensible how much he owed me, and that he would soon find an opportunity to talk with me at large. I return'd when the Council rose.

9. Wednesday. Din'd alone.

10. Thursday. Went to Council. Earl of Northumberland, Lord Barnard, and Sir William Lowther, sworn Lords Lieutenants for Northumberland, Durham, and Westmorland. Governors Thomas and Sharpe sworn for the Leeward Islands and Maryland.

Mr Ralph was yesterday with the Duke of Bedford: very well receiv'd but nothing positively settled. I think he has acted precipitately, but durst not restrain him for fear of becoming answerable for consequences beyond my power.

Din'd with Mr Furnese at Sir Francis Dashwood's. Return'd at night.

11. Friday. Din'd alone. Was surpris'd at dinner with a letter from Cary the surgeon that Mr Furnese was struck with an apoplectic fit that morning. I hasten'd to town: found him blooded, blister'd, and physick'd, but much better, and out of all danger. I return'd. [Wrote to] Cardinal Albani for Mr Anne Poulet.

12. Saturday. Went to see Mr Furnese, and found him quite recover'd. Return'd and din'd with Mr Breton, at Hammersmith, who came to town yesterday.

13. Sunday. Mr Forrester, and Lord Middlesex came to settle his Lordship's affairs,[1] and din'd here with the Messrs Sharpe, Breton, Thomson, and Dodington, who lay here.

14. Monday. Mr Dodington went away. We din'd alone, and came to town at night.

15. Tuesday. Mr Lee din'd here. Went to the Cockpit.

16. Wednesday. Was to wait upon the Princess. She was gone to Kew. Mr Breton din'd here. Went to Sir Paul Methuen's, Mr Waller's, and Lady Middlesex's. King went to Kensington.

17. Thursday. Was to wait on the Princess, she was going to Kensington. Din'd at Mr Mildmay's—Went to the Duke of Argyll's.

18. Friday. Was to wait on the Princess. Very kindly receiv'd: nothing material pass'd. Din'd alone. Went to Mr Bance's to meet a civilian about Mrs Lyel's codicil. Thence to Mr Furnese's, and Lady Middlesex's.

19. Saturday. Din'd alone. Went to Lady Middlesex's. Thence to La Trappe.

20. Sunday. Alone.

21. Monday. Alone.

22. Tuesday. Mr Falkingham din'd here.

23. Wednesday. Lords Carlisle and Feversham, Sir William Irby, Colonel Lyttelton, Mr Breton (who staid) din'd here—and Mr Hampden.

24. Thursday. Mrs D., Mr Breton, and I went to see Mr Gideon's, at Erith.

25. Friday. Lord Bathurst, Messrs Mildmay, Blombergle, and Sturt din'd here.

[1] See 12 June below.

26. Saturday. Duke of Argyll, Messrs Maule Fletcher, Vaughan, Sharpe, Oswald, Beaghan, Dodington, and Tucker din'd here. We went to town.

27. Sunday. Went to Court at Carlton House. Din'd alone. At Sir Paul Methuen's, Duke of Argyll's, and Lady Middlesex's.

28. Monday. Din'd at Lord Carlisle's. Came to La Trappe at night.

29. Tuesday. Dr Lidderdale din'd here.

30. Wednesday. Mr Boyle din'd here.

31. Thursday. Din'd at London. Went to Lady Middlesex's. Return'd.

JUNE

1. Friday. Din'd alone. Mr Breton came at night.

2. Saturday. Mr and Mrs Pitt, Mr and Mrs Gardiner, Lord Middlesex, and Mr Boyle din'd here. The Spanish Ambassador came in the afternoon.

3. Sunday. Ladies Hervey[1] and Murray, Miss Hamilton, and Mr Baillie din'd here.

4. Monday. Mr Breton went to town. Din'd alone.

5. Tuesday. Went to town by water. Din'd at the Spanish Ambassador's at Chelsea. Return'd by water.

6. Wednesday. Went to town, and return'd to dinner. Alone—.

7. Thursday. Din'd at Colonel Lyttelton's at Ealing. Brought Mr Breton back.

8. Friday. Mr Ralph din'd here.

9. Saturday. Lord Barnard, Colonel Vane, Sir Thomas Robinson, Messrs Furnese, Fanshawe, Thompson, Carey, din'd here. Mr Breton went away.

10. Sunday. Alone.

11. Monday. Alone.

12. Tuesday. Alone.[2]

13. Wednesday. Alone.

14. Thursday. Din'd at Twickenham with Mr Cambridge.

[1] Mollie Lepel, widow of John, Lord Hervey, and former mistress of Frederick, Prince of Wales. She was fond of D., who used to read novels to her aloud. (See her *Letters*, 1821, pp. 208, 289, and Cumberland's *Memoirs*, 1806, pp. 144–7.)
[2] Composed and dispatched a long letter (now in the Clements Library, Ann Arbor) to the Duke of Dorset pleading for reconciliation with Lord Middlesex. A later letter of 28 July, in which D. encloses Middlesex's accounts just before leaving for the country, shows that the Duke did not take up D.'s offer to act as intermediary.

15. Friday. I din'd at Lord Barnard's. Return'd at night.

16. Saturday. Sir Francis Dashwood and his lady, and Mrs Dodington din'd here. Ladies Shannon and Middlesex came in the afternoon, and Mr Breton went back with them.

17. Sunday. Din'd at Gunnersbury.

18. Monday. Mr Carey din'd here.

19. Tuesday. We din'd with the Earl of Stafford.

20. Wednesday. Mr Chamberlayne din'd here.

21. Thursday. Went to town. Din'd at Lady Middlesex's. Return'd at night. [Wrote to] Cardinal Albani and Mr Mann.

22. Friday. Day of the King's Accession. I went to Kensington, and return'd to dinner.

23. Saturday. Din'd here Lords Barnard and Montfort, Messrs Vane and George Vane, Furnese, and Thomson.

24. Sunday. Went to Carlton House. Return'd to dinner. Messrs Bance, and Tucker din'd here.

25. Monday. Mr Carey din'd here.

26. Tuesday. Lord Barnard, Colonel Vane, Mr Pelham, Mr Furnese, din'd here: Not one word about business so that I look upon that transaction to be over.[1]

27. Wednesday. Messrs Wyndham, Kelsal, and Breton (who staid) din'd here.

28. Thursday. Mrs D., Mr Breton, and I, went to see Esher.[2] Din'd at Kingston, and return'd.

29. Friday. Messrs Young and Beaghan (who staid) din'd here. Mr Breton went to town.

30. Saturday. Went to town. Mrs Dodington din'd, and staid here.

[1] See 16 March above.   [2] Horace Walpole's favourite villa.

JULY

1. Sunday. Lord and Lady Stafford, and Lady Mary Drummond, din'd here.

2. Monday. Din'd alone.

3. Tuesday. Sir Francis Eyles, and his lady and Mrs Egerton, and Mr Kelsal din'd here. Dr Sharpe came after dinner.

4. Wednesday. We din'd alone.

5. Thursday. Dr Sharpe went away. Mr Breton came:—we went with Mrs Dodington to see Lord Lincoln's and din'd at Ashley. I gave Mr Breton his bond for £400.

6. Friday. Mr Breton, and I went on horseback to dine with the Duke of Argyll, who din'd abroad. We return'd to dinner.

7. Saturday. I went to town, and return'd to dinner.

8. Sunday. I din'd at the Duke de Mirepoix.

9. Monday. Mr Ralph and four Tuckers din'd here.

10. Tuesday. We din'd with Sir Francis Eyles.

11. Wednesday. Messrs Campi and d'Acunha, and Mr Cambridge din'd here.

12. Thursday. We all din'd at Mr Furnese's.

13. Friday. Lord, and Mrs Edgcumbe, and Mr Furnese din'd here.

14. Saturday. I went to see Sir Paul Methuen, and return'd to dinner.

15. Sunday. Din'd here Duke de Mirepoix, Prince de St Severin, Comtes du Lude, Marquis Dufreville, Chevaliers de la Rocque, and de Belleisle, M. Duvelaer. I went to Kensington in the morning. Mr Stanley came.

16. Monday. Mr Carey came, after dinner.

17. Tuesday. Messrs Stanley and Carey went away. I din'd at Lord Middlesex's.

18. Wednesday. I pass'd the day with the Princess of Wales by her order. Extremely friendly and kindly receiv'd.

Conversation was chiefly of a domestic familiar nature. Nothing very remarkable in politics, except my observing that people who chiefly out of regard [to] her, had declin'd all opposition, and [were] very ready and desirous to contribute to the service of the Ministry, for all that, were still to remain in a state of proscription; that such people were pretty much snaffled by the apprehension that if they resented it they might be look'd upon as being in opposition to her, and the Prince, in a new reign, to whom their attachment and affection was inviolable and invariable; whereas it was hard to believe that the treatment their Royal Highnesses met with was so cordial and endearing as to oblige them to espouse the quarrels of the present Court, especially against those who were drawn into them from the treatment they met from their attachment to their Royal Highnesses and the late Prince.

She said, 'To be sure it was so', but was not so explicit upon the head as I wish'd. She gave into it, but rather seem'd to allow it than declare it. We had an hour's conversation with the Princess and I left her about ten o'clock.

19. Thursday. I din'd at Lord Edgecumbe's.

20. Friday. Mrs D. and I din'd at Mr Oswald's, at Wandsworth, and returned to Pall Mall.

21. Saturday. Din'd in Pall Mall with Messrs Dodington and Beaghan.—Went to Sir Paul Methuen's.

22. Sunday. Went to Carlton House. Return'd to dinner.

23. Monday. Alone.

24. Tuesday. I went to town, and return'd at night.

25. Wednesday. Messrs Furnese and Ralph din'd here.

26. Thursday. I went to town, and return'd [to] dinner. Alone.

27. Friday. Mr Carey din'd with us.

28. Saturday. We din'd alone.

29. Sunday. At $\frac{1}{2}$ an hour past three, Mrs D. and I set out from Hammersmith in our post chaise for Eastbury, where, thanks be to God, we arriv'd well, with out any accident, at six, exactly.

30. Monday. Lord Malpas din'd here. Mr Sturt came in the afternoon. The first, to desire my assistance for Dorchester; and the last, for the County.

31. Tuesday. Mr Drax din'd here.

AUGUST

1. Wednesday. Alone.

2. Thursday. A messenger to desire me to come to Bridgewater. I sent word that I would be there, on Friday; and sent to Mr Balch to go with me; Mr Crabb din'd here.

3. Friday. Mr Gresly din'd here. Lord Malpas came at night.

4. Saturday. Lord Malpas, Mrs D., and I din'd at Lord Shaftesbury's, who was determin'd not to go to the meeting at Dorchester to nominate the Knights of the Shire. Finding that I went, he was perplex'd; but more so by a letter he receiv'd at dinner from Lord Digby,[1] requesting him to go. We left him uneasy and irresolute.

5. Sunday. Din'd alone.

6. Monday. Mr Pitt din'd here.

7. Tuesday. At $\frac{1}{2}$ past five I set out in my chaise for Dorchester, where I arriv'd at nine to assist at the meeting to nominate the County Members for the ensuing [Parliament].
   Lord Digby was in the winter brought to me by Lord Hillsborough, from Messrs Pelham and Fox. He ask'd my assistance, as determining to stand on the Whig Interest; I told him that if no relation or person whom I had particular connections with set up, on the same interest, mine was at his service. From that time to this morning, I never saw Lord Digby, nor was consulted for him, by any friends of his. Soon after I came to the Antelope he came to me, told me he hop'd for my favour. I told him I had no other business there. He soon returned with Lord Ilchester; they both press'd me to stand with him, which I declin'd. Lord Milton (who also press'd me), Mr Drax, Trenchard, and most of the Whig gentry (as I was in the house appointed for the meeting, I suppose) came to me.
   I found that Mr Trenchard was to propose Lord Digby but that he and his uncle Ilchester had [not] consulted, nor concerted anything with anybody. I said that there could be no doubt of the Whigs

---

[1] Henry Fox's nephew, and a member of the Prince of Wales's household. He was sitting for Malmesbury, and was ultimately, in 1754, brought in for Wells.

carrying the election, if they resolv'd upon it; because I knew that near two thirds of the property was in their hands; and because I had done it for Mr Pitt's father, (who was hardly capable) when our property was much less.—But whether *they would resolve to go thro' it at all events* I did not in the least know. That I suppos'd that Lord Digby's adviser has ask'd and knew; if not, a Party Meeting should be held, and they should be ask'd.—I think everybody approv'd of this. Lords Digby and Ilchester both told me privately that Mr Pelham put Lord Digby upon standing. Afterwards, walking with Lord D. He told me that he, in great measure, laid aside the thoughts of it, but that a little before Parliament rose, Mr Pelham took him aside in the House, and said that he was inform'd it would certainly do and press'd him to go on with it. I said to my Lord, that I did not know from whom Mr P. had his information, but that it was not from me. That I would do him all the service I could, and all the return I desir'd was to remember that I was no ways consulted, nor advising, in this affair.

We went up to the Meeting about 12 o'clock. I believe of Whigs we might be somewhat more than 30 gentlemen. When the Tories came, we were about 100. Sir Robert Long, of Wiltshire, propos'd Mr Pitt. Mr Bingham return'd Mr Chafin's[1] thanks to the County, and excuses for declining, and then Sir Robert propos'd Mr Sturt, to join with Mr Pitt.—Mr Trenchard propos'd Lord Digby. Nobody said a word. Then Mr Francis Seymour, his neighbour, spake a few words in support of Pitt and Sturt, in order to keep the County out of *Ministerial Dependence.* To this nothing was offer'd on our side, till people began to move and were going to break up, when I thought it necessary to take some notice of that expression; which I did and concluded by saying that I should give my interest to Lord Digby only till I saw further. So it ended with very little spirit of their side, and none at all of ours.

I understood, and so did most gentlemen, that we were all to dine together. But it seems that Lords Ilchester, Digby, &c. had bespoken dinner at another house: to which we went; but our friends were not properly inform'd of it, so that several were left to them, or to shift for themselves, which was very bad management. Lord Ilchester left us at five, which I thought odd. I lay at Wolverton, and came to Dorchester before eleven next morning; which was

---

[1] The retiring member. George Pitt was the other sitting member.

8. Wednesday. After waiting 2 hours for Counsellor Gould he came in. I solicited him for his brother's interest at Bridgewater. He answer'd me, in a very reasonable, obliging, and gentleman-like manner; and gave a letter to his brother, in such terms that I have reason to think he will, heartily, support my interest; which will be of material use to me.

I din'd with Dr Daveney, and return'd in the evening.

9. Thursday. Din'd alone.—

10. Friday. At six Mrs D. and I set out for Bridgewater; got thither by 9 at night. A very hard journey for one set of horses.—

11. Saturday. Mr Balch and I went about near half the town.— The people did not care to speak out: tho' but few declar'd they were engag'd to Lord Egmont.[1]

12. Sunday.—I went, twice, to Church.—

13. Monday. So wet we could not stir out.

14. Tuesday. Mrs Dodington, Mr Breton (who came yesterday) and I, went to see Sir Charles Tynte, and from thence to Lord Egmont's, at Enmore.—We return'd to dinner:—I went round another part of the town, after dinner.

15. Wednesday. Went as far as the rain would permit: and

16. Thursday. Finish'd the round: this a week of the worst weather I ever saw, in August.

17. Friday. Mr Breton return'd to Cannons Lee; and at past ten, we set out from Bridgewater; and lay at Horsington.

18. Saturday. God be prais'd, we got home to Eastbury, pretty well, without any accident. The excessive badness of the roads, and weather, during the whole time, with the nature of the business, made it much the most disagreeable journey, and, I think, the most disagreeable week I ever pass'd.—

All this, trouble, vexation and expense, as well as that to come,

---

[1] Egmont, to D.'s great disgust, was proposing himself for Bridgwater against D. He had the Poulet interest on his side—see 7 Nov. 1753 below.

flows from a set of low, worthless fellows, who finding they shall not be brib'd without an Opposition, have prevail'd upon Lord Egmont to lend his name, to whom they will give one vote, that they may sell the other; without any chance, as things now appear, of making his election. This he does not see, nor that the Tories (tho' partly for other reasons) make his greatest strength. So that he is setting up an interest; which, if it could succeed, he could never sit in quiet with in that place. But tho' I think he has no chance at present; yet the uneasiness and expense will be the same, to me, as if he was sure of success.—

19. Sunday. ⎫
            ⎬ Alone.
20. Monday. ⎭

21. Tuesday. The Races. I din'd at Blandford.

22. Wednesday. Din'd at home.—Went to the race—but not to the concert at Blandford.

23. Thursday. The same.—

24. Friday. Alone.

25. Saturday. Mr Shirley, Lady Orford, in return from France, din'd here. Messrs Freke, Harris and Wise din'd.

[a day omitted]

27. Monday. Alone.

28. Tuesday. I din'd at Mr Drax's. Found Mr Breton at my return.

29. Wednesday. Alone.

30. Thursday. Lord and Lady Arundell, Mr Gage, and Mr Banks din'd here.

31. Friday. Alone.

SEPTEMBER

1. Saturday. Messrs Trenchard and Picard din'd here. Mr Freke came.

2. Sunday. The Forbes went away.

3. Monday. Alone.

4. Tuesday. Mr Shirley and Lady Orford came to dinner, and lay here.

5. Wednesday. ⎫
6. Thursday. ⎬ Alone.
⎭

7. Friday. Sir George Lee, and Mr Wood came to dinner.

8. Saturday. We went to Lord Shaftesbury's and return'd to dinner.

9. Sunday. Sir George Lee and Mr Wood went to town. Mr Tucker and Dr Sharpe came to dinner.

10. Monday. Alone.

11. Tuesday. Mr Tucker went home. Messrs Dodington and Beaghan, Breton and I went to Lady Orford's to dinner: lay there, and

12. Wednesday. Came home to dinner. Balch din'd with us, and return'd home.

13. Thursday. Mr Dodington, and Mr Blake din'd here.

14. Friday. Mr Carver, who broke his neck from a horse, was buried from Chettle at Ashmore. The bearers met at Chettle at 3 o'clock, and were Lord Arundell of Wardour, myself, Messrs Beckford, Grove, Okeden, and Chafin.

15. Saturday. Alone.

16. Sunday. Messrs Okeden and Drax din'd here.

17. Monday. Messrs J. Beckford and Bower din'd here.

18. Tuesday. Mr Wyndham came.

[a day omitted]

20. Thursday. About eleven, Mrs D. Dr Sharpe and I set out in the coach for Weymouth. Din'd at Piddleton, arriv'd in the evening.

21. Friday. Election of the Mayor. Mr Richard Tucker chose unanimously. We din'd with the Mayor.—Mr Sturt's auction next Monday.

22. Saturday. About ten, left Weymouth, and return'd to dinner.

23. Sunday. Alone.

24. Monday Alone. Went to Mr Bower's.

25. Tuesday. Went to Rushmore.

26. Wednesday. Went to Mr Sturt's. Mr Young[1] came.

27. Thursday. Messrs Breton, Sharpe and I rode to Mr Banks's and return'd to dinner.

28. Friday. Alone.—Mr Young quarrel'd with Mr Wyndham, in the most indecent manner.

29. Saturday. We made it up, and Mr Young went away.—

30. Sunday. Alone.—Excessive rain.

[1] Edward Young, the poet.

OCTOBER

1. Monday. Mr Wyndham went away.

2. Tuesday. Messrs Breton and Sharpe went away.

3. Wednesday. Mrs Dodington and I set out in the post chaise at quarter past five and arriv'd at Hammersmith at quarter past nine in the evening, without any accident. God be prais'd.

4. Thursday. Alone.

5. Friday. Went to town, to see Mr Pelham. He was gone to Cashiobury, returns Monday. Came back, din'd alone.

6. Saturday. Alone.

7. Sunday. Went to Carlton House—Return'd to dinner, at Gunnersbury.

8. Monday. Mr Fox was here and express'd great civilities on account of my behaviour to his nephew, Lord Digby, at Dorchester.

9. Tuesday. Went early to Mr Pelham; talk'd with him about Bridgewater. He gave me the strongest assurance of his assistance; promis'd to write, that night, himself, to Phil: Baker, to convince everybody of his friendship to me; and that the Custom House Officers shou'd be properly taken care of—I am persuaded he is sincere. I return'd to dinner. Lord Chief Baron Bowes, and Mr Carey din'd here.

10. Wednesday. Mr Frankland din'd here.

11. Thursday. Went to Mr Fox's, who was gone to the Duke's.— Din'd alone.

12. Friday. The Minister of Modena was here, to acquaint me, in many words, that if I did not like that Monsieur Venturini, who married a sister of Mrs Dodington, should be sent Minister hither he would employ him somewhere else.—I gave him in writing, to

235

transmit to his Court, that Venturini did not steal his wife.—That they were married in Holland with full consent of her family, that he had never seen her in England, and that I was glad to hear that his Highness was dispos'd to employ him at all: and should rather wish it was in England than elsewhere.—Mr Breton din'd and lay here.

13. Saturday. Mr Breton went away. We din'd alone.

14. Sunday. Din'd at Mr Frankland's.

15. Monday. Mrs Dodington and I went to town: found Sir Francis Dashwood; brought him to dinner, and sent him back to town.

16. Tuesday. Alone.

17. Wednesday. Ladies Yarmouth and Hoare were here. Din'd alone.

18. Thursday. Alone.

19. Friday. I went to Holland House. Din'd here, Lord Bolingbroke, Messrs Furnese, Hoskins and Carey.

20. Saturday. Alone.

21. Sunday. I went to Leicester House. I saw the Lord Chief Baron of Ireland in Pall Mall.—I return'd in the evening.

22. Monday. Coronation Day.—Went to wait on Mr Pelham, who has done all that can be expected hitherto, and promises to continue all his endeavours to support my interest at Bridgewater against Lord Egmont's Opposition. In this he has acted, and I am convinc'd will act, the part of a real friend. But I do not find that he has made any progress in the great point of smoothing my way with the King. I went to Kensington, return'd, and din'd alone.—

23. Tuesday. About twelve, The Princess and Lady Augusta, attended by Lady Middlesex, and Mr Breton only, did Mrs D. and me the honour to come to breakfast with us. After breakfast, we walk'd all round the grounds. We then came in, and they went into all the rooms but the common eating rooms. When we were

coming down stairs, I told Her Royal Highness that there was one room I had forgot to show them; they desir'd to see it, and found a cold collation (for it was near 3 o'clock). The Princess sat down very obligingly, and ate herself and made us all eat a very hearty very cheerful meal. She staid with us, at table, till near 5 o'clock, that the day began to decline.—She behav'd with infinite ease, humanity, and condescension.

24. Wednesday. I went to enquire after the Princess's health. Return'd to dinner; found Messrs Bruce and Brewer here.—

25. Thursday. Mrs D. and I went to town; Din'd at Lady Middlesex's, and return'd.

26. Friday. Alone.

27. Saturday. Mrs D and I came to town. Din'd alone, and lay there. —I went to Drury Lane play-house.—

28. Sunday. Went to wait upon and thank the Princess—very kindly receiv'd. Return'd to La Trappe to dinner alone—The Duke [of Cumberland] dangerously ill of a quinsey.

29. Monday. Alone.—The truth of the Duke's illness was a fall from a horse.

30. Tuesday. ⎫
              ⎬ Alone. The Duke well.
31. Wednesday. ⎭

NOVEMBER

1. Thursday. Alone.

2. Friday. Alone.

3. Saturday. Went to see Mr Ralph, who told me that he had made his peace with the Ministry, by the means of Lord Hartington, to whose favour he was recommended by Mr Garrick: that he was to have £300 per annum and £200 down, to repay to those he was engag'd with the money they had advanc'd him.[1] All which Mr Pelham had told me before; as also that it was against his opinion, but that his brother was uneasy about it and therefore he acquiesc'd.

4. Sunday. Took Physic.—Alone.—

5. Monday. Went to town. Call'd upon Mr Pelham, who was not come to town.—Waited on the Princess who was gone out.—Saw Lady Middlesex—Din'd at Lord Bath's.—Return'd at night.

6. Tuesday. Alone.

7. Wednesday. Saw Mr Pelham.—He told me that Lord Poulet went immediately out of town, from waiting:—That he had no conversation with him but a broken one, while he was waiting to get in to the King. That his Lordship told him he had seen his letter.—That if anybody had told him that he had said that Mr Pelham was for Lord Egmont, he was misinform'd. But that he (Poulet) was (and did not deny it) for Lord Egmont &c.—Mr Pelham replied that it was no matter how he was inform'd, but that at the Mayor's Feast publicly declaring that he (Pelham) was indifferent between the three, when his Lordship knew he had so explicitly declar'd himself in favour of me, and my friends, was very singular; as was his being for Lord Egmont, when he had offer'd, and promis'd both his brother and himself, to do as they desir'd him, which they told him was entirely to assist me, in every thing. —That he was call in to the King before Lord Poulet could make an answer.

[1] i.e. the Bedfords.

238

The King ask'd him about this election, and Lord Poulet's be-haviour: said that he knew he had made up with his son before he died, but did not know whether he did it by me, or Lord Egmont, but that one or the other had a hold upon him. Mr Pelham said that he knew nothing of his own knowledge, but by conjecture he imagin'd it might be by both; that he was oblig'd to be for Lord Egmont as thinking he would speak out more than I would choose to do; but that he believ'd that Lord Poulet's plan was, as far as he could contrive, that the election should fall upon Lord Egmont, and me.—The King said that he thought so too; but that was not enough; and ask'd him how he thought it would go. Pelham said that he did not find by me, that I was dispos'd to give up the interest: but when it came to much expense, and much trouble, which it must do, in the end, he suppos'd, as his Majesty did, that their design was to let me see my own election, and in that case, he could not say how it would go; for then he did not think he had a right, in the light I now stood, to insist on my engaging to go thro' that expense and trouble, to keep out an opposer, when my own election would be easy without it.[1]

I told Mr Pelham that I would be at a word with him; that the fact, and the interest was exactly as the King and he understood it. That as to the interest, my seat did not depend upon it. That I had nobody to come after that I could wish should be the better for it. To this he agreed. I added that when I did things, I never did it by halves. I profess'd attachment to him; that when I had any interest I meant to exert it against those who oppos'd his administration; that therefore I desir'd him humbly to assure his Majesty in my name, that my election was not the object, for that I would undergo the same trouble and the same expense, to keep out anybody that differ'd with his Ministers, as I would, if my own seat were in question, to secure him one that would support him. He promis'd me he would make the kindest use of it.

8. Thursday. The King came to St James's.—We remov'd to Pall Mall. I waited upon the Princess, who receiv'd me with great goodness; complain'd of the little regard had to her recommenda-tion of the late Prince's servants; said she suppos'd the Ministers meant great regard to her; meant it, but had not show'd it yet. I went to *The Old Batchelor*, at Drury Lane; The King there.

---

[1] i.e. D. could get himself returned for Weymouth.

9. Friday. Lord Mayor's Day. I breakfasted with Sir T. Robinson, where all the Foreigners.[1]—Din'd at Guild Hall—Lord Mayor disabled from attending by the gout: Alderman Benn officiated for him.—Nobody there, but the Lord Chancellor, myself, and the Judges.

10. Saturday. King's Birthday.—I din'd at Mr Pelham's.

11. Sunday. Went to Leicester House. Sir Thomas Robinson din'd here.

12. Monday. At the Exchequer Chamber to appoint the Sheriffs. Din'd Alone.

13. Tuesday. Din'd here Lord and Lady Stafford and Miss Beaghan. We went to the opera.

14. Wednesday. Sir Francis Dashwood din'd here.

15. Thursday. The Parliament open'd. I went to hear the Speech, which was very unexceptionable. I went to the House of Lords, where the Duke of Newcastle brought in a Bill to repeal the Act of last Session, in favour of the Jews. Drs Secker and Drummond of Oxford and St. Asaph, spoke for the repeal very well, with sentiments of charity, comprehension and liberty of conscience highly becoming them, and to the honour both of the Church and State.[2] Lords Westmorland and Talbot and Sir Fran: Dashwood.

16. Friday. Took Physic. Din'd here Lord Talbot and Sir Francis Dashwood.

17. Saturday. The Princess sent to me to attend her between 8 and 9 o'clock. Din'd alone. I went to Leicester House expecting a small company, and a little music: but found nobody but Her Royal Highness. She made me draw a stool, and sit by the fire with her.
  Soon after came the Prince of Wales, and Prince Edward; and then the Lady Augusta, all quite undress'd, and took their stools and sat round the fire, with us. We sat talking of familiar occurrences of all kinds, till between 10 and 11, with the ease and unreservedness and unconstraint, as if one had dropp'd into a sister's house that had a family to pass the evening. It was much to be

---

[1] i.e. the diplomatic corps.   [2] irony.

wish'd that the Princes convers'd familiarly with more people of
a certain knowledge of the world. And it seems an indication of a
good heart in the Princess, as if she resolv'd as far as it was in her
power, that the Prince should not forget those who were belov'd
by, and deserv'd well, of his father.

18. Sunday. Went to Leicester House. Din'd here Two Princes
Corsini, Lords of Huntingdon, Lincoln, and Stafford. Lord Stormont, Chevalier Peux, and Messrs Stanley and Glover.

19. Monday. Went to Hammersmith. Return'd to dinner here.

20. Tuesday. Went to the House of Lords. Repeal of the Jews Act
committed. Din'd alone.—Went to Council.

21. Wednesday. Din'd at St James's.

22. Thursday. Alone.

23. Friday. Went to the House. Repeal of the Jew Bill read the
first time. Din'd at the Ladies Poulet. Went to see Mr Gould:
receiv'd but little satisfaction.

24. Saturday. Din'd here Lady Middlesex, Messrs Masham and
Bludworth.

25. Sunday. Messrs Okeden and Glover din'd here.

26. Monday. Went to the House. Din'd alone. At Sir Paul
Methuen's and Lady Middlesex's.

27. Tuesday. Sir Hugh Dalrymple, and Messrs Oswald and Edward
Beaghan din'd here.

28. Wednesday. Din'd alone. At Dr Sharpe's and the Speaker's.

29. Thursday. Went to see the Duke of Newcastle: great assurances
of friendship.—To wait on the Princess.—Extremely obliging—
complains much of the Ministry showing no countenance to the
Prince's servants.—Wish'd they would say they would not; for
she is sure they can.—Din'd alone.

30. Friday. Princess's Birthday. Din'd at Sir George Lee's. All the
Ministers, and Great Courtiers.

DECEMBER

1. Saturday. Din'd alone.

2. Sunday. Din'd alone. Went with Dr Thomson to Lady Middlesex's, &c.

3. Monday. Mr Deverel din'd here. I went to Mr Glover's *Boadicea*: saw three acts;[1] and then went to wait on the Princess of Wales by her command; where I pass'd the evening. We had music: the Albuzi Serrifino, and la Visconti, sung.—Only Lady Middlesex, and myself, except the Prince and the Royal Children. The Princess extremely gracious.

4. Tuesday. Went to the House. A Motion, by Lord Harley, seconded by Sir Francis Dashwood, to repeal as much of the Plantation Act, as related to the Jews.—Division was Ayes—88. Noes—250.—Din'd alone.

5. Wednesday. Went to Mr Pelham's—nothing particular.—Messrs Drax and Pelham din'd here.

6. Thursday. Went to the Duke of Newcastle's: Nothing particular.—Din'd here Mr Venturini and Mrs D's two brothers and three sisters. Lords Burlington and Thanet died this week.

7. Friday. The same company din'd here.

8. Saturday. Din'd at Lord Carlisle's.

9. Sunday. Din'd at Dr Louis da Cusitia's. Went to the Speaker's.

10. Monday. Din'd alone.

11. Tuesday. Saw the Duke of Newcastle. Show'd and convinc'd him that my trouble and expense at Bridgewater was only to keep out a man who oppos'd those to whom I had attach'd myself: That my own seat was not concern'd in it. That the maintaining the interest there was, to me, nothing, having nobody to leave it to.

[1] There were five.

He was perfectly satisfy'd with it. I then told him that in these matters, those that would take money I would pay and not bring him a bill. Those that would not he must pay; and I recommended my two parsons of Bridgewater and Weymouth, Burroughs and Franklin. He enter'd into it very cordially, and assur'd me that they should have the first Crown livings that were vacant in their parts, if we would look out and get him the first intelligence.

I then just touch'd upon what had pass'd between Mr Pelham and I. He profess'd his knowledge and approbation of the whole. I said that I must think, that so much offer'd & so little ask'd in such hands as theirs and at a time where that commodity was particularly marketable could not fail of removing at least resentments, and obtaining pardon, which language I was willing to hold to my own Sovereign, but to no other. He was very hearty, and cordial, and protested that everything should be done to show their true regard and friendship to me. He did seem to lay no great stress upon difficulties with the King. I concluded by telling him, that I had no desires of being in favour with the King, or even well with him, or about him; that all I desir'd was that he and his brother might be able to say, that the King left me to them— that was all my price. He answer'd very cordially—to appearance. Din'd alone.

12. Wednesday. I carried the Princes Corsini to dine with the Earl of Stafford, at Turnham Green. Met the Duke of Norfolk, and Mr Howard his nephew.

13. Thursday. Din'd alone. Went to Council.

14. Friday. Din'd here, Messrs Balch, Mills, Allen, Towgood, and Hill.

15. Saturday. Dr Sharpe din'd here. Went to Lady Middlesex's, and Sir Paul Methuen's.

16. Sunday. Mr Glover din'd here. Went to the Speaker's.

17. Monday. Went to Hammersmith. Return'd to dinner. Mr Carey din'd here.

18. Tuesday. Was to wait on the Princess. Staid with her two hours. Much freedom and condescension. Rather too much of the

first, on my side.—Endeavour'd to explain to her (*by her order*) the present unhappy divisions in Ireland.—Beg'd her to make the Prince thoroughly master of it.—Told her that tho' I did not doubt but that the present heats would, somehow, and in appearance, be allay'd, yet I was sincerely griev'd at the consequences that, from indisposing numbers of a rich and thriving people most cordially attach'd to the Family hitherto, might arise to a new and young reign.—That I did not like the prospect.

She said 'No doubt of it', and with a visible alteration in her countenance to a mixture of fierceness and grief that I had never seen before, added 'We have other very disagreeable prospects'. She very suddenly recover'd her placidness of look and voice. I reply'd, as truth was, 'Indeed, Madam, I do not see any'. What then struck her, I know not, but it was forcibly. Perhaps it might be the Duke. She told me some instances of the Prince's feeling the subjection he was under. (I have since heard that Prince Edward complains of it, and of his brother's want of spirit.) I said it was to be wish'd he could have more company. She seem'd averse to the young people, from the excessive bad education they had, and the bad examples they gave.—She seems uneasy, and indeed her situation is very disagreeable, and much to be pity'd.

19. Wednesday. Mr Masham din'd here.

20. Thursday. Din'd alone. Went to the Duke of Argyll's.

21. Friday. Mr T. Beaghan din'd here. Went to Lady Middlesex's.

22. Saturday. Din'd alone.—

23. Sunday. Din'd at Lord Carlisle's. Went to Sir Paul Methuen's.

24. Monday. Dr Sharpe din'd here.

25. Tuesday. Sunday night, Earl of Home brought the account from Ireland that their Parliament had rejected the Bill for the Appropriation of the Surpluses (alter'd in Council here, by the addition of the King's Consent only) by 5 voices.—Dangerous event! and productive of more mischiefs than I shall live to see remedied.—Din'd alone.—Went to the Speaker's.

26. Wednesday. Went to Hammersmith. Dr Sharpe with us. Mr Bance and Mr Chandler one of the chief Dissenting Ministers, came to us, at dinner.

27. Thursday. Mr Bance went to town, and return'd to dinner.

28. Friday. Messrs Bance, Chandler, and I went to Mr Wilbraham's, in Lincoln's Inn, to consult upon a Chancery suit Mr Bance is engag'd in.—Return'd to dinner.

29. Saturday. Messrs Bance and Chandler went away after break-fast. We came to town to dinner.—Din'd here, Messrs Sharpe, Beaghan and Venturini.

30. Sunday. Din'd alone.

31. Monday. The Princess sent to me to wait on her in the evening. I went about eight. She was, as usual, extremely gracious to me.— The younger children came, about nine, to ask blessing. Soon after, the Princess, the Prince, Prince Edward, Lady Augusta, Lady Middlesex and I set down to cards at a penny a counter, till eleven when I retir'd. Mr Robinson din'd here.

1754

JANUARY

1. Tuesday. Din'd alone. Went to Sir Paul Methuen's, and Lady Middlesex's.

2. Din'd alone. Went to the Duke of Argyll's.

3. Thursday. Din'd here, the Princes Corsini, the Chevalr. Peux, the Earls of Middlesex and Carlisle.

4. Friday. Mr Bodens din'd here.

5. Saturday. Alone.

6. Sunday. Mr Cambridge din'd here. Lady Middlesex came to see me.

7. Monday. Mr Bodens. Mrs D. and I went to Hammersmith, and return'd to dinner.

8. Tuesday. Din'd alone. Went to White's, to a ballot for increasing the old Club; which pass'd in the negative, 34 to 10. Supp'd there.

9. Wednesday. Din'd alone. Went to the Speaker's.

10. Thursday. I din'd with Lord Hobart. Pass'd the evening with the Princess and the Princes, by her command. We had music. Nobody there, but Ladies Howe and Middlesex.

11. Friday. Mr Warburton din'd here. I went to Lady Carlisle's.

12. Saturday. Mrs D. and I went to Hammersmith. Return'd to dinner. Din'd alone.

13. Sunday. Went to Leicester House. Mr Vaughan din'd here. Went to Lady Middlesex's and Mr Furnese's.

14. Monday. Went to the House about a Breach of Privilege against Mr Byers. Lord Dupplin and Mr Dobbs din'd here.—

15. Tuesday. Din'd alone. Went to the Cockpit.

16. Wednesday. Mr Wyndham din'd here. Went to White's, and supp'd there.

17. Thursday. Waited upon the Princess: very kindly receiv'd: a deal of friendly talk about things in general. Din'd here, Ladies Susan and Rebecca and Mrs Poulet, Messrs Harris, Mildmay, and Mrs Mildmay.

18. Friday. Went to Mr Pelham's. Many assurances of friendship. Din'd alone. Went to the Duchess of Leeds, and Lady Middlesex's.

19. Saturday. We made up the Breach of Privilege between Sir William Codrington, and Mr Byers. Din'd here, Sir William Codrington, Messrs Byers, two Beckfords, Martin, Dawkins, Warburton, and Hugh Elwell. Went to Sir Paul Methuen's.

20. Sunday. Din'd alone, went to the Speaker's.

21. Monday. Din'd at Sir Henry Bellendine's.

22. Tuesday. Council about pressing seamen for the E. India Squadron, held in the King's Closet. Din'd alone. Went to a Committee of Council, at the Cockpit.—

23. Wednesday. Mr Beaghan din'd here. Supp'd at White's.— Earl of Huntingdon had a black ball.

24. Thursday. Din'd Alone.—a Sheriff of Middlesex came to see me. Went to White's. Earl of Hillsborough had three black balls. Supp'd and staid there till seven in the morning. Much talk with Lord Barnard: Strong assurances of the friendship, and regard of the Ministers for me. That they would do everything possible with the King—that nobody died to make room, and they could not turn out. Many instances of their pusillanimity, without perceiving it himself: his and their detestation of Mr Fox—G. Grenville's insolence in refusing to come to town—opposing the number of seamen, without the least notice to Mr Pelham. Pitt's

perfidy, and their making up with the Prince. That Barrington would not accept of being chose at Saltash, but would be chose at Plymouth, which was design'd for Admiral Clinton, Lord Lincoln's uncle. That Fox had ask'd Mr Pelham for the first vacancy in Treasury for Barrington, but had been absolutely refus'd. That Dupplin was to have it—and Lord Northumberland the first blue ribband.

25. Friday. Mrs Dodington and I went to Hammersmith. Mr Bodens din'd with us, at our return.

26. Saturday. Din'd alone. Lady Middlesex came to see me in the evening.

27. Sunday. At Leicester House. Din'd at the Spanish Ambassador's. Went to the Speaker's and Sir Paul Methuen's.

28. Monday. Din'd at Sir Richard Lyttelton's.

29. Tuesday. Went to the Duke of Newcastle's. Got the living of Broadworthy for Mr Burroughs. Din'd alone. Went to *Philoclea*, at Covent Garden House.—

30. Wednesday. Dr Sharpe din'd here.

31. Thursday. Council at St James's. Sheriffs appointed. Din'd alone.

FEBRUARY

1. Friday. Went to Hammersmith. Return'd to dinner. Messrs Furnese, Warburton, and Wyndham din'd here.—Went to Lady Barrington's.

2. Saturday. Mr Beaghan din'd here. I went to Lady Murray's.

3. Sunday. I staid at home. Mr Venturini, Mrs J. and Mrs G. Beaghan din'd here.—My great acquaintance poor Mr Hampden, died suddenly.

4. Monday. Din'd here, Sir Francis Dashwood, Messrs Furnese, Thomson, and Carey.

[Five days omitted]

10. Sunday. Din'd at Lord Middlesex's with Lord Cork.

[Three days omitted]

14. Thursday. Waited upon the Princess. She was sitting to Leotardi for her picture: Lady Augusta, only, with her. Din'd with Mr. Ellis. Went to Lady Middlesex's.

15. Friday. Din'd here, Lords Thanet, Hillsborough, Dupplin, Barrington, Sir Henry Bellendine, Messrs Townshend and Fane.

16. Saturday. Din'd at Mr Beckford's. Went to Lord Halifax's.

17. Sunday. Took physick.

18. Monday. Lords Middlesex Cork and Dungannon, Ladies Middlesex and Cork, staid here. Went to the Speaker's.

19. Tuesday. Mr Wyndham din'd here. Went to Lady Berkeley's.

20. Wednesday. Mrs Venturini, Mrs Dodington, Mr Beaghan, and I went to Hammersmith. He din'd here. Went to Mr Bance's.

21. Thursday. Mr Tucker din'd here.

22. Friday. Got Burroughs' livings of the Chancellor. Din'd at Mr Mildmay's. Went to Sir Paul Methuen's, and Lady Middlesex's.

23. Saturday. Went to Hammersmith with Mr Morgan, and brought him home to dinner.

24. Sunday. At Leicester House. Din'd alone.

25. Monday. Din'd at Sir Francis Dashwood's. Went to Lord Talbot's, who was ill.

26. Tuesday. Din'd here, Messrs Drax, Breton, Lisle, and Fremantle. Went to Lord Talbot's.

27. Wednesday. Went to St James's. Din'd alone. Went to Lord Talbot's, who was in bed. Thence to Mr Bance's.

28. Thursday. Council at St James's. The Judges attended. Were call'd in. A charge deliver'd to them, the King present, and in his name, by the Chancellor, to be by them given, on their respective circuits, against irreligion, immorality, murders, poisonings, &c. This was in consequence of a motion in the House of Lords, by the Bishop of Worcester for something to be done by the legislature, to this effect, in consequence of the last paragraph of the King's Speech, at the opening of the Session. Mr Venturini din'd here. Went to Lord Talbot's.

MARCH

1. Friday. Mrs D. and I went to Hammersmith. I return'd to dinner, at Lord Barrington's

2. Saturday. I went to Hammersmith. Return'd to dinner, at Mr Venturini's. Went to Lord Talbot's.

3. Sunday. Mr Rollinson din'd here. Went to Councillor Gould's (who, with Messrs Pratt and Sewell were made Kings Councillors last Thursday) and did not find him. Went to Lady Middlesex's and Sir Paul Methuen's.

4. Monday. Din'd at Sir Francis Dashwood's.

5. Tuesday. Went to Hammersmith with Sir Francis Dashwood, and Mrs D. Din'd alone. Went to the Cockpit.

6. Wednesday. As soon as I rose, receiv'd an account that Mr Pelham died, at six o'clock. Din'd at Lord Strange's. Call'd at White's.

7. Thursday. Messrs Furnese, Wyndham, Tucker, and Beaghan din'd here. I went to Lord Barnard's. Staid till 5 in the morning. Much talk. Agreed that if Mr Fox came into Mr Pelham's place, their interest was entirely undone.—That Fox had declar'd that he would have it; that he had serv'd up to it; and it was his due, and was resolv'd to give way to nobody.—That the Pitts, Lyttel-tons, and Grenfields [Grenvilles] had wrote a letter, that if Mr Fox had it, they would oppose.—That Lord Bath had sent a message to the Chancellor, that if Fox came in, old as he was, he would muster up a party, to oppose.—That he was sure Mr Furnese, I, and my friends, would do so, too.—That Fox was at Lord Harting-ton's between 7 and 8, on Wednesday morning.—That Hartington was for him.—That he thought the Duke of Grafton was so too, who had behav'd most infamously to Mr Pelham, for two years past; and was a most perfidious man.—That Mr Pelham led a most uneasy life—from his brother as well some family affairs.—That when Lord Barnard died, the Duke of Newcastle sent him a letter directed to the Earl of Darlington; and told him he must take it as the only mark then in their power, of their particular regard to

him.—That some time after the Duke propos'd him, and the Lord Chancellor to the King for that honour,—who refus'd both, told him he suppos'd he design'd to leave nobody on the baron's bench; and now that *he had cheated* Lord Barnard out of the settlement of succession to his estate, he wanted to make him amends, by promoting him to be an Earl.—The Duke went to Cambridge, for ten days, but made Mr Pelham give his word that he would not stir in this thing, during his absence.—Somebody acquaints Lady Yarmouth with it, who puts the King in better temper about it.—She bids Mr Pelham move it to the King—He excuses himself, upon his word, given to his brother.—She says they must agree that among themselves, for the King is prepar'd, and expects to hear of it.— Mr Pelham moves it, and it is favourably receiv'd.—The Duke returns and the moment he sees his brother, flies into the most violent passion, that he had told him a lie, broke his word, &c., with such intemperance, that Mr Pelham went away to the Solicitor General, till he cool'd.—Friends interpos'd, but the Duke, another day, flew into the same intemperance to Lord Barnard, and Mr Arundell, before his valet de chambre; that he would fourst[1] his brother, that he would make him know that he should not dare to do any thing, in his absence—&c.—and they did not see one another for a fortnight. This story shows the uneasiness of Mr Pelham's situation in his private life.—

Lord Barnard press'd me much, to suggest who I thought proper to fill Mr Pelham's place. I said, the Solicitor. 'That would not do— he would not take it—the people would not bear it.' I said, 'Then put a Lord at the head, and make a Chancellor of the Exchequer.' '—What Lord?' '—Why not Lord Carlisle?'—The best that he had heard nam'd. Any but Lord Winchelsea; his behaviour had been such to Mr Pelham that he could never sit at a board with him.— That if ever the Duke of Newcastle suffer'd him in any employment, while he had any power, he should look upon him as a very mean creature.—That the Duke of Devonshire was sent for, who went to Chatsworth, last Monday, but he doubted if he would come.— That Mr Pelham was my friend sincerely, had often mention'd me favourably to the King, and when I had executed what I was engag'd in, about the elections, he hop'd to be able to serve me; but wou'd not tell me so, till he was sure he could do it. (This I took for moonshine).

---

[1] Not in O.E.D.

As an instance of Mr Fox's perfidy to Mr Pelham [he] said that he set the King upon him to repeal the Place Bill, which Mr Pelham absolutely refus'd—and now, lately, upon the endeavour to repeal the oath in the Bribery Act, the day it was to be mov'd he was with Mr Pelham at two o'clock, and gave him his word that he would not speak for the repeal; then went to the House, and *did* speak for it. Lord Barnard concludes that he went from Mr Pelham to the Duke [of Cumberland], who commanded him to speak; and the rather, because being at the House himself, he saw Lord Sandwich in the gallery, and observ'd that as soon as Fox had spoke, that Lord went away.

I said he (Sandwich) was a most dishonest man; that the Duke of Newcastle was, at first, in raptures of fondness for him, and when he grew angry with him, Mr Arundell told him, 'twas his own fault, he had nothing to complain of: when he knew that he betray'd Chesterfield to him, what reason had he to think or be surpris'd that he should betray him to the Duke.

8. Friday. Din'd at Mr Grenfield's.—Went to White's.

9. Saturday. Went to wait on the Princess. We began by laughing, about the plays. I then told her that as I did not design to trouble her long, my message should be short: and it only was to put her in mind and desire her to remember, that at this time of changes, and all others that might happen, my first engagements were to her, and her House, to which, when she let me know her pleasure, all others were to give place, and should be subservient. She receiv'd it most kindly, and said she was thoroughly convinc'd of it: that no changes that could happen, ought or should make her and hers forget my friendship and attachment to them.

'And now, Madam,' says I, 'if your Royal Highness pleases, we will return to the play.' But she could not quit the subject.—Ask'd what I thought they would do: I said I had not seen anybody that could be suppos'd to have any direction; that I did not, in the least desire to be inform'd by Her Royal Highness but that to be sure she must have some lights about it. She said she had none. I said, that was a fault, and that she ought to have them.—That the Ministry of late years, had been like children round a fire, telling stories of spirits, till they frighten'd one another that they dar'd not look behind them.—That it was become necessary that she should give them courage.—That the people were very solicitous to see something that look'd, as if she had a share in it, and that her security was consider'd.—That I would not mention what was said, because particular names were mention'd, unfavourably.

She reply'd, 'What could she do? To get things in the hands of certain people, was as impossible as to move St James's House, and for anything else, what did it signify?' Besides, she suppos'd they knew where Leicester House stood: it was open. I said that means should be found to direct them; for what had happen'd to Mr Pelham would, sooner or later, and in less time, happen elsewhere. She said, 'Alors, comme alors.' I reply'd that she would be pleas'd to consider that she would have these and only these hands to work with, there, if she continued as she was; and it might create some difficulty to begin with those where there was so little correspondence, or connection. She said it was not an agreable prospect, she hop'd the King would do what was best; but she thought it would be Mr Fox, and she was very sorry for it. This great dislike of Mr Fox coming in, she repeated several times, in the rest of the conversation.

10. Sunday. Sir Francis Dashwood and Mr Glover din'd here.

11. Monday. Din'd at Lord Hillsborough's.

12. Tuesday. Din'd here, Mr Breton. Went to the play. I had good intelligence that the Princess took what I said to her very kindly and express'd herself very favourably of me.

13. Wednesday. Mr Beaghan din'd here. I went to the Duke of Argyll's.

14. Thursday. Din'd at Mr Stanley's. And here I must take notice of the extraordinary scenes that have pass'd since the death of Mr Pelham.

He died about six on Wednesday the 6th. Mr Fox was at the Marquess of Hartington's before 8 that morning. Negotiations began. The Duke of Devonshire was sent for the same day. He came on Saturday night the 9th. I was inform'd that as Mr Fox was supported by the Duke, and Princess Emily, to succeed Mr Pelham, &c., the plan to disappoint him was, to refuse the Treasury, but to offer him something that was better than the War Office; which they hop'd, and believ'd he would refuse; and then to incense the King against him, and show him, that Fox would take nothing that was compatible with the Duke of Newcastle remaining in power.—This I was told, but could not figure to myself what that Something was to be.—

On Monday the 11th at night, by the intervention of Lord Hartington, between the Duke of Newcastle and Fox, the King agreed that the Duke of Newcastle should be at the head of the Treasury, Mr Legge, Chancellor of the Excheqer and Mr Fox, Secretary of State. I knew it, soon, the next morning, and finding *that* was the Something, thought it a Something that must ruin the Duke of Newcastle.

Tuesday night, this was declar'd to the Cabinet Council.— Wednesday night the 13th. Mr Fox had a meeting with the Duke of Newcastle when, as it afterwards appear'd, they differ'd about the powers that he was to be trusted with in his office.—For he understood, by Lord Hartington, he was to have the direction of the House of Commons—had acquainted me, that morning, by Mr Ellis, a Lord of the Admiralty, that he was to have the absolute direction of that House, but under the Duke of Newcastle and as his man, who was to remain in full power: with the whole confidence, and secret of the King. But finding, at this conference with the Duke of Newcastle, that either this was not meant; or that he was not to be trusted with sufficient powers to execute it properly, they parted dissatisfy'd; and the next morning, Thursday the 14th, he wrote to the Duke to be excus'd from accepting the seals of Secretary.

This news I met with at dinner, much surpris'd at it, as was the whole town. One side says he us'd, and wrote the most abject submissions, to get the seals. He says, that he only offer'd, as he really meant, to serve absolutely under the Duke of Newcastle and only requir'd sufficient powers to be able to do it, in the House, without exposing himself. I went to Mr Furnese's, and then home.

15. Friday. Mr Ellis came to me, with the avowal of Mr Fox to give me the material part of this account, adding that as a proof of what Mr Fox meant, he instanc'd Mr Craggs being Lord Sunderland's man, when he had the Treasury,[1] and was in full power, with the late King. And also that he had declar'd to the Duke of

[1] Craggs was Secretary of State (as it was suggested Fox should be) and led the Commons for Sunderland.

Newcastle that he never desir'd to touch a penny of the Secret
Service Money, or know the disposition of it, farther than as it was
necessary to enable him to speak to the Members without appearing
ridiculous. He ended with strong assurances of Mr Fox's regard
and friendship to me, and desires to have mine in return: this very
strong. I din'd with the Duke of Argyll at Mr Vaughan's.

16. Saturday. Was to see the Duke of Newcastle. Much company—
no opportunity to talk with him. This day came out a new commission of Treasury, such as I never saw. The Duke of Newcastle
in his brother's place, and the four former Commissioners none of
them Chancellor of the Exchequer. That remaining with Lord Chief
Justice Lee.[1]

17. Sunday. Din'd alone and did not go out.

18. Monday. Din'd here, the Earls of Coventry, Jersey, Temple,
and Hillsborough, Lords Strange, Hobart, and Barrington; Sir
Francis Dashwood, and Mr George Greenville. The talk was that
Sir Thomas Robinson was to be Secretary of State, and had refus'd
it—this was not believ'd. Lord Barrington staid after the company
and told me his transactions with Mr Pelham, relating to the
Treasury, and, last Thursday, with the Duke of Newcastle. He
states his promises from Mr Pelham too strong, if what Lord
Barnard told me be true—and by his conversation with the Duke
of Newcastle I think he will not have it this time; at least, not
before Lord Dupplin.

19. Tuesday. I was to wait upon the Duke of Newcastle, who with
great *seeming* kindness beg'd me to come to him, on Thursday, by
nine in the morning; that he was sensible of my friendship, and
would endeavour to deserve it. I said he certainly did deserve it,
but I hoped he would show the world that I had his. He replied,
that he would use all his endeavours. I din'd at Sir Francis Dashwood's.

20. Wednesday. Din'd alone.

21. Thursday. Went to the Duke of Newcastle's. Began by telling

[1] H. B. Legge was in fact appointed Chancellor of the Exchequer in April: a piece
of finesse.

him that I consider'd, and respected the weight he must lie under, of different kinds at this time; therefore should never trouble him, but when it was absolutely necessary, and never long.—That I was come, to assure him of my most dutiful affection, and sincere attachment to him, simply, having no engagements to make me look to the right or the left—also, to repeat my readiness to comply with the engagements I had taken with his brother which I understood to be with him, and I suppos'd he would continue to approve. But that what had happen'd made it necessary to recapitulate them, though he knew them.—That the engagements on my side were: to give him all the little interest I had, toward the electing the new Parliament—I did it in the county of Dorset, as far as they pleas'd to push it—I engag'd also specifically, to chuse two members for Weymouth, which he desir'd might be a son of the Duke of Devonshire, and Mr Ellis of the Admiralty—I suppos'd he would confirm that nomination: but that was nothing to me: I was to chuse two of his nomination, which, now, was fallen to him, so he might name whom he pleas'd.—That I was also engag'd to exclude Lord Egmont from Bridgewater if I could, of which I would give him a farther account when I knew his pleasure upon this first part; because there might be mention made of that transaction in the Closet, and there were some particularities attending it, that 'twas probable he might not be acquainted with.

He assur'd me of his friendship and affection, in a solemn and dejected manner; knew his brother was sincere to me; knew all our engagements and look'd on himself as party to them; would do everything in his power to comply with them, and agreed to his nomination of Lord G. Cavendish and Ellis, and hop'd they would be agreable to me.

I proceeded to the article of Bridgewater which I said was thus: Long after my mutual engagements with Mr Pelham, when Lord Egmont made that unfriendly attempt, Mr Pelham ask'd me what would become of it. I said, that it need not affect my election, though it might destroy the Whig interest there, for ever; that the interest was very indifferent to me, for I did not expect to live to see another Parliament and had neither succession, relation, or friend, that I could, or wish'd to leave it to; but I ask'd him if it was indifferent to him, that Lord Egmont should come in there. He said, 'No, to be sure'; and hinted, besides his public opposition, great distaste to him, personally, as if something very dishonourable had pass'd between them: I avoided entering into that, and said that as he thought him his enemy, I thought myself oblig'd to oppose him, where I had any interest; that I was sorry it came so home to me, but that I design'd to do it. Some time after that, he told me that the King ask'd him if I design'd seriously to endeavour to keep Lord Egmont out of Bridgewater, having been told that it would be a matter of some trouble, and expence. Mr Pelham replied that he could not speak to his Majesty with any authority, but he thought I would: that I desir'd him, when next those matters came to be discuss'd, to lay me at the King's feet, and tell him that as I found it would be agreable to his Majesty I would spare no pains nor expence to exclude him: that thus it became my engagement to do it, if I can. That these were the engagements on my side with his brother. He saw I had not diminish'd them, and I was fully determin'd to perform them, let what would fall out on the other side.

He was very serious, and dejected, during the whole conversation, and threw in several warm expressions of approbation, and then said that he was loaded with too many things, at once, for one man to bear: that he had seen, and his brother had told him, how handsome my proceeding has been: that this was the most noble that could be imagin'd: that he had transactions with many, but none like this, and beg'd me to say what his brother had engag'd to do, and to tell him all that had pass'd, and how I understood it.

I said I must be excus'd—I cou'd not talk about advantages to myself that were to take their rise from my own assertion, only, when there was nobody to contradict me: I was afraid he would have enough of that, from others. It was sufficient that he was satisfy'd and that I had not whittled down the obligations that I was to perform. He press'd me still more strongly; till I told him that I would not talk of it at all, without reminding him, that I was absolutely determin'd to fulfil all the engagements I had taken, and repeated to him, without any regard to what might be done on the other side.—That it was the last transaction of my life, and therefore should suffer no ambiguity; they were too far gone to admit of any alteration, let what would happen to me. I could not refine them away; I thought myself bound by them, and would at all events, perform them; that my proceeding must be as open and clear to the memory of his brother with him, as they would have been with his brother if we had had the misfortune to lose his Grace. That even upon this footing, I had very little to say; for

I was sure he must know that his brother was to remove the personal misrepresentations that I lay under with the King, at a proper time, and to bring me into the service, in a proper manner.— That I never thought of fixing him down to a particular day, or a particular office, because, indeed, I meant more, I meant to come in, so as to live with them as an humble friend, under their friendship and protection.

He said very seriously, and warmly, that he would never assert anything as done, that he was not sure was done; but as to the King's dislike, we might waive that—it was impossible but that must give way; it could not withstand such a behaviour as mine; we might put it out of question: with two or three strong expressions more, to that purpose. He then ask'd me if his brother had engag'd to bring me in before the elections were over. I said, he had made me no such promise, that I never barter'd with him so as to pin him down to a day, or an hour, my views being to obtain their friendship &c as I had before explain'd to him. He said he always understood it so, and ask'd me, as there would be many changes, and they were oblig'd to cut the cloth into as many pieces as they could, if I thought I could come in, before the election. I said I did think I could. He said, he knew I might be trusted, and would talk very freely to me, and tell me how things stood, since I said I thought I could come in now: that the Secretary's office was settled, and that he had four positive engagements which were to Lords Hillsborough, Dupplin, Barrington and Mr Nugent[1]—but that he had not, and would not, promise any one of them, till it was done and settled with the King.

He then expatiated on the King's kindness to him, which, however, he imputed great part of, to the exigencies of the times: that his Majesty had advis'd him not to promise, and that he replied, that he should take care not to have himself quoted against himself. I said I understood the Secretary's office was design'd for Sir Thomas Robinson.—He said yes, and that for the business of the Northern Province (N.B. He is to have the Southern Province[2]) no man in England understood it better; that he was not happy at explaining himself, but no man knew more, or had better understanding. I said I knew him very well, he was a worthy man

[1] Hillsborough became Comptroller of the Household and Nugent a Lord of the Treasury soon afterwards. The other two had to wait for office until November 1755.
[2] D was correctly informed. The appointment was made two days later.

and I lov'd him. I said 'What if I came into the place he left?' [Commissioner of Trade] He consider'd a little, and said, 'Very well, pray, go on.' I said I would particularly support him in the House, where he would chiefly want it. He said he knew I would. I said, 'There is my old place, Treasurer of the Navy, that must be vacant: I should like that, better than anything—but', I added, 'why should I enter into these things; I leave it wholly with your Grace.'[1]

He said that by a strange fatality the direction of the House of Commons was fallen upon him, who had never thought of it; and he must expect that the great attempt would be, to show that he could not do it. Therefore he could not chuse by affection, but must comply with those who could support him there. I said I understood so and that I thought I might pretend to some abilities, that way; that in the Opposition, I was thought of some use there; that in Court, indeed, I never undertook much because he knew I never was supported; but now that I should be supported, I hop'd I might pretend to be as useful there, as my neighbours. He said that it was incontestably so. I said, that I would derogate from nobody, but considering the superiority of age, the offices I had gone thro', and my rank in the world; and adding to that, chusing six Members for them, at my own very great expence, without costing them one shilling, I thought the world in general, and even the gentlemen themselves, could not expect that their pretensions should give me the exclusion. He said, that what I did, was very great, that he often thought with surprise, at the ease and cheapness of the election at Weymouth. That they had nothing like it. I said I believ'd there were few that could give his Majesty 6 Members for nothing. He said he reckon'd 5, and had put down 5 to my account. I said it was so: but this attempt of Lord Egmont's made it six. He would observe I did not pretend to chuse two for Bridgewater; but by Lord Egmont's opposition, the two Members must be entirely owing to me; for if I did not exert my whole force to exclude him, he must come in, and the Court could have but one there. He thank'd me, said it was most clear, now it was explain'd, but he had not consider'd it in that light.

I said I must be excus'd from talking, any more, about myself; that I left it entirely to him, and to the King; that I was fully

---

[1] It was held by Legge. D. must have known of Legge's intended move to the Treasury.

determin'd to make this sacrifice to his Majesty, let him use me as he pleas'd; that I would keep out of the way of a personal affront; that I knew I had given no just cause of offence, but that I would not justify with his Majesty; that it was enough that he was dis-displeas'd, to make me think that I was in the wrong, and to beg him to forget it: I would not even be in the right against him, and I was very sure I would never, again, be in the wrong, against him, for which I hop'd his Grace would be my caution. He said, he would, with all his heart.—He took me in his arms, and kiss'd me twice, with strong assurances of affection and service. I told him I would go to Mr Ellis, and acquaint him. He desir'd I would, and from him, and tell him that he agreed to his brothers nomina-tion, but not to say anything, by way of compliment.

N.B. When I came in, the Duke had a quire of paper before him, upon which, at the top, I saw my name. He took notes of all that pass'd. Call'd in Roberts, show'd him the paper; told him he must write it fair, the notes in one column, for his use, the other, blank, to take the King's pleasure.

22. Friday. Din'd at Sir Richard Lyttelton's.

23. Saturday. The Duke of Newcastle resign'd the seals, and Sir Thomas Robinson receiv'd them.

24. Sunday. Those gentlemen kiss'd the Princess's hand. Mr Breton din'd here.

25. Monday. Din'd at Lord Talbot's.—Went to Sir Paul Methuen's.

26. Tuesday. Din'd at Lord Coventry's.

27. Wednesday. Din'd at Lord Barrington's, and found that not-withstanding all the fine conversation of last Thursday, all the employments are given away.

28. Thursday. Din'd at Lord Jersey's. Went to Mr Bance's, who was not well.

29. Friday. Din'd at Lord Hobart's.

30. Saturday. Mrs D. and I went to Hammersmith. Return'd to dinner alone.

31. Sunday. Lord Barnard kiss'd hands at Leicester House, as Earl of Darlington, Mr Charles Townshend for the Admiralty, Lord Chancellor was made Earl of Hardwicke.—Din'd here, Lords Bolingbroke, Strange, Hobart, Stormont, and Barrington, Comte Poniatowski, Messrs Stanley, and Cambridge.

APRIL

1. Monday. Mr Breton din'd here. Waited on the Princess in the evening, by her order. Music. Lady Falconberg and Mr Breton there only, except the royal children, and servants. Sir George Lyttelton as Cofferer, and Mr George Grenville as Treasurer of the Navy, kiss'd the King's hand.

2. Tuesday. Din'd alone. Went to the Cockpit. Short talk with the Solicitor who is extremely hurt, dejected, and dissatisfy'd with the proceedings.

3. Wednesday. Dr. Sharpe din'd here.

4. Thursday. Went to the House of Lords. Earls of Darlington and Hardwicke introduc'd. Mr Breton din'd here. Went to Sir Paul Methuen's, and Lady Middlesex's.

5. Friday. Dr Sharpe and Mr Breton din'd here. After dinner, Mrs D., the Doctor and I set out for, and lay at, Hammersmith.[1]

6. Saturday. Lord Strange came to breakfast: din'd alone.—

7. Sunday. Morning, at 5, Dr Sharpe, and I set out in my post chaise, and arriv'd at Basingstoke, before 11, where we took my coach, which carried us to lie at Salisbury.

8. Monday. Breakfasted at Salisbury and got to Eastbury, about 12 without any ill accident—God be prais'd.

9. Tuesday. Mr Gresly din'd here. Sent for to Bridgewater.

10. Wednesday. Alone.

11. Thursday. Dr Sharpe and I set out at 4 o'clock, in a post chaise; chang'd horses at Stalbridge, and went to Ansford Inn; took my coach, din'd at Piper's Inn, and got to Bridgewater in good time. Found as I expected, things very disagreably fram'd.

---

[1] Before leaving D, who had received a soothing note from Newcastle (not preserved), briefly acknowledged it and promised to wait on him after his election trip to Bridgwater (Add. MS. 32735, f. 46).

12. Good Friday.—Lord Egmont came with trumpets, noise, &c.

13. Saturday. He, and we walk'd the town: we found nothing unexpected, as far as we went.

14. Sunday. ⎫
15. Monday. ⎬ Spent in the infamous and disagreable compliance with the low habits of venal wretches.
16. Tuesday. ⎭

17. Wednesday. Came on the election, which I lost, by the injustice of the Returning Officer. The numbers were, for Lord Egmont, 119, for Mr Balch 114, for me 105.—Of my good votes, 15 were rejected: 8 bad ones for Lord Egmont were receiv'd.

18. Thursday. Left Bridgewater—for ever: got to Eastbury, in the evening.—

PART THREE

UNFORMED OPPOSITION

APRIL 1754 TO DECEMBER 1756

1754

APRIL

19. Friday. Din'd here Messrs Tucker, Arbuthnot whom we found here, and Mr Burroughs, whom we brought with us.

20. Saturday. Captain Arbuthnot went away. Mr Allen came in the morning, and Mr Towgood, in the afternoon.

21. Sunday. Mr Tucker went away.

22. Monday. Mr Towgood went away. Mr Gresly din'd here.

23. Tuesday. Mr Fleet din'd here.

24. Wednesday. Dr Sharpe, and I set out from Eastbury, in the Coach, about 5, and were at Stockbridge, before half an hour after 9; there we took a post chaise, and arriv'd, safe, at Hammersmith, by God's goodness, by half an hour after 6.

25. Thursday. Mr Breton din'd, and lay here.

26. Friday. Mr Breton went away. I went to the Duke of New-castle's. Receiv'd with much seeming affection.—Thanks for Wey-mouth, where I had succeeded, sorrow for Bridgewater, where I had not.—I told him that I would give him a detail of that whole transaction, in as clear, and short a manner as was possible, if he was, then, at leisure to receive it: but if not, and he thought it worth mentioning to the King, I would only give him the heads of it and he might say that I was to acquaint him with the proofs of those heads, at a meeting which he had appointed on purpose.

Accordingly I began by telling him that I had done all that was in the power of money, and labour, and show'd him two bills for money remitted thither, before I went down, one of £1000, one of £500, besides all the money then in my steward's hands; so that the election would cost me about £2500.—In the next place,—If the election stood, the borough was for ever, in Tory hands.—That all this was occasion'd by want of proper support from the court, and from the behaviour of the servants of Crown.—Upon Mr Pelham's death, seeing the multitude of promotions in which no notice was taken of me, and Lord Poulet acting openly against me, with all his might, seeing no check given to him, or encouragement to me, they so strongly concluded the Government to be indifferent, that five of the Customhouse Officers voted single votes for Lord Egmont.—The next head was—that in spite of all, I had a fair majority of legal votes, for that the Mayor admitted 13 bad votes for Lord Egmont and refus'd 12 good ones, for me: so that it was entirely in their own hands, to retrieve the borough, and get rid of a troublesome opponent, if they pleas'd.—That if the King requir'd this piece of service, it was to be done, and the borough put into Whig hands, and under his influence, without any stretch of power; for the cause was so clear, and indisputable, that instead of wanting their power to support it, nothing but their power could withstand it.—That if it was expected, I would lend my name, and my assistance here, and into the country, to rescue the borough, and deliver it into such hands as the King shou'd approve of; but that I, myself, would have nothing more to do with it. I had fulfil'd to the utmost the sacrifice of duty which I had promis'd, and propos'd to myself: I desir'd no retrieval, or acquisition of interest, and would absolutely be no farther concern'd, than as the canal to convey that borough into his Majesty's disposition.

He reply'd that they understood the borough to be lost; and also that it was entirely a party affair:—That Lord Shaftesbury had confirm'd him in it, and assur'd him that the violence of the Tories against me, was much inflam'd, by the assistance I gave, and offer'd to give to Lord Digby, last summer, in his appearance for the County of Dorset.—That they knew Mr Balch neither would, nor could support Bridgewater.—That nobody had acted like me, or consider'd the King and his service, in what I had done and now offer'd to do, so nobly, and disinterestedly, &c.

I said that what I had done was in consequence of what I had before declar'd to him *viz*: to show my duty to the King, and my earnest desires to pass the rest of my life, in his Grace's friendship, and protection; that I had back'd my fancy, and left the rest to him.—He made great professions of good wishes, good will, best

endeavours, &c. which weigh with me, as much as the breath
they were made of.—Return'd to dinner.

27. Saturday. Alone.

28. Sunday. Went to Kensington, and Leicester House. Din'd alone.

29. Monday. Alone.

30. Tuesday. Alone.

MAY

1. Wednesday. Mr Beaghan came.

2. Thursday. I carried him to town; and went to Mr Cooke's, on his election for Middlesex.—Din'd at Mr Furnese's, and return'd.— Found Mr Breton here.

3. Friday. Comte Poniatowski din'd here.

4. Saturday. Messrs Masham, Wyndham and Dashwood din'd here.

5. Sunday. Mr Stanley din'd here.

6. Monday. Went to town. Din'd at Sir Francis Dashwood's. Return'd.

7. Tuesday. Alone.

8. Wednesday. Din'd alone. Mr Lee came, at night, and lay here. [Wrote to] Mann and Cardinal Albani.—

9. Thursday. Went to town. Din'd at Mr Furnese's.

10. Friday. Din'd at Mr Stanley's.

11. Saturday. Din'd here, Lord Bolingbroke, Messrs St John, and Furnese, and Sir Francis Dashwood.

12. Sunday. Went to Leicester House. Din'd at Lord Middlesex's. Return'd.

13. Monday. Din'd here, Lord Talbot, and Sir Francis Dashwood. Princess went to Kew.

14. Tuesday. I rode to Kew to enquire after the Princess's health.— Din'd here Lord Carlisle, Sir George Lee, Sir William Irby, Messrs Fane, Breton (who lay here), and Bance.

15. Wednesday. We din'd alone.

16. Thursday. Comte Poniatowski and his friend din'd here.

17. Friday. Mr Breton went. Mr Bance call'd.—Din'd alone.

18. Saturday. Went to see the Speaker. Din'd here, Sir Everard Fawkner, M Parisot, and Dr Lidderdale.

19. Sunday.—Din'd alone.

20. Monday. Din'd alone. The Master of the Rolls died, yesterday.—

21. Tuesday. Went to town. Din'd at the St Albans.

22. Wednesday. Lord and Lady Cork breakfasted, and Mr Wyndham din'd here.

23. Thursday. Din'd alone.

24. Friday. Mr Venturini, Mr P. and Mr J. Beaghan din'd here.

25. Saturday. Din'd alone.

26. Sunday. Went to Gunnersbury. Din'd alone.

27. Monday. Din'd at Sir Francis Dashwood's.

28. Tuesday. Mr Breton came to dinner, and lay here. I receiv'd the Princess's commands to wait on her, at Kew, the next day.

29. Wednesday. Went to Kew, before 11. The Princess walk'd with me, till two. Much conversation about the Prince.—Wish'd he saw more company—but whom of the young people were fit? Wish'd he had acquaintance older than himself: durst not recommend for fear of offence: while he had governors &c., was under immediate inspection, all that they did not direct, would be imputed to her.—In a year or two, he must be thought to have a will of his own, and then he would, she hop'd, act accordingly.

Express'd great slight, and disregard for those in office, and her usual dislike for the King. We talk'd of his accumulation of treasure, which she reckon'd at £4,000,000: I told her, that what was become of it, how employ'd, where, and what was left I did not pretend to guess: but that I computed the accumulation to be from £12 to £15,000,000. That these things, within a moderate degree, perhaps less than a fourth part, could be prov'd, beyond all possibility of denial; and when the case should exist, would be publish'd in controversial pamphlets if troublesome times should arise, which I hop'd in God, would never happen.

She was very kind, and gracious to me. After dinner, Lord Bathurst, and Lord Moreton (who, with his son, and daughter she saw upon the road, and ask'd to step in) walk'd with us; they staid but little, and left us with her, Lady Augusta, and the two Princes. We convers'd till near eleven, when I return'd.

Mr Breton went to town in the morning. I found a letter from Mr Balch, acquainting me that he had brought Mr Burroughs with him, to lay the Bridgewater affair before the Ministry.

30. Thursday. We went to town, before dinner. Messrs Balch, and Burroughs din'd with us. I told them, that having laid the whole affair before the Duke of Newcastle, upon my arrival, and he having assur'd me that he would appoint a time to go thro' and settle it, which he had neglected to do, I would not go to him; but advis'd them to wait upon him; and that I thought the best way would be that Mr Balch should write a note to acquaint his Grace that he had brought Mr Burroughs with him, who in conjunction with himself, was best able to give him an account of the injustice the whole party labour'd under, who thought themselves well entitled to his Grace's protection, in obtaining that justice, which they were determin'd to prosecute. Therefore desir'd to know when they might wait on him, to lay that whole transaction before him.— Went to Sir Francis Dashwood, who return'd, ill, from Oxford.—

31. Friday. Parliament open'd: by Commission.—Mr Onslow propos'd for Speaker, by the Marquess of Granby, and Mr Thomas Pelham. I went without doors—very full House.—Mr Burroughs din'd with us.

JUNE

1. Saturday. Saw the Duke of Dorset. In the House. Messrs Balch and Burroughs din'd in Pall Mall. Mr Balch resolv'd to write the note I advis'd (of which I gave him a draught) and send it, that night. We return'd to Hammersmith.

2. Sunday. Din'd here Messrs, Mrs and Miss Mildmay.

3. Monday. Went to the Duke of Dorset's and acquainted him with my situation with the Ministry. Went to the House.—Mr West desir'd to speak with me.—Said that Mr Balch had wrote to the Duke of Newcastle (which letter he show'd me) who had appointed to see him on Thursday; but desir'd to see me, first. I told him that I would go to him, tomorrow. Return'd to dinner.

4. Tuesday. Went, early, to the D. of Newcastle's. He told me that he had receiv'd a letter from Mr Balch, but desir'd to advise with me, before he saw him.—That nothing was settled, or he should have sent to me, long before.—That he was against multiplying petitions, for reasons obvious to me.—That he knew nothing of Lord Egmont, but had heard that he at times talk'd as if he was willing to battle it: that if it should be made a point, he did not know if we were certain of carrying it; that Lord Egmont would make a party; that possibly, the Princess might wish he should be let alone, or at least, that those of the late Prince's Servants might be for him.

I said that I had laid this affair fully, before him, already; that he knew I push'd it, in the country, with such an expense, and trouble, so absolutely as a service which the King (as his brother told me) wish'd: that it had cost me £3,400. That I was fairly chosen, nor would the Returning Officer have dar'd not to return me, had he not been encourag'd by the servants of the Administration: that the borough was lost; and lost, solely by a Lord of the Bed Chamber,[1] and the Custom House Officers. That they might retrieve it, or not, just as they pleas'd; leave it in Tory hands, or recover it; get rid of Lord Egmont as an opponent, or keep him in, as a friend. I should neither be satisfy'd or dissatisfy'd with it; I should not be oblig'd

[1] It is not clear who is referred to here. Possibly the Earl of Lincoln.

by the one, nor disoblig'd by the other: I dealt clearly with him, and desir'd to be understood, without any ambiguity: I had told him this, before, and my opinion and resolution was the same.

He said he acknowledg'd it, and desir'd me to advise what was to be done. I told him I could not advise, because I did not know the truth of my own situation; it was time to come to a full explanation upon that head, for it must come to a decision: that I had done all the services in my power; and spent very great sums, of all which, they, now, had the benefit: that I had made no bartering bargains, but done it frankly, with a plain, avow'd and accepted intention to take off the edge of the King's ill grounded resentment, and prove my attachment to his Grace; to show myself his immediate friend. . . .

[Some lines are here torn from the manuscript, leaving only the words 'at the same time he was surly when a' suggesting that Newcastle's rejoinder was on the lines that the King was usually tractable, but surly when aroused.]

I reply'd, it must come to a conclusion, one way or another. If after accepting both offer and execution of all I could do, I was to remain under an absolute proscription, and exclusion from all favour, that every other subject of any rank might justly expect, I must do as I could, but it must be explain'd, and fully.

He said, he, himself, lik'd to deal explicitly and to understand clearly, what was expected: that he had laid my services before the King in the best manner he could, tho' some people (of which he would inform me afterwards) had endeavour'd to insinuate to His Majesty that I had not the power I pretended at Weymouth. I ask'd him, if he himself did not tell me in that room that he had declar'd to the King that the borough was redeliver'd into my hands, on the express condition to take his election of two, for *that time only*?[1]

[Corresponding lacuna in manuscript. The following words belong to the Duke]

. . . would do it in the best manner he was able. That it had been insinuated, and he had not said expressly, that he would; but had not said he would not. That if I had any view upon any particular

---

[1] This was, indeed, the understanding with Pelham, but there is no record of it in the interview with Newcastle (21 Mar. 1754 above).

thing, or office, he would move it, and try to get it in the most cordial manner.

I said, as to going to the King, I would postpone that consideration for a minute: that as to the last, he well knew I never thought of making bargains, that I left that matter totally to him.—He said that there were few things that a man of my rank could accept, and that none of them were vacant.

I said it was true, but I did not impute that to him. That as he was at the head of the Treasury, I should choose a seat there, if it was vacant, sooner than anything; but I could not take that: at the same time he would observe that I did not expect to be Privy Seal if Lord Gower should die; that I did not come to make bargains for this, or that thing or time. He had forc'd me, before I went into the West, [to say] that Sir Thomas Robinson's office, or my own again[1] (both which were then vacant) I should like very well: he gave them away, without considering me. I desir'd nobody to be removed, much less to die: he must think that £2,000 per annum would not make my fortune with one foot in the grave: that as to rank, I had heard that the King was odd about titles: that I had as much respect for the peerage as any man; but he could not but see, that in my situation, without succession, or collateral, a peerage to me was not worth the expense of new painting my coach.—That I desir'd to pass my life as his attach'd friend and servant persuaded that he would, as such, do me favourable justice, the first opportunity that offer'd.

He said that he understood me very well: that I would have no competitor in the House of Commons; I expected then any of the employments that I could take which should first fall; and added 'I suppose you will be disoblig'd, if you have not the very first that falls'.

I demurr'd a little at the oddness, and bluntness of the proposition, and did not well conceive the intention of it, but after a little pause said, 'That is a hard word, my Lord, I do not say say absolutely, That. There may possibly be reasons that my real friendship for you might make me acquiesce in: I will not say so hard a word, at once, the case will speak itself; but it must come to a positive issue. And now, my Lord, I must resume the offer your Grace made of going immediately to the King to demand a categorical answer whither he be determin'd, after all I have done,

[1] Secretary of State or Treasurer of the Navy.

275

and spent for his service, (of which he now reaps the whole utility) to suffer no return to be made me, when opportunity throws it in the way, but to exclude me from all the advantages I am intitled to, in common with the rest of his subjects, by my rank, tho' with much less services: as to his resolution, it must be known, but as you profess your sincere desire that I should be properly consider'd, it lies upon you to do it in the best manner, and at the properest time: I do not prescribe tomorrow or next day, this week or the next, but as this is the only obstacle, it must be known, absolutely, and in a reasonable time: if I am proscrib'd from amongst all my fellow subjects I must and shall submit to the King's pleasure with all possible respect: but as your Grace has re-assur'd me that you have represented what I have done, fairly and favourably to him, till I know it from your Grace, I cannot believe that so just, and generous a Prince would accept a poor subject's offers of service, and suffer him to carry them into execution at so great an expence, with a resolution absolutely to exclude him from all sorts of common favour. I thought it would be what never happen'd before, or to me only.'

He said he would do everything in his power; and did not imagine it could end so. I told him that I heartily wish'd it might not, but it must end one way, or another, it must not remain as it was; for I was determin'd to make some sort of figure in life. I earnestly wish'd it might be under his protection, but if that could not be, I must make some figure, what it would be, I could not determine, yet: I must look around me, a little, and consult my friends; but some figure I was resolv'd to make.

He said he would do his best to settle it to my satisfaction; he could not think it could end in a proscription.[1] I said I ought to hope so, for my own sake, but if he should not be able to obtain common indulgence for a friend whom he favour'd, and thought useful, and who had given such convincing proofs of his utility, I should be sorry for myself indeed, but I should also be sorry for him too. It was being upon a very indifferent footing, indeed I should be very sorry for it, upon his account, as well as my own.

He said he would do his utmost to prevent it from coming to that, for now he understood me thoroughly. And then desir'd that we might advise together, about the Bridgewater affair. I said, I

[1] 'How could he suffer this?' Horace Walpole's marginal note in his copy of the *Diary.*

thought that all attempts to quiet the Whig party there would be vain, without beginning by turning out the officers.[1] He seem'd very unwilling to go so far; and at last said that he knew I was a man of honour, and he would trust me with a secret, which I must never reveal, not even to the Duke of Dorset; and then after a multitude of precautions, and exacting engagements of honour from me not to divulge it, he told me that the truth was that he had a mind that this petition against Lord Egmont would not go on; and if I could assist him to bring that about, he should be much oblig'd to me: but if it should be known, it would be reported and believ'd that he had made up with Lord Egmont which was no ways true, for upon his honour, he had neither spake with him, or seen him, or had any negotiation with him; for he knew very well, that if the King was inform'd that the town was resolv'd to petition, and there was the least grounds to throw out Lord Egmont he would order him to push it with the utmost vehemence.

I said I had often told him it was no cause of mine; be it how it would, I should not take it as matter of payment, or dissatisfaction: that I would certainly keep his secret, which, however, everybody would see thro', if no justice was done; that I would do all I could with Mr Balch, and the town, to quiet them, but that without punishing the officers, I fear'd he would find it impracticable; which he would better judge of, when he saw Messrs Balch and Burroughs, on Thursday. What if he offer'd the alternative, and try'd to make the giving up the officers the price of dropping all farther proceedings? He said it was a good thought, and he must scramble off as well as he could. Captain Arbuthnot, and his wife, din'd here.

5. Wednesday. Lord Talbot, Mrs Talbot, Misses Talbot, and Chetwynd breakfasted here. Din'd alone.

6. Thursday. Mrs D. and I went to town. I saw Sir Paul Methuen, —and Messrs Balch and Burroughs, who had been at the Duke of Newcastle's. His Grace had talk'd them over; but nothing positive, not so much as punishing the officers; but told Mr Balch that he would send Lord Dupplin to him. While they were with me Lord Dupplin was at Mr Balch's, and soon after they met, talk'd very amicably, and agreed to meet here, next Tuesday. This haste to see Mr Balch was in order to learn all he could, that he might talk

---

[1] i.e. the Custom House Officers.

it over at Claremont with the Duke of Newcastle, between Saturday and Tuesday.

7. Friday. Captains Hardy and Horne came, about a prize cause. Mr Breton came.

8. Saturday. Mr Breton and I rid out. Mr Wyndham din'd here.

9. Sunday. At Leicester House. Mr Breton went. Din'd alone.

10. Monday. Walk'd to Lord Hillsborough's. Much talk. First about Bridgewater election.—Could not conceive the D. of N. could have the least difficulty in supporting a petition, wonder'd he was not most desirous of it.—If not, my friends would certainly support me.—I doubted.—He said that the tide of politics might have a little separated people, so that they might not be so ready to follow me in every political point, yet in anything personal he could not doubt but that the many that had liv'd with and been oblig'd to me, would support me heartily, and with all their power. —I still doubted.—He said that my relations, the Grenvilles and Lytteltons would, and he knew it from themselves.

  We thence fell upon other subjects, and he desir'd to know of me what I thought of their present situation. I said I could not judge of it, because I did not know it; but it seem'd to me very disjointed. He said he could not imagine anything like it. Everybody of consequence was dissatisfy'd. I said I could not conceive that, as they had just had everything divided amongst them. He said it was so, for all that: he not only knew it was so, but from his intimacy with them, he knew their reasons, which he would tell me, and would begin with Mr Pitt. That indeed he had no intimacy with him, but was told them by his bosom friend, Mr George Grenville, who was, also, his. That indeed if Mr Pitt meant money, I might well think he ought to be satisfy'd; but his passion was not that—it was ambition, power, of which he had no share; this made him very uneasy, which was highly increas'd by the late promotions. Instead of being acquainted with, and consulted about what was to be done, he was only inform'd what was done; instead of offering him his share, he receiv'd news that his most inveterate enemy was made Secretary of State: the next post brought him an account that Mr Fox had refus'd the seals, and Sir Thomas Robinson had receiv'd them.

I said that I supposed that they did not think Mr Pitt could possibly undertake the fatigue of an office of business from the state of his health. He said that Mr Pitt said he himself ought to be the best judge of that. Besides, Mr Legge, who could have no pretence to go before him, was made Chancellor of the Exchequer, just in the same manner. They should have offer'd him at least. They should have made him well with the King who was his enemy, which they had never taken the least care to do. That Legge, George Grenville, and Fox were his intimate friends, and he knew their thoughts from themselves; that as to Legge he acknowledg'd that he was promoted; tho' he did not much desire it: however, when he was put there, he thought that he should be supported: he expected to be at least as well with the Duke of Newcastle as anybody, tho' he was to act an under part; but he found himself, instead of better, not so well with him as the rest of his colleagues; that he knew nothing of what was doing, or to be done, and was not consider'd at all, in anything. That George Grenville was in the same way of thinking, and expected very different treatment, consideration, and communication, from his rank in the House of Commons. Besides if he had less reason to be displeas'd, nothing would make him easy while his great friend Pitt was dissatisfy'd. That as to Fox, he need say nothing: Fox says he was offer'd the seals with proper powers to be at the head of the House of Commons; and the next day, was told with some roughness, that he was to have none, nor to meddle with the conduct of the House, farther than as it related to his office. That he might have accepted, with honour, even upon those last conditions, yet having been offer'd, and accepted the office upon the first, he must have been a mean rascal to have submitted to it.

I ask'd him if, considering the suspicious temper of the D. of N. he thought he would be willing to leave Fox in the Closet, in any station, after what had pass'd. He said he believ'd not; but that Fox would meddle very little, and if he gave no particular offence, he thought the Duke could not get him out. And added that he and the rest of them should take very little share in Business, unless there was more trust, and communication than had hitherto appear'd. Ladies Binning, Murray, Miss Hamilton, Sir Francis and Lady Dashwood, din'd here.

11. Tuesday. Ladies Bath and Darlington breakfasted here. Lord

Dupplin came about Bridgewater:—We found that the Duke of Newcastle was a little more inclin'd toward a petition.—

12. Wednesday. Mrs Goldsworthy, Mrs Venturini, and the Marquis Menefoglio din'd here.

13. Thursday. Mrs D. and I went to London. Saw Messrs Balch and Burroughs, who had been at the Duke of Newcastle's, and were promis'd that the party should be supported, in the strongest terms. We return'd to dinner.

14. Friday. Mr Kelsal din'd here.

15. Saturday. Mr Burroughs came, and staid.

16. Sunday. Messrs Shirley, Tryan, and Breton (who staid) din'd here.

17. Monday. Messrs Breton, Burroughs, and I (Mrs D. in the coach) rode to Lord Harrington's. At our return, found Dr Sharpe, who staid.

18. Tuesday. Went to town, din'd at Mr Furnese's. Went to Council. Return'd.

19. Wednesday. Lady Orford came at 8 in the morning, staid with me above three hours. Her business was to lament her misfortunes, for that Mr Shirley and she were parted, of which she gave me a long account: the whole of which was that he insisted upon something independant, and she would part with nothing out of her own power.—

20. Thursday. Went to Town. Din'd at home. Went to Council, return'd at night.—This day put a cruel end to a long, and tender friendship.—

21. Friday. Lord Dupplin came, he said to talk about Bridgewater: but first, he must acquaint me that he had told the Duke of Newcastle what I had said, about myself: that I had offer'd a free, and unreserv'd friendship, that after what I had done, I thought myself well intitled to the treatment, and favour of a friend, and that it must be decided one way, or another. That the Duke seem'd to

desire it as much as I, understood it should be settled, and tho'
he did not explain himself to him positively on that head, yet he
[Dupplin] look'd upon it as a thing fix'd, and would, soon, be over.

I gave him proper thanks, and said that it could not remain as
it did; that the Duke was so generous as to press me to say what
his brother engag'd for; that I would not speak to my own advantage, when the only person that could contradict me was dead;
that, indeed, there was no bargain for particular things, friendship,
and connexion, was what I ask'd, and Mr Pelham said he was
equally desirous of. Lord Dupplin said that he knew that Mr
Pelham for above a year before he dy'd, look'd upon our union to
be as settled as any connection he had; always said that I was the
only man of business they had, and was resolv'd to attach me to
them. I said that I would tell him, tho' I had not said so much to
the Duke; that Mr Pelham said that I had a good deal of Marketable
Ware (meaning Parliamentary Interest) that if I would impower
him to offer it, all, to the King, without any conditions, he would
be answerable to bring it to a good account. That if this engagement had not been taken, the nature of the thing spoke itself.
Service is obligation, obligation implies return. Could any man of
honour, profess friendship, accept the offers of his friend's whole
services, suffer those offers to be carried into execution, avail himself
of their whole utility, and then tell him he could not or he would
not make him any return? Could there be such a character?
Supposing this gentleman had a master, whose affairs were
promoted by these services, whose concurrence was necessary to
this return, but was indipos'd to his friend: could he answer it to
him, or the world, when he found his master's resentments not
to be remov'd, if he did not advise his friend to take back his
offers, and apply them as he thought best, unless he chose to risk
them on an adventure for the return of which he could not be
answerable? These things spoke themselves, and all mankind must
see them in the same light. That be it how it would, it must be
thoroughly understood by the world. If this connection, and the
acceptance of my effectual services, was not ratify'd by effects that
justify'd them, I must be contented to pass for a dupe, and they, for
sharpers, the world would justly call me fool, and them by a much
harsher name, but I was prepar'd to bear it, if it should.—And this
particular deduction, and conclusion, I found means to repeat, two
or three times in the subsequent conversation.

We then fell upon Bridgewater. The Duke of Newcastle would do everything to support the party.[1]—Demurr'd upon petitioning only for fear of making it a handle, for forming an improper connection, at setting out.—I knew that those in considerable places differ'd amongst themselves and almost all disown'd immediate dependance, obligation, and allegiance to the Duke—and they might, on such an occasion, perplex, and form followings, without being seen to do it, &c.

I said I understood him, and after having strongly represented to him, that what I undertook, I had perform'd, since he acknowledg'd I was fairly chose; that I meant it as a service, if they were satisfy'd, I was; if they chose to make effectual, what their own dependants had obstructed, I would give my assistance, but was wholly unconcern'd in their determination: I said that I did not think that this case was liable to the inconveniences he had mentioned; for that I had reason to think that Mr Fox would not espouse, even privately, Lord Egmont against me; tho' I had not seen him since my return from the West. That I had been press'd, by several, with offers of service, to know if I would petition; that the Grenvilles &c. had given me to understand, that they would not only be for me, but actively so.—That I would own to him, in confidence, that I wish'd there might be no petition; that the Duke might think it no ill bargain, if he could *get* Lord Egmont, by suffering him to sit only, without any farther pretensions upon him, tho' at my expence; and may be, I may think so too; but I thought it impracticable; that if I were in his Grace's confidence, I should be oblig'd to tell him, that if Lord Egmont subscrib'd to that bargain, when the 14 days for petitioning were out, if he did not engage to gratify him (which would be no easy matter) the 15th., it was my opinion, he would break with him, the 16th.

He said much of Lord Egmont's falseness, and bad behaviour to Mr Pelham, who told him [Dupplin] that he was so gross a flatterer, to him, when he brought him in, for Weobley, that it was very shocking; and show'd him a letter of his, in which he writes that he was happy in having found a man, in whom he could have an *implicit faith*—with a great deal more of this kind. He then enter'd into the means of managing this affair of Bridgewater, one way, or the other. I said I could say but little to it, after what I had said: that my being in their confidence, or not, must and would a good

[1] i.e. the local caucus at Bridgwater.

deal, decide of the complexion of that affair. He said he always look'd upon that, as done: to be sure that must be decided, before any measures could be taken, with effect. I told him that one way came across me, and only one, to make all things easy; but charg'd him, as a man of honour, never to mention it as a thought or suggestion of mine; because it was not so much as my wish, and the suggestion might be construed to imply the wish: that the expedient was, if anything should happen, or be form'd, that could make room for me, in the service, before the meeting of the Parliament, that would vacate my seat, and I could neither petition, nor stand for Bridgewater; but I enjoyn'd him never to mention this, seriously, (for it struck him much, and made him, for a few minutes, very thoughtful) nor at all as coming from me, for I really meant, only as a pleasantry between him and me, that rose on a sudden.

I went to Kensington to Council. The Lord Chief Justice, the Master of the Rolls, the Comptroller, the Treasurer of the Navy, and the Cofferer, were sworn of the Council: it has hung these three months since they had their offices, before the King could be brought to admit them. Messrs Dobbs and Morris were sworn as Governors of Carolina, and Pennsylvania. Messrs Burroughs and Balch din'd here.—

22. Saturday. Messrs Wyndham and Tucker din'd here. The Speaker came in the morning.

23. Sunday. Inauguration Day. Went to Kensington and Carlton House. Din'd alone.

24. Monday. Lord Hillsborough and Mr Fox came. Messrs Sharpe and Tucker din'd here. Sharpe staid.—

25. Tuesday. Lord Halifax din'd here.

26. Wednesday. Comte de Poniatowski, Messrs Balch, Tucker, Burroughs, din'd here.

27. Thursday. Din'd alone.—

28. Friday. Mrs D. and I call'd upon Mrs Oswald. Din'd alone.—

29. Saturday. Mr Balch was to see Durand's house. Messrs Wyndham, Tucker and Breton, who staid, din'd here.

30. Sunday. Mr Beaghan din'd and lay here.

JULY

1. Monday. Mr Breton went away. I rode to Mr Fox's and Lord Hillsborough's. Return'd and din'd alone.

2. Tuesday Went to town to Lord Dupplin, about Bridgewater business. He said that he had told the D. of N. all that I said to him; had explain'd the nature of the friendship I offer'd in contradistinction to the inconnection, and inconfidence of the others, in office; that the Duke approv'd of, and desir'd it, and meant to effect it; that he press'd him to end it with the King; for that when the proscription was taken off, and the King had accepted of me, the Duke might declare that I was in his connection and under his protection, and that he was at liberty, and would do me justice, the first opportunity that should happen; and then, he [Dupplin] could have the pleasure of communicating everything he knew and heard, with me confidentially, and should look upon me, and himself, and the Attorney and Stone (*who was by* when he talk'd to the Duke) as one person.

I said I could not imagine any reason why Stone should be indispos'd towards me—He cried, 'Indispos'd! Very much the contrary—he desires it very much, and so do all the D. of N.'s friends.'—I said if it ended otherwise it would be the most scandalous transaction that ever appear'd to the world and appear it must. He said it could not end ill—he look'd upon it as done, for he desir'd me to observe that the Duke did not hold up the King, at all, to him, or so much as intimate that he apprehended any difficulty from His Majesty. I beg'd of him to press the Duke to make an end of it, before I went into the West; that I would wait on him before I set out, and earnestly desir'd that it might be entirely settled.

Went to Sir Paul Methuen's, and return'd with Mrs D. to dinner.

3. Wednesday. Din'd alone.

4. Thursday. The Archbishop of Canterbury was here. I din'd at Gunnersbury.

5. Friday. Lord and Lady Stafford were here, with Lord Fairfax and his daughter. Mr Carey din'd here.

6. Saturday. Three Misses Beaghan, and their brother, Mr and Mrs Lowrie, and Miss Hamilton, Messrs Breton and Bance din'd here.

7. Sunday. Mrs D. and I went to town—I to Carlton House. Return'd, and din'd alone.

8. Monday. I went to Town.—WROTE. Saw Sir Paul Methuen. Return'd. Mr Kelsal din'd here.—

9. Tuesday. I rode to Mr Kelsal's, where we din'd. My horse fell with me. I receiv'd no hurt but a small contusion on the thigh. I hope I know, and acknowledge the Goodness that sav'd me.

10. Wednesday. I went to London. Wrote to P.[1]—Return'd to dinner.

11. Thursday. Din'd with the Archbishop of Canterbury at Croydon—

12. Friday. Went to Lord Stafford's. Mr Tucker din'd here.

13. Saturday. I went to town to see Lord Dupplin, who was here, at the same time. Mrs D. came.—We return'd to dinner alone.

14. Sunday. Mr Breton din'd here.

15. Monday. Sir Francis Eyles, Lady Eyles and Mrs Egerton, Mr Kelsal and his two daughters and Mr Carey din'd here.

16. Tuesday. I came to town. Saw Lord Dupplin, who protested he thought that the Duke of Newcastle sincerely meant to connect himself with me. Din'd at Gunnersbury.

17. Wednesday. Mr Beaghan din'd, and lay here.

18. Thursday. Went to the Duke of Newcastle's. After he had talk'd indecisively, about Bridgewater, of which I gave him the hearing, I desir'd to know positively, what I was to expect. He told me that he had laid all my services before the King, in the fullest manner; but it did not satisfy him; that he endeavour'd to lessen my credit at Weymouth; that the Duke reply'd that he

[1] ? Pitt.

thought His Majesty himself told him that the borough was put into my hands, at the renewal of the Charter, on condition of choosing two that he should name, *for that time*. The King could not deny it: but upon the whole, would not receive me to any mark of his favour.

I said that as it was so, I receiv'd it with that respect, and resignation that became me towards my Sovereign. That after such offers receiv'd, suffer'd to carried into execution at the expence of between £3, and £4,000 and availing themselves of the services, I did not believe such a conclusion had ever happen'd, but I submitted, and must act as opportunity and accidents should direct. He express'd much sorrow; protested the sincerity of his endeavours; said that the best of my friends would say, that what would not do one day, might do another. I said that I could not judge of that. But if he imagin'd that I would remain postulating amongst the common herd of suitors, and expose myself to suffer twenty unworthy preferences more, to get nothing at last perhaps, certainly nothing that I wanted: *that* was impossible: I would as soon wear a livery, and ride behind a coach in the streets. These words, I again repeated in the course of the conversation. We parted very civilly. Return'd to Hammersmith. Signors Celesia, Mavelia, Menefoglio, and Sir Francis Dashwood din'd here.

19. Friday. Mrs D. and I came, and lay in town. I din'd at Sir Francis Dashwood's. I went to the Attorney-General: told him what had pass'd, and desir'd him to be a witness that I look'd upon myself as free of all engagements, after such a return, and expected to have no hints thrown out of breach of faith &c., whatsoever party I might take. He said, I was undoubtedly, free.—But could not believe it could end so:—protested that he was sure the Duke of Newcastle had represented everything in the most favourable manner, tho' he should not wonder if I did not believe so. I said, that all things consider'd, it was pretty hard to believe it. He said he agreed to that, if they on their side, did not return to the charge, till they carried the point. They must do it, &c., which was very civil, and insignificant: We parted.

20. Saturday. Messrs Carey, and Beaghan din'd here.

21. Sunday. Went to Messrs Poulet, and Lowrie. To Carlton House, Lady Middlesex's, and Sir Paul Methuen's. Din'd alone.

22. Monday. I din'd on board Sir Francis Dashwood's vessel *The Fortune*, at Deptford. The *Dunkirk* was launch'd at Woolwich for the entertainment of the Prince of Wales. Return'd to Hammersmith, at night.

23. Tuesday.

24. Wednesday. } Alone.

25. Thursday.

26. Friday. Set out, early for Eastbury, and arriv'd safe, there, the same evening by God's goodness. Found Mrs Venturini, and Beaghan, there.

27. Saturday. Alone.—

28. Sunday. Colonel Harvey, and Captain Okeden, and Mr Drew din'd here.

29. Monday. Lady Orford came, with a long account of the quarrels, and parting between her, and Mr Shirley. She staid here.

30. Tuesday. Alone.

31. Wednesday. Lady Orford went to London, in order to go to France. Din'd alone.

AUGUST

1. Thursday. Mr Gresley din'd here.

2. Friday. Din'd alone. Dr Taylor, Mrs Allen and her two sons, came.

3. Saturday. Colonel Harvey din'd here. Mr Richard Tucker came.

4. Sunday. Mr Tucker went away.

5. Monday. Dr Taylor, &c. went away.

6. Tuesday. Alone.

7. Wednesday. Mr Crabb din'd here.

8. Thursday. Lord and Lady, Mr and Mrs Arundel din'd here.

9. Friday.

10. Saturday. } Alone.

11. Sunday. Messrs Okeden and Harvey, din'd here.

12. Monday. Mr Fleet din'd here.

13. Tuesday. The Drax family, and Mr Baldwyn din'd here.

14. Wednesday. Messrs Drummond, and Black din'd here.

15. Thursday.

16. Friday. } Alone.

17. Saturday.

18. Sunday. Mr Freke din'd here.

19. Monday. Mr and Mrs Dodington came.

20. Tuesday.

21. Wednesday. } Alone.

22. Thursday. Mr and Miss Sturt, Mr and Mrs Beckford, and Miss Pitfield din'd here.

23. Friday. Lord and Lady Shaftesbury; and Miss Ewer din'd here.

24. Saturday. Mr and Mrs Fleet din'd here.

25. Sunday. Alone.

26. Monday.

27. Tuesday. } Alone. Mr and Mrs Dodington went away.

28. Wednesday. Din'd at Mr Drax's.

29. Thursday. Din'd at Mr Sturt's.

30. Friday. Alone.

31. Saturday. Mr and Mrs Tucker, Drs Sharpe and Smith, and Mr Giddy, came.

SEPTEMBER

1. Sunday. Alone.

2. Monday. Alone.

3. Tuesday. Din'd at Mr Arundell's.

4. Wednesday. Mr Banks din'd here.

5. Thursday. Messrs Tucker &c. went away.

6. Friday. Monsr Celesia came.

7. Saturday. Din'd at Lord Shaftesbury's. Mr Shirley came.

8. Sunday. Mr Stanley came.

9. Monday. Mr and Mrs George Shirley, Mr and Miss Sturt din'd here. Mr Stanley was sent for to Bath, on the death of his grand-mother.

10. Tuesday. Alone.

11. Wednesday. Messrs Breton and Wyndham, came.

12. Thursday. Alone.

13. Friday. Mr Gresly din'd here.

14. Saturday. }
15. Sunday. } Alone.

16. Monday. Mr Crabb din'd here.

17. Tuesday. Alone.

18. Wednesday. Mr William Sharpe, Mr and Mrs Waine came.

19. Thursday. Alone.

20. Friday. They and Mr Wyndham and I went to Weymouth. Din'd with Mr Tucker.

21. Saturday. Mr John Tucker chosen Mayor of Weymouth.

22. Sunday. Mr Wyndham, and I return'd to dinner, at Eastbury.

23. Monday. Colonel Harvey, Messrs Okeden, Drax, Mr and Mrs Fleet din'd here.

24. Tuesday. Alone.

25. Wednesday. Mrs D. and I set out at 5 minutes past 5 o'clock and got to Hammersmith by half an hour after seven, without any accident, thanks be to God. We stopp'd near an hour at Basingstoke.

26. Thursday. Alone.

27. Friday. The coach came, with Mrs Venturini, & Beaghan.

28. Saturday. Went to town, with Mrs Venturini. Saw Marquis de Paolucci. Return'd to dinner.

29. Sunday. Went to Carlton House. Return'd to dine.

30. Monday. To Mr Furnese's. Din'd alone.

OCTOBER

1. Tuesday. Carried Mrs Venturini to London. My coach carried her to her husband's house—where she was refus'd the door.

2. Wednesday. Mr Breton din'd here.

3. Thursday. Went to Mr Cooke's, at Hanfield.

4. Friday. Return'd to dinner.

5. Saturday. Went to town. Saw Sir Paul Methuen.

6. Sunday. Din'd here, Lord Hillsborough, Messrs Lowrie, Clements, Breton, Beaghan, Sir Henry Bellendine.

7. Monday. Alone.

8. Tuesday. Call'd upon Lord Hillsborough. Much free talk.— nobody in office, satisfied, or would act, beyond their particular department.—Nobody impower'd, or would take the lead.—Mr Pitt had seen the Duke of Newcastle for an hour, and went back to Bath. The Duke would have enter'd with him into the American expedition, to dislodge the French from the Ohio: Mr Pitt said, 'Your Grace, I suppose, knows I have no capacity for these things, (being disatisfy'd that he was not made Secretary of State) and therefore I do not desire to be inform'd about them.'—He is likely to resign, but not go into opposition.—Fox and Pitt, are willing to see the first, at the head of the Treasury; the other, Secretary; but neither would assist the other.—Ask'd if that was not a virtual union.—Near it: Mr Pelham had the address to play the one against the other: the Duke had not.—He [Hillsborough] had talk'd to the Duke of Newcastle about this, who told him all would go well: let them do the duty of their offices.—He said he had told the King that he had not much to expect from his first rank, in the House of Commons, (meaning Fox, Pitt, Legge, Grenville, &c.) but he had an excellent second rank, (meaning him, Hillsborough, Barrington, Dupplin, Nugent, Charles Townshend &c.)—That West, Secretary of the Treasury had been with him. Express'd his opinion that they could not go on; that he saw many of the City, that it was an

unanimous opinion it could not; that opinion, however founded, was of great weight; that he had told this to the Duke, who said he knew nothing of the matter; all would go well. The King does not speak to the Duke of Dorset; yet it is possible he may go, again, to Ireland; The Duke of Grafton wants to send his son-in-law, Earl of Hertford, thither. All This is Astonishing—

9. Wednesday. Alone.

10. Thursday. Din'd at Lord Hillsborough's. Lady Hillsborough, Lady Caroline and Mr Fox, Sir Henry Bellendine, Mr Clements and I. Much drink, which Mr Fox promoted. Sir Henry Bellendine and Mr Clements went away about eight. We there staid till one, and then went to sup with the ladies. I have hardly met with such a conversation, where there never was a connection, but rather a coldness.

[Here the Diary was laid aside until May 1755]

1755

MAY[1]

THIS is an abstract of the letters of the Governors of North America to the Court, as far as the 31st of March. Braddock will put himself at the head of the Irish Regiments, and the provincial troops, and immediately attack the French forts, upon the Ohio. They made, together, about 2,300 men.

Shirley will propose to Braddock, an attack upon the Niagara, at the same time by his and Peperel's regiments, commanded by themselves. If this be thought impracticable, that Braddock join them, leaving only a few men to make a diversion.

In aid of this expedition, Shirley proposes to his colony an attack upon Crown Point, and to erect a fort upon the eminence near it.

The four colonies propose to raise:

Massachusetts Bay	1,200
New Hampshire	500
Connecticut	1,000
Rhode Island	400
	3,100

but determine to wait the resolutions of New York, New Jersey, and Pennsilvania. Mr Pownal is sent Commissioner to them. Colonel Johnson, who is a Sachem among the Six Nations, will carry two or three hundred of them with him, and so engage them in the war.

Shirley was to meet Braddock, the 4th of April at Annapolis to concert all these things.

It was concerted between Shirley and Lawrence to dispossess the French of all their forts at Beausejour; and on the north side of the

---

[1] The *Diary* was here resumed in two separate notebooks, one of which contains supplementary, and to some extent, repetitive, entries for May, June, and July only. The text here given combines the two versions, giving the fullest entry for days where there is a choice.

Bay of Fundy. To this intent, 2,000 irregulars are rais'd in New England, and with 14 pieces of cannon, are to be landed in Nova Scotia, the first week in April, there to be joyn'd by such regular troops as Lawrence shall approve of. Monkton to command the whole.

Sloops appointed for intelligence—New York grants £45,000 thus appropriated:

To fortify New York . . .	£20,000
Albany	£ 6,000
Senect[ady] . . .	£ 3,000
For securing Kinderhook . . .	£ 1,000
For a fort, on Hudson's River . .	£ 600
To replace the money sent to Virginia	£ 5,000
For refreshment of the King's troops .	£ 5,000
	£40,600

Holborn with one ship of 74 guns, four of 70, one of 60, and one of 20, to reinforce Boscawen, sail'd the 11th instant. Off the Lizard 14th.

About Monday the 26th instant we understood here that six of the ships of war (French) were return'd to Brest. So that 9 with the men on board, and 3 in fighting order, are gone on.

On 22 April Mr Boscawen, with 11 ships of line, was out of sight of Portsmouth, victuall'd for America. He was to take up a regiment at Plymouth. Clear'd the Brest Squadron, about 20 ships of line and some frigates, sail'd to the West.

7. Pass'd the evening at Leicester House. The Princess was clear the D. of N. could not stand as things were. Desir'd that it should be understood that Leicester House had no communication with Newcastle House; but not that she said so, because it would be told at St. James's House, where she desir'd to avoid all disputes.

9. Mr Pitt came to Lord Hillsborough where Mr Fox was; who stepping aside, Mr P. thinking he was gone, declar'd to Lord H. that all connection between him and Mr Fox was over, that the *ground was alter'd*, that Mr F. was of the Cabinet, and regent, and he left expos'd &c—That he would be *second* to *nobody*, &c—Mr Fox rejoyning the company, Mr Pitt, heated, said the same, and more to him: that if succeeded, and so made way for him [P.] he

would not accept the seals of Secretary from him. That would be owning an obligation, and superiority, which he would not own. He would owe nothing but to himself:—and much more very high and very strange conversation.—Fox ask'd him what would put them upon the same ground: he said, a winter in the Cabinet and a summer's Regency.

He talk'd the same over again to Lord Hillsborough who endeavour'd to soften matters; but he was unalterable; and desir'd Lord H. as a friend to take an opportunity to tell Mr Fox that he wish'd there might be no farther conversation between him [P.] and Fox about it; that he esteem'd him, but that all connection was over between them

15. Notwithstanding what pass'd at Lord Hillsborough's Messrs Fox and Pitt have had another conference—not so alienating, but not satisfactory. I have seen neither, so do not know the particulars.

17. Set out for Horton, from Hammersmith. Got thither by 3 o'clock. There was Lord Halifax, Colonel Johnson, Lord Dupplin, and Mr Wright the Surveyor, and Mr Cumberland.

18. Came Sir Charles Hardy, and Mr Isted.

19. Lord Dupplin went away, early, and the

22. I return'd to Hammersmith, by 3 o'clock.

I had much conversation, during this visit, with Lord Halifax. The insufficiency, falseness, and meanness of the Duke of Newcastle's Administration, we entirely agreed in. The imminent necessity of the quite contrary in the present dangerous state of our country, we much lamented. The remedy we could not find, tho' we agreed, that neither the Duke nor the country could go on, without other management, or other hands. I advis'd him to think of it, seriously: he said the D. of N. was his near relation; he wish'd him well; had serv'd him honestly; had asserted the rights of his own office; but had enter'd into no cabals against him; that the Duke had sometimes us'd him kindly, sometimes not so: had oblig'd him, and sometimes, granted, but so as not to oblige: that he had, frankly, told him, and all this, and had press'd upon him, that it was impossible he should go on with these hands, oblig'd as he might think them, and disoblig'd, as they thought, or at least profess'd to think, themselves; that he would do it again, but without hopes of success; tho' he thought the Duke saw his danger, and would try to do something before the winter; for his (Halifax's) part, he saw nothing to help him, but my friends, Talbot, Dashwood, and me.

I said that I did not know how he could come by us, unless he would show us a real intention to extricate this country from the distress he had so much contributed to bring upon it: and then, that he (Halifax) should have the seals, with sufficient authority to carry those intentions into execution; or else would engage with us, to force him to a compliance.

He then said that he had represented the usage he had met with, to the D. of N. both as his near relation, and his friend; the unworthy preferences—Lord Holderness, very incapable—then Mr Fox—then Sir T. Robinson, every way, most unfit, and under him, once at the Board where he presided—making Mr Fox of the Cabinet which he refus'd him, under pretence that the King would not.—Allowing Mr Pitt's claim to the seals of Secretary, by making excuses, and laying it wholly upon the King's dislike:—Expressing much alienation to Mr Pitt and Mr Fox, and the Grenvilles. The arrogance of the first; the falseness, and cunning of the second who would deceive the D. of N. by pretending to be his friend.

I said the Duke would deceive himself, for Mr Fox did not pretend it, would be sorry to have it thought so, and declar'd he neither had nor would have any obligation to him—but that it behov'd him (Halifax) not to acquiesce under these pretensions of either, for by that means, they would become realities, against him, and in case of any alterations, (which, by some means, must, now, soon happen) they would acquire a foundation, if not success.

He said that unless the D. of N. made a new system, he was sure he could not go on; but if those should succeed, it would be a very flimsy, and short administration; for neither the nation, or the people of quality would confide, or acquiesce in either of them.— That he had felt the danger of suffering those groundless pretensions to establish themselves, but knew not how to help it; and therefore he had told the D. of N. since he saw he would not trust him in business, and was continually putting people before him, he expected some mark of distinction, and demanded the Garter. That he boggled at it, that Lord Carlisle was to have it, that Lord Northumberland insisted upon it—that he would do his best, but that he (Halifax) had no friend, at Court, but himself. That he reply'd, he did not know what he meant by that: that he never thought it necessary to apply to whores, and knaves: but in short, he must have it; or quit his office; did not care it should appear done in a pique, for both their sakes, and therefore desir'd he would propose, and insist upon it with the King, and if the King absolutely refus'd it, to tell him so, upon honour, and he would take a proper time to quit the service; which would prevent its appearing to the world that the Duke had not the power of a Minister, or that he laid down out of resentment. The Duke said that he would not for the world, draw such a thing upon the King, but would do his best to serve him, &c.

I said I wish'd he had put his weight rather upon a share in Government, and a power to serve his country, at this exigence. He said it was nothing; he was persuaded that the D. of N. had never mention'd it to the King. That he would, again, press him to think of his own security, for as it was, he could not stand.—Much kindness, and protestations of friendship, and desires to unite, and act with me, &c. That the Duke trusted the Chancellor no more than him and suffer'd difference of opinion from him, as impatiently.

23. Went to Kew to enquire after the Princess's health. Met Lord Egmont in the ferry as I return'd. Din'd in town, at Sir Francis Dashwood's.

24. Saturday. Din'd here, Lords Carlisle and Hillsborough, Messrs Fox, Breton, and Sir Francis Dashwood.

26. Monday. Din'd here, Messrs Tucker &c, and Messrs Shirley and Kelsal.

27. Tuesday. Was with the Princess by her order. We had much conversation alone, both in the morning, and the evening; in which I think all was said that my memory could suggest to me upon the present state of affairs. The weakness, meanness, cowardice, and baseness of the Duke of Newcastle—all which she echoed in the strongest terms. The impossibility that he could stand without a new system. This too, she declar'd she was fully convinc'd of, and said, she was so persuaded of his falseness, and low cunning, that if she design'd to go into the next room, she would not trust him to conceal it, if she meant it should not be known.

I laid before her the necessity of a new system: that I found people would not bear this; that I believ'd there was no new one form'd, but that I saw there was such a disposition, that it would end in one, of some sort or another; that what most retarded it was that people were guessing at *her*, and were tender at pushing at anything she might be disoblig'd by, and resent another day; that I myself, had enter'd into no engagements, with anybody, and was not fond of doing it, but was on such a foot with the most efficient, that I thought they would hardly come to any fix'd plan, without acquainting me with it: that I thought it absolutely necessary to attempt a settlement, not only for the present but that might, with small alterations, last when *a certain event* took place; for that it would be a melancholy thing if under a young King (who must have his pleasure) and the pressure of a war, when efficiency, and immediate action was requir'd, instead of consulting what was to be done, we must be struggling who should do it: that therefore it was to be wish'd, that some system, so mix'd as not to be disagreeable to her, should be convey'd to the Duke of Newcastle, with intimation, that if he would embrace it, he might not only be supported, *now*, but find protection *another day*: if he would not, he must be left to his enemies, and must expect none now nor *then*: that my meaning was to lead the King into it, without his knowing it, and make him consent to it to make his own affairs easy without knowing whence it arose, or the extent of it: that I wish'd to avoid all disturbances, and it was that, and that alone that made me think of any thing that was to continue such a creature as the Duke of Newcastle at the head of affairs, an hour; either now or then.

She signified her entire approbation of all I had said, by several short interruptions and then said, that she was, and long had been, much affected with the melancholy prospect of hers and her son's affairs: that she desir'd it should be understood that Leicester House had nothing to do with Newcastle House: but not that she said so, because then, it would immediately be carried to St James's House that such a settlement as I mentioned, was, no doubt, much to be desir'd, but how was it to be obtained? There were a hundred good reasons that tied her hands from interfering with the King; those about her children were obvious enough; that if she was to stir, it would make things worse; she saw no way to extricate herself.

I said that it was extremely delicate; that whenever I thought of it, I laid it down, that something must be done, and yet, that she must neither be seen nor heard in it: that upon so delicate a foundation, such a sort of confidence was requir'd, to act, that was above my capacity, such a one as I did not aspire to: that I thought men were wanting: that I was satisfied the nation had still great resources, that even parts were not wanting, but character, and experience in business, was: that the D. of N. had the ball at his foot[1] when his brother died, and might have made a lasting and advantageous settlement for himself, and the country, but had not endeavour'd to oblige one efficient man, besides his known enemies: that there was no violence, no oppression, no particular complaint; but the nation was sinking by degrees, and there was a general indisposition, from the weakness and worthlessness of the Minister, who would embrace everything, and was fit for nothing.

She said the Duke of Newcastle was a coward; that she was glad to hear me say that the nation had still great resources. People told her that it was undone; she did not think so, but, if there were both resources and parts too, if they could not both be exerted, what did it avail? That she saw, and much lamented the consuming state of the nation which I mention'd: that it was of infinite consequence how a young reign set out, that it made her very uneasy: that she was highly sensible how necessary it was, that the Prince should keep company with men: she well knew that women could not inform him, but if it was in her power absolutely, where could she address him? What company could she wish him to? What friendships desire he should contract? Such was the universal profligacy, such the character and conduct of the young people of distinction, that she should be in more pain for her daughters, than for her son, if they were private persons, the behaviour of the women was so indecent, so low, so much against their interest; by making them so cheap.

This and much more (with no very high opinion of His Majesty) took up above two hours before dinner, when the Prince, and Prince Edward came in, from riding, and she retir'd, to get her clothes, for dinner.

About six, after drinking coffee with Lady Charlotte Edwin, we were sent for to walk. Their Royal Highnesses, the Princess, the Ladies Augusta and Elizabeth, Lady Charlotte, Comte de R——, and I. The shape of the day seem'd to be, to leave the Princess to me; for the rest of the company always kept before, or

[1] One of the earliest examples of this phrase.

behind. After making the tour of the ground, and showing me the improvements, she propos'd going into the King's gardens: there she again began the same subjects; we talk'd of several people's private characters; the general indisposition; the dangers of the wars; from thence the inability of the D. of N., her dislike and contempt for him; the impossibility of his standing, as he was now situated. Something should be thought of, and soon—the summer was the time. The winter was not so proper for concerting things. I said that in summer, indeed, people's steps were not so much observ'd, and particularly this summer, as the King was abroad.

She again express'd her astonishment at the D. of N.'s conduct, and said she could not conceive who were really, truly, the persons whose advice he depended upon. I said, I really had never heard of anybody, but those whom public fame had made notorious, which were Messrs Murray and Stone. She said that if it were so, they were very bad politicians, unless it were true, that they were at bottom the Jacobites they were so strongly represented to be, and did it to carry on the consuming system. I said, that was impossible, that their understanding, their actions, and, above all, their interest made it so.

She said that nobody but God could judge of the heart; that for her, she did not give any credit to those reports: spoke in favour of Murray's abilities, but nothing, one way or the other, of Stone. Two things she said that were remarkable, from the inference: talking of what the D. of N. ought to do: 'But then', says she, 'he will say, "the *party* will not come into it"': the party, this, and the party that: but I could never understand what the party was; I have endeavour'd to learn, and I could never find that the party was anything else, but the Duke of Devonshire, and his son, and old Horace Walpole.' N.B. The Duke of Devonshire was the cause of the Duke [of Cumberland's] being in the Regency this time; and insisted upon his being left sole Regent at a meeting, where were the Duke of Newcastle, the Lord Chancellor, the Duke of Grafton, Lord Waldegrave, and old Horace Walpole.

The other was, on my commending the Prince's figure, and saying he was much taller than the King. She said, 'Yes, he was taller than his uncle.' I said in height it might be so, but if they measur'd round, the Duke had the advantage of him. She reply'd it was true, and she hoped it was the only advantage that he would ever have of him.

In the half hour between her dressing, and dinner, Mr Cresset did me the favour to come to me; and to my very great surprize, enter'd at once into the wretched management, and inabilities of the D. of N. That he had every thing in his power, for himself and the country, when his brother dy'd; that he had fool'd it away.— Lavish'd all upon his enemies, &c., just what the Princess said.— The monstrous expense of this armament and yet insufficient; tho' well made by those who had it in charge, *when* they were *permitted to act*; but infinitely blamable in the Minister, who delay'd that permission so long and thereby occasion'd this vast, unnecessary expense in arming, and inability of doing it properly, in the time.— Why not be prepar'd or at least forward in your preparations, in the Autumn? Then, everything might have been done, completely, and at the usual expense.—That it was impossible to stand as it was. For the same would happen when the war came upon the Continent in Europe:—Hanover must be protected, but it would be in the same way; a number of expensive, useless engagements enter'd into in a hurry, too great for the country to bear, and yet, by that hurry, ineffectual to the end, which might be attain'd by a reasonable plan, upon reasonable terms. Just such, was the last war, ruinous in the expense, unsuccessful in the end, for want of consideration, and a reasonable plan at the beginning.— But one saw—*All* was *going one way*.—That it was a sad prospect for those who wish'd well to the Prince.—That the poor Princess was very uneasy at it, &c.—

All this is so; and it is as certain, that the Duke [of Cumberland] is full as much indispos'd to the D. of N. as the Princess, and the amount of it all will be—Nothing—

The King, the Princess, the Duke and the chief people in employment, and (except the King) all, avowedly, hate and despise the D. of N.—The King delegates his power to him. The Princess and the Duke, from private dislikes, (trifling ones, I believe) and the chief people in employment, from this strange situation of the Royal Family and from great unwillingness to venture their emoluments, will not unite in bringing about the single thing in which, perhaps, they all agree.—

Is not this political prodigy a surer forerunner of the fall of a state, than a comet?—

28. Wednesday. Alone.

29. Thursday. Went to town. Din'd with Mr Furnese. Had a long conversation with Lord Temple. Took much pains to persuade me that they were, all, very well satisfied with Mr Fox, tho', to jealous minds, there might be pretence for suspicion; from appearances, and the consequences of their different conduct: that they had no suspicions, and were willing he should try the same conduct for 2, 3, 4, months; but thought something must be settled before the opening of the Session. They are desperate with the King, and have not been able to get possession either of Leicester House or of the Duke of Cumberland.

30. Friday. Din'd at Sir Richard Lyttelton's, at Ealing.

31. Saturday. Alone.

JUNE

1. Sunday. Went to Carlton House. Din'd at Lord Temple's, with Messrs Pitt, Stanley, James and Henry Grenville, and Sir Richard Lyttelton.

2. Monday. Din'd at Lord Halifax's. A turtle, and much company.

3. Tuesday. Mr Breton din'd here.

4. Wednesday. Alone.

5. Thursday. A most extraordinary meeting at the Admiralty, about Greenwich Hospital. Din'd at Sir Richard Lyttelton's, at Ealing.

6. Friday. Mr James Grenville din'd here, and held the same language, more at large.

7. Saturday. Din'd at Hillenden, Mr J. Grenville's.

8. Sunday. Alone.

9. Monday. Sir Thomas Robinson din'd here.

10. Tuesday. Lady Tyrawley din'd here.

11. Wednesday. Alone.

12. Thursday. Mrs D. and I breakfasted at Mr Kelsal's. Mr Breton din'd here.

13. Friday. Din'd at the Duke of Argyll's.

14. Saturday. Mr Kelsal din'd, and lay here.

15. Sunday. E. went abroad.[1]

16. Monday. Alone.

[1] Mr. East, D.'s protégé, and perhaps illegitimate son. Numerous letters from his mother, Mrs. Anne East, are among D.'s papers. The young man carried with him an introduction from D. to Voltaire. See p. 337 below.

17. Tuesday. At Mr Fox's. Din'd with Sir Francis and Lady Dash-wood.

18. Wednesday. At London, with Lord Halifax and Sir Paul Methuen. Din'd alone.

19. Thursday. Din'd alone.

20. Friday. Messrs Breton and Thomson din'd here.

21. Saturday. Alone.

22. Sunday. Went to Carlton House. Mr Masham din'd here.

23. Monday. Dr Sharpe came. Carey.

24. Tuesday. Mr Breton din'd here.

25. Wednesday. Alone.

26. Thursday. Mrs D. and I went to town, left Dr Sharpe there, and return'd to dinner.

27. Friday. Mr Breton came to dinner, Mr Glover came, and lay here.

28. Saturday. Din'd at Mr Kelsal's, with the Duke of Argyll.

29. Sunday. Mr Fox pass'd the morning here. Very much talk to no purpose. None of them dare come to any resolution. Was assured by the Duke of Argyll, that Stone was not well with the Princess—had it from West that the D. of N. upon West's pressing him to make up with *him* [Cumberland], said that Stone was always advising the same thing, and had lost himself, at his own court, by it:—Said that the Duke [Cumberland] was with the Princess, on Sunday the 22nd and propos'd to her taking the Prince with him to Portsmouth: which she approv'd of, and desir'd him to ask the Prince himself.—He did, and the Prince agreed to it, but not with so much eagerness as might be expected.—On Monday, Lord Waldegrave sent word he would wait on the Duke to settle the journey, on Tuesday morning; but by that time, the Princess had alter'd her opinion, and sent to put it off, on pretence that it might give umbrage to the King. Fox refines, and is much dissatisfy'd with

this transaction: The Duke does not, and says it is only from a resolution she had taken not to be accountable for anything with the King. But Fox is very uneasy, and very solicitous to unite the Duke and the Princess and it is the only sound ground. But I think it will be exceeding difficult, if possible, to effect.

30. Monday. Mr Glover went to town and return'd at night. Lord Bute din'd here.

JULY

1. Tuesday. Mr Glover went. Din'd alone.

2. Wednesday. Mr Breton din'd here.

3. Thursday. Alone. Duke [of Cumberland] went to Portsmouth.

4. Friday. Mr Wyndham din'd here.

5. Saturday. Mr Breton din'd here.

6. Sunday. We receiv'd the news that Mr Beaghan died yesterday. Mr Venturini din'd and lay here. The Duke return'd from the fleet.

7. Monday. Sir Paul Methuen came. Alone.

8. Tuesday. Rode to town. Din'd alone.

9. Wednesday. Mr Wyndham din'd here.

10. Thursday. Rode to town. Din'd alone.

11. Friday. Alone.

12. Saturday. Went to Mr Fox's, and din'd at the Duke of Argyll's. Mr Glover came at night.

13. Sunday. Mr Breton din'd here.

14. Monday. Captain Beaghan din'd here. Mr Glover went in the morning with me to town and return'd at night.

15. Tuesday. Din'd here Dean Bruce and his son, Messrs Breton and Rich.
    This morning came the news of taking the French men of war, in America. Captain Holwell of the *Gibraltar* dispatch'd from Admiral Boscawen brought the following advices: That the Admiral fell in with, and chas'd a considerable time, four French ships of war, but lost them in a fog, and they got into Louisbour . The

rest, take in the words of the Gazette.—Letters from Admiral
Boscawen of the 22d. inst. give an account, that the 10th of that
month, the *Alcide* of 64 Guns, and 480 Men and the *Lys* of 64 also,
but mounting but 22, having 8 Companies of land forces on board,
being separated from the squadron commanded by Monsieur Bois
de la Mothe, fell in with the English fleet, off the Banks of New-
foundland. There was a skirmish between those two, and the two
Frenchmen, in which the two last were taken.—The *Dauphin
Royal* who had been in company with them, disappeared in the
fog. Holborn joyn'd Boscawen on the 21st inst: the day before
Holwell was dispatch'd. This seem'd to speak plain enough, and
put an end to the doubts, and dilatoriness of our proceedings in
Europe, which are most remarkable: viz:—when Fox was here
the 29th past, he told me that a courier was arriv'd from Hanover,
the night before, or that morning, which brought an answer to
the letters they sent, praying to know if, in case France should
reject their last proposals, or give an illusory answer as usual, they
might send out our fleet, and with what orders; 'What the answer
is', says he, 'I shall know on *Tuesday*, when the Regency meets.'—
and which I suppose I shall not know when I think of enquiring
about it.

16. Wednesday. Din'd here Lord Halifax, Messrs James Grenville,
Sewallis and Thomas Shirley, and Deering. Lord Halifax told me
that the D. of N. had again mention'd his resolution to come to
some settlement. That Mr Pitt did not insist absolutely, upon
being Secretary; but that there was great unwillingness to speak
out, or come to him (D. of N.)—That he (Halifax) said he did
not wonder at it: if he was not in earnest, why did he send him
positive terms, or desire a conference? Could he think that Pitt
would open himself upon hints, and to such messengers? (He, since,
told me, the person was Mr. Yorke.) That the D. in a former conference, had express'd *much flattery for me*, *much concern* that I should
make a speech against him; resolution to make up with me; and
enquiries when I went into Dorsetshire; and that in this conference,
he cry'd out of himself, 'We must have Dodington.'—Thus far,
Lord Halifax; and it was all that he knew relating to Mr Pitt.

And to render intelligible what follows, and may follow, with
relation to that gentleman, I will throw what I know of his situation
all together: his extraordinary conference with Mr Fox at Lord

Hillsborough's, may be seen under the article 9th May. The other conference, at Holland House, tho' a little more courtly, was not more satisfactory, and has never been renew'd. It seems that a little before the King went, old Horace Walpole, either officiously, or sent, try'd to bring Mr Pitt into temper.—That the D. of N. desir'd it, would, had done, everything in his power to serve him according to his wishes, he must not be inflexible &c.—He said he was not, and did not insist upon the seals, now, but would be contented, as a proof of the D.'s sincerity, if he would take off all marks of proscription, that the King should agree that when any vacancy happen'd he should have the seals, and should, in the meantime, treat him upon that foot. In this way he would not desire that any vacancy should be made for him, &c. Old Horace seem'd to give in to this.

And here let me insert that Fox told me that Lord Hartington told him that he had it from Old Horace himself, that the D. was very angry with him, for having advanc'd so far, and said he had gone farther than his commission, or than he (D.) *could go, if he would, or would go, if he could*, but nothing came of it. Then came on these extraordinary conferences, which I confess, I do not yet understand: *I know Mr Fox* imputes it to a design of fixing himself with the Princess, and that in order to do that, it became necessary to declare off with him Fox, as the D. of Cumberland's man: I do not think so, it is too refined for me; I think nobody but Cresset (if he) is in a settled confidence of measures (if there be any) with the Princess, and so I told him.

In this state then, I suppose, Mr Yorke found Mr Pitt, when he seem'd so cold, as the Duke represented him to Lord Halifax, when he sounded him by his Grace's order. But the real ouverture, and answer was as Mr James Grenville told me (from Mr Pitt, in effect, tho' not avowedly) was assurances of friendship, and affection: resolution to bring about everything he wish'd, as soon as it was possible: desirous that they might talk together, they should soon agree &c. *This* not by positive message, but by insinuation. The answer was: that as to friendship, and confidence, that was entirely over: 'twas loss of time to talk any more in that style. That if ever those assurances were to be carry'd into execution, and realities, it was a doubt whether they would be accepted. That he would take, or hold nothing as a favour from the D. of N. and will never owe him any obligation. That therefore he saw no use of meetings, or conferences; but if he was really in earnest, and meant anything, why did he not propose plainly the three things: what was the work he expected to be done; who were the gentlemen he propos'd should do it; and in what stations he design'd they should act. When he was clearly inform'd of those three points, he should be able to give an answer; after he had consulted his friends, gentlemen of honour and efficiency, whether it was to be undertaken, or not, and upon what terms.

18. Friday. Din'd here Mr Supple, Mr Venturini, and Mr P. Beaghan.

19. Saturday. Alone.

20. Sunday. Went to Carlton House. Talk with Mr Fox. Brought Sir Francis Dashwood and Lady, and Mr Stevens, to dinner.

21. Din'd with the Duke of Argyll, at Mr Fox's. When the company was gone, he told me that he was sure that Mr Pitt had made up with the Princess; had it in mind, when he declar'd off with him. That he had long cultivated (above 6 months) an acquaintance with one, no way connected with D. of N.,[1] with whom he had had the first confidential conference since he saw me. That in talking of things of that court, I think he call'd it 'his court', to that person, he said that he had heard that Stone was not so well as usual there, what could be the reason of it? The person answer'd, 'Shall I tell you? I fear you will not like it, but as you command me I will. I take it to be from thinking him too much in your interest.'—The same person told him (who, he says, some times converses with Cresset) that Mr Pitt was better at that court than usual: to what degree, or by what means he did not know; but that he found Cresset spoke more favourably of him than he us'd to do: He then (Fox) went on to say that Lord Egmont was thought to have the chief management there: and that the Prince was much fonder of *him*, than of any other man living.

I said that Mr Pitt might have sent offers of service, (and by Lady Charlotte Edwin, whom my women relations, the Grenvilles, and Temples had been making court to), all the winter and that they had been very civilly receiv'd, and return'd: but that there had been any communication, or proposition of measures between them,

---

[1] Horace Walpole, in his copy of the *Diary*, opines that this was Lord Waldegrave.

or even an audience, I did not believe. Maybe I might think there were no settled measures; but if there were, I thought neither Pitt, nor Egmont, had the secret, or the management of them, but Cresset only, as yet.—What then could this transaction, either real or imaginary, amount to, but refinement? Could it influence Mr Pitt's acting in public, or his, Fox's, in consequence?

Then we enter'd into the present state of affairs: and he told me that the courier that came the 28th past with the answer from Hanover, which was expected should be a decisive one, as to the sailing of the fleet, brought back a letter which was neither wrote by Lord Holderness, nor dictated by the King, but was certainly sent from hence by the D. of N. (to gain so much time for inaction) as a proper return for the King to make. For it acquaints them that the King cannot give any positive orders about the operations of the fleet till they had fully inform'd him of three particular things, which he, Fox, said he had forgot, but were trifles. That they had answer'd those questions: and humbly advis'd his Majesty to leave the direction of the fleet to their discretion: and that, by the return of the courier, he had done so: that now, till they had digested something positive, they did agree to send this order to Sir Edward Hawke, that he should sail with about 16 ships of line, to Torbay, and there expect farther instructions. That these farther instructions were to be drawn up by Lord Anson, and Sir Thomas Robinson: that the Duke of Cumberland had said that if they had any prospect of getting a peace, he had nothing to say; but if they were convinc'd it must be war, he had no notion of not making the most of the strength, and opportunity you had in your hands. That afterwards, in a window with the Dukes of Marlborough and Newcastle, the last said that what the Duke had said, was full of very good sense, but that he was not entirely, of that opinion; that Lord Granville was absolutely against meddling with trade, he call'd it vexing of your neighbours, for a little muck; but that the D. of N. was by no means of that opinion, but thought some middle way might be found out.

Ask'd 'What?' Said that to be sure Hawke must go out, but that he might be order'd not to fall upon them unless he thought it worth while. Answer'd that sure Hawke was too wise to do anything at all, which others, when done, were to pronounce he ought to be hang'd for. Reply'd, 'What if he had orders not to fall upon them, unless they were more together in number than ten?'—

Was answer'd that the return'd part of the Brest Squadron, now at Lisbon, is but nine.—Said that he meant *that* of merchantmen only; to be sure he must attack any squadron of ships of war.— Ask'd what was a squadron, said three ships or more.

This absurdity is inconceivable.—What orders they will give to Hawke tomorrow, I shall not go out of my way to enquire

22. Tuesday. Monsieur de Mirepoix set out by one o'clock this morning.—The sole question is whether France will submit to purchase the getting home her trade and sailors, and having the winter to tamper with Spain, at the expense of a little reputation in tamely suffering an insult, for a while. If she should, I verily think his Grace would not incline to be rude. This way of Monsieur de Mirepoix's departure looks as if they would take it with a high hand: which may render Hawke's instructions a little more explicit.

ONE THING Mr Fox assur'd me of yesterday, which surpriz'd me very much. He said that the Russians hitherto had refus'd our subsidy. As also, the Queen of Hungary had refus'd, absolutely, both our money, or to have any thing to do with us, saying it is our quarrel, she will not be concern'd in it: the French she is sure will not meddle with her, and therefore she will send no troops into Flanders, if we would be at the whole expence. He said, that upon his telling the Duke that the D. of N. was for a naval war and thought of no provision for a war on the continent, His Highness laugh'd at him, and said it was because he could get nobody to take his money; and that he order'd of his own authority, that more money should be offer'd to the Russians than the Regency knew of, or the King (as he suppos'd).

I press'd Fox much, (who did not seem to feel the force of it) to try if we could fix such a fact on the D. of N. which is not only criminal in itself; but if it were approv'd of afterwards, would be sufficient to frighten him out of his wits for having acted extra-provincially. I was surpriz'd that he did not see it in the same light, and I shall press him again. About this time there was talk of recalling Boscawen and leaving Holborn to command.

22. Tuesday. Lord Halifax breakfasted here. Din'd alone.

23. Wednesday. Rode out. Din'd at Mr Furnese's.

24. Thursday. Din'd alone.

25. Friday. Sir Paul Methuen came. Din'd alone.

26. Saturday. Din'd here Duke of Argyll, Earl of Bute, Messrs Fletcher and Kelsal.

27. Sunday. Mr Venturini din'd here.

28. Monday. Messrs Breton and Kelsal din'd here, the last staid. Last night, news from America.

29. Mr Venturini din'd here. Yesterday I had an account that Captain Loring in a schooner left Boston on 26 June, and arriv'd at Portsmouth the 27th inst. with news that the New England troops, 2000, and regulars 500 commanded by Colonel Monkton, had taken Beausejour, after a siege of four days, and another fort in Baye Vesta, the forts well provided with cannon of 12 pounds. He is proceeded up the River St John. This was the 17th June. The prisoners, in all near 600, are sent to Louisbourg, which is reported to be very short of provisions. There is sufficient force left to block it up.

30. Wednesday. Alone.

31. Thursday. Went to town. Mr Breton din'd here.

AUGUST

1. Friday. Messrs Sharpe and Forrester din'd here.

2. Saturday. Din'd alone.

3. Sunday. Was at Carlton House. Saw Lord Temple there, who assur'd me that neither Mr Pitt nor he knew, or had heard one word more than what Mr James Grenville had acquainted me with.

I also saw Mr Fox there, and he told me that the D. of N. was angry with the Duke, and would hardly speak to H.R.H.—and that he (Fox) had not chang'd a word with his Grace since he saw me last.—That the Hessian Treaty was sign'd, and that Hawke's orders were of the compromising kind. Which is saying all that is weak, and ruinous.

4. Monday. Lord Halifax came. He goes to settle at Horton tomorrow.—Was with the D. of N. at dinner, on Saturday, and yesterday, again, by the Duke's desire.—The Duke did not tell him Hawke's instructions, but finds they are not to meddle with the trade, nor is sure they may attack the men of war, unprovok'd.—Thinks they will, by no means, declare war, if the French do not; what signifies taking a cock-boat?

At last, he took the Duke into another room, and told him that as he had laid before him the state of his affairs, and given him his sincere opinion, which his Grace seem'd to approve of, at the time, but had, he believ'd, never thought of since, he would trouble him no more upon that head.—That he thought himself very ill us'd; but if his Grace thought he could go on without any settlement 'twas well. He thought it impossible, and tho' he had, hitherto, been very lucky, yet the whole would certainly break about his ears.—The Duke said that he still approv'd of what he (Halifax) had advis'd, and was of the same intention to do it, but could settle nothing till the King came. He reply'd that was his Grace's affair, that he did not care, if he made Mr Pitt Secretary, but if he made any alteration that he (Halifax) expected to have justice done him, he was a wretch, a nobody, he would be of the Cabinet, and have access to the King, if anything was done. The Duke said he was surpriz'd to hear him talk so, and went on, as if it was laying under

new difficulties, to which he reply'd that he found it was more
necessary to talk so than he at first thought it; for by his surprize it
was plain that his Grace never thought of it at all.—That tho' a
lover of an active life, yet, in the way he was treated he was weary
of it, and would quit it, if justice was not done him.—That they
flatter'd him extremely, on the success in Nova Scotia; but that
they neither consulted, nor told him the least hint of what use they
design'd to make of it, whether at all, or how to prosecute it.—That
he found that Boscawen was coming home, and he believ'd that the
D. of N. understood that part of the squadron was to come with
him, and a force equal to what is in Louisbourg, (6 ships, it seems)
to be left, for a time. That he, Halifax, oppos'd this strongly; said,
'If the force to be left is but equal, suppose the French should come
out, and beat them, is it impossible? Suppose the squadron under
la Mothe, at Quebec should know that there was but an equal
number left, might they not fall upon them, and be join'd by those
in Louisbourg, was that impossible?' That they certainly were
straiten'd in provisions, and if a superior force remain'd there, in
probability, the place must fall to us. The Duke said the ships
could not winter there: Lord Anson was of that opinion.—He said
that he did not mind Lord Anson's opinion, against fact: he would
maintain that the whole navy might ride the whole winter, in
Halifax Harbour, with the utmost safety; That the *Albany* sloop
had been there, these five years, had cost as little in repairs, as any
other vessel, and is, now, gone out again. The reasoning seem'd
to be thus: if you leave those seas, the French will come away, and
Louisbourg be victuall'd; if you leave but a small force, it will be
in danger, from the ships there, and from a junction of those got
into the Gulph of St Lawrence. The French cannot remain there in
November, without being frozen up. You can stay, because the
harbour of Halifax never is frozen, or very slightly: you are at sea,
from thence, in seven hours, so need never have the same ships out,
above a week at a time: so that if the French appear, you take them;
if not, you freeze them up, and their numbers add to the want of
provisions in the place.—The D. of N. press'd him to give him these
hints in writing.—Would not.

5. Tuesday. Alone.

6. Wednesday. Pass'd the day at Kew. The Princess has had nothing
of Hawke's instructions or any thing else communicated to her:

express'd her dissatisfaction at it. Inveigh'd most bitterly against the not pushing the French everywhere: 'Sure the people would not bear it, when the Parliament met.' I said I believ'd they would. she said, 'Sure the Parliament would never bear the suffering the French to bring home their trade, and sailors, &c.' She saw the terrible consequences of it, and of a patch'd-up peace, which must break out when the French had perfected their naval plan, and fall upon her son, young and unexperienc'd at the beginning of his reign.

I said I doubted if anybody would meddle; but if they should, '*I hope*, Madam, *you would not take it ill.*' '*I*', says she, '*No, indeed, very far from it. I am sure I have no reason, nor any thing like it.*' Very solicitous to push the war: wish'd Hanover in the sea, as the cause of all our misfortunes. I said that I presum'd to differ with her: that I was as ready to defend Hanover as Hampshire, if attacked on our account; thought it no incumbrance, if properly treated, and the only difference between me and the Ministers was not about the thing, but the manner.

She said she perfectly understood me; and it would be so, in another reign, but cou'd not be so in this. That in the manner it had been treated, it had been the foundation of all just complaints, and bad measures.

I ask'd her if she could account for Lord Anson and the Duke of Cumberland concurring in shortening Hawke's hands: the one as a Sea General unconnected, at least; the other, as a Land General, at open enmity with the D. of N. She said she could not: for that the Duke [of Cumberland] (tho' not to her, who had not much conversation with him) declar'd strongly for a *Naval* war. I said, that might be the language of good sense only, as being the popular cry; with hopes possibly, that a sea war might light up a land one. She said she thought so. That nobody knew what to do—no two people together—she sat still, thinking it the only prudent part as everybody was so disunited. I said that the general diffidence she describ'd, was cause of the infinite speculation, and refinement that now reign'd; for as nobody knew, so everybody was guessing each other; in which, H.R.H. had a principal part. She said sure nobody could stand clearer than she; that everyone must know everybody that she saw, and when. I laugh'd, and said I had some thoughts of writing her life, and transactions, as I pick them up, and presenting it to her, of which, I was persuaded, that she knew nothing at all.

She seem'd mightily pleas'd with the idea, and after laughing, took serious pains to convince me that she had no fix'd settlement, or connexions, at all (she may deceive me, but I am persuaded that she has no fix'd digested political plan at all: or regular communication in politics, with anybody, but Mr Cresset:)

N.B. The King has sent to invite the two Princesses of Brunswick to Hanover: they came, but their mother, (King of Prussia's sister) who was not invited, came with them. We talk'd of the match. Sure he would not marry her son, without acquainting her with it, so much as by a letter.—I said, 'Certainly not, as he had always behav'd very politely to her'. 'Maybe so, but how can this be reconcil'd?' 'Thus,' says I, 'Nothing will be settled there; but when he comes back, in conversation, and commending the Prince's figure, he may say that he wishes to see him settled, before he dies, that he has seen such and such young Princesses, and tho' he would settle nothing, without her participation, yet he could wish to see the Prince settled, before his death; & therefore, if she had no objection, he should think one of those Princesses, a very sortable party'—

She paus'd, and said 'No: he is not that sort of man.' But if he should settle it without acquainting her with it, she should let him know how ill she took it: and if he did it, in the manner I said, she should not fail to tell him plainly, that it was full early; that she had eight other children to be provided for: that she hop'd he would think of doing that; and not leave her eldest son eight younger children to take care of, before he had one of his own: that it was probable he would have so many, that hers could not expect to be taken much care of. This she was determin'd to do, whenever he spoke to her about it. Thought the match premature; the Prince wanted to mix with the world; this would prevent it: he was shy, and backward; this would shut him up forever, with 2 or 3 friends of his, and as many of hers. That he was much averse to it, himself. That she dislik'd the alliance, extremely; that the young woman was said to be handsome, and all manner of good qualities, and abundance of wit, &c. but if she take after her mother, (her father, the Duke of Brunswick, is a very worthy man) she will never do, here.

'Pray Madam, what is her mother, I know nothing at all, about her.' 'Why her mother is the most intriguing, meddling and also, the most satirical, sarcastical person in the world, and will always make mischief, wherever she comes. Such a character would not do with George, it would not only hurt him in his public, but make him uneasy, in his private situation; that he was not a wild, dissipated boy, but good-natur'd, and cheerful, but with a serious cast, in the whole: that those about him knew him, no more, than if they never had seen him: that he was not quick, but, with those he was acquainted with, applicable, and intelligent.

His education had given her much pain. His book-learning she was no judge of, suppos'd it small, or useless, but hop'd he might have been instructed in the general course of things. That she did not know Lord Waldegrave: and for Mr Stone, if she were to live 40 years in the house with him, she should never be better acquainted with him, than she was: she, once, desir'd him to inform the Prince about the Constitution; but he declin'd it, to avoid giving jealousy to the Bishop [of Norwich]. That she had mention'd it to him, again, but he declin'd it, as not being his province. 'Pray, Madam, what is his province?' She said she did not know, she suppos'd, to go before him up stairs, to walk with him, sometimes, seldomer to ride with him, and now and then, to dine with him. But when they did walk, the Prince generally took that time, to think of his own affairs, and say nothing.

Show'd me a letter from Hanover, that said the news of Boscawen's action, which came here on the 15th June, got to Hanover on the 20th. That Bussy had his audience the 17th and his courier of recall the 22nd, but was not gone, then, being the 25th June. Wish'd, extremely, that he was gone, for fear he should frighten them into some very unbecoming compliance, as he did, once, before.

Afterwards much talk with the Prince, about funding &c., and other serious things, who seem'd to hear with attention and satisfaction.

7. Thursday. Dr Sharpe, and I din'd with the Archbishop at Croydon.

8. Friday. Din'd here Mr Dean Bruce, and Dr Bruce, Dr Sharpe, Messrs Bludworth and Scot.

9. Saturday. Went to town. Din'd alone.

10. Sunday. Sir Francis and Lady Dashwood din'd here.

11. Monday. Alone.

12. Tuesday. Went to town. Din'd alone.

13. Wednesday. Carey din'd here.

14. Thursday. Went to Sir Francis Dashwood's.

15. Friday.[1]

16. Saturday. Return'd. Din'd at Gerrard's Cross.

17. Sunday. Went to Carlton House—Mr Glover here.

18. Monday. Was at Holland House, and had much conversation with Mr Fox. He said—That the Hessian Subsidy was ratify'd— That the D. of N. bid Mr Amyand read Lord Holderness's letter to the Regency, acquainting them that the King had made such a treaty, and bid him observe that his Majesty directed the Chancellor to set the seal to it: who only bow'd, and their Lordships sign'd it: without reading, and as a thing of course. That the first directions to Lord Anson and Sir Thomas Robinson to draw Hawke's instructions were, that he should take, or destroy all French ships of war but no merchantmen.—Contrary to the Duke of Cumberland's opinion. When they were brought to the select persons of the Regency, they had alter'd them, and restrain'd him from taking any but ships of line. The Duke [of Cumberland], in this little assembly, was expressing his dislike of the alteration, when the D. of N. came in; who interrupted his Highness by saying that he was glad of the alteration, because he knew that it was more conformable to the King's way of thinking upon these matters, and then desir'd his Highness to go on: who said that he knew his Grace had correspondences at Hanover which he did not communicate to him; but did not know that he had taken his Majesty's pleasure upon that head till now that he was pleas'd to declare it: that since it was so, he had too many tyes ever to say a word against his Majesty's pleasure, when he knew it. That when the instructions came to the bottom of the table, to be sign'd by him, Fox, he ask'd Lord Anson if there were no objections to them. Who said 'Yes, a hundred, but it pleases those yonder,' (looking to the upper

---

[1] A significant blank, no doubt indicating a West Wycombe meeting.

end) 'and will signify nothing, for the French will declare war next week, if they have not done it already.' 'But,' says I, 'that did not happen.' 'No,' says he, 'and therefore I am very sorry that I sign'd it: but in a few days the Duke was very desirous to have them alter'd, as well as the Duke of Marlborough, and myself: and in the morning, before the Regency met, he endeavour'd to have them extended, but without effect. When the Regency was over, the Duke of Marlborough and I desir'd to speak with the D. of N. and I told him how absurd I thought it, that we who had begun the war should suffer the hands to pass by us that are to be employ'd against us &c. I desir'd him to remember that I had made no objection at the Regency, but that I did, now, and to him privately, declare my disapprobation of these orders.' The Duke of Marlborough did the same. Who with Lord Anson din'd at Mr Fox's: while they were at table, a note came to Lord Anson to meet that evening, at the Duke's lodgings, which was to send directions to Hawke to seize or destroy everything French, trade or men of war, between Capes Ortegal and Clear: and so it, now, stands.

Said that beside the Hessians a subsidiary treaty was concluded with Russia, as he understood, tho' he had not heard—directly from Williams. Did not speak out, about that correspondence. That the subsidy was £100,000 pr. ann. for 4 years, he thought, to hold in readiness 50, or 60,000 men, which, when we employ'd, we were to pay £500,000 pr. ann. for. That he suppos'd that there would be subsidies to Bavaria, and maybe others. That he had of late, had opportunities of conversing much with the Duke of Devonshire, occasion'd by his son's affairs. That he was open, and vehement against all subsidies whatsoever, that the nation could not carry on a naval war with France, or support Hanover: that it must take care of its self. That we had follow'd the Kings politics too long, the nation could not support the expense of both, the King must be told so. That the D. of N. held by nothing but absolute submission, must not, would not, contradict the King in anything.

That Lord Granville told the D. of N. that he would be serv'd himself, as he, and his brother had serv'd him, Granville; they would not abuse him, themselves, but would set still and rather encourage it, than defend him. That he knew, positively, some considerable people, not suspected of an inclination to differ, who would be absolutely against all subsidy whatsoever. Did not name them nor would, to him, Fox. Said that talking this matter of subsidies over with the Duke [of Cumberland], His Highness said in a word, that he was sorry for it, that the bent of the nation was strong against subsidies for Germany; that it would be brought to endure it, with much reluctance: that he laid no great weight upon the point of honour; it would not do with the bulk of the people; that we should see a strong exertion of power, on one hand, and a strong dislike, and restiffness on the other. I said I thought Hanover might and ought to be defended, the question was only who was to pay for it, and in what proportions? He said he was surpriz'd that I was not against all subsidies; I told him that those I should be for, would hardly be the ministerial ones; but desir'd to know what these Russians, &c. were to do? 'Why, to prevent the King of Prussia from attacking Hanover, in conjunction with the French.' I said the King of Prussia would not attack Hanover. He said he was glad to hear me say so: and hop'd I could make it out. I said that was time enough for that, and for my ideas of defending Hanover, that he might believe that I had not given myself the trouble to digest my thoughts with very great exactness, much less, to put them into writing, but that whenever he came to act, I would lay everything I knew, before him, without reserve, but it was now useless to digest, and discuss what was never like to come into operation:[1]

[1] The entry appears to be incomplete and there is no entry for the next fourteen days: suggesting some pages excised.

SEPTEMBER

2. Mr Pitt came to see me, and acquainted me that he had seen the Ministers, and was to see the Duke of Newcastle, at his own desire, at 7 this evening.

He began by the Subsidies: that the Hessian, he knew of; for 8000 men a warrant for the levee-money was come to his office, that he would support a Naval war to the utmost: but, by no means, a continent one: The nation could not support both: it would carry us up to £7,000,000 the first year, and go on increasing &c.—'Twas bankrupcy. Regard should be had to Hanover no doubt, but secondarily. We should never lay down our arms without procuring satisfaction for any damage they should receive, on our account: but we could not find money to defend it by subsidies; and if we could, that was not the way to defend it. An open country was not to be defended against a neighbour that had 150,000 men and an enemy that could march 150,000 more, to back them. In short, many strong, ingenious and solid reasons, for making a stand here, and giving no subsidies; at all. That the King's honour would be urged, &c. and therefore if the D. of N. would be contented with this Hessian subsidy for this once; engage, *with proper security*, never to offer another, during the course of this whole war; let be treated as a single thing, and receive it as a compliment to the King for this one, never to be renew'd, or attempted again, but to be look'd upon as a putting a full end to continent subsidies, then—tho' it would not be right, yet he might not absolutely reject it but might ask other gentlemen's opinion about it: but for the Russian subsidy of £120,000 pr. ann. and £500,000 pr. ann. when we take the number of men into pay, which treaty, he heard, was sign'd, if not ratify'd, he could never come into it, upon any account: 'twas better speaking plain—there was no end of these things: it was deceiving, and ruining ourselves, and leading Hanover into a snare: for if 70,000 men would not be sufficient, we must take more, till they were sufficient, which would ruin us, or give them up at last when we had drawn a war upon them. That the D. of N. had made a person write to him, to say that the Duke was sorry that he was oblig'd to go to Sussex, the next day, but that the Chancellor did not go to Wimpole till Wednesday, and he should be oblig'd to him

(Pitt), if he would call upon the Chancellor, which he did. The Chancellor told him that he hop'd he would assist them cordially in their business: that the King had, indeed, taken prejudices that were disagreeable—, that steps had been taken to remove them, before he went; that they had been corresponded upon since; that they had not indeed, all the success they could wish, *As Yet*, but hop'd they should; that the King was very fond of Lord Holderness, and Sir Thomas Robinson; but if any accident should happen, if he would assist them cordially, possibly it might be brought about that they might get the seals for him, which he so much desir'd.

When the Chancellor had done, he reply'd that he must begin with his last words, 'the seals he so much desir'd'—of whom? He did not remember that he had ever apply'd to his Lordship for them: was sure he never had, to the D. of N. and did assure him that if they could prevail upon his Majesty to give them to him, under his present dislike, all the use he would make of them would be to lay them at his feet. That, 'till his Majesty lik'd it, and thought it necessary to his service, and till his ministers desir'd it (neither would happen) he would never accept of the seals. That he knew the King had said, lately, that he had intruded himself into office: that he, Chancellor, knew how much he was misinform'd, and if he would ask for any favour, it would be that they would inform his Majesty better.

The Chancellor was long, but he desir'd his Lordship to let him know what he was to assist in, what was their work: 'Why, to carry on the war they were engag'd in.' He said there was no doubt of his concurrence in carrying on the war, as it was a national one; and he thought that regard ought to be had to Hanover, if it was attack'd, upon our account. The Chancellor stop'd him short, there, and said he was extremely pleas'd that they agreed in their principles, and that both thought Hanover *should be defended*. He desir'd his Lordship to observe his words, 'That regard was to be had to Hanover', and then said all he had said to me before, as to our inability to defend it, and the impropriety of the defence, by subsidy—and that he would make it out against any military man. The Chancellor said that he understood that the Commons last Session, tacitly allow'd that Hanover must be defended: that in consequence of that acquiescence, there was a subsidiary treaty for 8000 Hessians, in the usual form, and there was also a treaty for a body of Russians. Then he said all that he had said, above, upon subsidies. What he put his finger upon was, that in reasoning, the Chancellor said, 'To be sure those things, (meaning subsidies) *should have their bounds*': that '*he was afraid they would not be very popular*'—and when he was enforcing the necessity of putting a total stop to them, and leaving Hanover to the system and constitution of the Empire, the Chancellor seem'd to acquiesce in the reason, but told him he must be sensible that talking in that manner would not make way with the King.

He persisted in not giving in to the subsidy and the Chancellor desir'd him to see the D. of N. and talk it over with him.—Said that if the Duke sent to desire to speak with him he would wait upon him; not else.—Thought that the Duke of Devonshire would oppose subsidies, and might be brought to do it in the House of of Lords.—Had seen the Duke of Bedford, who talk'd warmly and sensibly about it.—Went away fully determin'd to tell the D. of N. plainly that he would not come into the Russians, upon any account; nor into anything till he was well appriz'd of the measures, knew who were to carry them thro', and in what stations; and that the House was properly treated, and gentlemen were made easy that had a right to be so; had not seen Lord Egmont; knew he had been sent to with an offer of Sir William Yonge's place; hop'd he had given no positive answer.—Would acquaint me with the result of the conference he was to have that evening, with the D. of N. before he went back into the country; which he should do, tomorrow.

3. Mr Pitt came to acquaint me with the result of his conference with the D. of N.

That he had painted to the Duke, all the ill consequences of this system of subsidies in the strongest lights that his own imagination, heighten'd by my suggestions to him, furnish'd him with; had deprecated him not to complete the ruin which the King had nearly brought upon himself, by his journey to Hanover, which they should have prevented; *with their bodies.*—A King abroad, at this time, without one man about him that has one English sentiment, and brings home a whole set of subsidies!—That he was willing to promote the King's service, but if this was what he was sent for to promote, few words were best; nothing in the world should induce him to agree to these subsidies.

The Duke was long and perplex'd, would have persuaded him what a pretty figure he would make when he was a Cabinet Councillor. That the King was extremely pleas'd with both his Secretaries, but if any accident should make a vacancy, to be sure the King would be glad of his services, &c.

Mr Pitt said, that he did not desire such—vacancy, nor the office; that he had said when press'd about the House of Commons, that if they expected him, or anybody else, to do the business there, they must give them proper distinction and powers:—that in short, the Duke's system of carrying on the business of the House, he believ'd, would not do, but that 'while he had life, and breath to utter, he would oppose it': that there must be men of efficiency, and authority in the House, a Secretary, and a Chancellor of the Exchequer, at least, who had access to the Crown, habitual, frequent familiar access, he meant, to tell their own story, to do themselves, and their friends, justice, and not be the victims of a whisper: —That he esteem'd both the Secretaries, but he suppos'd something was wanting, or why was he sent for? If they were necessary to Government, no doubt they could carry on Government: and he should be glad of it, for his part, if the Ministry ask'd nothing of him, he ask'd nothing of them.

The Duke then said, that the system of subsidies, indeed, was not to be insisted upon, but two did not make a system; The King's honour was engag'd, and enlarg'd much upon that.—He reply'd, that he had a deep regard for the King's honour; but that the system of subsidies was so fatal, that he could not think of submiting to £100,000 without it was given by gentlemen who became pledges to each other, and to the public, that nothing of the like kind, should ever be offer'd again; and it should be publicly declar'd, and understood on both sides, that it was given, and receiv'd, as a mark of the affection of a ruin'd nation, to save the honour of its King, who had enter'd into a rash engagement: but for two, it was the same as twenty, and no persuasion should make him for it:—What if the Duke of Devonshire should begin the opposition in the House of Lords?—If he did, he (Pitt) would not conceal it from the D. of N.—he would echo it in the House of Commons, as loudly, and with all the powers he was able to exert. But was this all, were there no subsidies to be renew'd?

The Duke mumbled that the Saxon, and Bavarian, were offer'd, and press'd, but there was nothing done in them. That the Hessian was perfected, but the Russian was not concluded.—Whether he meant unsign'd, or unratified, we cannot tell, but we understand that it is sign'd. When his Grace dwelt so much upon the King's honour, Mr Pitt ask'd him, what if out of the 15 millions he had sav'd, the King should give his kinsman of Hesse £100,000 and the Czarina £150,000, to be off of these bad bargains, and not suffer the suggestions so dangerous to his own quiet, and the safety of his Family, to be thrown out, that would and must be insisted upon in a debate of this nature, where would be the harm of it? The Duke had nothing to say.—But desir'd they might talk it over again with the Chancellor. He said, he was at their service, but nothing could alter his opinion.

We then talk'd over whom we could engage; whom he had communicated this to? He said that Mr Legge was firm as a rock. He was shy about Lord Egmont but said he had seen him, receiv'd very kindly, seem'd to enter into the thing, but what might happen when offers were made, he (Pitt) could not tell. Desir'd me to apply to Lord Hillsborough, and Sir Francis Dashwood: I mention'd Oswald: he said, he thought he was in it. (If so, it must be by Legge). I ask'd him if he had communicated it to Mr Fox: He said, No, nor did not design to do it. He would tell me the whole of his thoughts of that matter:

That he wish'd Mr Fox very well, and had nothing to complain of; but that they could not act together; because they were not upon the same ground: that Mr Fox own'd to him he was not *sui juris* [*sc. generis*]—he did not blame him for it, but he who was could not act in connection with one who was not.[1]—He Pitt was ready last Session, to go any lengths, against the Duke of Newcastle— when it came to the push, Mr Fox own'd he could not; and went on, thro' the whole Session, compromising everything when it begun to pinch: The Reading Election; the Linen Affair; and when Ireland begun to be a thorn, Mr F's. great friend, Lord Harrington, was to take it out.—That by these means had taken the smooth part, and left him to be fallen upon; had rose upon his shoulders, but he did not blame him, and only show'd me how impossible it was for two to act together, who did not stand upon the same ground.

Besides, Mr Fox liv'd with his greatest enemies: Lord Granville, Messrs Stone and Murray: 'twas true he own'd it. But he (Pitt) would always act upon plain Whig principles, and would never have anything to do with Stone, or Murray.—That the D. of N. had told a great person that Mr Fox, very lately, had offer'd himself

---

[1] i.e. Fox was under formal obligations to Cumberland and was not his own master.

to him.—I said, I was confident it was false.—He said that he knew the D. of N. was a very great liar, and therefore, if Mr Fox deny'd it, he should not hesitate a moment, which he should believe.—I, then, said, that those who united in this attack, were to part no more, and therefore it would be proper to think what was to be held out to them, if we succeeded.—He declin'd that, and said that it would look to much like a faction: there was nothing 'country' in that:—If we succeeded, to be sure those who contributed must and would be consider'd, when, first, opportunity offer'd, but to engage for specifical things, and times, he thought no one man had any title, except myself; that for me, anything, everything that I lik'd, ought to be the common cause, and with me he was ready to enter into any engagements.

He then, express'd himself *strangely*, as to me: that he thought me of the greatest consequence, no man in this country would be more listen'd to, both in, and out of the House, &c.—&c.—That he was most desirous to connect and unite himself with me, in the strictest manner. Ever had the highest regard for my abilities.—We had always acted upon the same principles. He had the honour of being married into my relations, everything invited him to it, and a great deal more. That surpriz'd me very much, considering the treatment I have met with, for years, both from him, and those relations. It surpriz'd me so much, that all I said, was, that I was much oblig'd to him: but that he might depend upon it, that I would not even accept of his friendship, or any mark of his confidence, without meeting him more than half way.—Thus far, however, is lucky, and I am glad to find that I shall be supported in a step, that, for my own credit, as well as for the interest of my country, I must have taken, tho' I had met with no support at all.

11. Set out for Eastbury.—Arrived the 13th.

24. Account of the defeat, and death of General Braddock, on the Ohio.

Dodington to Henry Fox[1]

Eastbury
Saturday the 27th Septbr.
1755

Dear Sir,

I receiv'd the Honour of yours of the 23rd last Thursday the only

---

[1] Source: Add. MS. 38091, f. 61. The letter is a copy, but the date and address are in D.'s hand.

day the Post comes in here without returning in the Afternoon, which alone has prevented your receiving my thanks sooner.

That of all Those who are in the King's Service, or likely to be so you are one whom I most cordially wish to see in the first Rank is a truth that I hop'd to convince you of, by contributing both to the placing and Supporting you in it, & not by Words, and therefore I have been very sparing of them. You know you were the last thing I saw before I set out, and that I delay'd my journey a day, to have that Pleasure, since I have been here you will imagine I have seen nobody to agree, differ, or engage with.

My Opinion in many things must naturally be known to most of those I converse with: for as it is below the Administration to take notice of them, I have thought it below me to conceal them: but as to the particular manner of acting, in Pursuit and consequence of those Opinions, I have taken no positive Engagement, because I have not positively determin'd it in my own thoughts, nor will take any, till I have the Honour of seeing you, since you are pleas'd to make me some part of your Care in so noble and freindly a Manner: as such I look upon it: and receive it with Pleasure.

I never thought you could be a Looker-on, I never wish'd it: I always wish'd you should be an Actor, a Principal Actor, but where Honour and Reputation as well as Power and Profit, distinguishes the Part you appear in: for Dear Mr Fox believe an Old Man that Loves and esteems you, there is nothing else worthy of an honest, noble, well-regulated Ambition.

Nothing I hope, would have made me put such an air of Significancy upon myself as to have suffer'd you to make a Journey Hither, if I had design'd to stay the Autumn here, which you know I did not. I shall set out on Monday next the 29th instant and hope to get to the convent,[1] on Wednesday the first October where if I meet your commands when and where you will be attended you shall find your Poor Friend in nothing alter'd of his most Affectionate Regard for you and most desirous of showing you the true sense he has of the many kind, and friendly Offices you have bestow'd upon him.

I am with reall Affection
and Respect
Dear Sir,
Your most Faithfull, Humble,
servant
G. D.

---

[1] Another possible reference to Medmenham Abbey.

OCTOBER

1. Return'd to Hammersmith.

Henry Fox to Lord Halifax, Copy to Dodington[1]

Holland House
4 October 1755

My dear Lord,
    I call'd at your Lordship's Door, & should have been very glad to have had the Honour of seeing you before I went into the Country, where I am, this Moment, going, for ten days. I am coming into a situation that will, I hope, give me the Opportunities of cultivating what I have long aspir'd to, your Lordship's Friendship; and it is upon the good Will, and good Opinion of Persons of your Character, that I should wish to depend. Mr Dodington, who has known you longer, honours you above all Mankind, and I believe is as much inclin'd as you can be to make One in a political System with your Lordsp, Lord Hillsborough, and your humble servant; But how far his Opinion will permit him to follow his inclination, I do not know. I think him of great Importance, and I believe, to the forming or changing that Opinion your Lordsp. will go a great way. If your Lordsp. thinks the Measure, which will be the Question in Debate, (I mean the Defence of Hannover, by these two Subsidiary Treaties) just, or necessary, and to be given into, upon a Knowledge that it is to extend no farther, and would endeavour to engage Mr Dodington, your Lordship would do the Greatest Service to your Friends; and the King has given his Word, that he will no longer, put his negative on Mr Dodington, but will do what may be advis'd, that will be agreeable to him.
    I am sensible that I have ventur'd too far with your Lordship in a first Letter. But I hope, your Lordsp. will not only excuse this, but lett me go a great deal farther in the Progress of that Friendship, which is among the sincerest, and most ambitious Wishes of
My Lord,
Your Lordsp's
most obedient, oblig'd
& faithfull humble servant,
H. Fox

[1] Source. Add. MS. 38091, f. 63. D had dined with Fox on the previous night, and Fox reported to Newcastle in the same sense as the letter to Halifax—that D would come in with a little persuasion to overcome his scruples about policy.

5. Went to town. Talk'd with Lord Halifax.

6. He din'd here, and we settled his behaviour to the D. of Newcastle, on a letter to him, from his Grace,[1] pressing him to engage me in the King's service.

8. Went to town and din'd with Lord Halifax: he had been with the Duke of N. who press'd him much upon my subject, and beg'd him to obtain a meeting with me. I agreed to go to Newcastle House, next Friday.

10. Went, first, to Lord Halifax's, then, to Newcastle House. Was much press'd to come in, but absolutely refus'd being for the Russian Subsidy, on any account.

Dodington's Minute of the above Conversation[2]

'MY LORD,

I UNDERSTAND, by Mr Fox, and by a letter from your Grace to Lord Halifax, that the King is disposed to accept my services: and I am very ready to serve him, if I can do it, with utility to his Majesty and with honour to myself: for I do not want the service, either to mend my fortune, or for an introduction into the world; I want it for neither. I am come, therefore, my Lord, to know of your Grace, in what, and in what shape and situation his Majesty expects my services.'

He said it was true: and that the King had received what he laid before his Majesty of my zeal for his family, and of my abilities, much more favourably of late, than when he formerly had done all that he could with his Majesty, to——

'My Lord, I beg we may not look back: that, I am sure, will not advance any thing I came hither about.'

He said it was very obliging in me, to forget what was pass'd—but he must have his own thoughts about it.

---

[1] Dodington was not intended to see this letter at all. It was written on 4 October, following Fox's report, and particularly asked Halifax not to mention the appointment that the King had authorized to be offered to Dodington (the Comptrollership). D kept a copy for his file (Add. MS. 38091), and was thus prepared to hold out for something better.

[2] Printed in P.W. Appendix. That it is faithful in recording D's refusal to compromise on the subsidies is confirmed by Newcastle's letter to Hardwicke (Add. MS. 32860, f. 18)—'Mr Dodington protested against the Russian Treaty in stronger, and more explicit terms than even Mr Pitt himself.'

'And I mine, my Lord.'

He proceeded to say, that as Mr Fox was a person agreeable to me, the King had directed that Mr Fox should come to Dorsetshire to me, to settle matters, and that his Majesty would consent to any thing for myself, that I liked and should be agreed amongst us; not then knowing that I should be so soon at Hammersmith.

I said I had seen Mr Fox, and that he had spoke to me, in generals only, about public affairs, and his Majesty's favourable disposition to me.

He said he understood it so: and that Mr Fox had only reported that I was well disposed to enter into the service, and if measures could be made agreeable, I had no objection to men.—And that, if there was anything I liked, and would let it be known, it might be shaped out to my satisfaction, &c.

'My Lord, where there is no offer, no answer can be expected.'

He said, all would depend upon measures, if those could be made agreeable, everything would be made easy; and therefore it would be proper to go upon that.

'My Lord, if your Grace pleases, one thing at once. As you have no offer to make, you can expect no answer upon that head: and be pleased to observe that I have nothing to offer, and nothing to ask.'

'Why, to be sure,' he said, 'if what was thought of was not agreeable, anything else that I liked might be brought about: but what the King first thought of was the Comptroller's Staff.'

'My Lord, I will suppose I did not hear you, and as you have nothing to offer, and I have nothing to ask, there can be no answer, and we may shut the book.'

He said, that if they had known I should not have liked the Staff, it would not have been thought of.

'My Lord, it should not have been thought of.—If you please, my Lord, let us suppose that nothing specifical has been offered: and I repeat my expectation that your Grace will remember, that I have nothing to offer, or propose to you, and nothing to ask.'

He said, he understood it so: and that I came at his Majesty's requisition, who was desirous I should come into the service. And as for measures, they had no particular ones, but the two treaties with Hesse and Russia, which last had been negotiating these two years, (what he meant by that, I neither know, nor thought proper to ask) as he supposed Mr Fox had explained them.

Upon my answering in the negative, and saying that I did not believe that Mr Fox understood them thoroughly himself; his Grace began to enter into that with Russia; but I stopp'd him, by saying, that I supposed they were two subsidiary treaties, which, like all others, bargained for a certain number of men, for a certain time: so much subsidy to the Princes, and such pay to the troops, when called for.

'Yes—exactly so'—and then proceeded to show that the Russian treaty was the best, and only way to defend Hanover, and prevent a Continent war. That if Hanover was attacked for the sake of England, it ought to be looked upon as England, &c. and then would have gone on into the particulars, but I interrupted him, by saying, 'Then I would not lose your Grace's time in explanation, which can only affect the mode of the thing, and not the substance; I may possibly think of it, as of a dish dressed by your Grace's cook, the more palatable, the more unwholesome. But I will be plain with your Grace; I think this Russian subsidy to be ruinous to this country, of most dangerous precedent, most hurtful to his Majesty's true interest, and destructive of the interest of his family; at the same time insufficient to the ends proposed by it, and instead of preventing a Continental war, the most certain seed and foundation of it. And I can never think I am serving his Majesty by supporting it.'

'At the same time I will agree with your Grace, and am willing it should be understood, I am for defending Hanover, if it be attacked out of resentment to England, and that I not only never will consent to, but will hinder, to the best of my poor little power, the swords being sheathed, till Hanover be indemnified. I will go farther, and will allow without farther examination, that if it be now attacked, it is on the account of England:—but I do not think this Russian subsidy is the way to defend it, or to make the people fond of it. Besides, my Lord, your Grace knows, and I know, that (without this Russian subsidy) it will never be attacked.' He said, he wished he did; that if I could convince him of that, it would be the best news that had come to England a great while.

'I do know it, my Lord, and I thought your Grace had: unless we are to suppose that people will do the direct contrary to what they have promised, and engaged to do.'

'But at the same time I say this of the Russian subsidy, your Grace will observe that I *do not say* that I will be for the Hessian: I desire not to be misunderstood, or misrepresented.' Oh no! he understood me very well, and would be sure not to misrepresent me any where.

'My Lord, I will not be misrepresented. I do not say that I will approve of the Hessian subsidy, if there were no Russian, because considered by itself, 'tis a silly, unadvised step, the best one can think of it, or call it, is a job; 'tis so apparently of no significancy, and inadequate to the purposes held out; and nobody can think you in earnest when you declare them: but, however, as to that, there may be modes and qualifications, especially as *that* is ratified and concluded, (and your Grace says that you are not sure you shall get the other) and as great respect to, and desire to comply with his Majesty's word, when it was solemnly engaged, is our duty, as far as is consistent with our duty to our country; I say, there may, possibly, be found some temperament, in that case single, that might enable one to speak to gentlemen, and one's friends; and if, upon proper explanations, they were disposed to make so great a compliment, I should not endeavour to inflame, but rather, possibly, be inclined to acquiesce.' After a little, and not very material interruption, I resumed the discourse, and said:

'My Lord, I did not come here to dispute with your Grace: my opinion of the general tendency of these subsidies, both at home and abroad, will admit of no variation; and it is fit that I should acquaint your Grace, that as to the Russian, I will oppose it with all the little credit and efficacy I have, both in the House, and out of it: but I will do it with all the decency that is consistent with truth.' He said, they were convinced of the great decency of my behaviour on all occasions. And I went on to say, that as to the Hessians, I did not say that I would be for them: that point, however, might admit of some modification: but if they both came in, I would indubitably oppose both, for, whatever I did, I would do thoroughly.

After civil expressions of concern, that we did not agree in our opinion about measures, he let himself into the danger of provoking other maritime Princes to join France against us; from the present too openly professed doctrine of being masters of the seas: that Sweden and Denmark would, in conjunction with France, have a fleet of fifty sail in the Baltic, &c.—that we had the greatest fleet, the best provided, officered, and directed, that ever was: that I saw it could not be depended upon: they could not hinder squadrons from going out, and coming in, through the most winding, difficult passages, &c. I got up, and said, if we were not superior at sea, we must give it up: that I had taken up too much of his time, and begg'ed leave to recapitulate what had passed, that there might be no room for mistake, or misrepresentation: that, in the first place, as to myself, I had made no manner of offer, nor asked any thing, of anybody: that as to measures for the Hessian subsidy, I had no ways said that I would be for it, if it came single; but, in that case, it might admit of farther consideration; but if it was to be combined with the Russian, I would most certainly oppose both: that I had said I would oppose the Russian, to the utmost of my power, but with all the decency that truth would admit: that there remained but one thing, and that was not recapitulation, because I had not said it before, which was, that he should find, (though I did not know whether ever they told him one word of truth) he should find (if they did) that I opposed it solely from the unfitness of the thing, and not because anybody there thought fit to oppose it: that I should show it was from opinion, my own opinion only, and not from anybody's else; or out of dislike to, or against any body, that I opposed it. I was unconnected with any one, and would be so, upon this question: how long I should continue so I could not tell, but I was so now. Nobody had any demand, any right to call upon me, but one gentleman, a near relation of his Grace's, Lord Halifax; he had a right, and when he did call, at any time, and upon any occasion, I should always be ready to obey it.

After a little insignificant talk, and reciprocal civilities, we parted.

19. Preliminaries, which with the conversation at Newcastle House, are to be found among my papers.

THE PRELIMINARIES

What is hinted at for Mr Dodington, is more than he desires for himself; but without the concurrence of his Friends, and the following conditions for *them*, it is impossible for *him* to enter into any engagement.

Earl of Halifax to be of the Cabinet. Such provision in possession, or reversion, for Mr Furnese, as shall be agreed upon between him and Mr Attorney General.

Sir Francis Dashwood to be offered the Comptroller's Staff, or something that is proper for, and would be agreeable to him; if he can be prevailed upon to accept anything, which I very much doubt.

Lord Talbot to be comprehended. Mr Tucker to be provided for, at, or before the end of the Session.

Full liberty to oppose the subsidies, honestly and fairly; which is never to cause the least coldness, expostulation, or remonstrance.

Mr Dodington is also obliged to be of the Irish side of the question, about the linens.

It is presumed that there is to be no trifling; but that the correspondence and communication between Mr Dodington's friends and the Administration, is to be sincere, honourable, and unreserved.

NOVEMBER AND DECEMBER

NOVEMBER

7. Came to town.

13. Parliament open'd.

20. Messrs Pitt, Legge, and George Grenville receiv'd letters of dismission,—and James Grenville resign'd the Board of Trade.

DECEMBER

12 & 15. Debates in the Committee, and upon the Report, of the Subsidiary Treaties with Hesse Cassel and Russia.[1]

16. The D. of Newcastle desir'd to see me, next day.

17. I went to Newcastle House. With much assurances of confidential friendship, the D. told me that he had the King's leave to offer me the Treasury of the Navy: which I accepted.

19. Waited upon the Princess to acquaint her with what had pass'd. Receiv'd very cooly.[2]

22. Kiss'd the King's hand as Treasurer of the Navy.

23. Set out for Horton, and din'd there.

27. Return'd to London, before 6 o'clock.

---

[1] The Debate on the Address, which raged round the Subsidy Treaties, was one of the greatest in the century. The House sat until quarter to five in the morning. The speeches included a tremendous one from Pitt, lasting an hour and half, and the effort that made 'Single-Speech Hamilton's' nickname and reputation. Dodington, of course, opposed the treaties, but it was noticed that he did so half-heartedly. He could not, of course, accept office till the Treaties were clear of the Commons.

[2] 'No wonder'—Horace Walpole's annotation of the *Diary*.

1756

JANUARY, FEBRUARY, AND MARCH

JANUARY

13. Parliament open'd.

26. Question upon the dividing the Vice-Treasurership of Ireland into three. Propos'd and supported by Messrs Pitt, Potter, and their friends.

FEBRUARY

4. Sent for to Newcastle House, about the loan which fail'd from Sir T. Barnard's affectation of showing his superior credit and abilities, by raising money at a price that it is not to be had, in the quantity wanted. I subscrib'd £50,000 public money.[1]

Voltaire to Dodington[2]

A Monrion près de Lausanne
4 Fevrier 1756

Sir,

I was very sick in the month of January, at the foot of the Alps, when a handsome youth[3] did appear in my cabin, next to Lausanne, and favoured me with your kind letter, written in September: the date from Eastbury. . . .

The country about Geneva, which you have seen, is now much improved; noble houses are built, large gardens are planted. Those who say the world impairs every day are quite in the wrong—are quite in the wrong as to the natural world; 'tis not like the moral and political one.

---

[1] i.e. he underwrote this amount to be subscribed in the City.
[2] Source: Seward, *Anecdotes of Distinguished Persons*, fifth edition, 1804, vol. iv, p. 433. The original, once among D.'s papers, has not been traced.
[3] The 'handsome youth' was Mr East, D.'s protégé. See 15 June 1755 above.

Be what it will, I have pitched upon two retreats on the banks of that lake you are pleas'd to mention in your letter. I pass the winter by Lausanne, and the other seasons by Geneva, without care and without kings.

That country would not perhaps agree with a Frenchman of twentyfive; but it is most convenient to old age; when one is past sixty, the place of reason is a private station.[1] Yet, though I am mightily pleased with these lands of peace and freedom, I would gladly see another land of liberty before I die; I would have the honour to see you again, and renew to you my sincere and everlasting gratitude for all the tokens of kindness I received from you when I was in London.

My good countrymen have sometimes upbraided me for having too much of the English spirit in my way of thinking; it should be but just I should pay a visit to those who have drawn that reproach upon me; be sure, dear Sir, none was more guilty than you. I hope I should find you in good health, for you are born as sound and strong as Nature made me weak and unhealthy. I hope the evening of your day is serene and calm; 'tis the best lot of that hour: you have enjoyed all the rest.

> I am, with the tenderest respect,
> Sir,
> Your most humble and obedient servant,
> VOLTAIRE

12. American Blll read the First Time.

18. . . . . Second

20. Committed.

23. Reported.

26. Read the Third Time.
   N.B. Oppos'd with insufferable length, and obstinacy, by Mr Pitt and his friends.

MARCH

3. Ways and Means. Houses, Ale Licences, (Bricks being given up) and Plate.

---

[1] A favourite tag from Addison's *Cato*.

17. First Reading of the Plate Bill. N.B. Second Reading contested, and carried by 9 only.

29. Eight thousand Hanoverians mov'd for by Lord George Sackville.

[There are no entries for April]

MAY

5. The news came of the French landing at Minorca. Went to the

6. D. of N.'s—Who told me with much warmth, and anxiety that they had an account by the Spanish Minister, that the French *finish'd* their debarkation upon Minorca, the 20th April, that they had taken Mahon, and pretended to take St Philips, by the end of the month. And also, as soon as they had finish'd their debarkation, Monsr de la Galissonière stood out to sea, off the island, to intercept any succours: so that, before now, there must have been a naval action, between him, and Byng. He has 12 ships of line; Byng, 10, very good.[1]—I said, that as we were alone, 'twas astonishing that Byng was not there, a month ago.—He said he was not ready, that he was oblig'd to stay two, or three days for his last 200 men. That we had but 63 ships of line in Europe, and those still wanted 4000 men. That it was *impar congressus* that Mirepoix had told him that 30 of their ships would amuse 80 of ours.—That if Hawke, and Boscawen did not join, we had no naval force equal to what they have at Brest.—I ask'd 'Why were you not ready? Why have you not more ships, and more men?'—Said he had not the direction of the sea.—Laid a vast deal of blame, there—and without naming Lord Anson show'd himself extremely dissatisfy'd with him: but conjur'd me, upon my honour, not to mention to anybody, what he had said, upon that head—and concluded by insisting that the island must be retaken.

7. Estimate for the 8000 Hanoverians, without division. Call'd upon Mr Fox.—Full of concern.– He would have sent a squadron, and a strong one, the first week in March, but could not prevail.— Fears of the invasion, and *landing in Sussex, prevented.*—Lord Anson assur'd him, and took it upon himself, that Byng's squadron would beat anything the French had, or could have, in the Mediterranean.

12. Message for a Vote of Credit—No Division—but the Prussian Treaty (which made part of the Message) separated, and to be consider'd the 14th as it was.

[1] In fact Byng did not sail till 8 May from Gibraltar, and the engagement was not until 20 May. It was not true that the British ships were better found than the French: the reverse was the case.

17. I went to Council, at Kensington. Declaration of War with France agreed.

18. War declar'd. Mr Fox came to me in the House, and after saying that he must shortly come to me, to La Trappe, to talk a little; freely: for that he was very uneasy at the posture of public affairs and particularly with his own situation.—That the D. of Newcastle was unusually light, and trifling yesterday, when he din'd with him: extremely pleas'd with what he (Fox) declar'd on Friday last in the House, which was that Lord Anson authoris'd him to say, that the D. of N. never obstructed the sending sooner to the Mediterranean, (which was more, says he, than he could ever make him say, before) but that they were all agreed &c.—That therefore nobody blam'd him, that the City imputed nothing to him, as it was not his province—Fox ask'd him where he had that news.—Said from Garraways.—Reply'd, that if he (Fox) could believe anything he heard, the City was extreamly displeas'd with the leaving Minorca expos'd, and that in general, it would be ever true, that those who had the chief direction, in an administration, would bear the greatest share of blame, and that those deceiv'd him, who told him it was otherwise, now.—He still persisted that nobody thought him to blame, that, after the declaration, last Friday, the House of Commons were satisfy'd with him.—Fox reply'd that he did not know from whom he had his information of the House of Commons; but it appear'd plain to him, that when Mr Pitt charg'd the loss of Minorca upon his Grace, and that he (Fox) defended him as answerable but in an equal degree with others, that all friends hung their heads, and that not a man could be, or even seem'd, persuaded, that a squadron could not be sent sooner, or that all was done that could be done. That he defended him in everything he could defend him; in *one thing*, he never could, which was, in not believing it must be war, and not arming sooner.

Still, nobody could think *him* to blame—Mr Fox went on,—and said, that this intelligence came from Sir Thomas Robinson, who was very weak, &c.—That he thought he had fully answer'd all that could be expected; or that he had engag'd for, at coming in; hop'd I thought so too: but he found by the D. of N.'s whole behaviour to him, that he was not, at all, satisfy'd with what he had done.—Was it not true that the chief in an administration, would always be the most obnoxious?—I said, 'Yes, unless they had anybody to make a scape-goat.'—He seem'd alarm'd, ask'd me if I thought him likely to be a scape-goat, and dwelt upon it. I told him (as truth was) that when I said that, I had not *him* in any degree so much as in my contemplation, and had no apprehensions of any such thing.—He continued, and said he was very uneasy, that the country was in a sad way, but if it were in a better, those who had the direction of it could no more carry on this war, than his three children—that he, always, hinted at sending a squadron to Minorca sooner, That the D. of Cumberland press'd it, strongly, so long ago as last Christmas.

I, then, ask'd him what there was in a report that the Princes George and Edward were to be kept at Kensington.—He said he fancy'd that there was some grounds for it, but was not, in the least, trusted, or consulted with, about it; but he knew, (tho' not from them) that the D. of N. and the Chancellor had had two conferences upon that head, and tho' private conferences between them, was nothing new, for he suppos'd they had them every night, yet they had two, particularly, upon this subject; and he would tell me how *he* knew it: they were overheard in an entry, enough to learn the subject of those conversations, tho' not the result of them. That when everything was settled, he suppos'd Lords Holderness, Waldegrave, and himself should be call'd in, and when they were acquainted with it, then a minute of it was to be made, and carry'd to the King sign'd by them all, as their joint advice.—That he was ready to give his advice, and sign it, upon any of the King's affairs, how delicate soever; but whether he should sign, as his advice, what others had settled, and digested, without any way communicating it to him, was what he wanted to talk with me about, and know my opinion.

I thought this conversation much too delicate to be held in the benches; I, once, made him move his place, but he would go on.

21. Went to the D. of Newcastle's.—He would have talk'd about what pass'd the day before, in the House of Commons, upon the Committee of the Million Bill, which gives the Treasury the unprecedented power of borrowing it, without limiting the rate of interest. Sir George Lyttelton's candour in opening it made him acquaint the House with this dangerous, and unnecessary, innovation, which produc'd a debate and a division, where the Treasury rejected the limitation offered to be inserted, *but by one voice*. None

of us were acquainted either with the innovation, or Sir George's design to go into the Committee that day;[1] so that the numbers were but 37, and 36. I refus'd to talk of it, and told him it was too bad. He press'd me much to go down to the report; which I receiv'd coolly, and chang'd the subject to considering what new encouragement should be given a deputation of merchants having been with me, upon that head.—He desir'd me to talk with Lord Anson.—I then press'd him about Lord Halifax.—He express'd an earnest desire to keep his friendship, but protested he could no more get him a blue ribbon, than he could get the Kingdom of Ireland for me.—I said, I thought *that* was the mistake.—That tho' I wish'd he had the Garter, yet I never mention'd it, or meant it: what I meant, he knew, was the Cabinet; Lord Halifax, from station, services, merit had a right to it: his own interest loudly call'd for it: could not he do that?—He strongly declar'd that he would think of it, and do all he could, as soon as the Session was over—but he had talk'd with Lord Halifax's friends, and found that the Cabinet would not satisfy him.—I said, 'Put him in the wrong then—show you have done what everyone knows you can, and ought to do: and if at last, you are to break, break at least upon a point where you have some ground to stand upon, and not where you have none, not decline doing what you can do, because you do not attempt what possibly there may be some doubt about'.

He was very uneasy, and protested, with great earnestness, that he would do all that lay in his power to oblige Lord Halifax, as soon as the Parliament rose.

24. Militia Bill thrown out, by the Lords.[2]

25. Lord Chief Justice Ryder died.

[1] Lyttelton was Chancellor of the Exchequer. An interesting example of how business was not co-ordinated.
[2] Pitt had forced this bill for a national militia through the Commons in the teeth of the Government, as a demonstration against the subsidy policy for the purchase of foreign troops. Newcastle and Hardwicke killed it in the Lords, at considerable cost in popularity.

JUNE AND JULY

2. Heard that a message in writing had been sent to the Prince from the King offering him an allowance of £40,000 pr. ann. and an apartment in the Palaces of Kensington and St James's.—Answer full of high gratitude for the allowance but declining the apartment on account of the mortification it would be to his mother. N.B. He does not live with her, in town, or country.

N.B. The Duke of Newcastle gave me these papers, on the 21st, at Claremont. The same day the Spanish Ambassador had an account of an engagement between Byng, and the French in the Mediterranean.[1]—He had 13 ships of the line, 5 frigates: they 12, and 4 frigates. It lasted 4 hours, when by the advantage of the wind, the English stood out of gunshot, and were out of sight, next day.

9. Settled at La Trappe.

18. Parliament met, and was farther adjourn'd.

23. We had a good account of Byng's affair, by a letter from Consul Miller[2]: andabout an hour later his own dispatches arriv'd which gave no satisfaction at all.

Fox to Dodington[3]

H. House
June 23rd

. . . You will observe how like Galissonière's account was to this of Bing's, *mutato nomine*. I own I cannot but suppose this, as far as it goes, authentic, and as all the accounts from France agree that the seige of Fort St Philip's is not at all advanced, what if we should at last save it? This is the first time I have indulged myself in such a supposition.

Bing's despatches, sent from Barcelona cross Spain to the Corunna, are not arrived.

---

[1] This was a copy of the French Admiral's dispatch on the inconclusive action of 20 May, which had been transmitted by the French Government to the Spanish Ambassador in Paris. It resulted in the decision to supersede Byng and publish, in doctored form, his report of 25 May.
[2] James Miller, Consul at Barcelona.
[3] Text of this letter taken from *H.M.C. Var. Coll.*, vol. vi. No original traced.

Fox to Dodington[1]

June 23rd

The despatches mentioned in Miller's letter are already come this moment, not all deciphered, but enough so to blast most of the hopes you and I conceived. He says he beat the French fleet, or rather that it was a drawn battle. But he says they are too strong for us, that the fort is invested with 17,000 men (in buckram I suppose)[2] so that a letter cannot be conveyed into the place; and that by the advice of a council of war he is going back to Gibralter to refit, wait for reinforcements and return. He hopes to make a more complete victory. Helas! Adieu! P.S. Captain Andrews of the *Defiance* is killed.

26. Mr Fox show'd me Byng's strange letter, and yet stranger Council of War.

27. Pass'd the whole day at Claremont, much strange talk.

JULY

15. D. of Newcastle din'd here, and brought the disagreeable news of the loss of Fort Philip.

24. Set out for Eastbury: lay at Stockbridge.

25. At home.

[1] Ibid.
[2] The reference to Falstaff was justified. The whole French land force was well below this figure.

AUGUST TO OCTOBER

Dodington to Fox[1]

Eastbury
30 August 1756

I know nothing of public affairs but from the public papers, which represent them in a state of perplexity which I do not see sufficient grounds for; but if those gentlemen are at all well-informed, and they should, in any the least degree, be in such a state as to make people think that their friends can be of any use to them, you will please to remember that if you send your commands to La Trappe you will find one that is much more ready to do than to say.

But in truth, the state of my poor dear country is not the cause of my writing, tho' so pathetically set forth by those gentlemen, but their report of your ill-health, which a little alarms me, is the real motive of this letter; and if you can order Mr Tucker to send me word that you are well, it will be a more agreable piece of news to me than all the ministerial intelligence you will ever be able to send me as long as you live.

P.S. My duty to Lady Caroline and any young lady you may find in the neighbourhood.

As to Exertion, I sincerely do not conceive how it can be exercis'd without knowledge; especially in Things which I imagine to be so intricate, that one must be learning, when one should be acting. But more of This, when we meet, for I am honestly, your Friend to serve You, when you shall want one; but I do not think you do, yet, and I hope you never will.

I am, with sincere, and affectionate Respect
Dearest Sir &c

P.S. I did not write nor do I now to open a Correspondence. I expect you should employ your Time better than in writing to me.

Dodington to Oswald[2]

Eastbury
21 September 1756

Tho' I presume you take me for the Pretender by your great care not to hold any Communication with me either by speech, message, or letter, in your private capacity; and though in your publick capacity

---

[1] Add. MS. 38091, f. 67. 'Those gentlemen' refers to Pitt and his supporters.
[2] Oswald MS. 43 Oswald was at this time a Commissioner of Trade under the Earl of Halifax.

you use me like a Dog, (which you will find I shall not submitt to) yet I trust the Lord will touch your stony heart, and that you will relent and remember that there is such a person as Noll Bluff in the world, who is still, and like always to remain, your most faithful servant; and is now going to drink your health with the Corporation of Weymouth.

OCTOBER

1. Set out from Eastbury, lay at Bagshot.

2. At La Trappe. Note from Fox that things went ill.

3. Heard Oswego was taken.[1]

5. Went to Council. 55,000 seamen declar'd.

Dodington to Oswald[2]

La Trappe
Sunday Night [October 10
1756]

Dear Sr.

The proposition came from Mr F. upon the D's expressing great desires to gain P. The plan was, that F. would resign to him, take any other employment, *not of the Cabinet*, & assist, as far as he was able, in Parliament: this past, some months ago: and bears the appearance of friendliness, both in the act & its consequences. I, by no means answer for its sincerity. I have wrote to Ld. H. I confess I think our private as well as publick situation, very comfortless; as to the last, the difference is extreamly immaterial between having no resources, of having them, without any prospect of practicability to make use of them. I shall be very glad to see you tomorrow, & am ever, most faithfully.

Yours
G.D.

11. News of the Prussian victory.[3]

---

[1] Captured by the French, 14 August.
[2] Oswald MSS. 45. 'F'. 'P'. and 'H'. are Fox, Pitt, and Halifax.
[3] Lobowitz, fought 1 October. This initiated the war on the Continent.

Dodington to Oswald[1]

La Trappe, Tuesday [12 October
1756]

Dear Sir,

I am at your service on Fryday next, all day, & if it be equally
convenient to you, will pass it, here or at your house, which you
like best. If you chuse the first, bring all the papers &c that we can
want: if the last I will bring mine.

Yours most affectionately,
G.D.

The Kg of Prussia has wrote to his Mother, on a leaf torn out of his
pocket book, dated 1st Oct. that he has beat Marechl. Browne à platte
coutiere, lost 2000 men; the Austrians 4000. Place, between Aussich
& Lossowitz. Four Prussian Generals killed. Prince Lobkowitz
prisoner to Prussia. Prussians—35,000—Austrians about double the
number.—The King came up the night before the battle.—All this
comes confirm'd from Dresden & I suppose you knew it before.

14. Din'd with Mr Fox, who is in an extraordinary state.[2]

Dodington to Oswald[3]

La Trappe Saturday night
(October 16 1756)

I hope you caught no cold. Lord President carried the message, &
the paper; they were not well receiv'd, but the answer was not
decisive, yesterday; His Lordship was to bring some farther resolutions, today, which he did while I was there. I might have known
what they were, if I would have staid, but I beg'd to be excus'd: the
whole is inexpressibly disagreeable to me.

However his Lordship, or the place he came from may be dispos'd
it will be difficult to make the gentleman trust the Duke. In that
case, will the person design'd to succeed him, accept? can he without
encrease of power, & alteration of measures? will the Duke encrease
the one? can he alter the other? Comfort me a little if you can. My
heart sinks at the prospect of the private uneasiness we are plunging
into, & the broad ruin that is rushing upon our poor country.

His Lordship would keep me to tell me that Colnl. Lentulus arriv'd,

---

[1] Oswald MSS. 46.
[2] He sought permission to resign on the following day.
[3] Oswald MSS. 48. 'The message and the paper' were Fox's resignation, taken to
the King by Lord Granville, the Lord President. 'The gentleman' is, of course, Pitt,
and 'the person' Fox.

last night, from the King of Prussia, to give the King a verbal account of the battle. It was a compleat victory; General Brown behav'd extreamly well, as did the Austrian Troops: but after an obstinate resistance they were forc'd to give way, in the afternoon of Friday the 1st inst. The Prussians pursued them all that evening, & the two following days, till Monday when they drove them into a safe camp, where they are ready to attack them, if they shall venture to peep out. Colnl. Lentulus brings, also proofs of the King of Poland's behavior sufficient, it is said, to justify the King of Prussia's to him.

Farewell,

Yours faithfully and affectionately,

G.D.

Fox to Dodington[1]

Dear Sir,

I had a good deal of serious discourse with H.M. yesterday. The Chancr. did not come to town till last night. The D of N did not know his own mind till then, if he does now. H.M. kept his temper therefore, and is open to any future Behavior he shall think proper. Pitt came to town this morning. I know nothing more, & therefore had nothing to trouble you with. I believe, without knowledge, reflection will have brought you from what seem'd to be your opinion on Saturday, that things will be accommodated. What will be the Event I know not, nor am in any Degree Master of it. It is in other Hands, and I am *not* sorry for it.

Adieu

H. House. Octr 19 1756

Dodington to Fox[2]

La Trappe
Tuesday [19 October 1756]
Past 9 at night

Dear Sir,

The more I consider this whole Matter, the less I must confess, I can form any determin'd Judgment of it, and its Consequences. The serious Conversation you are pleas'd to mention must, I should think, furnish Materials that may be decisive; but as I do not show the particulars, I cannot pretend to judge in what Manner, and can only form the most ardent Wishes that it may be to the Advantage of the Publick, and your particular Satisfaction.

I am &c.

[1] Add. MS. 38091, f. 69.   [2] Add. MS. 38091, f. 70.

19. Mr Pitt sent for to town, and came.

Dodington to Oswald[1]

La Trappe Wednesday morng.
past 8.
[20 October 1756]

Dear Sr.

I receiv'd a letter yesterday, from Lord Halifax,[2] such as I did not quite expect, & am very sorry for. Late last night, I receiv'd a much more extraordinary note, from Mr Fox: both of which I will show you, if you will ride this way, this morning, or to dinner, or whenever you care to take that trouble.

Yours entirely
G.D.

26. He (Pitt) returns, rejecting all terms 'till the Duke of Newcastle was remov'd.

27. The King sent for Fox, and told him that the Duke of Newcastle would resign, and bid him think of an Administration. Fox met Pitt at the Prince's levée; who declin'd giving him a meeting, or treating with him, at all.

29. Went to Council. Parliament prorogu'd till the 2nd December.

31. Duke of Devonshire sent into the country to Mr Pitt who gives the exclusion to Mr Fox.

[1] Oswald MSS. 47.

[2] Halifax's letter of 18 October refusing to come to town in response to D.'s appeal for support is summarized in *H.M.C. Var. Coll.*, vi. 36. Halifax said he proposed 'enjoying my retirement here till I see reason to think my presence in town will be of use'.

NOVEMBER AND DECEMBER

NOVEMBER

1. Din'd at Lady Hervey's.

2. Saw Lord Hillsborough, who fancies the Court will not submit to Mr Pitt. I think otherwise.

3. Saw Lord Halifax who thinks Mr Pitt's demands are agreed to: he will go on with them.

4. Found the Duke of Devonshire, after having agreed to accept the Treasury with Fox as Chancellor, went to settle it with the King, and came out with Legge for his Chancellor. This is incredible but true.

9. Came to town.

11. Duke of Newcastle resign'd.

12. Mr Fox resign'd. Duke of Devonshire kiss'd hands for the Treasury.

15. Duke of Devonshire was here, and left word he would come again tomorrow. I sent him word that I would wait on him.

16. Went to Devonshire House.—The Duke told me that he was forc'd by the King to take the employment he held.—That he was order'd to go to Mr Pitt and know upon what conditions he would serve.—That in the arrangements he and his friends made, my office was demanded. He was very sorry,—had no hand in it.— Behav'd very civilly &c.

DECEMBER

1. Din'd at Lady Hervey's.

2. Parliament open'd.

21. Mr Wyndham and I set out for Lord Halifax's.

PART FOUR

THE NEW REIGN

FEBRUARY 1757 TO JULY 1762

1757

FEBRUARY AND MARCH

FEBRUARY

18. Motion for £200,000 for an Army of Observation in Germany agreed to without division, or debate.

Mr Tucker had agreed with Mr Geo: Grenville &c to be Paymaster of the Marines, and Governor Grenville to be chose in his place.[1] The King sent to Fox to know if he could prevent it: and if he thought I would interpose. Fox said, he suppos'd if his Majesty commanded me, I would: He order'd Fox to speak to me: he did, and I stopp'd it: this the first step to turning out Lord Temple.

23. Admiral Byng's affair brought into the House by Sir Francis Dashwood, by moving for an explanation of the 12th Article of War (22 Geo. 2 cap 2). Coldly receiv'd, and withdrawn.[2]

MARCH

Fox to Dodington[3]

[Endorsed] Mr Fox the 12th
March 1757

Dear Sir,

What can I do? Can I speak to Lord Halifax without such authority as may justify me at all Events in what I say to Him.

I not only authorize but desire you to converse with Him on the Subject, and if you please to say that it is by my Desire and on this foot.

[1] Tucker had been brought in by D. to be Cashier to the Treasurer of the Navy when D. got the Navy Office. Now he was trying to make his own bargain with the incoming Grenvilles instead of going out with his master.
[2] D. himself took part in the campaign to save Byng—despite his membership of the Government on whose shoulders Byng sought to put the responsibility for the fall of Minorca. On measures he was consistent, and he had opposed the provision under which Byng was condemned.
[3] Source: Add. MS. 38091, ff. 72, 73. Printed in *H.M.C. Var. Coll.*, vi. 37.

That I wish the King would dismiss Pitt, Lord Temple &c., that I think no one of the late Ministers can now succeed them, but that such a Ministry should be form'd as the late Ministers may support, and as the People can not complain of. That the Secr. of State must be in the H. of Commons; that if the D. of Devon will stay there is no place but first Lord of the Admiralty for His Lordship who could fill that place, that I should advise you to succeed him, and that Oswald should be Secr. of the Admiralty. That the *conciliabulum* should consist of the Dukes of Devon and Bedford, the E. of Halifax, Lord Mansfield, & the two Secretaries. This is my Notion, & if every body will act the part assign'd them, I can answer for the Success. If because they will not, or for any other reason H.M. is forced to keep these Gentlemen 2 Months longer, I shall look upon them as complete Conquerors, and Leicester House the Court. I shall not go to it, but I shall struggle no longer against it. Adieu, My Dear Sir; as soon as I know H.M. Determination you shall know more, or that there is nothing more to be known.

Saturday Morning.

Fox to Dodington[1]

March 15, 1757
[endorsed as received 16 March]

Dear Sir,

I understand Lord T. [Temple] had an unkindly audience in which H.M. did by no means yield; but I understand they do not intend to resign upon it. So now things tend to delay again; and you and I think alike of the consequence of that. I am the less anxious, because tho' you may not see Lord H's Refusal[2] in so strong a Light as I do, yet, my dear Sir, if We can not change his mind, it is much the same thing; and I will not, upon consideration, give myself leave to imagine that what you can not do with him, the Duke of Bedford can. Pitt &c. have, by their faults and want of judgement, put themselves into our power; it is now our turn by the same means to make them again Masters. It is however neither your fault nor that

of Yours Ever
H. Fox

---

[1] Source: Add. MS. 38091, ff. 74, 75. Printed in *H.M.C. Var. Coll.* vi. 38.
[2] Halifax had refused to come into this scheme: See his letter of 13 March to D. Ibid.

Dodington to Fox[1]

Near 12 at Night
Fryday the 18 March [1757]

Dear Sir,

The gentleman was wth me this Morning and din'd here, afterwards. He told me what had pass'd between You and Him, yesterday, in the House.—You have done what Nobody else could have done.— He gave me an Account of the Letter he wrote you this Morning.—I like his setting forth the Difficulties of the Undertaking & the decent Diffidence he expresses of himself, as it ends in an absolute Obedience to His Majty's Pleasure even in that Particular. The Hitch in the last Part I do not like so well, I mean insisting upon a Gentleman's giving his Word that he would concurr; Because it is but childish, at best. For if *that* was all the Assurance he had to rely on for his Concurrence, our Friend, himself would not tell You, or Me, that he would give sixpence for his Security. I hope, & believe, therefore, that it is only dropp'd in, Here, because he has so often laid so much Stress upon it, to us. However, I would humbly suggest, whether this Letter, or Part of the Contents of it, might not be made such an Use of, with the King, as to extort a positive Declaration of the Concurrence in Question.

Were not the Subject too serious, it would make one smile to suppose that any Body could, really, think that a Gentleman's Word could add Security and Strength to his acting for his own Interest & Safety who never in his Life, kept it, one Moment, *when he thought* it came in Competition with the One or the Other. If such a Paradox should defeat so wise, & great a System, I shall look upon it as the Fatality of the Times. I have heard that Lord Mansfield does not, so warmly approve, as it were to be wish'd. I hope it is without Grounds; or, at least, that he will not discourage it.

I am just come home, & have heard that la Cerda, the Portuguese Minister to France, is come hither for a little Time. I would Catch, like a drowning Man, at the smallest Twigg, that could possibly, shoot out into a Peace, but should be very desirous that my Friends should have the making of it.

I am &c.

P.S. I go to la Trappe, early, tomorrow morning, and shall return on Sunday night.

---

[1] Source: Add. MS. 38091, f. 78. 'The Gentleman' here is probably Sir Thomas Robinson.

Fox to Dodington[1]

Sunday Night
[20 March 1757]

Dear Sir,

I wish I could agree with you that Ld. H. mention'd the idle promises of another, *pro formâ* only: But we may probably see; for a positive Declaration will be requir'd on the D. of N's part, and perhaps declin'd, Lord Mansfield I am told approves of no *pezzo termino*. I believe he approves of nothing that may sooner or later make his Patron again a Minister. Be at the House tomorrow, & I will inform you; and besides I intend there to call upon the Ministers for a contradiction of the prevailing Lye that is industriously spread, of an intended Message for English Troops to be sent to Westphalia. They say Pitt woud not carry such Message & is Perforce to be turn'd out. Adieu. Put the inclos'd in your Drawer, & 100£ in your pocket which give me tomorrow.

Yours Ever
H. Fox

[*The Diary resumes*] The Duke of Newcastle who had resign'd would not stir: the King grew impatient to get rid of the Ministry *he had impos'd upon himself*: threw himself upon Fox to form a new Administration: agreed to begin by dismissing Lord Temple: I propos'd Lord Halifax for the Admiralty, the King agreed to it, and I was to negotiate it, with him.

Mr Fox and I had a long conversation about this settlement. Agreed, that as the Duke of Newcastle, to whom the first place, and the nomination to the others, was, several times, offer'd and press'd, even by the King himself; by Message refus'd to act, *as yet*, an Administration should be form'd, where a first place should be ready to receive the D. of Newcastle but none of the old Ministry should come in at first, 'till the enquiry was over, &c. Duke of Devonshire at the head of the Treasury, Lord George Sackville to be Secretary;—I declin'd being Chancellor of the Exchequer, but if Lord Halifax accepted the Admiralty, I agreed to accept of the Board of Trade. The King still eager for the change. N.B. All this while, Lord Halifax, upon whose friendship, and concurrence I depended from repeated assurances, and to whom I had communicated all this transaction, without authority, *till now*, had privately seen, and negotiated with D. of Newcastle and taken measures to defeat it

[1] Source: Add. MS. 38091, ff. 79, 80.

with him: what makes this the more surprizing is, that always before, at that time, and ever since, he has spoke of the D. of Newcastle to me, and to others as a knave, and a fool in the strongest terms.

21st, or near it, Fox call'd upon Messrs Pitt, and Legge, and made them disown the prevailing lie spread by their friends, of troops being to go from hence with the Duke into Germany, they both, in their places, disown'd any knowledge, or belief of any such proposition. N.B. Somebody, in less than 3 months, gave above a million of English money, and sent what was call'd 10,000 [a little above 7000] English soldiers, to that very army when commanded *by another Prince.*

The Ministers after all their threats, not pushing the enquiry, Fox mov'd for it, to be enter'd upon, in a Committee of the whole House, on the 19th of April; which was evidently throwing it into contempt. Submitted to without the least hesitation.

Fox came to me, to see Lord Halifax, and told him that Sir Thomas Robinson accepted the seals, by the King's command;—that Lord Mansfield approv'd the system, and said in the strongest terms, that the Duke of Newcastle ought to do so too. Lord Halifax acquiesced upon that condition: but understood, I suppose, by his private dealings with the Duke of Newcastle that Robinson was not to accept, writes to him, who writes, in answer, that he has had some talk about that matter, but not having receiv'd an account how his answer was taken, cannot give his Lordship the information he desires; but wants to see him. Lord Halifax goes from Pall Mall, where he din'd; returns, and reports that Robinson, with a most submissive preamble, had sent an absolute refusal, (but not disapproving the plan) and added, that he could not, must not, would not accept.—So all is at a stand.—

24. Din'd at Lord Barrington's.—Went to Lord Halifax's, who had wrote to Fox that he would accept, if Robinson took the seals, which he knew Robinson would not take.

26. Message from the King to the Duke of Newcastle to offer him, again, to come in: if not, to say if he would support the present plan: if not that, to name what plan he would support, but to speak positively, for His Majesty would admit of no more evasive answers. We think, however, he will have one; and therefore think it most advisable to force Robinson to be Secretary.

APRIL

5. Lord Winchelsea kiss'd hands for the Admiralty.

6. Mr Pitt dismiss'd. Fox, and I order'd from the King, by Lord Holderness, to come to kiss his hand as Paymaster of the Army, and Treasurer of the Navy.[1] We wrote to the Duke of Cumberland our respectful thanks and acceptance of the offices, but thought it would be more for his Majesty's service not to enter, publicly, upon them, 'till the enquiry was over.—Which His Majesty agreed to.

N.B. The Duke of Newcastle prepar'd, and all along inform'd by Lord Halifax, (who ought not to have done it) joins Pitt, takes the Treasury, makes Pitt Secretary again, Lord Temple Privy Seal, Lord Anson at the head of the Admiralty, &c. and tells Lord Halifax that it is settled that he should be third Secretary for the Plantations, which was his object, and for which he had overturn'd the whole plan. Lord Halifax tells all his friends of it, goes to Court, talks to Pitt about it as a thing settled; Pitt star'd at him, and told him very coolly, and very truly, that he never had heard one word of it: and that he did not conceive that anybody had a right to curtail his office to that degree which was, already, too much encroach'd upon, by the Board [of Trade].

Lord Halifax, cover'd with confusion, goes away in a rage, writes an angry letter to the Duke of Newcastle, goes to the King, complains, meets no great comfort, resigns, asks one or two things for his friends, and is refus'd. The Duke of Newcastle behaves (as Lord Halifax says) with the utmost meanness: owns he had not spoke to Pitt about it: and that the reason was, *Pitt look'd so much out of humour that he durst not.* Lord Halifax talk'd of the D. of N. everywhere in the most opprobrious terms, as the object of his contempt, and detestation; but as he had not fill'd up the office, his Lordship, about Michaelmas, took it up again, just as he left it.

The King kept his word with Fox, and made him Paymaster:— but was not pleas'd to do so with me.

Thus ended this attempt to deliver the King from hands he said he did not like, in making them more his masters; and all this,

[1] See Hillsborough to D. 2 Apr. 1757 (*H.M.C. Var. Coll.* vi. 39). The letter contains the most profuse assurances on behalf of Fox that he will stand by D.

from Lord Halifax's duplicity, which drew a greater affront upon him than I ever remember offer'd to anybody. From the Duke of Newcastle treachery, and ingratitude, who after having given his word to the King that he would never join Mr Pitt, but by His Majesty's consent, forc'd him to consent: and by the King's timidity, who dares not support anybody, even in his own cause.

11. Sir Paul Methuen dyed, at 3 o'clock this morning.

JUNE AND JULY

Dodington to Fox[1]

La Trappe, Thursday night
[2 June 1757]

Dear Sir,

I Hear you were come to Town, but not much more inform'd of the settlement of the Administration than the King Himself.

How long is this Gentleman to trifle with his Sovereign Benefactor? and to Keep our Country in suspense, you of too much consequence, I of too little to be trusted with or admitted to the Honour of Supporting Him. I know nobody that ought to decide for you but the King: I am sure nobody shall decide for me but you.

Farewell. I will take the first opportunity of waiting upon you and am very faithfully and affectionately,

Yours
G.D.

Dodington to Fox[1]

La Trappe 3 June 1757

Dear Sir,

I humbly thank you for your Note. I must, ever, think that the King stands equally engag'd in Honour, tho' not in Interest, to Both of us, for the two Paymasters' Offices. If it be necessary to the System you are entering into, to leave me quite out, I have nothing to say to That.—If I am to have an Equivalent, I think they ought to settle it with you, at the same time, for with Them, I will have nothing to do.

Dear Sr,
Yours, most Affectionately,

Fox to Dodington[2]

Fryday night [3 June 1757]

It is impossible to recollect & you, Dear Sir, would be sorry to read half the absurdity I have heard this Day. The D. of Newcastle went to the King not to accept but to desire till Tuesday to determine because Lord Hardwicke do's not come to town till Monday.

[1] Source: Add. MS. 38091, ff. 81 and 82. Copies in D.'s hand. Fox's intervening note is missing.
[2] Source: ibid., f. 83.

If He accepts, it is against the Advice of all his Friends, yet He will accept & let those Friends make his Situation ten times worse than it would be if they did not meddle. But He is to act against their Advice, yet they are to advise Him. I in the mean time will not be of the System (as you will persist to call what they do who never had a System). I will take what I take from the King. He is certainly engag'd in Honour to you as well as to me. And therefore that Settlement too must be with Him. But they cannot settle it with me, nor I with Him as yet, for I am sick of what passes, & will neither see Him nor them more, till I kiss his Hand, & that I ever shall kiss it, is doubtful.

Adieu

Fox to Dodington[1]

[6 June 1757]

The D. of Newcastle has been with the King, to know what Terms he may offer Mr Pitt; whom, together with Lord Hardwycke, and Lord Bute, he is to meet, tonight.

The King gave the Duke little Encouragement to think he would condescend to such Terms as They wou'd accept; and the Duke gave the King as little, to imagine He would come in without Them. His Grace is to be at Court to morrow, when *according to present Appearances*, they will part, for good, & all, for the King complains of himself, for having permitted so long Delay. But the very Reverse of this Conjecture may prove to be the Event. Incertus, non perturbatus. I'le go to Dinner—Adieu—

Dodington to Fox[2]

La Trappe
Fry day morng 10 June
past 8 o'clock

When we parted, I went to carry Lord Leicester to Ken Wood, who kept us drinking, There, till nine. Not a Word said, of what had pass'd, or was passing.—I mett Rigby yesterday, in Hyde Park, who stopp'd me to tell me that Lord H had resign'd.—Am I to wish you Joy, & of What? If I am, I do it cordially, & will support you, in every honourable Thing—Usque ad Internecionem—in whatever Shape you like best, either in, or out.

Yours most faithfully,
G.D.

[1] Source: ibid., f. 85. Copy in D.'s hand endorsed 'sent on to the Earl of Hillsborough'.
[2] Source: ibid., f. 86. Copy in D.'s hand.

[*The Diary resumes*] In this year, in the months of June or July (I think the 18th), I am not sure which, Sir George Lee told me (which was confirm'd afterwards by Lord Halifax) that he had been more than once solicited to be Chancellor of the Exchequer to the Duke of Newcastle in the Administration he was then negotiating. That he consented, not without difficulty (and other large conditions, he might have added). That the Friday, I think, before Whit Sunday he was at Newcastle House, and the Duke told him that all was settled in general with the King, and he was to be Chancellor of the Exchequer.—Show'd him what he said was the list in detail, which he was going to carry to the King at Kensington; and desir'd to see him next morning.

Upon Sir George's telling him that he was to go next morning to his brother in Bucks, the Duke press'd him to stay. Ask'd if he did not go to the House of Lords from Kensington.—Yes—. Sir George met him there, and the Duke told him all was settled, and the King agreed in form to his being Chancellor of the Exchequer, upon which they parted, Sir George being to return Monday or Tuesday.

When he came back, he found the system was entirely alter'd, and another Chancellor of the Exchequer (Legge) made part of it. And he further told me that he never had any communication of any sort from or with the Duke of Newcastle, either by word of mouth, note, message, or common friend, since parting with him at the House of Lords, till Sunday the 16th July, the day but one preceding our conversation, when he came and sat down by him at Leicester House, and with all the ease and familiarity of an old friend, communicated his no news to him.

16th July Lord Halifax came to La Trappe, and told me the following history of his friend Legge.

Instigated, I suppose, by his Lordship and Oswald, who hop'd to enhance their favour with the Duke of Newcastle while the negotiation with Mr Pitt was open, by their bringing over so considerable a person; and following the low, shuffling, disposition of his own heart, a little before Easter he met the Duke of Newcastle at Lord Dupplin's, coming in at the back door, thro' the Park, at nine o'clock. That meeting pass'd in assurances of good-will to each other, and went no farther. That the Duke propos'd another, which Legge was afraid to venture, but the correspondence was kept up by message. This treaty (if it had taken place) was for

Legge to come in without Mr Pitt, if he persisted in his exorbitant demands.

The Duke chiefly treated with Mr Pitt by the Primate of Ireland, Stone; one day in the beginning of the negotiation, when Lord Bute and Mr Pitt were in conference with the Primate, and insisted upon very extravagant terms, he beg'd them as a friend, to be a little more moderate, and before they went so far, to consider if they were quite sure of *all* their friends. They were surpris'd, and said they thought so. He reply'd that he thought otherwise, and could, if he would (*for he was authoriz'd to do it*) tell them a very different story. Pitt insisted upon knowing it, or would treat no farther. Upon which he told them this private transaction of Legge's with the Duke of Newcastle.

This occasion'd great coldness to Legge at Leicester House; which, as soon as he perceiv'd it, gave him great uneasiness. At last (I think from Lord Halifax) he found out that in return for thinking of leaving his friends for the Duke of Newcastle, the Duke of Newcastle had betray'd him to his friends. He would have expostulated with them, but they would not, and negotiation taking place in their favour, they bid him take Exchequer Seals under the Duke of Newcastle, and enter into no farther eclaircisse-ment. He has done so, detested by Mr Pitt and Leicester House; acting under one whom he hates, who hates him, and has betray'd him; breaking faith with Lord Halifax, without whom he engag'd not to act, and with Oswald, to whom he had pledg'd his honour never to come into the Treasury without him.—And all this for Quarter Day!

Narratives of the Attempt on Louisbourg and the 'Secret Expedition' to Rochefort[1]

Late in the year 1756 Lord Loudoun sends home a scheme for an attack upon Louisbourg; approv'd, and acquainted that his demands for the execution of it shall be comply'd with, early in the year.

January, 1757. Transports with troops from Ireland arriv'd. But as there were not public houses enough to billet them, the

---

[1] These narratives follow D.'s account of the ministerial crisis, the last part of which was obviously written in retrospect, and at some points are intermingled with it. They are here given as a connected whole. The text makes it clear that D. abandoned day to day entry between February 1757 and the end of the year. The Louisbourg narrative, with its sidelights on colonial discontent with the home Government, is wholly omitted by Wyndham.

private ones would not receive them. Lord Loudoun thought it unreasonable that troops sent for the defence of the Province, after the fatigues of such a voyage, should lie in the streets, and therefore oblig'd the private houses to receive them. This was the foundation of the ill will, which broke out more violently, on the embargo laid.

3rd March, on all outward bound ships, in order to prevent any intelligence going to the enemy—and also—the profit of those who had freighted corn for England. However, this ended in restraining all Governors from embargoing any ships bound for England, and for the future.

In this month Lord Loudoun met the Governors of Pennsylvania, Maryland, Virginia, and North Carolina, at Philadelphia, settled with them a plan of defence, which was all he requir'd of them when he went against Louisbourg.

27th. He left Philadelphia.

April. Chiefly spent in getting together about 90 sail of transports, for 5,800 regulars.

5th May. All, ready: waiting for Holborne.

25th. All the troops embark'd, and fell down to Sandy Hook.

5th June. Lord Loudoun embark'd, but having heard that there were five French ships of the line cruising off Halifax, resolv'd not to sail without further intelligence. Sent two ships, they return'd without seeing the French: so he resolv'd to sail, with Admiral Hardy's ship only for convoy, the 20th: and arriv'd safe at Halifax the 30th. If he had been met with—certain destruction.

9 July. Holborne, with 6,200 men, arriv'd. They, then, sent for intelligence of the state of Louisbourg, and in the mean time, exercise the troops.

30, 31 July, 1 August. Troops embarking, and embark'd.

4th August. A French schooner brought in; said to be bound for France with dispatches which were dated in July, importing that there were 17 ships of the line in the harbour, and 7,000 men in the garrison. N.B. This was look'd on *here* as sent out on purpose to mislead, because they did not destroy her papers.

11th, Lord Loudoun reembark'd, leaving three battalions at Halifax, and one up the Bay of Fundy.

16th, the whole fleet sail'd, and got to Sandy Hook the 20th. Fort William Henry taken in his absence.

The Admiral approach'd within two miles of the batteries of Louisbourg: as soon as the French Admiral saw him, he made the signal to unmoor, which as soon as our Admiral saw (knowing them to be 17 to 15) he made off, immediately.

11th September, being reinforc'd by two 70-gun ships and two 60-gun ships, which made him 19 to 17, he return'd to look at them again.—Found them just as he left them, and left them just as he found them.

Thus ended an expedition, for want of a fleet's arriving in time, which was acknowledg'd to be the necessary foundation of it, and agreed upon nine months ago.

★   ★   ★

Secret Expedition was founded on the information of one Clarke, a Lieutenant in the Train, who told the Ministry that he pass'd through the place [Rochefort] some years ago and was shown the works as an English officer, by order of the Governor—that the ditch was dry, the fortifications, garrison &c. such as might be taken by storm.

This was believ'd: and then, without the further examination of any one person but a French pilot, Thierry, General Mordaunt was sent.

9th [September 1757], they sail.

20th, arrive near Rochefort.

23rd, take Aix. Mordaunt proposes landing at, and taking, Fort Fouras. Thierry offers to bring a ship within 400 yards of the fort, and lay her in soft mud at ebb (which it appear'd, afterwards, he could not do). Hawke refuses a ship.

24th, spent in sounding for another landing. One found, four miles off, call'd Chaldaillon.

25th, Council of War. Question, if the ditch was dry? Pilot of the *Neptune*, who had liv'd several years at Rochefort, said he knew it was wet. The French pilot confirm'd it. Clarke persisted it was dry. Ask'd, in case it were wet, could the place be taken by escalade? Says no. Council unanimous that the attempt upon the place was impracticable.

The difficulties of landing at Chaldaillon were very great. The transports could not come within a mile and a half of the shore—the ships of war not within a league. There was a row of sand banks upon the shore, sufficient to conceal a number of men. The pilot who had liv'd there said that he had known a western gale blow off-shore for seven weeks together; so stiff that no boat could land upon the coast.

However, Mordaunt, tho' refus'd the protection of one ship, terrify'd with the fate of Byng, resolv'd to land where he could try to take Fouras and look at Rochefort.

26th, and 27th, spent in looking for better landings: but finding none he embarks his troops the

28th, at night, but the wind made it unadvisable to land.

Next day Hawke declar'd that if Mordaunt would take upon himself the consequences of keeping the great ships out at that season, he would stay; otherwise he must go home. Mordaunt would not do that; so they return'd together, 1 October, landed 6th.

Thus ended this expedition, contriv'd with such secrecy that everything necessary to its success was a secret to the contriver himself.

As a proof of it, a year afterwards, when Mordaunt, (who certainly should have had living witnesses of the futility of the plan, and the foundation it stood upon) had been brought to a trial, and also worried by all the low Court flatterers and scribblers, it happen'd that Captain Dennis took the *Raisonnable*, commanded by the Chevalier de Rohan, and Mr Fox told me, that being with Lords Waldegrave and Gower together, they both told him that Dennis had assur'd them separately that his prisoner told him that he (the Chevalier de Rohan) was, at that time, in Rochefort—or la Rochelle (the Lords in comparing notes had no other doubt in their narrative); that they had 7 or 8,000 men there at least; that there was 3,500 men behind the sand banks, and a mask'd battery at each end; that if we had landed when we first appear'd, we should have embarrass'd them. But they thought themselves betray'd, when they found we did not land at the time we attempted it.

*   *   *

On September 18 Mr Martin call'd upon me at Eastbury. Said that Holborne was very willing to agree with Lord Loudoun in not attacking Louisbourg. That Anson, since he came in last, told the Ministry that Holborne went out with no better stomach to fight than Byng. That at a meeting of the Lords, Newcastle, Hardwicke, Holderness, Anson, and Mr Pitt, upon the ill success of the Duke[1] in Germany, it was propos'd to send the armament then going against Rochefort to the assistance of His Royal Highness in Germany; that every man was for it, except Mr Pitt, who insisted that if the resolution was to prevail, minutes of the meeting should be taken, and his dissent enter'd. Upon which they desisted; but no one would acquaint the King with the result. Mr Pitt was left to do it himself.

He told me farther that the King said his revenues were seized, that he was £800,000 in debt, and that the army must disband if not supply'd from hence; and that Mr Pitt had consented to give him £100,000, and £20,000 to subsist his daughter.

[1] Cumberland. On 8 September, after his defeat at Hastenbeck, he capitulated under the Convention of Klosterzeven, which destroyed both his military reputation and his domestic political prestige.

NOVEMBER AND DECEMBER

NOVEMBER

5. King of Prussia beats Monsieur de Soubise at Rossbach.

25. The French fleet of 17 ships of the line return from Louisbourg to Brest: very sickly.

DECEMBER

5. King of Prussia beats Count Daun at Lissa.

20. Breslau surrenders.

29. Lignitz surrenders.

After the Battle of Hastenbeck, and the disowning of the Duke and the Convention of Closterseven by the King; late in the autumn of 1757 the Hanoverian army again take the field commanded by Prince Ferdinand of Brunswick, and, December 29, take Marbourg Castle.

1758

JANUARY TO JUNE

JANUARY

18. Message by Mr Pitt for a Supply to keep the Hanoverian army together.—Granted—£100,000.

In this month Messrs Hawkins, Arundell, and Duke Hamilton. Princess Caroline buried.

FEBRUARY

19. Admiral Boscawen sail'd.

25. Monsieur du Quesne taken, by Admiral Osborne's squadron.

APRIL

16. Schweidnitz surrendered.

MAY

3. General Keith, King of Prussia, Prince of Anhalt, enter Moravia.

12. Admiral Boscawen arrives at Halifax.

27. Trenches open'd before Olmutz.

28. Admiral Boscawen sail'd for Louisbourg with 12,900 regulars. *Above 16,000 provincials rais'd and ready, but without arms, or general.*

JUNE

1. Commodore Howe sail'd from the Isle of Wight with one 70-gun, three 50-gun ships, several frigates, two transports having on board 16 battalions, 9 troops of light horse, all preparations for a

siege, and commanded by the Duke of Marlborough, Lord George Sackville, General Waldegrave, &c. Lord Anson sail'd the same day.

5 and 6. Arriv'd in the Bay of Concalle, near St Malo, burnt a few ships of no great consequence, and several small craft, which were on ground. All fir'd by the light horse.

12. After staying about six days without attempting St Malo, after hearing there was a body of about 10,000 men assembled, or assembling, in the neighbourhood, they reembark'd, with the loss of two or three men of a side. They continu'd in or near the Bay of Concalle till the men began to grow sick, ragged, and lousy, from want of room in the transports: and were reduc'd to a quart of *stinking* water per day.

19. Parliament prorogued.

28. We heard that the Austrians attack'd the Prussian convoy the 28th inst with a good deal of success: the head of the convoy got to the camp the 29th, but

30. Siege of Olmutz rais'd.

JULY

1. King of Prussia march'd back into Bohemia. And our expedition that set out the 1st of June came back. When it was known that they were return'd, it occasion'd great disputes among the Ministers whether they should land or not; which lasted until Wednesday the 5th, when at a meeting of the Cabinet it was determin'd that they should land, (as sickness began among them) while provisions &c. were preparing for them (which might as well have been sent to them). These orders were sent the sixth.

7. They disembark'd. At this meeting of the 5th there was great difference of opinion: Lord Granville declar'd he was always for distressing France upon the Continent. Experience had taught him to have no great expectations from expeditions: meant no reflexions upon the late ones, or to make his court, for he wanted nobody, his duty alone made him speak &c.

Mr Pitt said he had sufficiently show'd he was for supporting the Continent by paying an army of 50,000 men for its defence—that he had consented to send 10,000 men more, from hence—but still thought that expeditions, and keeping France in alarms upon the coast, was the most effectual way to distress her—that expeditions had always succeeded.—'Did you not take Port l'Orient, if St Clair would have accepted it? Did you not take Rochefort last year—it was entirely at your disposition? Have you not taken St Malo?' &c. Lord Ligonier said to Lord Granville, 'Your Lordship must admit . . .', Lord Granville cut him short with, 'My Lord, I will admit nothing: your Lordship is apt to admit, but I will admit nothing.'

10. The horse and dragoons were to encamp upon Black Heath, in order to embark for Emden. The 10,000 men Mr Pitt allow'd for Germany were 6 regiments of horse and 6 battalions, *viz*:

Blue Guards	9 Troops of 40		
Bland's	6	„ „ 55	
Mordaunt's	6	„ „ 55	
Scots Greys	6	„ „ 55	
Sir Charles Howard's	6	„ „ 55	
Cholmondeley's	6	„ „ 55	
		2,010	

Hay		
Kingsley		
Husk		
Napper	each 900	5,400
Stuart		
Brudenel		
		7,575

These troops to be commanded by the Duke of Marlborough; Lord George Sackville, General Waldegrave, all having deserted the expedition. Lord George said he would go no more buccaneering: the King refus'd to let him go to Germany, but was oblig'd to submit. They have also taken the three first regiments above, and half the light horse, from the expedition—but Prince Edward is on board.

15. Din'd at La Trappe Lords Halifax, Buckingham, and Barrington, Comtes de Viry and de la Perrière, Sir Thomas Robinson and his son, and Mr Oswald.

18. Din'd here, Comte de Viry, Lord Bute, Sir Richard Lyttelton, Mr Breton.

20. Went to town to see the man.[1]

25. Din'd at Lord Bute's at Kew. Mr Pitt there at dinner.

27. Din'd here Messrs Cumberland.

28. Din'd at Lord Hillsborough's.

29. Din'd at Mr Bodens', with Lords Halifax and Barrington.

26.
28. }Part of the troops arriv'd at Emden. The expedition again put
31.   to sea.

Having laid our own affairs pretty much together, I must now return to the Battle of Crefelt. [On the] 2nd the left wing of an army, double in number, entirely defeated, commanded by the Comte de Clermont: by Prince Ferdinand of Brunswick. The 7th,

---

[1] Significance of this entry is obscure.

King of Prussia, in retiring with his whole army, destroys and takes a great magazine of the Austrians, at Leylemissel. Marches on by Coningsgratz with various successes. About the 15th, the Russians commanded by Brown were got to Great Glogau. The 21st, a squadron of 20 Russian, and 10 Swedish ships of the line, with transports for 13 or 14,000 Russians, to land in Pomerania, appear in the Baltic—*To our great surprise.*

30. Set out from La Trappe, and lay at Lord Buckingham's, in the forest.

AUGUST

1. Arriv'd at Eastbury.

2. Mr Warburton, and his niece, came.

3. It appears by the Duke of Marlborough's manifesto to the magistrates of St Malo, that he threatens them with burning the country in his possession if they do not order the inhabitants back to their houses, and direct them to send proper persons to him, to settle contributions. They did not obey his orders; and he, in too much haste to return to put his threats in execution.

4. Said that the Admiralty receiv'd an account *from France*, that on the 22nd June, after 2 days siege, Boscawen had taken the light house battery, which commands the harbour.

Account that on the 25th June, there was an engagement between 18,000 of Prince Soubise's army, and 6,000 Hessians: the last defeated with great loss.—The Landgraviate abandon'd, and the Landgrave again oblig'd to leave it.

The Government have an account of the arrival of the *Vanguard*, at New York, with 6 vessels *loaded with Arms*, &c. for the provincials who had waited for them near 3 months.

Siege of Olmutz lasted 34 days after the trenches were open'd. 27,900 discharges of cannon, 27,300 bombs. The expedition of Moravia, up to raising the siege, suppos'd cost the Prussians 15,000 men—

11. Rode to Lord Shaftesbury's, and back to dinner.

14. Account that Cherbourg surrender'd the 8th inst. Troops, being two regiments, withdrew. About 27 ships in the harbour: 30 Pieces of brass cannon taken.

19. Din'd at Mr John Pitt's.

21. Receiv'd an account that Louisbourg was taken 26th July. All the ships in the harbour destroy'd: *viz.* two of 74 guns; three of 64; one of 50; five frigates. Amherst came into Halifax the day Boscawen sail'd out.

After having demolish'd the bason, and the forts, our troops left Cherbourg the 16th inst. without any molestation, tho' 'tis said there was a great body of troops in the neighborhood.

22. Messrs Tucker and Pengree din'd here.

23. Mr Pengree went in the morning. Mr Richard Tucker din'd here, and went away with his brother in the evening. Howe's squadron in Portland Roads the 19th.

24. An account of Abercrombie's unsuccessful attack on Crown Point, 12th July. Kill'd, wounded, and missing, above 1,900. Lord Howe kill'd.

29. Din'd at Mr Drax's.

31. Howe re-sail'd from Weymouth.

SEPTEMBER

1. Din'd at Mr Okeden's. Assassination of the King of Portugal.

4. An account that an express arriv'd the 1st inst. with news of a compleat victory gain'd by the King of Prussia, (who had join'd Count Dohna with part of his army) over the Russians near Custrin. 15,000 kill'd; 6,000 prisoners, and 100 cannon taken—This on the 25th August.
   The troops that disembark'd near Emden the 2nd past, and immediately march'd to join Prince Ferdinand, met the first detachment of the Hanoverians at the Camp of Cosfield, the 14th inst.

5. Dr Thomson came.

8. Din'd here, Lord Shaftesbury, Messrs Sturt, Napier, Ewer, Walters.

11. Mr and Mrs Drax din'd here.

14. Din'd with Mr Sturt.

16. Receiv'd an account that our troops landed the 4th inst. at Lunaire Bay. Burnt 20 vessels. Were to march to St Guildo, the 9th. To reembark the 10th at St Cast, by Matignon.
   Lady Bath died the 14th.

17. First account of the repulse, since it happen'd the 12th inst. between Matignon and St Cast. What did they do there? Return'd to Portsmouth the 18th.

19. Sir William Codrington din'd here.

20. Went to Weymouth.

21. The election of the Mayor.

22. Return'd to dinner.

23. Mr Gresly din'd here.

26. Mr Arundell on a visit. Messrs Freke and Fleet din'd here.

27. Mr Banks din'd here.

OCTOBER

1. Messrs Chafin, Okeden, and Good din'd here.

2. Mr Gresley din'd here.

6. Mr Warburton and his niece went away. Mr, Mrs, and Miss Ridge, and Mr Cumberland came.

10. They went away.

15. Mr Wyndham and I set out from Eastbury at near 5 o'clock in the morning, and got to La Trappe, a little after 8. I was told by a gentleman that said he had it from Colonel Cary, that upon landing at St Lunaire, Colonel Clerke told him that his (Clerke's) plan was first that Lord Howe should batter the forts of St Malo, while they of the land were to take the town by escalade—that being impracticable. Secondly, that they should go to St Bride where they were to find, and burn, 300 ships—finding only as many fishing boats as might be worth £40, or £50. Thirdly, they were to march farther into the country, to intimidate the French, who had nothing but a few militia to defend them.—Soon after they were beat by a number of regular troops inferior to theirs.

16. Mr Breton din'd here, and return'd.

18. Rode to Lord Bute's.

19. Din'd here Messrs Cumberland and Ridge.

20. Din'd here Sir Francis Dashwood, and Mr Shirley.

21. I din'd at Bushy, Lord Halifax's.

22. Mr Breton came. Heard of the misfortune of Messieurs d'Issemberg and d'Oberg, by the Prince de Soubise's army:

With Prince Ferdinand	Batlns.	37	25,900
	Each	700	
	Squad:	59	7,080
	Each	120	

With Oberg   Bat.   21 ⎫
                   Each   700 ⎭ 14,700

                 Sqd.   21 ⎫
                   Each   120 ⎭ 2,520

Cavalry   9,600 ⎫
Infantry   40,600 ⎭   50,200

This was the state of the army about this time.

24. Mr Breton went. I was this day inform'd from good hands, that our English troops alone, in Germany, cost us £43,000 per month. Their pay said to be, (I have not cast it up) £17,000. Their extra demands, as provisions, &c. amounts to £26,000.

25. Brought news of the King of Prussia's defeat, at Hochkirch, the 14th. My poor acquaintance Keith, and Prince Francis of Brunswick, kill'd.

30. A mail from New York, brought letters from General Abercrombie, from Lake George of the 8th and 10th past, that Colonel Bradstreet with 3,103 men (154 regulars only) had taken Fort Frontenac; he landed without opposition the 25th August, they surrendered the 27th. A square fortress of 100 yards, 110 men in it—demolish'd to the ground. Goods and provisions to the amount of 800,000 livres. Taking of vessels from 8 to 78 guns. The value of this seems to be the distress of their garrisons from the loss of these provisions. Duke of Marlborough died at Munster, the 26th inst.

NOVEMBER AND DECEMBER

NOVEMBER

1. I rode to London, and return'd to dinner.

3. All the Cumberland family, and Miss Ridge, din'd here.

4. Rode to Ken Wood, and back to dinner.

10. King's Birth Day. Din'd at Lord Gower's.

11. Mr Glover came.

13. He return'd. Commodore Hughes sail'd.

20. Came to Pall Mall.

21. Din'd at Lord Hillsborough's.

22. Messrs Beaghan, Mr Tucker, din'd here.

23. Parliament open'd by commission. Lord Middleton and Sir Richard Grosvenor mov'd and seconded the Address.—Universal approbation of all that has and all that shall be done.—King of Prussia's victories worth all we have given: those he will gain worth all we shall give. Thus this country seems to think at present. Din'd at Lord Buckingham's.

26. Seiz'd with a violent cold.

28. Din'd here, Messrs Shirley, Stanley, Vaughan.

30. Forc'd to go to Court to find Lord Bute, but could not.

DECEMBER

1. Found myself much better—walk'd above an hour in the park, and din'd with very good appetite, at Mr Stanley's; from thence, went to Lord Mansfield's, and coming home was seiz'd with a

violent pain, in the ear, and side of the head, with a relapse, worse than the first attack.

6. Voted 91,446 men for the land &c. and £2,636,803 to keep them.

13. The conspirators taken up for the assassination of the King of Portugal, the 3rd September.

1759

JANUARY AND FEBRUARY

JANUARY

19. News came that the French were driven from Fort Duquesne.

21. The Princess of Orange at the Hague in her 50th year.

29. Commodore Keppel writes from Goree Bay that the 28th December last, he took the fort there, without resistance.

30. Din'd at Lord Hillsborough's.

FEBRUARY

1. Din'd here Lord Talbot, Sir Jacob Downing, Messrs Elliot, Martin &c.

7. Din'd at Lord Gower's.

8. Din'd at Sir Jacob Downing's.

10. Din'd at Lord Buckingham's.

12. Din'd at Lady Hervey's.

14. Admiral Holmes sail'd in the *Somerset*, for America.

15. Din'd here, Lord Gower, Duke of Bedford &c.

16. An account that Bompart sail'd from Brest the 21st January with 7 ships of the line, 3 frigates, and 15 transports.

18. Saunders pass'd by Plymouth, join'd by the *Windsor*, *Dublin*, and *Lizard*. The squadron under him, Holmes, and Durel will consist of 25 ships of the line, 10 of them in America.

26. Din'd at Mr Ellis's with Lords Gower, Waldegrave, &c.

27. Din'd at Sir Jacob Downing's, with Mr Fox &c.

28. Din'd here, Mr Ridge.

MARCH

6. Came express from Guadalupe, Captain Tyrell and Mr Townshend, with despatches from the Admiral Moor and General Hobson dated the 30th January, giving an account that Hughes arriv'd at Barbados the 4th January. They left it the 13th, arriv'd and landed at the Negro Point the 16th. The 17th the General had the ground between that and Fort Royal, (about four miles) reconnoitred. Sent to the Admiral to land the heavy artillery at the Savannah before Fort Royal, and he would force his way to them. The Admiral let him know it was impossible, but offer'd to land the artillery at Negro Point where they then were and to lend him 400 sailors and 300 negroes to draw his cannon where he pleas'd. The General reply'd that there were two very steep ravines between them and the fort that were unpassable by artillery, and that it was 18 miles round to their head; so he desir'd him to send the boats, which he did, and they reembark that night.

The General inform'd the Admiral that he thought it for the service to attack St Pierre, which the Admiral readily comply'd with. The 19th they enter'd the Bay, and upon examining the coast the Admiral thought the town might be burnt, but was doubtful about taking it, and thought also, if it was taken, the keeping would weaken the army, that they would not have numbers to send out sufficient to destroy the country at any distance. So they both agreed to attack Guadalupe, and appear'd before Basseterre the 22nd. The town consists of a few wooden huts, which were abandon'd by all the inhabitants, and every thing of value that was portable, carried off. They soon silenc'd the batteries, and landed the 23rd and burnt the town, but had not penetrated into the country which is defended by a strong pass, which the Governor, with what force they have, was retir'd to, and resolv'd to maintain, when the express came away.

9. The French say the Marquis de Laval arriv'd from the East Indies with an account that Monsieur de Lally had taken Fort St David's in June 1758 with 720 English and 1700 Seapoys and a great quantity of artillery. The fleet was one King's ship of 74 guns, 8 belonging to the Company from 50 to 60 guns—one of which was lost. Pocock had 7 of the line. They engag'd twice: after the second, in which the English had the best, the French anchor'd the next day (August 4th) before Pondicherry; remain'd there till the 3rd September, arriv'd at the Isle of France 13th November, and was join'd by the *Minotaure*, *Illustre*, and *Actif*. This is the French account.

12. Din'd at Lord Granby's.

13. Din'd at Admiral Osborne's.

14. At home.

15. At home.

16. Din'd at Sir Richard Grosvenor's.

22. The appeal of the *Teresa*, a Dutch ship, heard. The forming the sentence put off till the 29th. N.B. None of the Ministry there.

28. Din'd at Mr Rigby's. Ladies Coventry, Northumberland, Betty Waldegrave &c.

29. Sentence upon the *Maria Teresa* to restore the cargo, for want of evidence that the property of the French. The ship was restor'd by the Court below.

APRIL

5. The appeal of the Dutch ship *America* was heard. She was con-demn'd, ship, and cargo, as French: going directly to St Domingo, unloading there; reladen by Frenchmen for their own account; returning directly to France; and by them order'd to throw all their papers overboard, if attack'd by the English; which she did.

15. Admiral Boscawen was seen off the Lizard.

23. The King went to Kensington.

25. An account came that our army, under Prince Ferdinand was defeated in endeavouring to attack the French lines, at a village call'd Bergen, near Frankfort, that cover'd them—

MAY

7. Bayne in the *Spy* arriv'd. Middle February Moor took Fort Lewis—27th Hobson died of the flux.—Barrington, who succeeded, finds nothing to be done on the side of Basseterre, left a garrison in the citadel, and sail'd with Moor to St Louis, which they were in possession of, the 6th March. He writes that he had about 2000 men left fit for service when he began to write. Two days after, just as the ship sail'd, he adds in a postscript that since he began his letter he had 180 men taken ill. He was preparing, (after leaving garrisons in the two forts), to sail for North America to refresh the remainder of his men.

10. The vase was put upon the column.[1]

16. Lord Halifax was with me, and told me that the D. of Newcastle was extremely glad of having a vacancy in the Treasury by making Lord Bessborough Post Master, that he might take Mr Oswald; and that all was settled. But that Lord Bute came to him, in the name of all of them on that side of the Administration, and told him positively that they would not consent to Oswald's being in the

[1] i.e. in the garden of La Trappe, a monument to his wife.

Treasury; and the rather, as they knew he was not his man, but was suggested to him by Mr Legge. Which the Duke, very much frighted, was pleas'd to own. They added that they thought they had as good a right to recommend as anybody and they expected it should be Mr Elliot of the Admiralty: The Duke did not acquiesce absolutely, in the nomination, but did in the exclusion.

JUNE

2. Parliament prorogued.

6. Admiral Saunders sail'd from Louisbourg with Generals Wolfe and Townshend. Durel sail'd up three weeks before.
[*The Diary was here discontinued until October 1760*]

Dodington to Sewallis Shirley[1]

Eastbury 15 Septr
1759

Dear Sir,
    I thank you for the Honour of yours of the 11th Inst.
    Tho' I do not rely upon the Papers as very faithfull Historians, nor look upon every thing they relate as fact to be so, already; but I think the greatest part of it like to be so very shortly. The Luck of the French at sea, & their ill Behaviour at Land, gives me, who always hated them, the most sensible satisfaction. Surely the infamous Figure they have made upon the Continent, both of Europe, and America, must draw the Contempt of all mankind upon them.
    Well, my good Friend, now recollect what your Poor Friend said, when he gave in to the Support,[2] & pointed out the Method of Carrying on this Warr. This is a Warr truly national, pure, and unmix'd with any other Interest or Consideration. 'Tis your own Warr—keep it so—if we had done so, is it not probable that we might have had a glorious, and Advantageous peace before last Xmas? Is it not certain that we from the success of that Method only must have such an one before the Next?
    Now that we have shown that what he propos'd was the proper object and attainable within our Reach, by the Means he pointed out, for we have not only sacrificed 30 Millions of Monies and 30,000 Men upon the Continent of America, but we have added ten supererogatory Millions upon the Continent to preserve the Interest and power of the Ministry: we have succeeded fully in Both Thank God.

[1] Source: Dodington MSS., from D.'s draft.
[2] i.e. the subsidies to Continental powers.

Lett us leave off while we are well & before we are oblig'd to sacrifice our works of necessary Duty to our Acts of supererogation: lett us clapp up a good English Peace while we may, & not be forc'd to cover our Losses in Germany by our gains in America, for as to that Part of your Measures, believe me, we are in the Case of a Fine young Woman who has swallow'd something that (like the little Book in the Revelations) is Sweet in the Mouth but Bitter in the Belly. She will struggle hard, sweet Girl! to prevent, or protract a Discovery; but while she strains to lace it down Before, it rises upon the Hipps, & after all her Endeavours it ends in something that her Family has Nothing to do with, & ought not to own. If Pr. Ferdnd. has cover'd our Weakness in Westphalia, you see it breaks out in Lusatia &c, & if the K. of Pr. should lace it up there, Lett the Prince take care, one against two is not sure to win, always; it is true (& I rejoyce, I pride myself in it) that with the Help of our Money, & a Very gallant Body of our Coutrymen He has beat the French about the Field, but let us remember he has not beat them out of the Field.

Poor Lord George.[1] I hear he begins again—Virum volitare per oras—he was burnt, this week, at Salisbury.

I so cordially wish you Health, that I do more for it than you. I pray, & would fast for it, if I thought it would establish it: I believe you think that one would do you as much good as the other, but will do neither for yourself.

Yours &c.

[1] Lord George Sackville, whose conduct at Minden had prevented Prince Ferdinand from beating the French out of the field, instead of merely about it. This was the second case—Byng's being the first—of a commander connected with a family D. was friendly with suffering disgrace. On 8 April of the following year D. wrote to Lord Chancellor Bowes a full account of his attempts to defend Lord George (*H.M.C. Var. Coll.* vi. 41).

1760

OCTOBER

Dodington to Lord Talbot[1]

Eastbury
4 October 1760

I have sat down several times to thank you, my Dearest Lord, for the best cordial I have receiv'd of late years, but my age and infirmities would not obey me. I hope you will far exceed me in the first, without ever feeling the last. But in spite of them both, I do thank you, and from a full effusion of affection for your very kind and inspiriting letters; for I am more fond of a warm place, alas, in the heart of a man, than a woman, of honour; and had rather enjoy the tender intercourse, and hear the cherishing voice of friendship, than all the applause of the most flattering blast of fame's trumpet can bestow.

This country has undergone such a surprizing variety of changes of late, that the imagination can hardly keep pace with it: from the most tame state of inactivity to the most extensive rapidity of action, and by transitions as rapid: from negotiating, pocketing affronts, and examining what wood the stick was made of, that broke our heads, till it was too late to resent it; to hectoring, searching, plundering, and breaking everybody's head we met with, with the first thing that comes to hand, without considering what may be the consequences of such turbulent behaviour: from a war of our own, which we were well able to support without any ally, and for an object where we were deeply concern'd; to a war of other people's, which we are not at all able to support, and for an object we have nothing to do with.

A complication of inconsistencies so sudden and extraordinary, puts me upon reflecting by what steps any war becomes necessary—how that necessary war was converted into the present—how it has, and does appear to me; and how I think it has affected this country—by what means it is likely to come to a conclusion, and in what condition we shall be found at the end of it. I shall lay them before you, my very dear Lord, confus'd as they arise, secure that with you

---

[1] Source: Dodington MSS., in D.'s draft. From the corrections it appears possible D. intended this long letter to be printed as a pamphlet.

389

mistakes will meet with indulgence [and weakness with improvement].

If we look back upon the two last Administrations, no doubt a war (but not this war) was become unavoidable in fact, but promising in prospect. But the war this Administration is now making, was certainly just the contrary, avoidable and unpromising.

During the long Administration of Lord Orford,[1] the interest of the House of Walpole, not of England, was the centre of action. In that House there was neither Admiral nor General. They well knew that if either of those Great Officers should prove eminently successful, he would expect more consideration and power than they were dispos'd to part with out of the family; and if they were successful, the officer would sink into oblivion, and the miscarriage would recoil upon them with its whole weight. What then could be the result but expedients, temporizing, conniving at affronts to maintain place, and at the same time, cast a veil over the humiliating foot it stood upon? Having turn'd the fleets and armies that were to protect or revenge the violation of it, for want of hands of their own, to govern them, into instruments of parliamentary corruption.

It is true that the commercial advantages of a long peace enriched the nation, which with the domestic abilities of the Minister, disguis'd at home at least, the tameness that preserv'd it. But the narrow spirit of avidity, and abilities to acquire, depress'd the more noble and necessary, and I hope the more national, spirit of defence: and the subsequent unmeaning Administration of the Pelhams has demonstrated this truth, that wealth without a proper spirit in the possessors to guard and defend it, is a temptation to enemies, instead of being a protection and security against them.

That Administration then, not knowing the tendency of the principles they acted upon, or that national reputation was national riches, thought to preserve the last at the expense of the first; and by that inglorious mistake drew upon us those open encroachments, and violation of treaties, and those slighting and contemptuous answers, when we presum'd to remonstrate against them, that in my opinion made a war not only advisable but necessary. I declar'd so, very publicly, at a time that there were great differences of opinion, both about the thing itself, and the manner of carrying it on: I not only gave my opinion for the thing, which I suppose admitted no doubt; but was averse from that mean, dishonest, contemptible beginning of it, by plundering the French merchants. I not only gave my opinion for the thing, but afterwards enter'd, very copiously, into the methods of carrying it on:—

---

[1] The first of the 'last two Administrations' referred to above: the other being that of the Pelhams.

It is the war of Great Britain solely, unmix'd with any interest or quarrel of the Princes of the Continent. You are equal to it without their help: 'tis your own war: keep it so.

They heard, and treated me, as Juvenal says, *ut pueri Junonis avem.* But I am, still, of the same opinion, and believe I shall continue so, unless you will take the trouble to help me to a better.

These were the causes, I think the real ones, that produc'd the absolute necessity of a war; such a war as I insisted upon in public, and which we were fully equal to: a marine, commercial, colony war.

But when you had retriev'd your own losses at a game you understood, what induc'd you to venture losing all back again, at a game where you have no chance, only to retrieve the losses of others? What could prevail upon you to take the whole weight of the German war upon you, when the Electorate was secur'd by the Convention of Closterseven, made by electoral directions, and to all the benefits of which England was entitled, without any share of the disgrace? This will appear as clear and plain to all the world, by the incurable wound it has fix'd upon us, as it does now, to me, when the present malady of the moon has fully subsided; till then, it would be fruitless and invidious to mention it.

The Colonies no doubt ought to be defended, but then they should help themselves, as far as they can; as children of one common mother, they should have one common interest, and not only help themselves but help one another. I have reasons to believe that they do these things very ill: they contribute but little themselves, and in any necessaries that are to be provided, or furnish'd for the defence of their brethren that are in danger, they make their bargain as well, and keep it as ill, as if it was made between the Cabinet Council here and their great support, the Common Council of London. I am not sure that this war would have brought France so low as the victorious Marlborough war would have done, if there had been honesty enough to have concluded it by the glorious conditions offer'd and sued for at Gertruydenberg; but it would have forc'd her to feel that we had spirit to resent, and power to revenge, insults, to repel encroachments, to make her respect our friendship, and not dare wantonly to invade our just rights; which is as low, I think, as it is necessary, *for us,* to reduce her.

For those that have more to fear from her, when they are attack'd, let them exert all their strength to defend themselves and reduce her territorial dominion; when we are convinc'd that they have done all they can, and all is too little, then perhaps we may find it our interest to assist them in such manner, time, and proportion as we judge convenient and can afford, always at our own option, not at theirs;

but never take the burden from their shoulders to lay it upon our own.

With respect to the light the war appears in to me: I must frankly own I am not *transported* with it. The ruinous expense of men and money it has brought upon us, has with use greatly sunk the value of the advantages we have gain'd, and if the account were made up in a mercantile way, I am not sure that the balance would appear in our favour: reputation we have got—no man rejoices more in it or thinks it more invaluable. I see the world, even those whom I know to be eagle bred, and can look upon the sun, are dazzled with the glory of our success &c. I am glad of them but I must confess I am not dazzled with them. Where the uncommon bravery of the executive can alone excuse the rashness and inconsiderateness of the direction: where the success of an expedition is owing to the disappointments of the main object from want of sending a proper force —where a place is taken when the general writes to the government, the day of the attack, that it cannot be taken and it's pity to expose so many gallant men to no purpose. When the commandant in the place after it was taken, writes also that it is not tenable and that he will get out of it as soon as he can to save his garrison; when he keeps his word and is beat back into the place and forc'd to keep it till the enemy could run away without a sally, or one shot fir'd, or a sergeant's guard aboard the ships they were afraid of.—When I see all these stupendous events, I am not much dazzled, but I am very much and very agreably surpris'd with the gallantry of our countrymen, and as much but not as agreably surpris'd that our hands are so much better than our heads.

It seems as if to avoid the ill consequences that flow'd from the want of spirit in the last Administration, the present had gone as far beyond the mark and adopted heroism as the characteristic of their administration: so far I agree with them that the more of it the better in the execution, but I am not so fond of it in the first concoction. When indeed I figure to myself Mr Hawke surrounded by all the terrors a tempestuous sea and approaching darkness can present to the view or press upon the mind: outrunning half his gallant squadron and crowding every sail to rush upon an enemy equal to his whole force, in a bay to which he was an utter stranger, to save the noblest province in Europe—I am not only dazzled, but I am exalted, I am transported with the heroic behaviour of my countrymen; but I am not much transported with those who left that noblest province so expos'd and defenceless that nothing less than that heroic behaviour could have sav'd it.

I shall conclude this picture with the most agreable feature in it to me, which is the figure the French have made through the whole war. I revel, I exult in the ignominy of that once formidable, always impertinent nation *cujus optimus fallere et effugere est triumphus.*— I rejoice to see them disgrac'd by sea and by land: *Europa atque Asia pulsi.* But I do not rejoice to see them ruin us without one manly or noble action, but by our own folly in following them where we have no legs to carry us.

To show you how I think this war has affected us up to the end of the present year, I must refer you to the state of the revenue I have troubl'd you with, which goes no farther than 1760; where it leaves you a bankrupt in my sense without one shilling of revenue, or even surpluses for the supply of 1761. I would only add the exhausting of the people, the most dreadful article of all in the human arithmetic, and the price of labour: but the first will be soon replaced after a peace, and the other as soon as may be, I hope, but not very soon, reduc'd.

As to what will bring the war to a conclusion, I suppose it must be what has carried it on, money, your money, and a profuse quantity of it. You cannot go on, you must at the expense of half what you are worth, buy a peace: you cannot buy it of France, she has losses to retrieve: you cannot buy it of Austria, she has territories to regain: Russia has more resentment than interest to gratify, you must buy it of her, and at her own price: I fancy you have tried already and made some advances to your satisfaction, or else she would have made more advances to the satisfaction of her allies whom you cannot withstand while they remain united. Avail yourselves therefore immediately of the flood of popular confidence and credulity. Put your hand into their pockets without mercy, purchase a peace at any rate, and tell them they give peace to their enemies. The fools will believe you, though they bought it with almost all they have, and will spend what is left in bonfires and rejoicings.

As to the last point, which is the condition the war will leave us in at its conclusion: that is a point of a very complicated nature: some certainty in it, some speculation, and a good deal depending upon the time when the peace shall take place. Suppose then it should commence from Lady Day next, I presume when the whole debt of all kinds is brought together up to that period. it will amount to about £120,000,000, which making allowance of the 3½ p.c. will amount to about £4,000,000 per annum mortgage upon your estates for ever. Thus you will be pleas'd to observe that whatever the debt may be when the peace takes place, the supply of the next year cannot be much less than £15,000,000: to get home, disband, and lay up your armies and fleets, discharge the debt of the Navy &c. &c. &c.

and provide for the current service of the year; of which the land tax at 4s (no very auspicious beginning of a peace), the malt, and the sinking fund, will hardly furnish £5,000,000: so that £10,000,000, or £300,000 per annum will come as an additional charge upon your estates.

This calculation is upon a supposition of a peace by next Lady Day. But if the alliance holds and we are to furnish out another campaign (which God forbid) we must raise £27 millions at least, and at 4 per cent at lowest, which is a farther mortgage of £680,000 per annum, for you have not one shilling to receive either from land, malt, or sinking fund for the services of the year 1761. All which, supposing the peace to take place the 1 January 1762 will amount to a tax upon your estates of above £4,500,000 for ever. I may possibly have stated the National Debt too high, having no paper here; 'tis easy for you to set it right and make the proper deductions of interest; and then let who will endeavour to disguise it. This will be the true state of the revenue at any of the above-mention'd periods.

But what will be the state of trade at a peace, trade to the pretence of which in the late administrations, you sacrificed the honour of your ancestors, and now when that spirit begins to rekindle (which is wholly owing to the new part of the Ministry, and I highly honour them for it) you still give up all subordination to trade and look upon every merchant as your master; how will this trade stand, that is to repay with usury the most enormous expenses it has occasioned?

Trade then no doubt has greatly flourished during this war (and the merchants more, by dipping in all the combinations and monopolies for every sort of furnishment for carrying it on) and the reason is plain. You have been masters at sea for the annual expense of £4,500,000 besides a vast debt incurr'd; the colony trade of France (of little profit, but vast importance as the foundation and nursery of her marine) totally destroy'd; her very lucrative European trade much narrow'd and embarrass'd; the trade in general of neutral countries interrupted and precarious while the two greatest powers sweep the seas; but as soon as it is peace the trade of France will fall into its old channels and her marine consequently begin slowly, I hope, to revive. The commerce of the neutral nations will retake its full and uninterrupted career without any obstruction or new burden upon it. What new advantages to your trade the peace will bring with it cannot be known till we know the conditions; but these considerations must naturally lower and break in upon that full tide or rather monopoly of trade which you vainly aim at and more vainly proclaim you do: but you will be much less able to encounter this returning rivalry when you find yourselves loaded with the additional interest of £50,000,000 possibly if you do not make peace soon; or of about £30,000,000 whenever it is made: far the greatest part of which will ultimately fall upon the labour or the materials of your manufactures. These difficulties and disadvantages your trade will have to struggle with at the conclusion of a war carried on at such a lavish expense for the support of it in pretence, but in reality I fear, a very great part of it for other purposes.

And now from this state of your revenue and trade arises another consideration, purely conjectural, I hope groundless, and a cloud only arising from the depression of age and solitude to sadden the imagination. Suppose after the full enjoyment of all the advantages that full peace can give, when we are in full possession of all we can expect or pretend to, and have nothing to ask of the Gods but 'propria haec ut munera faciunt'—suppose I say, that finding their estates so heavily loaded and their trade from which they were taught to expect relief, so irretrievably embarrass'd, the people should grow a little restless and inquisitive, and upon enquiry of what had brought them into these uneasy circumstances they should be told it arose from expenses necessarily incurr'd to procure and secure to them the advantages of the government they enjoy'd, might it not be possible that if upon too nice an inspection they should imagine that the advantages do not preponderate, they might grow out of humour with and by degrees indifferent to a government they were forc'd to support at an expense which they think beyond its value? Would not this be a most cruel and even dangerous situation for a young virtuous prince, unless your noble friend[1] takes care to put people of some experience and abilities, but above all of decided integrity about him, that with a moderate degree of talents and application will do great things?

The effects of the Westphalia armies are included in the vast expense they create; I know of nothing else they do but run up and down and ravage one part of a miserable country to attack and defend another.

This is the light that I see things in at present, possibly a good deal discolour'd by the late hour of the day and the depression of spirits that naturally clouds it. I think and hope I am impartial, I am sure I ought to be indifferent to the fate of a country to which I have no obligation and in which I rather vegetate than live or belong to; my inutility to her service is decided here and I have frequent intimations to remove which are every day less unwelcome as I contemplate the prospect before me, but as you continue to interest yourself for her welfare, I must ever wish her happiness and prosperity though I cannot contribute to it.

[1] Bute.

Your truly illustrious and amiable father, my dearest Lord, was partial to me and show'd it by leaving me the most valuable legacy in his power to bestow, your friendship; I will not forfeit it and am sure I cannot lose it, but I must now soon resign it and leave you where your virtues instead of being (as they were design'd) an ornament and support, will be a reproach to the country and the age you live in.

Farewell my very dear Lord, may the goodness of God surround and cover you, yours most faithfully and affectionately,

[unsigned]

P.S. I have just receiv'd information that the expenditure of the Navy this year, stated from the Votes at £5,611,708, is in reality £7, 000, 000.

[*The Diary is resumed*] 25. The King died, suddenly, between 7 and 8 in the morning.

27. I receiv'd an account of it;[1] the same day sent Tuffin to town, with a letter to Lord Bute.

Dodington to the Earl of Bute[2]

27 October 1760

I have just receiv'd an account of the late King's death by Mr Breton. I do not lay my duty and congratulations at His Majesty's or Her Royal Highness's feet by letter, because I hope to do it by a more agreable hand, from your Lordship's goodness in charging yourself with it.

In this day of pretensions, my Lord, you will not be surpris'd to find mine: but that it may be neither improper nor importunate I beg leave to put it entirely into your Lordship's hands: for myself I am just as you always knew me, desirous to oblige, willing to be oblig'd, and grateful for obligations. For the rest your Lordship will know how little I am good for, how much I have to say for myself, and I am sure are so generous as to feel (and I hope, therefore, will use your good offices to prevent) the mortification it must be to me, not to receive some mark of the Royal favour as an approbation of my services in a Family, to which your Lordship, I believe, thinks that my heart as well as my duty, attach'd me, in the most cordial manner.

Her Royal Highness was ever my most gracious Mistress, I am not conscious to have done anything to incur His Majesty's displeasure. Whatever favour, therefore, your Lordship shall think me worthy to receive, or becoming to the Crown to bestow, I shall acknowledge, with great reverence and respect to the hands it comes from, and the most sincere gratitude for your Lordship's favourable and efficient good offices.

[unsigned]

28. Set out from Eastbury.

29. Arriv'd at Pall Mall.

30. Kiss'd the King's hand.

---

[1] D. was at Eastbury.
[2] Dodington MSS. Copy in D.'s hand.

NOVEMBER

1. Messrs Glover din'd here, and went with me to La Trappe.

3. Return'd to Pall Mall.

6. Agreed with Mr Olmius.[1]

7. Merchants' address. Messrs Shirley, Stanley, and Glover din'd here.

8. Went to La Trappe.

9. Return'd at night. The King's bowels carried to Westminster.

10. His body carried thither.

11. Buried.

13. Went to Lord Bute.

14. Went to wait on the King, in his closet.

Dodington to Bute[2]

Friday, past 3 o'clock
[14 November 1760]

My dear Lord,

Not yet knowing which are your leisure hours I chuse to write what has pass'd: and then to begg to know, if it would not be proper to wait upon her Royal Highness, and if tomorrow morning or evening would be least troublesome, and if I might not submit to her Highness, all that pass'd, as my wish and duty is. I shall send your Lordship tonight, or tomorrow, an Address that I would present from Weymouth. I will draw it in some thing a different style; if you do not approve of it we will send them a common one, like the rest.

Your Lordship's ever dutifully and affectionately,
but in a great hurry
GEO. DODINGTON

[1] At the ensuing election John Olmius became one of the members for Weymouth. The long mortgaging of two seats to the Pelhams came to an end: Welbore Ellis and Cavendish were displaced: and for the first time Dodington nominated to all four seats. The members were Dashwood, Olmius, Glover, and John Tucker.

[2] Source: Institute of Historical Research, London, transcript of the original in possession of the Marquess of Bute.

Enclosed was the minute of Dodington's interview with George III

When I came into the Closet, I said, 'Sir, I was encourag'd to take this liberty, or I should not have presum'd so far: and I can assure your Majesty that I do it with as much reverential duty, as the meanest subject can approach the greatest Prince with: but Sir when I reflect upon the many happy days I have pass'd with your Majesty, when you were young, and were the delight of us all, I cannot look upon myself as quite a stranger to your Majesty and therefore, as my attachment to your Royal Father and Mother, was cordial and sincere, I must own, that I much wish to receive some mark of your Royal Favour, as an Approbation to the world, that my services, tho' useless, were not disagreable to your Royal Family.'

The King, by his looks and gestures, show'd most gracious condescension, while I spoke, and then was pleas'd to say, that he was desirous to do some thing that would show his goodness to me; that Lord Bute had hinted to him what I desir'd and that when those things happen'd, he would think of me, and had (or would) order Lord Bute to put him in mind of me.—I said that I receiv'd the favourable expressions he us'd towards me, with infinite gratitude: that as to offices that carried great pecuniary emoluments with them I fear'd his Majesty would be press'd upon, for them, by many with great eagerness, if not indecency. That money was not my passion, that my sole ambition was the good opinion of my sovereign whom I rever'd, in the Person of a Prince, whom, when he was young, I presum'd to love; and if I should be so happy as to be thought worthy of the honour he had been pleas'd to hint at, it was all I wish'd.

His Majesty again assur'd me that he would think of me, and that I might depend upon it, that there was nothing at all in his mind, against me. I, then, beg'd one word more, and said—'Sir, tho' I have presum'd to decline office, as I do not find my parts and abilities as yet much impair'd, if, in the course of things there should arise any thing where your Majesty should think I can be of any use to you, if you will be pleas'd to communicate your Royal commands to me by Lord Bute, to whom I am bound by the strictest tyes, of most sacred and unalterable friendship and service, I beg your Majesty to believe, there is nothing so difficult or laborious that I will not cheerfully assist and serve in, either in private opinion, or publick execution, with as much zeal, integrity, and resolution, as if I held the highest and most lucrative office, your Majesty has to bestow.'

I think he seem'd pleas'd with this last part, I hope he was not offended.—These were all the words—my own I will swear to, and I believe His Majesty's are pretty exact.

15. Was to wait on the Princess, at Leicester House. Went to La Trappe.

16. At La Trappe.

17. At Court to get Mr Tucker presented.

18. Mr Ellis was with me to let me know that the Duke of Newcastle was willing to see me about the election of Weymouth. I deferred giving an answer immediately. Din'd at Almack's with Lord Talbot &c. Parliament open'd. The Commons only swore.

19. Wrote to Lord Bute to settle the answer to the Duke of Newcastle.

Dodington to Bute[1]

Pall Mall
the 19th Nov 1760

My dear Lord,

I do not trouble your Lordship in person, but my heart is not less gratefully and unalterably with you.

I receiv'd a message, yesterday, by Mr Ellis, from the Duke of Newcastle to wait upon him, on Friday morning to settle the Election of Weymouth: I defer'd my answer, on pretence of speaking to Mr Tucker: but it must be (unless you command the contrary, before you rise from dinner) that I beg to be excus'd from troubling him, my interest at Weymouth being engag'd to gentlemen who I do not doubt will be agreeable to his Grace, because I am sure they will be acceptable to his Majesty.

This will be my answer, and I hope you will not forbid it, but will provide in a proper manner to fill my seat if at a proper time, by the King's goodness, it should become vacant,[2] for, in short I neither can, nor ever will belong to any body, but the King, the Princess, and your Lordship: lett what will happen, I will have nothing but from the hands I most respectfully revere, and the good offices of those I most cordially love.—And this, once, for all, and no more of it.

I have it from good authority that a peerage is granted to Sir Thos: Robinson instead of Ellis's place.

[1] Source: Institute of Historical Research, London, transcript of the original in possession of the Marquess of Bute.
[2] By D.'s elevation to the peerage.

I was to pay my duty to her Royal Highness last Saturday, to acquaint her with the most gracious reception I mett with from His Majesty. Her Rl Hs receiv'd me with so much benevolence and condescension that I want words to express it: but shall not want zeal to acknowledge it, if ever a day should come when so poor an instrument can be of any use.

Farewell God preserve you
Your Lordship's ever most dutifully and affectionately,
GEO. DODINGTON

20. Mr Ellis came for the answer, which was, that I beg'd to be excus'd troubling his Grace, because my interest for Weymouth was engag'd to gentlemen who I could not doubt but would be agreable to him, because I had reason to believe they would be acceptable to the King.

21. The Commons presented their Address. Din'd alone, and went to La Trappe at night.

22. Lord Bute sent to desire to see me at my house in Pall Mall. I went early to town; he staid two hours with me: much serious and confidential talk; repeated instances of his most generous friendship. Fresh assurances of the King's benignity, by his Majesty's order. Return'd to dinner, but lay in Pall Mall.

23. On Sunday.

24. Went to Court. Saw the Speaker at night.

25. At home.

26. Went to Lord Mansfield's.

Dodington to Bute[1]

26 November 1760

My dear Lord,

In consequence of what we last talk'd about I send you a list of the Boroughs and members now serving for them, where the Crown by virtue of its officers has either the absolute nomination or very much the superior influence. I believe it is far from being correct, for I have so long and with so much success endeavoured to forget these things (which brought me nothing in return but dissatisfaction) that they

---

[1] Source: Dodington MSS. (draft). The letter as sent (unvaried) is in the Bute MSS., but the enclosure is missing.

are all out of the way, both in my drawers and in my head: but my zeal for the King's service and independence would I believe recall some of them, if you should think it necessary.

It is not my wish that H. My. should interpose directly or indirectly where the interest is in any private gentleman as such; but during the two last reigns a set of undertakers have farmed the power of the Crown at a price certain under colour of making themselves responsible for the whole, have taken the sole direction of the Royal interest and influence into their own hands and applied it to their own creatures without consulting the Crown or leaving any room for the Royal nomination or direction.

This only I think should be prevented and prevented before they can pretend that it is settled and the persons promised, and these gentlemen should not be suffered in my opinion to engage the interest of the Crown without previously taking H.M.'s pleasure as to the nomination where he has the power; and the recommendation of support where he has the influence of such of his My's friends and servants as he not they shall approve of.

I do not know whether they have as yet mentioned anything to the King upon this subject; but I presume it cannot be too soon to lay before H.M. every thing that may the better prepare and enable him to execute his royal pleasure in a point of so much importance to the future ease and quiet of his reign.

What may be the weight and influence of your Lordship and your friends is another consideration. As all that is required is an immediate dependence upon the King and nobody else, I should think a standard so honourable firmly held up, could not fail of drawing many and very considerable persons to enlist under it.

I trouble you with these thoughts from what you mentioned here the other day, but I will go no farther. You know I am a ghost that never appears till he is conjured up nor speaks till he is spoke to; your Lordship has the power of evocation and can give me substance and speech whenever and wherever you please. In the meantime wherever I am, as long as I am anywhere at all I shall always be my dear Lord, yours most faithfully and affectionately—

27. Went to the Princess's drawing-room.

28. Presented the Weymouth address.

29. Lord Bute came hither by appointment. Staid a great while. I press'd him much to take the Secretary's office, and provide otherwise for Lord Holderness. He hesitated much, and said if that

were the only difficulty it would be easily remov'd, for Lord Holderness was ready, at his desire, to quarrel with his fellow-ministers, from the slights and ill usage he daily experienc'd, and go to the King, and throw up, in seeming anger, and then he[1] might come in without seeming to displace anybody.—I own the expedient did not please me. Much kindness and friendliness to me. Went to La Trappe at night.

30. At La Trappe. Mr Fleet there.

[1] Bute. This is in fact what happened, Bute succeeding Holderness as Secretary of State the following March.

DECEMBER

1. At Pall Mall.

2. At Council Lord Huntingdon, and Mr G. Townshend sworn. The King had a dangerous fall with his horse.—No hurt, by God's goodness.

3. At Council.—Sign'd a letter to check the Government of Ireland for not sending over a Bill of Supply, as is always the form, before their dissolution on the demise of the Crown.

4. Din'd here, Lord Buckinghamshire, G. Townshend, Bellendine, Dashwood, Macky, Vaughan, Stanley. Much dissatisfaction at the King's making Lord Fitzmaurice, Aide de Camp; and the measure of bringing country Lords and considerable gentlemen about the King, as Lord Litchfield, Mr Berkeley, &c. ridicul'd by the creatures of the Administration.

5. Din'd at Lord Halifax's.

6. At home.

7. At home.

8. At home. The Duke of Richmond, resign'd the Bedchamber, which he had just ask'd, because Lord Fitzmaurice was put before his brother. Din'd here, Lord Halifax, Colonel Johnston, Messrs Oswald, Shirley, Breton. The Duke of Richmond's affair much canvass'd. Lord Halifax said that the Duke assur'd the person he had it from, that the King sent, and offer'd him the Bedchamber, which was not so.

The whole affair, as I had it from Lord Bute was this. The Duke, after having talk'd very offensively of the Scotch, &c., on the promotion of Sir Henry Erskine, ask'd, in a private audience of the King, to be of his Bedchamber: His Majesty gave him a civil, but not a decisive answer, and acquainted Lord Bute with it, who told him that the Duke's quality, and age, made him a very proper servant for his Majesty, upon which Lord Bute was order'd to let him know that the King accepted his service, which he did and then let him know his behaviour about Sir Henry Erskine particularly offensive to him, Bute. The King was angry that he was not told before; and Lord Bute said that he thought the Duke a proper servant for his Majesty, as such recommended him, but not as his friend.

The Duke came to see Lord Bute to thank him for his good offices, and to disown all political connections with Fox: Lord Bute said that the King had no manner of objection to Mr Fox, and that himself had a great regard for him personally; but fairly told him that the King knew how he had talk'd about Sir Henry Erskine's affair, and of him, Bute, in particular; which the other endeavour'd to palliate, and said had been much aggravated.

10. Din'd at home. W.B.[1]

11. At Leicester House. Din'd at Almack's.

12. At St James's. Din'd at Sir Francis Dashwood's.

13. Din'd at home, lay at La Trappe.

14. Came to dine Lady Harrington. Return'd at night.

15. Came to town. Lord Bute desir'd me to call upon him, on Wednesday morning.

Dodington to Bute[2]

15 December 1760

My dear Lord,
    I am very unlucky. I did not come from La Trappe till 5 o'clock. I shall bring you a magnificent and convenient principal story which I have planned for you tomorrow morning by 9 o'clock unless you forbid me by letting me know what other day will be more convenient to your lordship.
    I am exerting all my endeavours to get as many members as I possibly can. For God's sake do not suffer all the King's interest to be employed against his power. If it be not thought proper to raise an Army, let us at least secure a phalanx devoted to duty impenetrable by malice and faction which I am very sure are implacably and indefatigably at work with all their powers and in every place.
                                                        I am etc.

---

[1] Significance obscure.   [2] Source: Dodington MSS. (draft).

16. The Frekes and Okedens din'd here.

17. Much talk with Lord Bute. Came to Pall Mall after Court, and staid till past four. Messrs Bodens, Wyndham, and Breton. Lord Bute desir'd me to call tomorrow, for a minute.

18. Call'd upon Lord Bute. Went to the Drawing Room. Sir Francis Dashwood declar'd for Weymouth.

19. Went with Mr East to Sir Francis Dashwood's. Din'd at Mr Forrester's with Lord Litchfield, Sir Francis Dashwood, Sir Henry Bellendine, Mr Macky.

20. At one Lord Bute here, till dinner. Much talk about setting up a paper—and about the Houses in case of resignations. I went to La Trappe.

21. Mr Breton and Mr Glover there. The last full of admiration of Lord Bute: applauds his conduct, and the King's, says they will beat everything; but a little time must be given to let the madness of popularity cool. Not determin'd about political connections, but I believe he will come to us.

22. At Pall Mall. Wrote to Lord Bute.

Dodington to Bute[1]

Pall Mall, past 1 o'clock
Monday 22nd Dec. 1760.

I am return'd from my convent my dear Lord and shall not go back till I have had the happiness of seeing you, which cannot be at dinner tomorrow because Lord Masham dines here by return from his own house.

I have seen Glover who is charmed with your behaviour, but more with what he hears of your master's. The points we agree in are that if he goes on with these moderate but manly exertions of power directed to national purposes, he will beat you all together and be your master in spite of your teeth—that you will become a common tavern toast and reduced to the now forgotten state of dependent servant to an independent king. His notions in case of aggression are bolder and I like them better than my own.

[1] Source: Dodington MSS. (draft).

I shall see Whitehead on Wednesday, but only see and talk with him in general.—You will think a little farther what you would have done and when, before we enter into particulars with these people, as I feel and am sure you gain ground, I am less in a hurry.

The more I think of the conversation of last Saturday about single resignations and even combined aggressions, the more I am confirmed in my opinion that nothing should be done that can justly be imputed to precipitation, nothing be delayed that can be imputed to fear of them. I think I can show you as good a House of Lords as they can make, uniting all that can or will unite; and for a House of Commons upon the noble principle the King sets out with, I am persuaded the attack can be made but by one man who will not be followed by half a score. This I say in case of aggression, which I think and hope will never happen. However as I think they will dropp off, e'er it be long, you will be pleas'd to think with yourself only, & your Royal Master, of proper Persons to fill up the first Rank with you, in case of Death or Desertion.

Remember, my noble and generous Friend, that to recover Monarchy from the inveterate Usurpation of Oligarchy, is a Point too arduous and important, to be atchiev'd, without much Difficulty and some Degree of Danger, tho' None, but what attentive Moderation, & unalterable Firmness, will certainly surmount.

Will you give me your Mr Worsley to chuse at Weymouth? If you will tell him so, when you think it proper time, it will be an easy Seat, both in the Manner and the Expence.

What I am going to write, I never saw upon Paper, myself, nor is it fitt any body should as yet, but You—unless you have a mind to make the King or the Princess Laugh.

> Quoth Newcastle to Pitt, 'tis in vain to dispute,
> If we'd quarrel in Quiet, we must make Room for Bute:
> Quoth Pitt to his Grace, to bring That about,
> I fear my dear Lord You, or I, must turn out:
> Not at all, quoth the Duke, I meant no such Thing,
> To make Room for us all, we must turn out the King.
> If that's all your Scheme, quoth the Earl, by my troth,
> I shall stick by my Master, and turn ye out, Both.

Farewell. God preserve you for my Sake, and for the Sake of my Betters. &c.

23. Lord Bute was here, we weigh'd all things and tho' after long discussions we parted without any decision, I think he inclines much to it. Din'd here, Lord Masham, Messrs Bodens, Breton, Sterne, Sharpe, Mallet.

24. Din'd here, Mr Whitehead. Went to La Trappe.

25. At La Trappe alone. Wrote to Lord Bute.

Dodington to Bute[1]

La Trappe   Xmas Day 1760

My dear Lord,

The inclos'd will be printed, if not disapprov'd of: if we attack, we must attack smartly, and the Fire must be kept up.

I have seen Elliot, manly, practicable, and affectionate. We have talk'd ourselves into our former opinions; and think your Lordship will be of the same, soon, either from Choice or Necessity; but if not, Both of us, I am sure, shall most chearfully concurr in yours.

These ludicrous Queries, and my late Conversation with Elliot, put me upon thinking of some very serious ones, which you may read, burn, and forgett, if you please, but not the Truth of the warm Heart they come from.

Queries

1st.   Is *this* to be look'd on as the Administration?

2nd.   If it is, can the People (would you have them) look upon it otherwise than as an Administration that they know the King hates?

3rd.   Is it not then to be apprehended that Malevolence may be apt to impute the long Continuance of such an Administration to Fear?

4th.   If this is not the Administration, will not the people conclude that there is *One Man* behind the Curtain that governs the whole Country, without appearing?

5th.   Will not that one Man, soon, stand in an invidious Situation, and become responsable, in their opinion, for all that he suffers his Enemies to do?

6th.   When those Enemies find that their power expires with the War, will They be in Haste to bring it to a Conclusion?

7th.   Or will they not privately hang upon the Wheels of government, when the easier they move, the faster their Dismission approaches, and be able to clogg them much more effectively, as well as imperceptibly, when every office in the Kingdom, is in their own, or their Creatures' Hands?

[1] Source: Dodington MSS. (Draft). The enclosed political article, no doubt by Whitehead, is missing.

8th. What Numbers can the Best Man expect will stand by their Colours long; or what Inducement is there for Volunteers to enlist, if they see that the Honour of Attachment only, is to be their Reward, while all the Honest Advantages of it, are to remain to the Friends of his Enemies?

9th. Does it not, therefore, seem adviseable, if not necessary, either to form an Administration, or to take an Open, Leading Part with the Principal Share of Disposition and Direction in this Administration, if it is to continue for any time?

Tuus sit Amice quod optas
Explorare Labor mihi jussa capissere fas est

I shall be in Pallmall on Saturday morning before you come from Kew, in Case you should have any Commands; if you have none, I begg you would not think of calling.

Your Lordship's most faithfully,
[unsigned]

27. Came to Pall Mall, in the morning. He came, much talk, about Lord Egmont, whose election I undertook to secure, if the King commanded me, on refusing him the peerage. Answers to my Queries of the 25th.—City Militia.—Demand of the Lieutenancy for the whole Corporation: Dukes of Newcastle and Argyll flattering Bute with the King, and offering to act under him.—Duke of Chandos's pretensions.—King of Prussia to rise at the head of Ferdinand's army—Duke of York's establishment.

Lord Egmont's affair is thus. The 26th inst. I receive a letter, letting me know that Lord Egmont had lately wrote to his steward Biddlecombe, with orders to show the letter to the Mayor of Bridgewater, wherein he lets him know that it was probable, and would be determin'd either the 23, or 24th. (which was the date of my letter from Bridgewater) there would be an election there: in which case, he should put up Lord Perceval in his room &c. This, to me, appear'd so strange that I ask'd Lord Bute about it. After putting me in mind that he had told me, a week ago, that there never was a thought of making Lord Egmont a peer, or that even any application had been made, he said, that very lately, he thought the day the King went to the House (which was Tuesday, 23rd inst. or the day before), Lord Egmont had been with him and beg'd earnestly to go into the House of Lords—that his election at Bridgewater was very uncertain—that he was very ill, & spit blood—was very much dejected, &c. That he, Bute, told him there was very little encouragement. And told me that the King was very little dispos'd. Ask'd me what I would do in his election. I said, 'Throw him out'; he seem'd to think it hard he should be in neither House. Perceiving that, I said that if the King would keep him out of the House of Lords, and he, Bute, desir'd it, I would secure his election at Bridgewater: he reply'd that it was too much to give up family interest. I said, 'Nothing is too much that is useful, where friendship is real, and mutual.' There it now stands. Went to La Trappe.—

28. At La Trappe.

29. Return'd to Pall Mall.

30. Mr Kelsal din'd here.

31. Went to the Duke of Argyll's—

Dodington to Bute[1]

Pall Mall
Wednesday night
[31 December 1760]

By the enclos'd just receiv'd, Lord Bute will see the state of Lord Egmont's interest. Binford, there mention'd, is, by much, the most considerable of that party.

If want of interest to gett into our House be a sufficient reason to gett into the other, no man's pretension to a peerage can be better grounded: but if His Majesty does not think it necessary to bring him into the House of Lords, Lord Bute may, if he pleases, still bring him (or probably, any body else) into the House of Commons for Bridgewater, by signifying his commands to one whose pleasure and pride it is, and ever will be, to obey him.

[1] Source: Institute of Historical Research transcript of original in possession of the Marquess of Bute.

1761

JANUARY

1. Din'd at Lord Hillsborough's.

2. Lord Bute came. Said he was sure that the Ministry had some glimpse of getting off this system by setting up that of abandoning Hanover and applying the money to distress France into a peace; that they would by their popularity, force this measure upon the King, who must lose a great deal of his. I told him (as truth was) that this measure was the only sound one to get out of the war—that I had, yesterday, begun to put my thoughts upon it into writing, to persuade him to obtain powers of the King to carry it into execution:—that my only doubt was, whether the new Parliament should not be suffer'd to meet only to declare in the Speech, (which must circulate thro' the kingdom) that the King found himself involv'd in this war to which he had, no way, contributed. That seeing the bent of the nation so violent, he had acquiesc'd in, without approving it, persuade that they would soon feel, if they did not see, their error; that he was convinc'd that this way of defending Hanover would ruin this country without defending that, and therefore would no longer expose his regal dominions to such hardships for fruitless attempts to defend his electoral ones; but would leave them in his enemies' hands, and apply the expense to force him to a reasonable peace by means more probable, and proper to attain that end.

He paus'd a good while, and did not say positively that he could, or could not, get the King to consent to this system; but return to say that he thought the Ministry had an eye that way. 'If it should happen,' I said, 'it would be irresistible', but there was one way to defeat the use they propos'd from it, which was to put himself at the head of it, in a great office of business, take the lead, and the merit of bringing with him the true British Principles of making war, peace &c.

He said that he was sure they look'd that way, he hop'd, and believ'd that they would not easily come at it.—That I always talk'd of them as if they were united, whereas they neither were, nor could be; that the D. of N. most sincerely wish'd peace and would go great lengths to attain it—that Mr Pitt meditated a retreat, and would stay no longer than the war. For my part I think they will continue the war as long as they can, and keep in, after it is over, as long as they can; and that will be as long as they please, if they are suffer'd to make peace, which will soon be so necessary to all orders and conditions of men, that all will be glad of it, be it what it will, especially from those who have all the offices, and the powers of office: all which can never end well for the King and Lord Bute.—

He, then, show'd me a letter to Lord Egmont, which he wrote in the King's presence. He tells him that the King is resolv'd to make no more peers, at present, than those now before him: that if his Lordship thinks his personal application to His Majesty will make him alter that resolution, he hop'd his Lordship would take that step—and then added, 'If you think your election uncertain, and I can be of any Service to you in it (*as I think I can*) your Lordship may command me.'—I hope he will not accept it.—

He said he was persuaded that it would be seen, this very winter, if they endeavour'd to prolong the war, for he thought the King of Prussia himself, would insist upon their making a peace, even a separate peace. This, I confess, I do not understand. We agreed about getting runners, and to settle what should be dispers'd.— Went to the Duke of Argyll's.

3. Carried Mr Wyndham to La Trappe.

4. At La Trappe.

5. Came to town at night.

6. Din'd at Lord Hillsborough's.—At the Speaker's.

7. Messrs Wyndham, Bodens, and Thompson din'd here.

8. At the House. din'd at Almack's.

9. Din'd at Sir Francis Dashwood's. Lord Bute came, show'd me Lord Egmont's letters. He is displeas'd, but desires to know if

he is to understand His Majesty refuses him the peerage for ever, or for this time only.—We are quit of him.

He thinks the French will make a separate peace upon the present foot: I think not—and endeavour'd to show him, that nothing but ruin could flow from our persisting in our present measures: nothing could produce peace, but withdrawing from the Continent. That it must be: either from necessity; or being drove into it by those who brought this ruin upon us; or carried to the foot of the Throne by the united voice of his Majesty's best subjects:—that at all events, it ought to appear that the giving up Hanover was his Majesty's own system, and therefore in case any thing that look'd that way should be stirr'd, he should be prepar'd to take the lead, and that he, and I should begin it in the House of Lords.[1] I wish I may have convinc'd him.

I had wrote, and then mention'd Lord Talbot's son-in-law, to succeed Boscawen who was dying: he was sorry I had not thought of it sooner, but had agreed to fill his place by a remove out of the Board of Trade.—I try'd to get the Jewel Office for him, by an arrangement for Sir Richard Lyttelton;—but in vain.—Wish'd to have some coffee house spies, but I do not know how to go about it.

10. Din'd here Lords Eglinton, and Litchfield, Shirley, Dashwood, Elliot, Glover.—Admiral Boscawen dy'd. Told Glover of Weymouth.

11. Went to La Trappe.—Return'd to dinner.

12. Went to Court.—Din'd alone—Duke of Argyll's.

13. Went to the House.—Alone—at the Opera.

14. Went to Court. Messrs Wyndham, and Kelsal din'd here.

15. Went to Court at Leicester House.—At the House on Lord Marischall's petition. Din'd at Almack's.—At the Duke of Argyll's—

16. Lord Bute came. Said that he was, now, sure that Pitt had no thoughts of abandoning the Continent; that he was madder than ever.—Uneasy with Talbot—that he would have put the Steward's

[1] This makes it clear that D. had already been promised the peerage he received in June 1761.

staff the first day, if he could.—That he had heard that Talbot thought Granby could persuade his father to quit it; that otherwise he could not accept of it, on account of the friendship between him and Granby.—That he would make an excellent officer to reform that most corrupt office.—That in whatever he should do for his friends, he should always, at the same time, consider the service of his Master, and the public. I press'd him much for Talbot. He said he had marks of all the distinctions that were going—the Council, accepted, and refus'd—in the promotions of peerage, an earldom; that he perceiv'd that he meant a place much more than he, Bute, wish'd—was sorry for it—that he was violent, and I might depend upon it would be impracticable in business.—That he had us'd him unkindly. I said all I could, and from my heart.

I touch'd again upon Rice. He said he thought the Board of Trade no improper beginning.—I agreed—that, possibly might be shap'd out. I said the offer of anything, directly from him, accepted, or not accepted, I thought would be very kindly taken. That Henley ow'd being made Chancellor, from Keeper, entirely to him—that he had brought his letter to show me.—I beg'd him to keep that letter as well as some others he had shown me, properly labell'd, and ty'd up; for the ingratitude of mankind might make it of use to have preserv'd them. He laugh'd, and said he had met with some, already, and then told me Martin's impertinent conversation at the Admiralty, before a dozen people, about the line drawn between the Scotch and the English, and that it ought to be continued, &c.

Said that he must see the Duke of Newcastle to settle with him about the elections, shortly.—That, to those who had propos'd to him to unite with the Duke upon conditions, he had said that he could agree to no conditions till he saw Talbot, Dashwood, and Charles Townshend, (which last, he said, had sworn allegiance to him, *for a time,*) had such places as he wish'd.

As to the army, he wish'd he could talk with an impartial officer: that he thought the King of Prussia, and Prince Ferdinand were as popular as ever. I said that I thought the King of Prussia began to be very little so: that there was something so servile in the education of an officer, that if he found out what he wish'd to hear he might be sure of hearing nothing else.—That I thought Prince Ferdinand was become as impopular in the army, as he was, once, popular—that he was accus'd of three great heads of malversation:

the first that he had exacted complete pay for incomplete corps; the second, that not one shilling of all those devastating contributions had been carried to the public account. The third that he had receiv'd good money, and paid the troops in bad, to a very great amount, at a great discount. That this last was an affair mercantile, and of exchange; that I would undertake to find those who should lay it open to the world beyond contradiction, if it were true.

His notions about the war are very singular, and I believe, not thoroughly digested. He thinks they will make a peace on the present footing, if we go on conquering their islands, &c.—I, that they will never make peace with you till you withdraw your troops actually, or that they think you design it.

He thinks that withdrawing your troops would make a peace, or enable you to carry on a war much cheaper, and by national means, for national ends, but what compensation is to be made to Hanover? I said, according to the damage done, and the foundation must be how much heavier their taxation has been than what was rais'd by their natural Prince. He said that if we made this separate peace, we must, still, pay the King of Prussia, which would make the war look yet more unnational. I thought not: 'But then', he said, 'we must stop here, and think of conquering no farther.'—I said I saw nothing to conquer; that France had as much lost Martinico as she could lose it—that the public had not receiv'd a sixpence from the duties, nor the particulars from their estates these two years, &c. He said all the produce came home in neutral ships—but return'd to the difficulties of indemnifying Hanover, if the troops were withdrawn, and the peace made—which makes me doubt whether the King can be brought to abandon Hanover, for a time, which seems to me to be the only way to secure a good peace to that country as well as this.

17. The Keeper made Chancellor the 15th.

18. Came to town: Din'd with the Duke of Bolton. At Lady Harrington's.

19. Mr Balch din'd here.

20. Din'd at Sir Francis Dashwood's.—

21. Din'd at Lady Hervey's.—At the Duke of Argyll's.

22. Din'd at Almack's.—At home.—

23. Din'd here, Messrs Wyndham, Bodens, Kelsal, Sir Thomas Robinson.

24. Din'd here, Messrs Glover. Went to La Trappe.

25. Return'd the

26, and din'd at Lord Litchfield's.

27. At home.—At the Burletta.

28. Din'd with Lady Hervey.—At the first night of *The Married Libertine*.

29. At Almack's.

30. Din'd at Lord Barrington's. Lords Anson, Harrington, Albemarle, Gower, Edgecumbe, Hertford, Bessborough and General Waldegrave.

31. At home.

FEBRUARY

1. Sunday. At Home.

2. Lord Bute came. Dissatisfied with the clamour about the beer,
at the playhouse the day the King was there. I told him intelligence
I had just receiv'd, that Mr Pitt had told Mr Beckford, last Friday,
that all was over, and he would have no more to do. He said (as I
had said before) that he did not believe it; that he had not seen him
this fortnight, but seen Beckford, lately, who dropping in conversation that he wish'd to see the King his own Minister, Lord Bute
reply'd, that his great friend Mr Pitt did not desire to see the King
his own Minister, and he might tell him so, if he pleas'd; that it was
very indifferent to him, if every word he said was carried to Mr
Pitt. I ask'd him if he knew why the Parliament was kept on so
long. He said he thought it was the better for him, his friends had
the more time to look about them, that the Duke of Newcastle was
desirous to have it end. I ask'd if he had settled the new Parliament
with him. He said he had not seen him for some days, but suppos'd
he should, and would bring his list with him. That what were
absolutely the King's boroughs, the King would name to, but
where the Crown had only an influence, as by the Customs, &c.
he could be refus'd the disposition of it, while he staid in. That
he had told Anson that room must be made for Lord Parker, who
said that they were quite full. 'What,' he said, 'what, my Lord, the
King's Admiralty boroughs full, and he not acquainted with it'—.
That Anson seem'd quite confounded, and knew not what to
answer.—Was not for pushing them as yet, for if the peace was a
bad one, as it must be, they would certainly proclaim that it was
owing to their dismission, who were not suffer'd to bring the great
work to a happy conclusion, by those to whom the glorious successes
which had hitherto attended their conducting of it, were entirely
owing. In short, he seem'd to think that nobody could stand such
a peace as must be made upon the present system, but those who
had brought us into it, and were the authors of it.

3. At home, at the Burletta.

4. At Sir Francis Dashwood's to dinner.

5. Din'd at Almack's.

6. At Home.—Lord Bute was here. Talk'd over Charles Town-shend's being Secretary at War, and Dashwood's succeeding him.—Seem'd resolv'd to come into Administration, but not yet. We agreed that if there was nothing irregular to be done, the Parliament would be the King's, let who will choose it; said that it was easy to make the Duke of Newcastle resign, and did not at all apprehend that he would do it in a hostile way, or make those he chose make an opposition. But who was to take it? He seem'd not to think it adviseable to begin there. I said I saw no objection; but if he thought there was he might put it into hands that would resign it to him when he thought it proper; but that he must begin to be a public man by taking something, or else the objection would be the same at ten years' end. Said the Holderness knew nothing they were doing, for these last ten days, and therefore he begun to think with me that it was possible Pitt might resign.

7. Went to La Trappe, and din'd alone.

8. Came to Pall Mall, at night.

9. Went to introduce Mr V. Poulet to Lord Bute. After the visit much talk—about the Bill the Irish had, at last, vouchsaf'd to send over. I thought it no Money Bill, so did he, but said that he, and Bedford, were the only two of the Cabinet who were of that opinion; so that it would be accepted. I said I was sorry for my friend the Chancellor and the two Chief Justices, who thought it so little a Money Bill that ought not to have been sent (they meant a Supply) that they would not sign it: and now, upon our acceptance, would be expos'd to all the fury of impopularity. He then said that in talking to the Duke of Newcastle about places, he told him that Dashwood must have Charles Townshend's place when he left it for the War Office—that he told him, with truth, that he did not bring Dashwood as a creature of his, that he did not know that

[here the Diary ends]

Dodington to Bute[1]

the 9th Febry 1761

My dear Lord,
    I have communicated to Lord Talbot, in the best Manner I could,

[1] Source: Dodington MSS. (Draft).

your kind Intentions. My Answer is, that Mr Rice being out of Town, he cannot tell whether the obliging Proposal would be accepted, or not—that he thinks it very kind, and obliging on the Part of Lord Bute.—I hope this will produce what I most wish, I am sure nothing can increase the Warmth of my Heart to ye both, and I trust, nothing will ever diminish it.

Since I saw your Lordsp I have been with the Chancellor, and studied Patents which I shall lay before you, as short as I can, but with great Truth, and Exactness. The King signs the Warrant, prepar'd by the Sectry of State to the Attorney Genl to make out Bills containing Grants of the Honours he pleases to bestow, the Attory transmitts them to the Privy Seal who transmitts them to the Chancellr—. The Chancellr is oblig'd by Act of Parliament to putt the *Recepi* upon them the same Day that he receives them which compleats their Validity as to Rank, Privilege &c.

Should he receive all these Patents on the same Day, they would all be Peerages of the same Date, as the law makes no Division of a Day, and the House of Lords must place the Persons they are granted to, which I by no Means presume to advise, but if it pleas'd His Majy would please me very well.

The next point is, that when James the first created the Baronets, he made an Ordinance which settled Precedency, which has always been observ'd in which he fixes the Rank of Privy Councillors to be before the second Sons of Viscounts, and next to the eldest Sons of Barons: it is at the end of Selden's Titles of Honour, may be you have the book, least you should not I send you a faithfull Copy. This Ordinance fixes the Precedency of the Chancellr of the Dutchy over the Ch: Justice of England, of the Mr of the Rolls over the Ch: Justice of the Common Pleas, and several others now in question, and is look'd upon as of as much Authority in these cases (all, intirely subject to H. My's good Pleasure) as anything but an Act of Parliament.

Hillsborough and Lytelton, created together—Hillsborough, the Precedence, because he had it before. Hardwick, and Darlington, Earls: Hardwick the Precedency, because his Office gave it him, tho' his Barony much younger.

Most of the Gentlemen are very young. Permitt me to say that neither their Age the opinion of the World, their Manner, Rank, or Company in Life, the Offices they have gone thro' or their Parliamentary Interest in their Countries give them any Pretence to go before your poor Friend at present. I must hope that the King will not give them a Precedency in our new Situation which they cannot claim in This. He does us all, very high Honour, and higher to me,

I admitt, than to any of them, but I trust that by your favourable Representation H. My will not lessen the Honour he does me to add to theirs a Precedency which, if he does not give them, they cannot complain, over one who will not complain, if he does.

I am, &c.

[unsigned]

P.S. I will have an answer from Rice as soon as I can.

Dodington to Bute[1]

Cockpitt. Wednesday
1 o'clock [?10] April 1761

I am just come from the Duke of Newcastle's—told him that I was well assur'd of the sincerity of the good correspondence between your Lordship and his Grace: that I was satisfy'd it would last as long as I liv'd: (I hop'd much longer) that in that confidence, & upon those terms, I came to offer him my services & as I knew you look'd upon his friends as your own, I hop'd he would look upon me as one of his &c.—Great professions of sincerity & dependence upon your Lordship: & great civilities, and assurances of good will to me.

I have just read the little pamphlett; what was immediately address'd to you is left out: you do not want it, I confess: the much you have done for the country, & the little you have claim'd, has made even envy fond to adopt you: But do not your countrymen[2] want it? Should not that invidious distinction be stigmatis'd and exploded by all honest means, as much, as publickly, & as soon as possible? Why must they, with full as good natural abilities, much more cultivated, & improv'd, in general, by application & industry, suffer by narrow prejudices that nothing but numbers can defend one moment?

Your ever faithfull & affectionate
M.[3]

(Enclosure)

Why I use the term *Minister* only is because your attack is partialy confin'd to a *particular* one, but who, it is well known, is far from ambitiously arrogating to himself the *sole*, and *arbitrary guidance* of our *measures*, however a late Ministerial *Vizier* may have resented his

[1] Source: Institute of Historical Research transcript of original in possession of the Marquess of Bute.
[2] The Scots.
[3] D.'s peerage as Lord Melcombe dated from 6 April.

not being permitted to exercise in a free country, this *unconstitutional* authority.[1]

Dodington to Bute[2]

La Trappe
May 29th 1761

I have obeyed your commands, my dear Lord, as I am sure I always shall do, with pleasure & I believe with admiration. Judge what effusion of heart the poor gentleman must feel on receiving such honours—benefits so totally unexpected & unsolicited by anything but humble merit in distress, when I, the canal only of so much goodness still feel pleasure from the stream of benevolence that flowed through me.

To dry the tears of affliction & to call forth those of gratitude & gladness are lessons that nothing but the noblest sensibility of heart can teach or learn.

I have been munificent at the King's and your Lordship's expense and added greatly to the poor man's happiness by indulging him with a proof of the Royal approbation, in a copy of your Lordship's letter.

Till now I found old age supportable enough from the infirmities it brings with it, which ensure the shortness of its duration: but now my most gracious sovereign & my most generous friend have turned that consolation into regret. This is indeed a reign to make life dear to a virtuous mind; for tho' virtue is no doubt above royalty & awful wherever it is stationed, yet it is never upon its throne but in the heart of Kings. May the only superior being ever watch over the most perfect of his works.

Fare well my dear Lord
believe me ever sincerely yours &c
MELCOMBE

Bute to Dodington[3]

[16 June 1761]

My dear Lord,

Late as it is I can't go to bed without imparting to you, a piece of intelligence, that teases me extraordinarily, while I hate myself for suffering it to do so, & I think it highly improbable;

---

[1] This enclosure refers to Whitehead's pamphlet *Ministerial Influence Unconstitutional* referred to in the earlier part of the letter. The 'Minister' is of course Newcastle, and the 'Ministerial Vizier' Pitt. The whole note is of some verbal interest, since it contains the first apparent use of the word 'unconstitutional'—recorded by *O.E.D.* as 1765 (Blackstone).

[2] Source: Dodington MSS. (Draft). I have not been able to trace the preceding letter from Bute, or the piece of patronage to which it refers.

[3] Source: Dodington MSS.

it has been reported to Lord Shelburne that your Lordship attempted to supply His vacancy in Wycombe without his knowledge; there is not a man in the kingdom for whom I entertain a warmer friendship, & whose character, spirit, & talents I have a higher opinion of, therefore you must not be surpris'd if the least surmise of this nature puts me in a flurry as I [*indecipherable*] to disjoint persons I wish to see cordially united. Be so good my dear Lord, as to let me know what you imagine could have given rise to this report, for if (as I incline to believe) it prove entirely groundless, it will render me extremely happy.

> I am ever with the greatest regard
> Your Lordship's
> Most obedient
> Humble Servant
> BUTE

Monday Night.

Dodington to Shelburne[1]

Tuesday 16 [should be 17] June 1761

My Lord,

I give you this Trouble, to ask your Lordship's Pardon for the involuntary Offence, which if it were voluntary, I should not forgive my self, or deserve it of your Lordship.

I am apprehensive that your Lordsp. has been told that I endeavour'd to fill the Vacancy occasion'd by your Peerage, without your knowledge: my Lord, when the Intention is innocent, the naked, & undisguis'd Truth is the best Excuse.

I engag'd, & disappointed Mr Lee contrary to ye universal Expectation, in an Election at Bridgewater: More sensible perhaps than I ought of the Disappointment, I receiv'd a Letter from the Ch: Justice his Father, acquainting me of the Vacancy, that your Lordsp's brother was not of Age, & earnestly praying me to recommend his son to my old Friend Mr Waller. I did just what I was desir'd, & did not trouble your Lordsp. because I was not desir'd; not in the least apprehending that an Application to Mr Waller could be wrested into any Meaning but by his Recommendation to obtain your Lordship's, without the least Imagination that any farther Step could or ought to be taken without it. I did not imagine it would succeed but

---

[1] Source: Dodington MSS. (from the draft). The original letter is in the Bowood MSS. The incident, which was Dodington's attempted intrusion of a candidate in Shelburne's borough of Wycombe, was the subject of conversation between the two peers when they found themselves paired in the coronation procession. Shelburne pinned Dodington down, and got the answer 'when did you know anybody get out of a great scrape but by a great lie' (Fitzmaurice, *Shelburne*, i. 15).

I thought I might show my good Will serve a Gentleman I had been so unlucky to disappoint without offence to any body, because I imagin'd nobody could think me so ignorant as not to know that your Lordsp's Nomination was absolute, There, or so absurd as to wish it less so, considering the very cordial, and sincere Respect I bear you, both on your own Account, & of those with whom you are most intimately connected.

This my Lord, is the undisguis'd Truth of the whole Affair; and if any Expression has been intimated to you, that can be interpreted into a contrary Meaning (as I think there cannot) it is the Effect of Haste and Negligence, & not of Intention, & I return, as I begun again to ask your Lordsp's Pardon, most earnestly entreating your Lordsp. to be perswaded that instead of attempting or wishing to lessen your Honour, Influence, & Consideration no man living wishes more cordially the Encrease of them all than myself on my own Account, on the Account of my Friends, & of my Country. I hope to have the Honour of waiting on your Lordsp. to morrow, before the Lever to assure you with how much Truth, & Respect I am.

My Lord &c.

Bute to Dodington[1]

[26 June 1761]

Lord Bute presents his compliments to Lord Melcombe. Lady Bute carrys her coachful on Sunday to breakfast at Kew, he takes Elliot, & Knight & Worsley meet him there; and if we were not so numerous & were sure of dining before four we should not hesitate to stay at Le Trapp.

Friday night

[The outing led to an accident in which D. appears to have had a narrow escape]

Bute to Dodington[1]

[29 June 1761]

My dear Lord,

I need not tell you that I am extremely anxious to know how you find yourself today. I protest I am as much afraid of all that your politeness made you go through yesterday as of the accident itself. Lady Bute charges herself with all that part of the misfortune & waits with the same impatience that I do for the return to this note. May it bring us good news that we may rejoice in the greatest escape ever happened to man.

[1] Source: Dodington MSS.

I am with the greatest regard my dear Lord your most obedient and humble servant,

BUTE

Monday Morn.

Dodington to Bute[1]

La Trappe
the 29th June, 1761

My Dear Lord,

The Rebuke I mett with, yesterday, was over paid by the kind concern Lady Bute, and you, were pleas'd to Express for me: the Ladies made the fore part of the Day, much more agreeable than the part that follow'd, & I am proud to be allow'd to think that it is necessary to assure them that all fear of Consequences is over.

I owe my Life to you, my Dear Lord, and I am glad of it: when one is, already, in debt more than one can pretend to pay, one does not care how much it encreases. If you had not stop'd me, at first, I really think you would have Lost a True Servant; Indeed if you had not Laid Hold of me, I must have sunk, in every sense; and not content to raise me, you have, now, broke my fall, even at the expence of Hurting your self, which, I trust, will soon be over. His honest Love, and prayers for your prosperity, is all you can have (and you have them, most cordially) My Dear Lord, from your ever faithfull, and affectionate.

MELCOMBE

P.S. I hope to have the Pleasure of dining with you to morrow, at Dashwood's; but do not stay for me, for I must be in the only Court where the Padronaura[2] is not known.

Dodington to Bute[3]

La Trappe Sunday [19] July 1761

My dear Lord,

Permitt me to ask, at what hour and how your Lordship goes to the christening at Deptford, on Thursday next: for as I find by Lord Anson, that I am to be one of your shadows, I should be glad to be as near my substance as I can without being inconvenient.

Your Lordship's ever, with
most faithfull affection

MELCOMBE

[1] Source: Institute of Historical Research transcript of the original in possession of the Marquess of Bute.
[2] Patronage: no doubt a reference to the 'purified' Court of George III.
[3] Source: *ibid.* The 'christening' relates to the renaming of the *Caroline* yacht as the *Charlotte* in honour of George III's proposed bride, to whom he had announced his engagement on 8 July.

424

Dodington to Bute[1]

La Trappe, Tuesday Evening
[7 October 1761]

My dear Lord,
　I sincerely wish your Lordship joy of being deliver'd of a most impracticable colleague, his Majesty of a most imperious servant, and the Country of a most dangerous Minister. I am told that the People are sullen about it.

　Be that as it may, I think it my duty to my most gracious Sovereign, and my generous friend to say, that if I can be of any service to either in any thing that is most dangerous and difficult, I am most ready to undertake it, and shall esteem it the more as it partakes of either or of both.

I am, my dear Lord, ever &c.
M.

Bute to Dodington[2]

Wednesday Night
October 8 1761

My dear Lord,
　Whatever private motives of uneasiness I might have in the late Administration, I am far from thinking the dissolution of it favourable, in the present minute, to the King's affairs. Without entering into the causes of the war, it is sufficient to observe, that it was a national one, and that the honour of the Nation is oblig'd to support its allies. You, my dear Lord, cannot dislike it more than I do; but as we have to do with a most treacherous enemy, whose infamous prevarications have been so lately experienced, we must act with redoubled vigour and spirit, before we can hope to bring them to such a peace as, from our repeated conquests, this country has a right to expect; such a peace as I (with this load of responsibility) durst put my name to. This being so, the change of a Minister cannot at present make any remarkable change in measures. I sigh after peace, but will not sue for it; not out of pride, or from motives of self-preservation (though both might without dishonour be urged), but from a thorough conviction that begging it from France is not the readiest way to come by it.

　The King has pitched on Lord Egremont to entrust with the Northern Seals. Mr George Grenville[3] is in his present office to take

_____

　[1] Source: *Seward's Anecdotes of Distinguished Persons* (1804), ii. 366, referred to under the wrong date of 6 October in *H.M.C. Var. Coll.* vi.50. The impracticable colleague is, of course, Pitt.
　[2] Source: Seward, op. cit., p. 369.　　　　　　[3] Treasurer of the Navy.

the lead in the House of Commons (but this is between us alone). They are both, as your Lordship knows, congenial to me.

I shall not fail to acquaint the King with the very frank and generous declaration you made. Indeed, my good Lord, my situation, at all times perilous, is become much more so; for I am no stranger to the language held in this great City: Our Darling's resignation is owing to Lord Bute, who might have prevented it with the King, and he must answer for all the consequences (which is, in other words, for the miscarriages of another system, that Pitt himself could not have prevented). All this keeps up my attention, and strengthens my mind, without alarming it; not only whispers caution, but steadiness and resolution (wherein my noble friend's assistance will no doubt prove a real comfort to me). Adieu, my dear Lord! My subject has insensibly led me to write a long letter where I intended to trouble you with a few lines. I am, with the greatest regard,

Most affectionately yours,
BUTE

Dodington to Bute[1]

La Trappe
October 8 1761

My dear Lord,

I know the nobleness of your heart, and as your Lordship knows the sincerity of mine, I shall not endeavour to disguise the simplicity of it, but shall give you my thoughts of what you do me the honour to write about (which I did not expect) naturally as they arise, and shall only premise that my veneration to the King, and my love and gratitude to your Lordship, shall have no bounds.

I am sorry to differ in opinion with you, because I am sensible it is not the way to be agreeable to you; and I wish much to be so. But I look upon the late event as an obstacle remov'd, and not as one added, where peace is to be treated. Your Lordship may remember some months ago, when you sometimes did me the honour to talk to me about business, I said I thought Mr Pitt would never make peace, because he never could make such a peace as he had taught the Nation to expect. I suppose that he now sees that we are within a year or two of an impracticability of carrying on the war upon the present footing, and may think, by going out upon a spirited pre-tence, to turn the attention and dissatisfaction of the public on those who, at a ruinous expence, are to carry on his wild measures, and whom they have been taught to dislike, by a total abandonment of the press to him and his creatures, which I humbly hope you will now think to employ better.

[1] Source: Seward, op. cit., p. 369.

I can say nothing to the treachery and prevarication of France in the late negotiations, being, as your Lordship knows, totally ignorant of all those transactions. I entirely agree with you, that we must act with redoubled vigour in carrying on the war, to obtain a proper peace; but it may be a doubt whether carrying it on in the same manner may be prudent, or even long practicable.

I agree also with you, that where honour is pledg'd, it must be maintain'd. But whether, after what we have done to support our allies, we cannot maintain it at a less expence than ruin to ourselves, without effect to them, may be worthy of consideration.

I am sensible I am writing upon a subject I am in no ways inform'd about. The mention of it made in your letter drew me into it. I have done. As you approve of the war, in what manner soever you carry it on, I shall never say a word more against it, in public or private, but will support it, whenever I am call'd upon, as well as my distance from the scene of business will allow me. I told you I would do so (after having told you my own opinion) when you did me the honour to command me to be your friend. Indeed my dear Lord, I wish and mean to serve you, and I am sure I never will disserve you, which, I fear, is as far as my poor abilities will go.

I am glad the King has given the Seals; and as you approve of it, I suppose they are well dispos'd of. The sooner it is public the better. I wish they had been given as soon as they were resum'd.

I think there can be nothing in the House of Commons. If there should, Mr Grenville, without all doubt, will do his best.

The insolence of the City is intolerable. They must, and they easily may be taught better manners. I was bred a monarchy-man, and will die so. And I do not understand that men of that rank are to demand reasons of measures, whilst they are under His Majesty's consideration. As to you, my dear Lord, I am sure you may laugh at them, and know, that the moment they are threaten'd with the King's displeasure, those that were at your throat will be at your feet.

I am frighted at my letter: 'tis a book, and would be a folio if I allow'd the effusion of thought that pours in upon me.

Forgive me this once; I will never again trouble you about these affairs till you open my mouth. In all situations, I sincerely pray for your welfare: none either of us can be in, shall ever deprive me of the honour and satisfaction of being,

My dearest Lord,

Your ever faithfull and affectionate,

M.

Dodington to Edward Young[1]

La Trappe
October 27th 1761

Dear Sir,

You seem'd to like the ode I sent you for your amusement: I now send it you as a present. If you please to accept of it, and are willing that our friendship should be known when we are gone, you will be pleas'd to leave this among those of your own papers that may possibly see the light by a posthumous publication. God send us health while we stay, and an easy journey!

My dear Dr Young,
Yours most cordially,
MELCOMBE

Love thy Country, wish it well
    Not with too intense a Care,
'Tis enough that when it fell
    Thou its ruin didst not share.

Envy's Censure, Flattery's Praise
    With unmov'd Indifference view;
Learn to tread Life's dangerous Maze
    With unerring Virtue's Clue.

Void of strong Desire, and fear,
    Life's wide Ocean trust no more,
Strive thy little Bark to steer
    With the Tide, but near the Shore.

Thus prepar'd, thy shorten'd Sail
    Shall whene'er the winds increase,
Seizing each propitious Gale,
    Waft thee to the Port of Peace.

Keep thy Conscience from Offence
    And tempestuous Passions free;
So, when thou art call'd from hence
    Easy shall thy Passage be—

Easy shall thy Passage be,
    Chearful thy allotted stay,
Short th'account 'twixt God and thee,
    Hope shall meet thee on the way.

[1] Source: Young's *Works* (ed. Doran), 1854, p. 83, gives the letter; the text of the poem is taken from Bodleian Western MS. 28578, f. 161, which is Malone's transcript of D.'s original.

Truth shall lead thee to the Gate,
Mercy's-self shall let thee in,
Where, its never-changing State,
Full perfection shall begin.

1762

Bute to Dodington[1]

February 10 1762
Wednesday Night

My dear Lord,

Your Lordship's letter, though wrote with your usual politeness, has too much of the air of reproach, and conveys too sensibly the idea of a broken promise not to surprise a person of my warm temper, and of my most kindly regard to your Lordship. . . . I will not call to mind any occurrences that passed from the death of the Prince of Wales to that of the late King, for I not only buried them in oblivion myself, but endeavoured to eradicate them elsewhere. Thus much, indeed, I must affirm; all former habitudes were so broken off between your Lordship and me at the demise that you certainly could not call on me for acts of friendship, and yet my conduct ever since has been that of a sincere and steady friend. . . . Your friend, my Lord, was not forgot; Windsor and Westminster were neither of them in my power to procure him; the first vacancy in Worcester or Canterbury I ever intended to be at your Lordship's disposal. . . .

I own, and that without blushing, I have been unfortunate in the means I have for years taken of cementing friendships and procuring attachments; others, with much less trouble, perhaps without my honesty, succeed better . . . but I repine not; conscious of my own feelings, conscious of deserving better treatment, I shall go on, though single and alone, to serve my King and country in the best manner my poor talents will allow me; happy, too happy, when the heavy burden that I bear shall be removed and placed on other shoulders.

Dodington to the Duke of Newcastle[2]

Pall Mall Friday Morning,
12 Feby 1762

My Lord,

I was, yesterday, to wait on your Grace, to thank, not solicit you,

---

[1] Source: *H.M.C. Var. Coll.* vi. 51. D. had sought, in a letter of 8 February, for a canonry for a clerical protégé—one Jones.
[2] Source: Add. MS. 32934, f. 303.

for I look'd upon the Favour[1] as receiv'd, from the first Moment it was promis'd, and from thence dated my Obligation to your Grace.

Give me no share, my dear Lord, in your exemplary Goodness to our poor Friend's most helpless Daughter, but that of having laid her sad state before your Grace; that feeling Heart knows no Merit in procuring Relief for Distress, but naming it.

I feel myself oblig'd to your Grace, and I have a Heart sensible of Obligations, but I feel that the Title you are pleas'd to give me to your real Friendship is the greatest Obligation I can receive from you.

Long may you live, my dear Lord, to enjoy the Pleasure of doing Good, and such Returns as may invite Those you leave behind to follow your Example.

> I am with the most sincere Duty, Gratitude, & Respect
> My Lord,
> Your Grace's
> most faithfull
> humble Servant
> MELCOMBE

Dodington to Doctor Thomson[2]

27 March 1762

... But waving a subject to which you are so superior a judge, I come now to the motive of this address to you. That motive I fairly confess to you is downright vanity. Weak as I am, I could not, on the perusal of the *Papers Relating to the Rupture with Spain* and of the most impudent and lying *Observations on these Papers*,[3] resist the temptation of invoking your testimony, I mean *in petto* to yourself, of the justness of my conjectures. Allow me then for once to consider you as my Court of Record. Did not I early, and in time, point out to you that spring of action to our Ministers which has since appear'd in the course of the Letters between Lord B and Lord Ch[4] as clearly as if I had been what, I thank God, I never was, nor even desire to be, admitted to the Cabinet Council? Did not I tell you in the plainest terms that the key to the new Administration would be found to be just what Pitt and his advocate upbraids them with (and in that deed he does not lie); their taking him for their *'example'*! Gracious and Almighty God!

[1] A pension of £500 a year for Mrs. Judith Hop.
[2] The original of this extraordinary letter, which was formerly in the Broadley Collection, has not been traced. The incomplete text is taken from L. C. Sanders, *Patron and Place-Hunter* (1919), pp. 266–72.
[3] The first had been laid before Parliament on 29 January previously; the second was a pro-Pitt pamphlet by Wilkes.
[4] Bute and, probably, Lord Chancellor Hardwicke.

him, him for their example! And yet it is so. The same tenor of councils. The same rage of acting vaguely on the mob-trap plan of doing something to be talk'd of no matter how little to the purpose! The same waste of blood and treasure upon *a la volée* expeditions, of which even the *success*, I repeat it, even the *success*, can contribute nothing essential in our favour to the sum of things. Could we even take ten Martinicos and ten Havannas it could, in all human probability only be so much the worse. While the German system continues to hang its dead weight upon us, everything is against us even to our successes: nor ought we ever to be surpris'd whenever that weight shall come to be felt, as feel it we could not yet if the wheel should run down with more rapidity than it has been wound up. And this very fellow whose levity, whose prostitution has made even the field of victory hollow under us, will, from that fatal neglect in his successors of immediately at once laying open to the nation the horrors of his continental measures and applying all the remedy in their power, be enabled to insult them for their compliance to his mad schemes and for their confessing that they took their 'example' from his *spirit*! that *spirit* which was so despicable, since there was not a grain of judgment went with it. Add too that his spirit was at bottom as false as his oratory and his oratory as false as his politics. . . .

Have you seen the *Continuation of the Address to the City*? I think that you mention'd the first part to me.[1] The writer is certainly a man of sense. Be this remark'd, without the least partiality in me to him for sousing the D of N and his puppet. One material observation has, however, escap'd him. After stating in a very clear light that collusive game, or rather that gross bungling juggle between those two *Great Men*, he might very well have added that his Grace after long using P as his tool was now at this moment that I am writing, employing him as his *scare-crow*; his Dragon to frighten children from those golden apples of Government of which he has made himself the dispenser. Mark him holding up P to Lord B and Co. as much as to say *'If you are not good children and do as I bid you I will bring the old Fee-faw-fum in again'*; and, *Nota Bene*, bring him in he would in spite of their teeth: a circumstance the power of which he owes to themselves, to their indolence, to their letting the most glorious occasion slip them of gaining a popularity on the strength of which they might have safely bid defiance to his Grace, to his Bully, and to the fools of both; at the same time that they would have done besides infinite honour to themselves, infinite service to their king and country. You know what I mean, that recall of our troops from Germany with

[1] *The Address to the City* and the *Continuation of the Address* were anti-Pitt and pro-Newcastle pamphlets.

all the coolness and all the concomitant requisites to render that step, a politic, a safe, and an honourable one. Should you here stop me by saying *they could not be recall'd*. Let that be granted. So much the better; such a circumstance would open the eyes of the nation. At least the Ministry would have had the honour of letting the nation into that curious secret of the army being in pawn for their reckoning. The fault could not have been THEIRS.

You cannot sure have seen the *Papers Relative to the Rupture with Spain*. What do you think of them? Are they not wonderfully instructive? My being taken in by those awful words prefix'd to some of the letters '*Most Secret*' to expect what I did not find, something very clever and very important, a little disgusted me, since most certainly, all due allowance being made for time and circumstances, they contain'd nothing but what might without the least impeachment of discretion have been, at the moment of their arrival, pasted up in the gateway of the Escurial. This mock-mysterious air reminded me naturally enough of the whispering scene in *The Rehearsal* between the Gentleman-Usher and the Physician for which Bayes accounts thus: 'Because they are SUPPOS'D to be POLITICIANS and MATTERS OF STATE must not be divulg'd'.[1] However, I blame neither of the Ministers for this absurdity. A part was given them beneath a candle-snuffer's from a creature of whom I never think, with his theatrical oratory, but I figure to myself a strolling buskineer ranting away before the kitchen fire to the greasy cook-maid and three country bumkins, a scene I once saw. Of such a wretched part, then, what could they make more than they did? For absolutely, the writing, in some parts, is very well, and proves that they both deserv'd a better opportunity of displaying their talents.

But to say the truth it is not the talents that are now so much wanted as SPIRIT. I do not mean, you may be sure, such a false spirit as that of his most unserene, mob-royal Highness, but that un-adulterate publick spirit, the very term of which is almost become an archaism in our language. A spirit in short that dares in the teeth of a silly mob, whether of Court, country, or City, at least aim at restoring the British system, without which there is no salvation for this country.

But let that be as it may, do you only do me the justice to remember how practical, how noble, and how constitutional a plan I open'd the view of in that application to Parliament, which would have made the present Ministers the most truly great Ministers that this country ever saw. But remember too that I told you I was not idiot enough to expect that that plan would be pursued: that I was afraid

[1] Buckingham's *Rehearsal*, Act II, scene 1. Bayes is Dryden.

what could effectuate it would sink under the weight of the conjuncture, and indeed they realis'd my fears. From that fatal Wednesday when P fairly out-brasen'd a set of men arm'd with the most
damning matter against him; and the blasts from that cave of the
winds, his head, made the whole House bow before him, like corn
lodg'd by a storm, I knew what I was not to trust to on behalf of this
wretched country.

I bespoke and you know that I bespoke his successors sticking in
the slough into which he had plung'd them without their having
the spirit to flounder out of it.

Let them then with all my heart give themselves the marrow-bones
and cleavers for their sublime efforts of genius in treading in Pitt's
steps and taking him, as they are now fairly twitted with it, for their
example. They are doubtless in the right, if they can find nothing
better in their own heads, to cultivate that precious production of
his, the German war. It is a fine exotic, but let them take care it does
not in the end make Sodom-apples even of their fairest successes,
even of that of their grand expedition, which at the best will only
pass for a copy of the great original's. May they not, on the winding
up of things, instead of the '*universal shout and high applause*', hear

> from innumerable tongues
> A dismal universal hiss, the sound
> Of publick scorn!

Dii Meliora! I sincerely wish they may themselves not find their
mistake too late both for their country and themselves. But this I
know: at present thus stands the prospect. If Pitt was to go down to
Hayes and lock himself up in the contemplative solitude of his closet,
to plan, for his successors, that tenor of their conduct which would
bid the fairest to make him regretted, and to force him into power
again, I defy him, nor has he talents enough for it, to frame a plan so
likely to produce such an event as that which has been indeviously
pursued ever since his abdication of the Ministerial throne: or to
descend from buskins, ever since his doing as Fanny Murray[1] and
others have done before him, his retiring from *Public Business* and
living upon an annuity.

I wish for their own sake that the members of the Tory engraftment
would consider that in the way things are going on they are sure of
all the blame in case of an unfavourable issue; and that, in neither
event, will they have the honours of history, or the opinion of the
people in their favour.

But once more all the wretched temporising of theirs, all this idle
expectation that brings will conform themselves not to their command

---

[1] The celebrated courtesan.

of them by their conduct, but to their being content to wish such a conformity, flows *not* from want of sense, *not* from want of good intentions, of all these I do them the justice to believe they have enough but to that bane of all *great* procedure, the miserably mistaking the forms of business for the spirit of it, the shadow for the substance; as if, in short, to do any good, thinking was not as necessary to acting, as acting to thinking. At present one would imagine the People of Britain had declared an implacable war against thinking, as if thought was their greatest enemy, an enemy too they do not serve as they do the French, fairly encounter it, but decline it. In short, it is inconceivable the courage that is nowadays requir'd not to be an idiot. The men of the first rank and distinction in the State are absolutely so fool-ridden as not to dare to follow the dictates of their own heart, of taste, of sense, of worth, of honour, for fear of the laugh of fools at them for being particular, that is to say for not being like *them* as if that unlikeness would not of itself be a merit, or at least a suspicion of merit. . . .

Bute to Dodington[1]

[9 April 1762]

My dear Lord,

I expected you yesterday, according to promise, but am afraid there was some mistake. I am sorry to hear you are not well. I am by no means so: and begin to think that a little more of what I have gone thro' for some time past, will prepare me for a longer journey than I should chuse at present to take; I am in short more down, & have lost both sleep & appetite; both rather necessary. If you are not engag'd to morrow & care to eat your mutton here, I should be extremely glad of your company,

I am my dear Lord with the greatest Regard
Your most obedt. Humble Servant
BUTE

Friday night past seven

Dodington to Bute[2]

Pl Ml 13 Apr. 1762

My dearest Lord,

I sett down the Overflowings of a most affectionate, and gratefull Heart opprest with Anxiety too sharp to be supprest without giving

---

[1] Source: Dodington MSS.
[2] From the draft, heavily corrected, in the Dodington MSS. There is no corresponding letter in the Bute collection, so D. may have carried out his intention of never sending it. Much of the phraseology echoes the letter to Thomson of 27 March above.

a Vent, tho' I have design it [n]ever should come under your Inspection.

I know the Splendor of your Birth, the adventitious Splendor of your Fortune, with what Grace it reflects upon you, now, what Dignity, when it was more moderate; Father, and Husband, indulgent, honour'd, and belov'd, a generous feeling Heart, fraught with all the Embellishments of the most cultivated Education. I know all this, & rejoyce that I do know it: I am sensible at the same time that this Knowledge furnishes a proper Handle to say 'If all this be true, why do you trouble your Friend with Ministry, & Politicks, why not advise him to turn his Eyes inward, & enjoy the Happiness, the Grandeur, the Independance of his own Situation?' I answer, because there is one Point behind, which is the greatest Glory the human Heart can feel that is still incumbent upon him to attain, & which till it is attain'd barrs the Enjoyment of all the rest.

God has given us a Prince with a Heart to make the Happiness of Millions, and you, my dear Lord, under God, have taught him to shutt up every Door to his own Happiness, but thro' the Happiness of Millions. This is wanting, greatly wanting. Rank, Fortune, Graces of Body, and Mind wait to produce their effect; till you have open'd the Way, & secur'd his Happiness you cannot establish your own.

I will now tell you, with the reserve [*illegible*] last June, that I think the Storm, which I have long seen gathering round you, is ready to burst, and the ill success [*illegible*] on you both; and no one proper Stepp taken to defeat it. The People are intoxicated with Conquest, his Partisans take effectual Care to combine the Idea of Mr. Pitt with it; his Party rises, they attack you publickly, in all Conversations, & now, in writing, personally, in the strongest and most audacious Manner.[1] Does the Body of Office assist them in all this? No—Does it lift a Finger against them? Yet less. They observe a worse than Spanish Neutrality, & tho' 'tis probable they may at present, have no Compact with your Enemy, yet they will not, most certainly, show you their own Family Compact, among themselves (which I believe would be found more offensive than the Spaniards' one) as they find you are in no Danger of your declaring War.—Would they have Mr Pitt again?—No—but they desire to have that Phantom follow'd enough to intimidate you, if you offer to break thro' their Measures of Government, or interfere with their Disposition of the Emoluments of it, by which, alone, they know they can be defended: but if you were to go too fast in the One, or meddle at all with the Other, they would in my Opinion, rather have Mr Pitt than you, because they wou'd think, in the first place, that he might be a little humbl'd by

---

[1] 'reproach you with following their example' (D.'s note in margin).

Adversity, & in the next that they could better struggle with his Popularity, transitory & ill-founded, than on your Credit with the King, built upon the solid Foundation of Honour as well as Inclination.

These are some of the reasons why Office (in the Hands the King is pleas'd to suffer it to remain) will never stirr one Step towards opening the Eyes of the People to the Destructiveness of the present Measures, & the Necessity of salutary ones. Other Reasons for abetting Pitt's Party are, that you will be driven either [to] meet this Phantom of Popularity (which has no body) your self, with your few firm Friends which experience may make them think you will not venture upon; or else to adopt their System without your own Friends (who cannot follow you) and then they will say that you are as deeply dipp'd as They; Mr Pitt's Party will insult you with following their Example, & you must employ the whole Weight of your own great Character, Abilities & Credit in the Closet, to absolve them, & justify yourself. For as you have never your self, or suffer'd the Press, to declare your determined Resolution to break thro' this System (ruinous in one Part, and romantic in the other) as soon as possible; I fear it cannot be expected from the Gross Apprehensions of the World, to believe that you disapprove of what is done, when they see you doing the very same thing, without strong & palpable efforts to flounder out of the slough you were plunged into, by that Means, forcing the People to see who brought you into this fatal Situation that makes it impossible to gett out, without going thorough. Here will be Triumph enough for your Enemies, & your no-friends. The first will insult you with following their Example: the others will naturally, & certainly make you responsible for the whole of this most destructive System, if ever the Eyes of the People should be opened, & the Nation recover its senses & by that Means force the King to defend what neither he or you are in any Degree accountable for, & ought not to have left the least [*illegible*] guilty of one hour upon the minds of the People.

Thus fetter'd they will not dislike to see you with the Seals, alone, unsupported, while They, & their Creatures divide all the rest, & are enabled, by wrangling, worrying, overbearing, to force the Acquiescence of the Crown to their System, by you, which they could not do by themselves.

This, tho' bad, is not to me the worst. It is the duty of the manly Friendship I owe you, void of Art or Interest, to lay before you all my fears at this alarming conjuncture. This picture would not be a welcome one, even from a welcome Hand, and mine, I am sensible, is become an unwelcome one; since the middle of the Summer, I found such an Alteration, not in your Kindness, my dear Lord, but in your Confidence, which

437

would have been very grievous if the consciousness of my unswerving attachment to you had not supported me. The Head may be a little impair'd, but I am sure the Heart is faithfull, & affectionate, and I should have hoped that the Goodness of the One might have allow'd for the Weakness of the Other. I do not insist upon a totally new System, & as I have said above a new System cannot take place without New Hands, for These cannot give up the old one without passing Condemnation upon themselves, the Authors of it, for servile & interested purposes. I perceive that you impute this Vehemence at Bottom to a desire, & an eager one, to gett a Place; I do not wonder you should be told this, I do, that you should believe it. But as I feel that I owe the Diminution of your Confidence to this false Impression, I owe to myself the Justice to say, That my Fortune is just sufficient to support the Rank that you, my dear Lord, have rais'd me to, & to have no stain of Injustice upon my Memory, to make me repent the Friendship you honour'd me with. Money has no charms for me, I have neither Passions or Time to employ it, or any body to leave it to; What then, should make me sollicitous about a place? Indeed, why wish it unless your Service, or Credit calls for it? Perhaps the World might think they do, but if you do not, I do assure you, my dear Lord, that I will never take one, from any other hand, for any other reason.

Bute to Dodington[1]

18 April 1762

Lord Bute presents his comps to Lord Melcomb. He is engag'd till Tuesday when he hopes to have the honour of his Lordship's company & should be obliged to him if he could let him peruse the pamphlet in the meanwhile.
London.

Dodington to Bute[2]

La Trappe
Sunday Morning 18 April 1762

Lord Melcombe with his duty to Lord Bute flatter'd himself he should have had the Honour of laying these very imperfect Papers before his Lordsp, himself, who alone, can explain & supply their Imperfections, as he alone directed the putting them together. However he has order'd them to be stitch'd as they are, & sends them in obedience to his Lordship's commands; but humbly insists that

[1] Source: Dodington MSS.
[2] Source: Dodington MSS. (Draft). The enclosure, whatever it was, seems to be lost.

they may not be seen by any other Person whatsoever till he has the
honour of waiting upon his Lordship on Thursday, at the Office, or
in Audley St, to receive his decisive Orders, either for Alteration,
Addition, or Suppression, which shall be punctually obey'd.

Dodington to Bute[1]

[28 April 1762]

The inclos'd Note (if you approve it) fully takes off all your
Scruples about using the term *Minister* in the Singular Number thro'
the Whole: it must be so, in the Body of the Pamphlett, for the Whole
is not at the Ministry but at you Alone; & you have no Right to
involve them in your Defence which must be Disapprobation &
putting as speedy an End as prudence will Admitt of to the German
War, & which they will not, indeed cannot, disown.

Bute to Dodington[2]

[28 April 1762]

My dear Lord, I have strong reasons against the publication of this
minute, & I have some remarks to make, that I must by word of
mouth communicate, when will you dine with me; will tomorrow
suit you.   B
Wednesday Night

Dodington to Dashwood[3]

La Trappe Fryday
[28 May 1762]

Dear Sir,
I have been too ill all night, & am so still, to use my own Hand,
which I beg you not to mention to any one of our Friends.
Tell Lord Bute I would have chosen Mr Grenville in obedience
to his Commands, if I had not been prevented by the unexampled
as well as unexpected Behaviour of a man who owes everything to
me. I am glad Lord Bute & you have taught him to behave with the
Submission which becomes his Rank, & Situation.

[1] Source: Dodington MSS. (Draft).
[2] Source: Dodington MSS.
[3] Source: Egerton MS. 2136, f. 156. The docketing appears to be Dashwood's
who played a part in the affair, and the collection of papers of which it forms a part
is his. This last electoral incident of D.'s life was a proposal to bring in Grenville,
who had just been appointed Secretary of State, and whom D.intensely disliked, for one
of the Weymouth seats occupied by Tucker. Tucker at first refused to comply, but
was compelled to do so. See Smith, *Grenville Papers*, i. 448–9, which makes the dating
clear. Only the signature, extremely shaky, is in D.'s hand.

I take no manner of Merit in it, with Lord Bute, or Mr Grenville, to which last, I never had, nor ever will have any obligation. Mr Tucker has found the only way (I did not think there had been one) of serving Lord Bute, without obliging me.

> I am ever most affectionately
> Dear Sir,
> Your most faithfull
> humble Servant
> MELCOMBE

Dodington to the Mayor and Corporation of Weymouth and Melcombe[1]

3 June 1762

Gentlemen,

Tho' you were acquainted with the great & deserv'd Mark of Favour which his My intended to bestow on Sr F. D. yet no Publick Application could be made to you, 'till it was carried into Execution. I therefore take the Liberty, again to recommend my best Friend to your Favour, not warmer in Inclination, tho' increas'd in Abilities, to be the Friend, & Servant of the Corporation & Towns of Weymouth, & Melcombe.

I will confess that the many Obligations I have to you All & the repeated Marks of your Goodness & Affection to me upon all Occasions, make me look upon this Application as Matter of Form, not doubting your Condescension to my humble Request.

But no Mark of Respect shall ever be wanting, on my Part, to show my Regard for you, & I seize with Pleasure, every Opportunity to declare my Sense of all your Favours to me, & to assure you, that the little Time I have to live, I will never cease to exert my warmest Endeavours, to promote the Interest, Service, & Satisfaction of you All.

Dodington to Bute[2]

La Trappe Wednesday 6 o'clock.
[? 10 June 1762]

My dear Lord,

I was at Table when I receiv'd the Honour of your Lordship's. I will wait upon you on Fryday, if I am able. I hope you dine at Dashwoods, tomorrow.

[1] Source: Egerton MS. 2136, f. 44—a copy transmitted to Dashwood, whose formal re-election was required on his appointment as Chancellor of the Exchequer.
[2] Source: Bute MSS.

I much esteem the attention of your Note, but I detest the Contents.—most unseasonable, undecisive, irritating, provoking, at the very time that decision, or good humour, is most absolutely necessary to us, proper to sink concessions on that side the water, & to heighten demands on this *mad* side.

However, if they will speak out upon the rest, & the only obstacle is St. Lucie, I will sign the preliminairies that give it upp, & defend it, if alive, agst. all the knaves, & fools, & mad men they have made.

Forgive the first, hasty, & possibly, very weak thoughts of your poor friend, who truly loves you, which is all he is capable of.

Your Lordship's, ever faithfully & affectionately

MELCOMBE

Dodington to Bute[1]

[? 13 June 1762]

Joy Joy Joy to my Dearest Lord, this is the greatest happyness I could wish for in this life, & as think [*sic*] my self much better, I hope to enjoy it, many a day, with my noble friend, for I have no view in life, but to live with my dear, & noble friend, in that state of elevation Health & Happyness which he deserves.

Wyndham, who is fully to be trusted, is not my amanuensis, but one whom I can answer for, with my life.

Farewell my dearest Lord,

I am, as I ought to be,

ever yours, most faithfully,

MELCOMBE

La Trappe
Saturday night.

Bute to Dodington[2]

[19 June 1762]

My dear Lord,

A thousand thanks for the heads you sent me, they are & will furnish matter for very serious consideration. I have invited the Chancellor to meet me at Kew tomorrow about ten, I hope you will

---

[1] Source: Bute MSS. From another letter in the Bute MSS., from Richard Glover to Bute, dated 12 June 1762, it is clear that D. was currently being offered the Admiralty, whence the joy in this letter. Glover assured Bute that D.'s appointment would be completely acceptable 'in our quarter'—Exchange Alley, from which he wrote.

[2] Source: Dodington MSS.

make *one* for I wish much to talk over the very important business of Monday.¹ I am ever with the greatest regard My dear Lord.

                                                 Your most affectionate etc.
Saturday   BUTE

*Bute to Dodington*²

                                                      13 July 1762
                                                           Kew

My dear Lord I am extremely concerned to hear you are still so much out of order. I hope however, to hear things are better, tho' I expect I must not hope to see you here today. If you are too weak to come out I will endeavour to call on Thursday in my way to Kew. I am all alone here & have the paper your Lordship sent me at present before me. I spoke to the King about Dr Thompson,³ & have orders to give him the same sallery as the physicians but to pay it myself that he may not lose part of it by fees. I have a quarter ready for him whenever he calls on me. I long to impart most interesting news received 3 days ago in which my noble friend will rejoice with me.

---

¹ No doubt the Cabinet held on that day, which discussed the French peace terms. D. had already been summoned to the Cabinet held early in June (see Sedgwick, *Letters from George III to Lord Bute*, pp. 112 and 118).

² Source: Dodington MSS. This news no doubt related to the progress of the secret peace negotiations. See Sedgwick, op. cit., p. 121. A fortnight later (29 July) D. died.

³ To make him a supernumerary Court physician, the payments being borne on the Secret Service account.

Note to the Index

THE index is designed (by including brief biographical particulars) for the avoidance of excessive annotation of the text of the Diary, as well as normal reference purposes.

These biographical notes concentrate on the individual's career during the currency of the Diary, and some identifications are necessarily uncertain. Dodington does not always make it clear—naturally enough—which of several possible persons of the same name a given entry refers to. Examples are the numerous Pitts and Churchills, and Dodington's even more abundant Irish relations by marriage, the Beaghans. Nor was Dodington's spelling of names so consistent that one can always confidently decide whether a given mention concerns Hitch Younge the M.P. or Edward Young the poet: Walter Carey, the Pelhamite placeman, or Cary, the specialist in the treatment of hernia. In such cases the spelling of the name in the text has occasionally been amended to accord with what appears most probable. Where Dodington consistently uses an eccentric spelling for a name (e.g. Poulet for Poulett) this has been preserved and the name indexed under Dodington's spelling in [], followed by the spelling now orthodox.

Despite these difficulties the preparation of the index has enabled many affiliations in Dodington's circle to be traced: the Sharpes, two of them Privy Council officials, and one of them Dodington's favourite clergyman; the borough-owning official Fanes, with their relationship to Dashwood; the Draxs, whose daughters married so well.

Individuals are indexed under the name (or in the case of peers, title) by which we first meet them in the Diary. Married women are indexed under their husbands' names, maiden names being given in ( ).

Places are indexed primarily for their parliamentary interest. An entry listing the plays Dodington attended during fourteen years illustrates his and the Prince of Wales's taste, as well as the versatility of the Prince's troupe of actors.

Index

[Abrieu] Abbreu y Bertodano, Joseph-Antonio de (*c*. 1700–75), Spanish juris-consult and minister in London, 26, 71, 76, 93, 96, 122, 135, 136, 248.

[Abercrombie] Abercromby, James (1706–81), General; Commander-in-chief in America during a portion of the Seven Years War; engaged in a disastrous attempt to capture the French Fort Ticonderoga, and was recalled, 376, 379.

d'Acunha, Senhor Luis, Portuguese Minister in London, 159, 226.

Albani, Alessandro (1692–1779), Cardinal; Vatican librarian and connoisseur; nephew of Pope Clement XI, 79, 86, 93, 99, 130, 135, 142, 188, 221, 225, 270.

Albemarle, George Keppel (1724–72), 3rd Earl of, soldier; M.P. Chichester 1746–54; served mainly under Cumberland (in whose court he had a post) and commanded the invasion of Havana 1762, 416.

[Aldsworth] Aldworth-Neville, Richard (1717–93), M.P. Reading 1747; Wallingford 1754–61; Tavistock 1761–74; Under-Secretary of State under Bedford 1748; secretary to Paris embassy, 73.

Allen, Thomas, nephew of Speaker Onslow, 130, 182, 201, 243, 267.

Allen, Mrs. Thomas, wife of the Speaker's nephew, 131, 132, 168, 288.

Almack's, 398, 405, 412, 413, 416, 418.

Amelia, Princess (1711–86), 'Princess Emily', 2nd daughter of George II; died unmarried, 25, 174, 180, 181, 205, 254.

America, 292. Preparations for Braddock's expedition, 294–5. Naval actions in, 307–8. Capture of Beauséjour, 313. Halifax's views on, 315.

Amherst, Jeffrey (1717–97), later Lord Amherst, General; commanded the American expedition, 1758, which conquered Canada, 375.

Amyand, Claudius (1718–74), Under-Secretary of State 1750–6; Commissioner of Customs 1756–65; M.P. Tregony 1747–54; Sandwich 1754–6; brother of George Amyand, the government contractor, 319.

Ancient Music, Academy of, 23.

[Andrade] Andrada, M. de, diplomat, 26, 71.

Andrews, Captain Thomas, R.N. (d. 1756), 345.

Anhalt-Dessau, Prince Moritz von (1712–60), Prussian general, 370.

Anne, Princess of Orange (1709–59), daughter of George II and wife of Prince William V of Orange.

Anne, Queen, 65.

Anson, George (1697–1762), 1st Baron Anson (1747); M.P. Hedon 1744–7; Junior Lord (1745–51) and First Lord (1751–6) of the Admiralty; Admiral of the Fleet 1761–2; Hardwicke's son-in-law, 9, 62, 113, 204, 311, 315–16, 319, 341, 343, 360, 368, 371, 416–17.

Anstruther, Sir Philip (1678–1760), Governor of Minorca 1742; Lieutenant-General 1745, 103–5, 113–14, 146.

Arbuthnot, A. Marriot (1711–94), Admiral; engaged in battle of Quiberon Bay; commanded American station 1779–81, 267.

Argyll, Archibald Campbell (1682–1761), 3rd Duke of (1743); Earl of Islay 1705; Lord High Treasurer of Scotland 1705; a supporter of the Union; Scottish representative peer 1707; Lord Justice General 1710; Lord Register of Scotland 1714; Walpole's manager for Scotland 1725; Scottish Lord Privy Seal (1725) and Lord Keeper (1734–61), 25 n., 31, 61, 67, 69, 72, 91, 93, 101, 109, 138, 139, 140, 143, 148, 151, 158, 159, 182, 188, 217, 222–3, 226, 244, 246, 254, 256, 304–5, 310, 313, 409, 410, 412, 413, 415.

Arthur, Mr., 162.

Arundell, Henry Arundell (1717–56), 7th Lord Arundell of Wardour, Wiltshire landowner and leading Roman Catholic peer, 80–81, 129, 168–9, 232–3, 288.

Arundell, Lady (Mary Bellings) (1716–69), 81, 129, 168–9, 232.

Arundell, Hon. Richard (*c*. 1696–1758), M.P. Knaresborough 1720–58; place-man and ministerial supporter. Brother of Lord Arundell of Trerise and brother-in-law of Henry Pelham, 130, 252, 288, 290, 370.

Arundell, Mr., 377.

444

INDEX

Ashburnham, John Ashburnham (1724–1812), 2nd Earl of; Lord of the Bedchamber; Ranger of St. James's and Hyde Parks 1753–62, 122, 163.

Aston, Lady (Elizabeth Pye), widow of Sir Willoughby Aston, Bt., 182.

Augusta, Princess (1737–1813), eldest daughter of Frederick, Prince of Wales; married (1764) Karl Wilhelm Ferdinand, Duke of Brunswick, 73, 136, 165, 173, 174, 197, 236, 240, 245, 249, 272, 300.

Augusta, Princess of Wales (1719–72), of Saxe-Gotha; married (1736) Frederick, Prince of Wales, eldest son of King George II; mother of the future King George III, and of several other children; appointed regent (assisted by a council) for her son in case he should succeed while still a minor; patroness of the Leicester House circle; at various times, a friend and condescending mentor of D. Birth of her son Frederick William, 68–69, of Caroline Matilda, later Q. of Denmark, 129. Her conduct on her husband's death, 106–9, 110, 111, 113, 147, 148, 163, 186, 209, 215, 222, 238–9, 240–2, 245, 246, 247, 249, 263, 270, 295, 305–6, 309, 314, 397–9, 400–2. D.'s major interviews with, 164–5, 173, 174–80, 189–96, 197–201, 202–5, 227, 243–4, 253–4, 298–302, 315–18. Discusses her son's education, 190–3, 202–5, 207–8, 271–2, 318, 336. Dines with D., 235–6. Her views on the Newcastle Ministry, 298–302. Approached by Pitt, 310–11. Referred to, 6, 7, 12, 13, 14, 21, 26, 33, 42, 47, 54 n., 60, 61, 62, 63, 72, 74, 76, 86–88, 89–91, 92, 93, 104, 115, 121, 126, 129, 136, 141, 142.

Augustine, Dr., 135.

d'Ayé, Marquis, Portuguese Minister in London, 90, 91, 96, 98.

Ayscough, Rev. Francis (1700–66), Clerk of the Closet to Frederick Prince of Wales, tutor to Prince George and (1761) Dean of Bristol. Had been tutor to George Lyttelton, whose sister he married, 65.

Baillie, Mr., 224.

Baker, Philip, 235.

Baker, Sir William (1705–70), London alderman and business man; M.P. Plympton Erle 1747–68; adviser to Newcastle and Rockingham on American affairs, 135.

Balch, Robert (1725–79), M.P. Bridgwater 1753–61, 173, 201–2, 206, 229, 231, 233, 243, 264, 268, 272–3, 277, 280, 283, 415.

Baldwyn, Mr., 288.

Baltimore, Charles Calvert (1699–1751), 4th Baron; M.P. St. Germans 1734–41; Surrey 1741–51; Gentleman of the Bedchamber to the Prince of Wales 1731–47; Cofferer to Prince of Wales, and Surveyor of the Duchy of Cornwall 1747–51; Junior Lord of the Admiralty 1742–44; Proprietor of the Colony of Maryland; married a sister of Sir Theodore Janssen, the magnate, 24, 25, 26, 28, 30, 33, 35, 41 n., 46, 47, 54–55, 59, 68, 70, 74 n., 83, 135 n.

Bance, James (1694–1755), clothier and banker; M.P. Westbury 1734–41 and 1747–8; Wallingford 1741–7; director of the Bank of England 1731–55, and of East India Company 1722–30; a leading dissenter, 8, 22, 26, 32, 34, 36, 42, 44, 61, 63, 67–68, 70–72, 75, 82, 92–93, 101, 108, 113–15, 122, 124, 138, 140–42, 151–2, 158, 160, 182, 189, 202, 217, 222, 245, 249–50, 261, 270–1, 285.

[Banks] Bankes, Henry (1700–76), landowner and barrister (K.C.); M.P. Corfe Castle 1741–62; Commissioner of Customs 1762; a Tory, 9, 11, 78, 80, 167, 232, 234, 290, 377.

Barbar, Edward (d. 1756), Captain R.N., 9, 82.

Barnard, Henry Vane (d. 1753), 2nd Baron, 217, 251.

Barnard, Henry Vane, 3rd Baron, see Vane, Henry.

Barnard, Sir John (1685–1764), business man and economist; M.P. London 1722–61, 337.

Barrington, Colonel, 386.

Barrington, Daines (1727–1800), lawyer and antiquary; son of 1st Viscount Barrington, 197.

Barrington, William Wildman Shute (1717–93), 2nd Viscount; M.P. Berwick 1740–54; Plymouth 1754–78; Lord of Admiralty 1766–54; Secretary-at-War 1755–61, 9, 31, 82, 103, 122, 151, 159, 187, 189, 202, 205–6, 248–9, 251, 256, 259, 261–2, 292, 359, 373, 416.

Barrington, Lady (Mary Lovell) (d. 1764), 249.

Barry, Spranger (1719–77), Shakespearian actor; played successfully at Dublin; then under Garrick at Drury Lane, and with Mrs. Cibber at Covent Garden, 61, 211.

Barton, Dr. Philip, Canon of Christ Church, 131.

445

Comyns, Mr. and Mrs., 161.
Constituencies, Parliamentary:
Bridgwater, 32 n., 34 n., 168 n., 170–1, 173–4, 201 n., 229, 231–4, 235–6, 238–9, 242–3, 257–8, 260, 263–4, 267–9, 272, 278, 280, 282–3, 284, 409–10, 422.
Dorchester, 228.
Dorset, 228–30, 235, 257, 268.
Ilchester, 9.
Lyme Regis, 9.
Old Sarum, 5.
Plymouth, 248.
Poole, 169.
Saltash, 248.
Shaftesbury, 10.
Weobley, 282.
Westbury, 8 n.
Westminster, 26, 30–32, 162 n., 188.
Weymouth, 32 n., 90, 92, 124, 145, 154–7, 169–70, 220, 234, 243, 257, 260, 267, 274, 285–6, 291, 347, 398, 400–2, 406, 407, 413, 439–40.
Wycombe, 422–3.
See also Elections.
Cooke, George (1705–68), Tory lawyer and politician; M.P. Tregony 1742–7; Middlesex 1750–68; candidate for Westminster 1749; Joint Paymaster-General 1766, 31, 60–61, 108, 141, 171, 270, 292.
Cope, James (1709–56), diplomatist and son of General Sir John Cope, 109–10.
Coram, Captain Thomas (1668–1751), philanthropist; native of Dorset; ship-builder in Massachusetts 1694; merchant in London 1720; trustee for Georgia 1732; planned colonization of Nova Scotia 1735; advocated establishment of Foundling Hospital in London opened 1745, 48.
Cork, John Boyle (1707–62), 5th Earl of (1753), 249, 271.
Cork, Lady (Margeret Hamilton) (1710–58); wife of 5th Earl and heiress daughter of John Hamilton of Co. Tyrone, 249, 271.
Cornbury, Henry Hyde (1710–53), Viscount; eldest son of 4th Earl of Clarendon; M.P. Oxford University 1732–51; Baron Hyde of Hindon; said to have been Gentleman of the Bedchamber to Frederick, Prince of Wales, 25.
[Cornwall] Cornewall, Velters (1696–1768); M.P. Herefordshire 1722–68; vehement Tory, 43, 158.
Cornewall, Mrs., 69, 158.

Cornwall, Prince of Wales's revenue in, 64–66, 109, 199.
Corsini, the Princes, 241, 243, 246.
Cotton, Sir John Hynde (1688–1752), or Madingley, 3rd Bt.; M.P. Cambridge 1708–22 and 1727–41; Cambridge-shire 1722–7; Marlborough 1741–52; Lord of Trade and Plantations 1712–15; Treasurer of the Chamber 1744–6; Tory and Jacobite, 25, 26, 28, 45, 107.
Coventry, George William (1722–1809), 6th Earl of; M.P. Bridport 1744–7; Worcestershire 1747–51, 125, 256, 261.
Coventry, Maria Countess of, 385.
Crabb, Rev. John (d. 1749), Rector of Tarrant Hinton, minor poet, and contemporary of D. at Oxford, 10.
Crabb, Mr., 78, 80, 129, 131, 229, 288, 290.
Craggs, James, the younger (1688–1721), Secretary of State 1718; friend of George I and of Alexander Pope; implicated in South Sea scandal, 255.
Crawford, John Lindsay (1702–49), 20th Earl of, and a Scottish representative peer, 34.
Creed, Sir James (c. 1695–1762), lead merchant; M.P. Canterbury 1754–61; follower of the Duke of Newcastle, 125.
Cresset, James (d. 1775), private secretary to the Dowager Princess of Wales, 165, 173, 187, 192–3, 302, 309, 310, 317.
Cresswick, Dr. Samuel, Dean of Wells, 124.
Crowle, Richard (c. 1699–1757), M.P. Hull 1754–7; legal representative of the 'Independent Electors of Westminster', 153.
Cumberland, Richard (1732–1811), poet, playwright, and politician; private secretary to Lord Halifax in the Board of Trade; Under Secretary 1761; Clerk of Reports in the Board of Trade; Secretary to the Board of Trade 1776; wrote sentimental comedies, an epic, some tragedies, and two novels, 296, 373, 378, 380.
Cumberland, William Augustus (1721–65), Duke of; 3rd son of George II, 24, 33 n., 44 n., 108, 139, 175, 180–1, 185, 194–5, 197, 201, 208, 218, 235, 237, 244, 253–4, 301–3, 305–7, 309, 311–12, 314, 316, 319–21, 342, 359–60, 368–9.
Curzon, Sir Nathaniel (1727–1804), Bt.; M.P. Clitheroe 1748–54; Derbyshire 1754–61; created (1761) Baron Scarsdale, 87.

INDEX

Cusitia, Dr. Louis da, 242.

Cust, Sir John (1718–70), Bt.; M.P. Grantham 1743–70; Clerk of the Household to the Prince of Wales; Speaker of the House of Commons 1761–70, 69, 70, 83, 114.

Dalrymple, Sir Hew (1712–90), Bt.; M.P. Haddington burghs 1742–7; Haddingtonshire 1747–61, 124, 211, 241.

Damer, Thomas, of Winterbourne, related to both the Henbury Churchills and the Sackvilles, 81.

Damer, Mrs. Thomas, 81.

Darlington, Lord, see Vane, Henry.

d'Artagnan, Count, 44, 62.

Dashwood, Sir Francis (1708–81), 2nd Bt. (1724); M.P. New Romney 1741–61; Weymouth 1761; after travel on the Continent, entered the household of the Prince of Wales; Treasurer of the Chamber 1761–2; Chancellor of the Exchequer 1762–3; Keeper of the Wardrobe 1763–5; joint Postmaster-General 1766–81; leading member of the Dilettanti Society (1736) and arch-master (1746); F.R.S. 1746; D.C.L. Oxon. 1749; founded so-called 'Hell-fire Club'; 1st Colonel of Bucks militia 1757; succeeded his uncle John Fane (q.v.) as 15th Baron Le Despencer 1763, 7, 8, 31, 57, 58, 60, 61, 62, 63, 64, 68, 69, 70, 72, 73, 77, 80, 82–83, 85, 86, 96–97, 101, 104, 109, 110, 113, 114, 116, 117, 121, 122, 124, 125, 133, 135 n., 136, 146–7, 149, 150, 152, 154, 158, 160, 181, 205, 210, 211, 217, 221, 225, 236, 240, 242, 249–50, 251, 254, 256, 270–2, 279, 286–7, 297, 298, 305, 310, 318, 319, 326, 334, 355, 378, 398 n., 404–5, 412, 413, 415, 417–18, 424, 441. Stands for Weymouth, 406, 440. Letter to, 439.

Dashwood, Lady (Sarah Gould), wife of Sir Francis Dashwood, 7, 8, 77, 158, 225, 280, 305, 310, 318.

Dashwood, Mr., 205.

Daun, Leopold Joseph Maria Count von (1705–66), Austrian field-marshal; defeated Frederick at Kollin (1757), but defeated by him at Leuthen (1757); again victorious at Hochkirchen (1758), but defeated at Torgau (1760), 369.

Daveney, Dr., 231.

Davison, Major, 212.

Dawkins, James (1722–57), archaeologist, artist, traveller, and Jacobite agent; M.P. Hindon 1754–7. Connected politically with the Beckfords, 137, 247.

Debates, Parliamentary:
Address (1749), 25; (1750), 96.
America, 338.
Army, 30, 36–42.
Bedford Turnpike, 42, 56.
Byng, 355.
Champagne imports, 202.
Dunkirk, 45–46.
Jewish disabilities, 240–2.
National Debt, 30.
Pall Mall paving, 116, 122–4.
Plate tax, 339.
Prince of Wales's Household, 116.
Prince of Wales's Tutors, 211.
Regency Bill, 116–17, 121–2, 175–6.
Subsidy Treaties, 143, 175, 336.
Vice-Treasurership of Ireland, 337.

[Deering] Dering, Sir Edward (1705–62), Bt.; M.P. Kent 1733–54, 108, 308.

Delaval, Sir Francis Blake (c. 1727–71); M.P. Hindon 1751–4; Andover 1754–68; brother of John Hussey Delaval, 1st Baron Delaval; volunteer in the expedition against St. Malo 1758; promoter of amateur theatricals, 104.

Dennis, Captain Henry, R.N., 368.

[Des Noyers] Dunoyer, Philip, French dancing-master, confidant of both Frederick, Prince of Wales, and the King's Household; 'a sort of licensed spy on both sides'; tutor to the son and godson of Lord Chesterfield, 59, 83.

Deverel, Mr., 242.

Devonshire, Duchess of (Catherine Hoskins) (d. 1777), daughter the steward to the Duke of Bedford, and wife of the 3rd Duke of Devonshire, 198.

Devonshire, William Cavendish (1698–1755), 3rd Duke of; M.P. Lostwithiel 1721–4; Grampound 1724–7; Huntingdonshire 1727–8; Lord Privy Seal 1731–3; Lord Steward of the Household 1733–7 and 1745–9; Lord-Lieutenant of Ireland 1737–45; retired from court after disagreement with Pelhams 1749, 96, 163, 214, 252, 254, 257, 301, 324–5.

Devonshire, 4th Duke of, see Hartington.

Digby, Edward Digby (1730–57), 6th Baron; M.P. Malmesbury 1751–4; Wells 1754–7; nephew of Henry Fox, 229–30, 235, 268.

Dillon, Henry (d. 1787), 11th Viscount Dillon, 44.

d'Issemberg, M., 378.

451

INDEX

Governor-General of French Canada 1752, 370.
[Durel] Durell, Captain Philip, R.N., 383, 387.
Duvelaer, Monsieur, 226.
Dyers, Miss, 31.

[Earl] Earle, Giles (1678–1758), politician; Colonel; client of Walpole and the 2nd Duke of Argyll; M.P. Chippenham 1715–22; Malmesbury 1722–47; Clerk-Comptroller of the Household 1720; Lord of the Treasury 1737–42; Chairman of Committees of Election 1727–41, 78.
Earthquakes, 48.
East, Mrs. Anne, 304 n.
East, Mr., 304 n., 337, 406.
Edgcumbe, Richard (1716–61), later 2nd baron; M.P. Plympton Erle 1742–7; Lostwithiel 1747–54; Penryn 1754–8; Lord of the Admiralty 1755–6; Comptroller of the Household 1756; friend of H. Walpole, wit, and gambler, 112, 226–7, 416.
Edgcumbe, Mrs., 226.
Edward Augustus, Prince (1739–67), 2nd son of Frederick, Prince of Wales; (1760) Duke of York, 85, 136, 148, 174, 178, 203, 240, 244–5, 300, 342, 409.
Edwin, Charles (c. 1699–1756), M.P. Westminster 1741–7; Glamorgan 1747–56; victor in the 'Independent Electors of Westminster' election, of 1741, with Admiral Vernon, 31.
Edwin, Lady Charlotte (c. 1704–77), daughter of the 4th Duke of Hamilton; married (1736) Charles Edwin; Lady of the Bedchamber to the Princess of Wales, 31, 34, 92, 173, 174, 300, 310.
Edwin, Lady Elizabeth, 173.
Egerton, Mrs., 226, 285.
Eglinton, Alexander Montgomery (d. 1769), 10th Earl of; later Lord of the Bedchamber to George III, 77, 143, 413.
Egmont, John Perceval (1711–70), 2nd Earl of; M.P. Westminster 1741–7; Weobley 1747–54; Bridgwater 1754–62, when raised to the British peerage. Lord of Bedchamber to Frederick, Prince of Wales, and his leading political adviser 1748–51; Joint Postmaster-General 1762–3; First Lord of the Admiralty 1763–6. Opposes D. in the Prince's Court, 47–56. Stands against D. at Bridgwater, 231–2, 235–6, 238–9, 257–8, 260, 263–4, 268, 273, 277, 282. D. agrees to support him, 409–10,

412–13. Referred to, 5, 11–12, 14, 23, 25–26, 28, 30, 59, 60, 69, 70, 74 n., 83, 96, 99, 101, 103, 114, 115, 143 n., 298, 310–11, 324, 326.
Egreland, Mr., 10.
Egremont, Charles Wyndham, 2nd Earl of (1710–63); M.P. Bridgwater 1735–47; Taunton 1747–50; Lord-Lieutenant of Cumberland 1751–63; Secretary of State 1761–3, 425.
Einsidell, Johann Georg (1730–1811), Graf von; Saxon diplomatist, stationed at St. Petersburg 1748, and London 1763, 10, 11, 26, 33.
Elections, Parliamentary:
Bridgwater, 263–4.
Middlesex, 60–61.
Oxford University, 101.
Reading, 326.
Westminster, 25–26, 30–32, 57–58, 98.
See also Constituencies.
Elibank, Patrick Murray (1703–78), 5th Baron (1736); brother of General Murray, 98.
Elizabeth, Princess (d. 1759), 2nd daughter of Frederick, Prince of Wales, 165, 73, 174, 197, 300.
Elliot, Lieutenant-Colonel George Augustus (1719–90), of the Horse Guards, later a general; defender of Gibraltar 1779–82, and raised to peerage as Lord Heathfield, 196.
Elliot, Gilbert (1722–77), M.P. Selkirk 1753–65; Roxburgh 1765–77; Lord of the Admiralty 1756–61; of the Treasury 1761–2; Treasurer of Navy 1770–7; a protégé of the Duke of Argyll, 382, 387, 408, 413, 423.
Elliot, General Granville (d. 1759), Lieutenant-General in the Elector Palatine's army, later Major-General in British service, 196.
Elliot, William (d. 1764), M.P. Calne 1741–54; Equerry to George II 1743, 33.
Ellis, Welbore (1713–1802), Ministerialist politician; M.P. Cricklade 1741–7; Weymouth 1747–61; Aylesbury 1761–8; Petersfield 1768–74; Weymouth 1774–90; Petersfield 1790–4; Lord of the Admiralty 1747–53; Vice-Treasurer of Ireland 1755–62, 1765–6, 1770; Secretary-at-War 1762–5; Secretary of State for America 1782; Lord Mendip 1794, 96, 124, 145–6, 154, 249, 255–7, 383, 398, 400–1.
Ellison, Lieutenant-General Cuthbert (1698–1785); M.P. Shaftesbury 1747–54, 35.
Elwell, Hugh, 247.

Glover, Richard (*cont.*):
146, 151, 183, 202, 205, 241–3, 254, 305–7, 380, 398, 413, 416, 442 n.

Godolphin, Sidney (1645–1712), 1st Earl of; Lord Treasurer under Queen Anne, 65, 198.

Goldsworthy, Mrs. (Philippia Vanbrugh), niece of the playwright and wife of Burrington Goldsworthy, Consul at Leghorn and Cadiz, 280.

Gollop, Thomas (1679–1758), Mayor of Weymouth 1758, 129, 130.

Good, Mr., 378.

Gordon, Cosmo George Gordon (1721–52), 3rd Duke of, a Scottish representative peer 1747–52, and father of Lord George Gordon, 170.

Gordon, Sir Thomas, 63.

Gottman, Mr., 166.

Gould, Henry (1710–94), lawyer; K.C. 1754; Baron of the Exchequer 1761, 78, 157, 231, 241, 251.

Gower, John Leveson Gower (d. 1754), 1st Earl; Lord Privy Seal 1744–54, 87, 174, 276.

Gower, 2nd Earl (1721–1803), *see* Trentham, Lord.

Grafton, Charles Fitzroy (1683–1757), 2nd Duke of; grandson of Charles II; Lord-Lieutenant of Ireland 1720–4; Lord Chamberlain 1724–57, 27, 251, 293, 301.

Granby, John Manners (1721–70), Marquis of; soldier; eldest son of 3rd Duke of Rutland; M.P. Grantham 1741–54; Cambridgeshire 1754–70, 69, 96, 272, 385, 414.

Granville, John Carteret (1690–1763), 1st Earl (1744); Lord-Lieutenant of Devonshire 1716–21; follower of Sunderland; envoy to Sweden 1719; Secretary of State 1721–4; Lord-Lieutenant of Ireland 1724–30; opposed Walpole 1730–42; Secretary of State 1742–4; Lord President 1751–63, 21, 24, 125, 137, 144–5, 311, 320–1, 326, 348, 372.

Grenville, Hon. George (1712–70), M.P. Buckingham 1741–70; Lord of the Admiralty 1744–7; Lord of the Treasury 1747–54; Treasurer of the Navy 1754–5, 1756–7, 1757–62; Secretary of State 1762; First Lord of the Treasury and Chancellor of the Exchequer 1763–5, 185, 247, 251, 253, 256, 263, 278–9, 282–3, 292, 336, 355, 425, 427, 439–40.

Grenville, Hon. Henry (1717–84), diplomatist, brother of George Grenville, and Governor of Barbados; M.P.

Bishop's Castle 1759–61; Thirsk 1761–5; Buckingham 1768–74; ambassador to Turkey 1761–5, 304, 355.

Grenville, Hon. James (1715–83), brother of George Grenville; M.P. Old Sarum 1742–7; Bridport 1747–54; Buckingham 1754–68; Horsham 1768–70; Lord of the Treasury 1756, 1757–61; Cofferer of the Household 1761–3, 304, 308–9, 314, 336.

Gresley, Mr., 229, 263, 267, 288, 290, 377–8.

Griffin, Thomas (*c.* 1693–1771), Admiral; M.P. Arundel 1754–61; suspended for negligence while commanding in the West Indies 1750; reinstated 1752, 149.

Grossa Testa, Abbé de, envoy of Modena in London, 26, 71, 76, 90, 96, 134, 135, 136, 235.

Grosvenor, Sir Richard (1731–1802), 7th Bt., later (1784) 1st Earl; M.P. Chester 1754–61; Mayor of Chester 1759, 380, 385.

Grove, William Chafin (1731–93), Dorsetshire gentleman; M.P. Shaftesbury 1768–74; Weymouth 1774–81, 9, 11, 81, 233.

Guernsey, Heneage Finch (1715–77), Lord; later, 3rd Earl of Aylesford; M.P. Leicestershire 1739–41; Maidstone 1741–7, 1754–7, 107–8.

Guadaloupe, Expedition against, 384–5.

Guise, General John (d. 1765), veteran and connoisseur; served under Marlborough, and subsequently in the expedition to Vigo and Cartagena, 134.

Haldane, George (*c.* 1722–59), M.P. Stirling burghs 1747–58; Lieutenant-Colonel 3rd Foot Guards, 103.

Hales, Stephen (1677–1761), divine, savant, inventor, and temperance propagandist; Fellow of Corpus Christi College, Cambridge; perpetual curate of Teddington 1709–61; incumbent of Farringdon, Hampshire, 1709–61; F.R.S. 1718; founder and vice-president (1755) of Society of Arts; Clerk of the Closet to the Dowager Princess of Wales, and Chaplain to Prince George (afterwards, George III) 1751; Trustee of the Colony of Georgia, 54.

Halifax, George Montagu Dunk (1716–71), 2nd Earl of, politician; Lord of Bedchamber to Prince of Wales 1742–4; President of the Board of Trade 1748–61; Lord-Lieutenant of Ireland 1761–3; First Lord of Admiralty 1762;

INDEX

subsequently Secretary of State and Lord Privy Seal. His part in Pitt's negotiation of 1755, 308–9. Converses with Newcastle about America, 314–15. Letter to, from Fox, 329. Negotiates for D. to enter office, 329–30, 334. Betrays D., 358–61. Resigns, 360–3. Referred to, 27, 45 n., 97, 185, 188, 197, 202, 249, 283, 296–8, 304–5, 312, 343, 347, 350–1, 355–6, 373, 378, 386, 404.

Hamilton, George (1698–1775), M.P. Wells 1734–5, 1747–54; Deputy-Cofferer to the Prince of Wales 1749, 33.

Hamilton, James (1724–58), 6th Duke of, 128–9, 143, 370.

Hamilton, Miss, 224, 279, 285.

Hampden, John (1696–1754), of Great Hampden; M.P. Wendover 1734–54, 58, 63, 92, 122, 133, 158, 189, 222, 249.

Handel, George Frederick (1685–1759), 147 n.

Harcourt, Mr., 169.

Harcourt, Simon (1714–77), 1st Earl (1749); present at Dettingen 1743; Governor to the Prince of Wales 1751–2; envoy to Mecklenburg for the King's marriage with Princess Charlotte 1761; Ambassador to France 1768–72; Lord-Lieutenant of Ireland 1772–7, 115, 178 n., 187–8, 190–3, 203, 207, 212.

Hardwicke, Philip Yorke (1690–1764), 1st Earl; Lord Chancellor 1737–56. Negotiates Pitt's entry to office, 322–4. Referred to, 22, 71, 87, 110, 137, 185, 187, 193, 204, 212, 240, 249–52, 261–3, 298, 301, 342, 362–3, 368, 419.

Hardy, Captain Charles (c. 1713–80), naval officer; M.P. Rochester 1764–8; Plymouth 1771–80; Governor of New York 1755–7; Rear-Admiral 1756; second in command under Hawke at Brest and Quiberon Bay 1759; Admiral 1770, 278, 296.

Harley, Thomas (1730–1804), grandson of Edward Harley, 2nd Earl of Oxford; M.P. City of London 1761–74; Herefordshire 1776–1802; Lord-Lieutenant of Radnorshire, 57, 205.

Harrington, William Stanhope (1690–1756), 1st Earl of; soldier and statesman; Secretary of State 1730–41 and 1744–6; Lord-Lieutenant of Ireland 1746–51, 280, 326.

Harrington, William Stanhope (1719–79), 2nd Earl of (1756); soldier; M.P. Bury St. Edmunds 1747–56; fought at Fontenoy, 416.

Harrington, Lady (Caroline Fitzroy) (1722–84), wife of the 2nd Earl, 405, 415.

Harris, John (1690–1767), of Hayne, Devonshire; Master of the Household 1741–67; M.P. Ashburton 1741–67, 35, 158, 232, 247.

Harris, Mrs. (Margaret Tuckfield) (d. 1754), 35, 157–8.

Hartington, Lord, William Cavendish (1720–64), eldest son of the 3rd Duke of Devonshire, and (1755) 4th Duke; M.P. Derbyshire 1741–51; Lord-Lieutenant of Ireland 1755–6; First Lord of Treasury 1756–7; Lord Chamberlain, 1757–62, 96, 125, 163, 185, 238, 251, 254–5, 301, 309, 350–1, 356, 358.

Harvey, Colonel Edward (1718–78), 3rd son of William Harvey of Chigwell, Essex; M.P. Gatton 1761–8; Harwich 1768–78; Lieutenant-Colonel 1760; Major-General, 1763, 287, 288, 291.

Harvey, Eliab (1716–69), of Claybury Hall, Essex, M.P. Dunwich 1761–8; barrister, patronized by Fox, 148.

Harvey, William (1714–63), M.P. Essex 1747–63; independent country gentleman, 147–8, 201, 218.

Harvey, 'Young Mr.', 182.

Hawke, Admiral Sir Edward (1710–81), M.P. Portsmouth 1747–76, when raised to peerage; present at Toulon (1744), Rochefort (1757), and Brest (1759); victor at Quiberon Bay 1759; First Lord of Admiralty 1766–71, 311–12, 314–16, 319–20, 340, 367–8, 392.

Hawkins, Christopher (d. 1768), of Trewithan, electoral agent of the Prince of Wales, and Vice-Warden of the Stannaries, 370.

Hawley, General Henry (c. 1679–1759), veteran and favourite of the Duke of Cumberland; had been present at Almanza (1707), Dettingen (1743), Fontenoy (1745), Falkirk and Culloden (1746); Governor of Portsmouth 1752, 194–5.

Hay, Lord Charles (c. 1700–60), army officer, brother of 4th Marquis of Tweeddale; M.P. Haddingtonshire 1741–7; commanded 1st Guards at Fontenoy, where he proposed the famous toast, and was wounded; Major-General 1757, 70, 74.

Hayter, Thomas (1702–62), Bishop of Norwich, 1749–61; Preceptor to George, Prince of Wales, 1751; Bishop of London 1761–2, 187, 190, 202, 212, 318.

INDEX

82; sailed with Anson 1740; in an action with the French off the St. Lawrence 1755; in Rochefort expedition 1757; blockade of Brest and Quiberon Bay 1759; Lord of Admiralty 1762–5; Treasurer of the Navy 1765–70; Vice-Admiral 1775; Commander-in-Chief North American station during American Revolutionary War; First Lord of the Admiralty 1783–8; Vice-Admiral of England 1792–6; victor of 'The Glorious First of June' 1794; Admiral of the Fleet and General of Marines, 179, 370, 376, 378.

Howe, Lady (Charlotte von Kielmansegge) (1695–1782), daughter of George I's mistress, the Countess of Darlington; widow of 2nd Viscount Howe, and Lady-in-Waiting to the Princess of Wales, 21–23, 27, 31–33, 35–36, 42–43, 58–59, 62–63, 67–69, 73, 75, 77, 83, 86, 87, 89, 91–92, 95–96, 99, 103–4, 136, 174, 246.

Howel, Parson, 35.

Hughes, Commodore Richard (1729–1812), 380, 384.

Huntingdon, Francis Hastings (1729–89), 10th Earl of; Master of the Horse 1760; Groom of the Stole 1761, 241, 247, 404.

Hurst, Miss, 7.

Huske, General John (c. 1692–1761); present at Dettingen, Falkirk, and Culloden; a favourite of the Duke of Cumberland and brother of Elis Huske, Chief Justice of New Hampshire, 27.

Hyndford, John Carmichael (1701–67), 3rd Earl of; diplomatist and Scottish representative peer; envoy to Prussia 1741–2; Russia 1744–9; Austria 1752–64, 62, 181.

Ilchester, see Constituencies.

Ilchester, Stephen Fox (1704–76), (1741) Baron, and (1756) Earl of; of Redlynch, Somerset, and Melbury, Dorset; M.P. Shaftesbury 1726–34, 1735–41; brother of Henry Fox, 229–30.

Inchiquin, William O'Brien (d. 1777), 4th Earl of; M.P. Windsor 1722–7; Tamworth 1727–34; Camelford 1741–7; Aylesbury 1747–54; Gentleman of the Bedchamber to the Prince of Wales 1744–51; Grand Master of Freemasons 1740–1, 21, 23, 27, 30, 31, 33, 42–44, 59, 60, 62, 63, 67, 68, 74, 96, 98, 100, 101.

Inchiquin (Anne Hamilton) (d. 1756), Countess of, 42.

Irby, Sir William (1707–75), Bt.; M.P. Launceston 1735–47; Bodmin 1747–61; Equerry to Frederick, Prince of Wales, 1728; Vice-Chamberlain to Princess of Wales 1736, and Lord Chamberlain to her 1760; married daughter of Henry Selwyn, 91, 93, 222, 270.

Irwin, Anne (d. 1766), Viscountess; daughter of Charles Scarborough, Clerk of the Green Cloth; Lady of the Bedchamber to the Princess of Wales, 69, 70.

Isted, Mr., 296.

Jackson, Charles, brother-in-law to George Dodington of Horsington, and father of Samuel Jackson Dodington, High Sheriff of Somerset 1763, 43, 44.

Jackson, Miss, 12, 74, 75.

Janssen, Stephen Theodore (d. 1777), business man, later 4th Bt.; M.P. London 1747–54; Sheriff of London 1749–50; Lord Mayor 1754–5, 44–45.

Jefferies, Miss, 23.

Jeffreys, John (1706–66), placeman; M.P. Brecon 1734–47; Dartmouth 1747–66; Joint Secretary to Treasury 1742–6, and Secretary to Chancellor of Exchequer, 84, 143, 151, 153, 187–8.

Jersey, William Villiers (c. 1712–69), 3rd Earl of; Chief Justice in Eyre South of Trent 1740–6, 256, 261.

Jicke, Mrs. and Miss, 78.

Johnson, James (1705–74), Bishop of Gloucester (1752) and Worcester (1759), 205–6, 212–13.

Johnson, Samuel (1709–84), the lexicographer, 35.

Johnson, Colonel Sir William (1715–74); expert in American Indian Affairs; Sachem of the Mohawks and Colonel of the Six Nations 1744; Commissary of Indian Affairs 1746; Member of New York Council and Superintendent of Indian Affairs 1755, 296, 404.

Jollyffe, Mr., Mayor of Poole 1753, 169.

Jones, Stephen Winthrop (1705–58), of Ireland; merchant, 81, 169.

Jones, Mrs., 10.

Keith, James Francis Edward (1696–1758), Jacobite exile and Prussian Field-Marshal, 379.

Kelsal, Henry (d. 1762), Chief Clerk at the Treasury; F.R.S. 1736; Commissioner for Taxes 1748 and 1760–2, 8, 9, 11, 43, 47, 62, 69, 72, 75, 86, 91, 115, 132, 133, 135, 136, 140, 141, 146, 148,

459

INDEX

Miller, James, Consul at Barcelona, 344–5.

[Mills] Mill, James (*fl.* 1744), soldier of fortune; Captain and 2nd in command of the East India Company's military forces in Bengal 1743; submitted project for the conquest of India to Francis, Duke of Lorraine, 1744; in his service as Grand Duke of Tuscany, 126, 133, 135, 139.

Mills, Mr., 243.

Milton, Joseph Damer, 1st Lord (1718–98), son-in-law of 1st Duke of Dorset; M.P. Weymouth 1741–7; Bramber 1747–54; Dorchester 1754–62, when raised to British peerage, 229.

Mine Adventurers Company, 65.

Mine Battery Company, 65.

Minorca: and General Anstruther, 146, 221; and Admiral Byng, 340–2, 355.

Mirepoix, Anne-Marguerite Gabrielle de Beauvau-Craon (1707–91), Duchesse de; wife of the French ambassador to London, 14, 21, 124.

Mirepoix, Charles Pierre Gaston Francois de Lévis (1699–1758), Duc de; French ambassador in London; Maréchal de France, 26, 34, 90, 91, 93, 96, 122–4, 132, 133, 139, 226, 312, 340.

Mitchell, Sir Andrew (1708–71), diplomatist; M.P. Aberdeenshire 1747–54; Elgin burghs 1755–71; Under-Secretary of State for Scotland 1741–7; British envoy to Prussia 1756; accompanied Frederick during the Seven Years War, 14.

[Monkton] Monckton, General Robert (1726–82), soldier; M.P. Pontefract 1751–4, 1774; Portsmouth 1778–82; served in Flanders 1742; Lieutenant-Colonel 1751; Governor of Annapolis, Nova Scotia, 1754; served in 1755 campaign in America; 2nd in command in Wolfe's expedition against Quebec 1759; Governor of New York 1761; sailed with Rodney 1762; after conquest of West Indian islands, returned to England 1763, 295, 313.

Montagu, Edward (1691–1775), of Allerthorpe, Yorkshire; M.P. Huntingdon 1734–68; grandson of the 1st Earl of Sandwich; Auditor to the Duchy of Cornwall, 33, 114.

Montagu, Mrs. (Elizabeth Robinson) (1720–1800), wife of Edward Montagu; the literary hostess, 33.

Montagu, John (1690–1749), 2nd Duke of; grandee; among his many dignities were the Lord-Lieutenancies of Warwickshire and Northants, and the Master-Generalship of the Ordnance, 44 n.

Montagu, Miss, 64.

Montfort, Henry Bromley (1705–55), Lord; M.P. Cambridgeshire 1727–41; prominent member of White's; gambler and suicide, 141, 143, 187, 217, 225.

[Moor] Moore, John (1718–79), later Bt.; naval officer; entered navy 1729; Commodore and Commander-in-Chief Leeward Islands station 1756; assisted in the reduction of Guadeloupe 1759; Rear-Admiral 1762, 384, 386.

Mordaunt, Sir Charles (1698–1778), 6th Bt.; M.P. Warwickshire 1734–74; Tory country gentleman, 122, 139.

Mordaunt, Major-General Thomas Osbert (d. 1782); served in the expedition against Rochefort, 367–8.

Moreton, Matthew Ducie (1700–70), 2nd Lord Ducie of Moreton; Lord-Lieutenant of Gloucestershire 1755–8; M.P. Cricklade 1721–2; Calne 1723–7; Gloucester 1727–8; Tregony 1729–32; Lostwithiel 1735, 272.

Morgan, William (1725–63), of Tredegar, Monmouthshire; M.P. Monmouthshire 1747–63; cousin and follower of the Cavendishes, 250.

Morris, Robert Hunter (*c.* 1700–64), Chief Justice of New Jersey 1738–54 and 1756–60; Governor of Pennsylvania 1754–6, 283.

Mostyn, Savage (1714–57), naval officer; Captain 1739; court-martialled for failure to engage two French ships off Ushant 1745; M.P. Weobley 1747–57; Comptroller of the Navy 1749; Vice-Admiral and 2nd in command on the North American station 1755; Lord of the Admiralty 1757, 9.

Mostyn, Mary Bridget, Maid of Honour to the Princess of Wales, 33.

[Mothe] Motte, Emmanuel Auguste de Cahideuc, Comte du Bois de la (1683–1764), French Admiral; Governor of Leeward Islands 1751; commanded relief expeditions to Canada 1755, 1757; opposed the raid on St. Cast 1757. 308, 315.

Munchausen, Gerlach Adolf (1688–1770), Freiherr von; Hanoverian Resident in London, 90, 94, 104, 136, 183–4, 204.

Munchausen, Madame von, wife of the Hanoverian Resident in London, celebrated frump, 23, 59.

Murray, Hon. Alexander (d. 1777), Jacobite, brother of Lord Elibank;

INDEX

Shirley, 14th son of 1st Earl Ferrers, 128–9, 151, 167, 170, 232–3, 280, 287.

Orford, Robert Walpole (d. 1751), 2nd Earl of, eldest son of Sir Robert Walpole, 109, 128 n.

Osborne, Sir Danvers (1715–53), 3rd Bt.; of Chicksands Priory, Bedfordshire; M.P. Bedfordshire 1747–53; married (1740) Lady Mary Montagu; Governor of New York 1753, but hanged himself shortly after taking office, 25.

Osborne, Admiral Henry (c. 1698–1771), naval officer; M.P. Bedfordshire 1758–61; present at Cape Passaro 1718 and Toulon 1744; Commander-in-Chief Leeward Islands 1748; in Mediterranean 1757–8, 370, 385.

Ostend Company, the, 126.

Oswald, James (1715–69), politician; M.P. Dysart 1741–7, 1754–68; Fifeshire 1747–54; Lord of Trade 1751–9; of the Treasury 1759–63; Privy Councillor and Joint Vice-Treasurer of Ireland 1763–8. D. attempts to enlist him for Carlton House, 98–102. Letters to, 346, 347, 348, 349. Referred to, 14, 69, 72, 77, 80, 87, 94–96, 105, 111–12, 139, 161, 223, 227, 241, 326, 356, 364–5, 373, 386, 404.

Oswald, Mrs. James, 72, 283.

Owen, William (d. 1793), bookseller in Fleet Street, 162.

Oxford, Bishop of, see Secker, Thomas.

Oxford, Edward Harley (c. 1699–1755), 3rd Earl of (1741); M.P. Herefordshire 1727–41, 110, 113.

Paolucci, Marquis de, Minister from Modena in London, 291.

Parisot, Pierre (1697–1769), friar and author of the anti-Jesuit *Historical Memoirs of the East Indian Missions*, which caused him to leave his order and live in exile, 271.

Parker, Thomas (1723–95), Lord; later 3rd Earl of Macclesfield; M.P. Newcastle-under-Lyme 1747–54; Oxfordshire 1755–61; Rochester 1761–4, 417.

Parliament, see Debates, Constituencies, and Elections.

Payne, Jane, Bedchamber Woman, 69.

Pelham, Griselda (1728–77), 173.

Pelham, Henry (c. 1695–1754), First Lord of the Treasury 1743–54; M.P. Sussex 1722–54. Negotiates with D. on Weymouth, 90, 92, 96, 145–6. Discusses D. rejoining government, 154–60, 163–5, 210–11, 219–21, 225, 292. Negotiates with D. on Bridgwater, 170–4, 235–6, 238–9, 243. Political

crisis on his death, 251–5, 269. D.'s opinion of his administration, 390–1. Referred to, 3–5, 87, 100, 108, 111–12, 147, 152, 176, 181, 185, 188, 204, 212–13, 217, 229–30, 240, 242, 247–8, 256.

Pelham, James (c. 1683–1761), M.P. Newark 1722–41; Hastings 1741–61; relative of Henry Pelham; secretary to Frederick, Prince of Wales, until 1737, 198.

Pelham, Thomas (1728–1805), later (1768) Baron; first cousin of 1st Duke of Newcastle; M.P. Rye 1749; Sussex 1754–68, 272.

Pembroke, Henry Herbert (1693–1750), 9th Earl of; Groom of the Stole to George II 1735–50; three times a Lord Justice; Lieutenant-General 1742; promoted erection of first Westminster bridge (1739–50); designed improvements at Wilton and elsewhere, 25, 27, 36.

Penant, Sir Samuel, Lord Mayor of London 1749–50, 22.

Pengree, Mr., 376.

Penruddock, Charles (1708–69), of Compton Chamberlayne, Wilts., 9, 10, 169.

Perceval, John James (1738–1822), Viscount; eldest son of the 2nd Earl of Egmont; M.P. Bridgwater 1762–9; succeeded as Earl of Egmont 1770, 409.

Perrière, Comte de la, 373.

Peterborough, Bishop of, see Thomas, John.

Peux, Chevalier, 241, 246.

Philip, Mr., 25.

Picard, Mr., 81, 233.

Piggot, John Bigg, of Brockley, 10.

Pinhorn, Charles, Mayor of Shaftesbury, 10.

Pitfield, Miss, 289.

Pitt, of Binfield, Mr., brother of John Pitt, 9.

Pitt, George (1721–1803), of Strathfieldsaye; M.P. Shaftesbury 1742–7; Dorset 1747–74; nephew of John Pitt of Encombe, ultimately Lord Rivers, 230.

Pitt, John (1706–87), M.P. Wareham 1734–47, 1748–51, and 1761–8; Dorchester 1751–61; Commissioner of Trade 1744–55; Lord of the Admiralty 1756–7; Surveyor of Woods 1756–63 and 1767–86, 10, 169, 375.

Pitt, Thomas (1707–61), M.P. Okehampton 1727–54; Old Sarum 1754–5, and 1761; elder brother of William Pitt; chief election manager for

INDEX

Temple, Hester Grenville (*cont.*)
married (1710) Richard Grenville;
mother of 1st Earl Temple and George
Grenville, 21, 181.

Temple, Richard Grenville (afterwards
Grenville-Temple) (1711–79), 2nd
Earl, and head of the Grenville connexion; politician; M.P. Buckingham
1734–41 and 1747–52; Buckinghamshire 1741–7; succeeded to his
mother's peerage 1752; First Lord of
the Admiralty 1756–7; Lord Privy Seal
1757–61; cousin and enemy of D., 185,
256, 303, 304, 314, 356, 358, 360.

Tessier, Monsieur de, French financier
and mimic, 26.

Teyward, Mr., 42.

Thanet, Sackville Tufton (1688–1753),
7th Earl of; married (1722) Lady Mary
Saville, daughter of the Marquis of
Halifax, 208, 210, 242.

Thanet, Sackville Tufton (1733–86), 8th
Earl of; married (1767) Mary Sack-
ville, granddaughter of the Duke of
Dorset, 249.

Thierry, French pilot, 367.

Thomas, Sir Edmund (1712–67), 3rd
Bt.; M.P. Chippenham 1741–54;
Glamorganshire 1761–7; Groom of the
Bedchamber to the Prince of Wales
1742–51, and an adherent of Lord
Talbot. Subsequently (1756–61) held
office in the Dowager Princess's household and (1761–3) under Bute. The
hero of the division on the Chippenham petition which brought down Sir
R. Walpole, 30.

Thomas, Sir George, Bt.; Governor of
the Leeward Islands 1753–66, 221.

Thomas, John (1696–1781), Bishop of
Peterborough; Fellow of All Souls
1720; Chaplain to George II 1742;
Bishop of Peterborough 1747; Salisbury 1757; Winchester 1761; Preceptor to George, Prince of Wales,
1752, 178, 196, 202.

Thomson, Dr. Thomas (d. 1763), physician and recipient of secret service
payments; in 1740's had a fashionable
practice, including Frederick, Prince
of Wales, and Pope as his patients; but
fell on bad times, and became D.'s
medical adviser and dependant; a
notable sloven. Becomes D.'s house
physician, 77. His 'disagreeable affair',
152, 157, 161. Letter to, 431. Referred
to, 12, 30, 36, 64, 66–68, 70–71, 84, 86,
89, 92, 129–30, 132–3, 147–8, 154, 160,
166, 170, 172–3, 181–2, 196, 216, 222,
224–5, 242, 249, 305, 377, 412, 441.

Thornhill, William (*fl.* 1737–55), surgeon to the Bristol Infirmary; nephew
of Sir James Thornhill, the painter,
216.

Tin Revenue, Frederick Louis's, 64–66,
70–71, 72–75.

Topham, Mr., 89.

Torrington, Viscountess (Charlotte
Byng) (d. 1759); daughter of Duke
of Manchester; wife of Pattee, 2nd
Viscount Torrington, 42, 75, 96.

Towgood, Nicholas, wealthy Wiltshire
clothier, 243, 267.

Townshend, Charles Townshend (1700–
64), 3rd Viscount; M.P. Great Yarmouth 1722–3; Lord-Lieutenant of
Norfolk 1730–8, 212.

Townshend, Charles (1725–67), politician; M.P. Great Yarmouth 1747–56;
Saltash 1756–61; Harwich 1761–7; son
of 3rd Viscount Townshend; educated
at Leyden; Lord of the Admiralty
1754–5; P.C. 1757; Secretary-at-War
1761–2; President of the Board of
Trade 1763; Paymaster of the Forces
1765–6; Chancellor of the Exchequer
1766–7, 25, 249, 262, 292, 414, 418.

Townshend, George Townshend (1724–
1807), later (1764) 4th Viscount; soldier and politician; M.P. Norfolk
1747–64; educated St. John's, Cambridge; fought at Culloden 1746, and
at Laufeld 1747; Lieutenant-Colonel,
1st Foot Guards, 1748; retired, owing
to differences with Cumberland, 1750;
supposed to have inspired pamphlets
criticizing Cumberland; brought in
Militia Bill 1757; Colonel and aide-de-
camp to George II; Brigadier-General
in Quebec expedition and, on Wolfe's
death, assumed command; P.C. 1761;
Lieutenant-General of the Ordnance
1763; Lord-Lieutenant of Ireland
1767–72; Master-General of the Ordnance; created 1st Marquis Townshend 1786, 103–4, 105, 113–14, 384,
387.

Trenchard, George (1684–1758), M.P.
Poole 1713–41 and 1747–54, 9, 79, 129,
140, 166, 169–70, 404.

Trenchard, Thomas, of Lychet, Dorset,
81, 229–30, 233.

Trenchard, Mrs. Thomas, daughter of
Henry Henning, of Pokeswell, Dorset,
81.

Trentham, Lord, Granville Leveson-
Gower (1721–1803), later (1754) 2nd
Earl Gower; politician; M.P. Bishop's
Castle 1744–7; Westminster 1747–54;
Lichfield 1754; son of 1st Earl Gower;

472

INDEX

Lord of the Admiralty 1749–51; Lord Privy Seal 1755–7; Master of the Horse 1757–60; Master of the Wardrobe 1760–3; Marquis of Stafford 1786, 26 n., 116, 121, 124, 125, 368, 380, 382–3, 416.

Trevanion, William (1727–67), M.P. Tregony 1747–67; Groom of Bedchamber to Frederick, Prince of Wales, 1749–51; Auditor to the Duchy of Cornwall 1751–67, 31.

Tryan, Mr., 280.

Tucker, John (c. 1713–79), M.P. Weymouth 1735–47 and 1754–78; Mayor of Weymouth 1754; D.'s political partner at Weymouth, and business associate; Cashier to the Navy during D.'s Treasurerships, 12, 30, 32, 34–36, 42, 54, 56–57, 61–62, 66, 68, 79–80, 89–92, 96, 105, 112, 114–15, 121, 124, 129, 130–1, 138–40, 142–3, 145, 147–8, 151–2, 155, 161–2, 168–9, 188, 196, 206, 214, 216–17, 223, 226, 233, 249, 251, 267, 283, 285, 289–91, 298, 335, 346, 355, 380, 398, 439–40.

Tucker, Mrs. John, 54, 80, 147, 152, 168, 216, 226, 289.

Tucker, Richard, son, or possibly brother, of John Tucker, M.P.; Mayor of Weymouth 1753, 9, 79, 80, 131, 140, 142, 226, 234, 288, 376.

Tucker, Mrs. Richard, 226.

Tudor, Mr., 169, 183, 197, 201.

Tuffin, D.'s servant, 397.

Tynte, Charles (1710–85), Bt. (1750); M.P. Monmouth 1745–7; Somerset 1747–54, 14, 32, 42, 64, 105, 122, 123, 139, 158, 231.

Tynte, Lady (d. 1758), wife of Sir Charles Tynte, 64, 123, 158.

Tyrawley, James O'Hara (1690–1773), 2nd Baron (1724); soldier and diplomatist; served under Marlborough; ambassador to Portugal 1728–41 and 1752–6; to Russia 1743–5; Major-General 1739; Lieutenant-General 1743; Governor of Minorca 1752–6; of Gibraltar 1756–7; General 1761; Field-marshal and Governor of Portsmouth 1763; Plenipotentiary in Portugal 1762–3, 26, 33, 34, 72.

Tyrawley, Lady, 304.

[Tyrell] Tyrrel, Arthur (d. 1794), Captain of Artillery, 384.

Uxbridge, Henry Paget (1719–69), 2nd Earl of; succeeded his grandfather 1743; a miser, 93.

Vandeput, Sir George (d. 1784), Bt.;

Opposition candidate for Westminster 1749, 30, 32.

Vanderdussen, Alexander, Lieutenant-Colonel on half-pay, 183, 197.

Vane, George, 158, 188, 225.

Vane, Lieutenant-Colonel Gilbert (d. 1772), brother of 1st Earl of Darlington; served in the '45; Deputy-Treasurer of Chelsea College, 142, 224–5.

Vane, Lady Grace (Grace Fitzroy), (d. 1763), daughter of the Duke of Cleveland and wife of Henry Vane, 3rd Lord Barnard, 207, 279.

Vane, Henry (1705–58), later (1753) Lord Barnard and (1754) Earl of Darlington; politician; M.P. Launceston 1726–7; St. Mawes 1727–41; Ripon 1741–7; Durham 1747–53; Vice-Treasurer of Ireland 1742–4; Lord of the Treasury 1749–55; Joint Paymaster of the Forces 1755–6. D.'s political conversations with, 218–20, 246–7, 251–3. Mentioned, 55, 140–1, 158, 160–1, 188, 197, 210–11, 213, 216, 217 n., 224–5, 256, 262–3, 419.

[Vaneck] Vanneck, Joshua (d. 1777), later Bt.; wealthy business man, 75.

Vansittart, Arthur (1726–1804), M.P. Berkshire 1757–74; son of Arthur Vansittart of Shottesbrooke; a Medmenham Franciscan, 169.

Vaughan, William (1707–75), M.P. Merionethshire 1734–68; Tory member of the opposition to Walpole; later inclined to support the Pelhams, 91, 138, 143, 223, 246, 256, 380, 404.

Venturini, Monsieur, D.'s brother-in-law, a minor diplomatist, 235–6, 242, 245, 249–50, 251, 271, 292, 310, 313.

Venturini, Mrs., née Beaghan, D.'s sister-in-law, 242, 249, 280, 287, 291–2.

Vernon, Mr., Jacobite draper, 205, 213.

Verschaffelts, Mr., sculptor, 161, 162, 218.

Viry, Francesco Giuseppe, Conte di (d. 1766), Savoyard diplomatist; Minister to Switzerland 1738, Holland 1749–54, England 1755–63, and Sardinian Foreign Minister 1764–6; in England moved in inner circles of government, and served as intermediary between Newcastle, Pitt, and Bute, 373.

Visconti, Giovanni Baptista Antonio (1722–84), antiquary, friend of Winckelmann and curator of the Museo Pio Clementino, 69.

Visconti, la, singer, 242.

INDEX

Oxford University 1758; tended to Jacobitism, 61, 96, 107–11, 113, 202, 240.

Weymouth, Mayor and Corporation of. Letter to, 440. *See also* Constituencies.

Wheate, Miss, 70, 77, 158.

Whitehead, Paul (1710–74), poet and pamphleteer; made his name with *Manners* (1739) and *Honour* (1747); had a minor post in Treasury, but also associated with the caucus of Independent Electors of Westminster; secretary to the Medmenham brotherhood, 67 n., 80, 407–8, 421 n.

White's Club, 125, 196, 246, 247, 251, 253.

Wilbraham, Randle (1695–1770), barrister; M.P. Newcastle-under-Lyme 1740–7; Appleby 1747–54; Newton 1754–68; related to the Thanets, to whom he owed his seat in Parliament, 245.

Wilkes, John (1727–97), politician and journalist, 431 n.

Willes, Sir John (1685–1761), Judge; M.P. Launceston 1722–6; Weymouth 1726–7; West Looe 1727–37; Fellow of All Souls; K.C. 1719; Attorney-General 1733–6; Chief Justice of Common Pleas 1737–61; Senior Commissioner of the Great Seal 1756–7, 11, 12, 24, 25, 70, 73.

William V, Prince of Orange (d. 1747), first hereditary Stadtholder of Holland, married to George II's daughter Anne, 136.

William VI (1751–1806), Prince of Orange, 148.

William Henry, Prince (1743–1805), 3rd son of Frederick, Prince of Wales; Duke of Gloucester and Edinburgh 1764; secretly married Maria, dowager Countess Waldegrave 1766, 70, 87.

Williams, Kyffin (d. 1753), M.P. Flint 1747–53, 10, 11, 35, 80, 161.

Williams, Sir Charles Hanbury (1708–59), diplomatist, wit, and satirist; M.P. Monmouthshire 1735–47; Leominster 1754–9; Paymaster of Marines 1739–46; envoy to Berlin 1750–1; to Poland 1751–5; to Russia 1755–7; committed suicide, 320.

Williams-Wynn, Sir Watkin (1692–1749), 3rd Bt. and leader of country gentlemen with a Jacobite tinge; M.P. Denbighshire 1716–41 and 1742–9, 13.

Wilmot, Dr. Edward (1693–1786), Surgeon to Frederick, Prince of Wales, 69, 105.

Winchelsea, Daniel Finch (1689–1769), 7th Earl of; M.P. Rutland 1711–30; Lord of the Treasury 1715–16; Comptroller of the Household 1725–30; First Lord of the Admiralty 1742–4 and 1757; Lord President 1765–6, 148, 252, 360.

Wise, Mr., 232.

Withers, Mr., 128.

Wood, Robert (c. 1717–71), traveller and politician; M.P. Brackley 1761–71; published *Ruins of Palmyra* 1753; *Ruins of Balbec* 1757; Under-Secretary of State 1756–63, 1768–70; member of Society of Dilettanti 1763, 233.

Wolfe, General James (1727–59), the victor of Quebec, 387.

Worcester, Bishop of, *see* Maddox, Isaac.

Worsley, Thomas (1710–78), of Hovingham Hall, Yorks., personal friend of Bute and George III, connoisseur and horse-breeder; M.P. Orford 1761–8; Callington 1768–74; Equerry to George II 1743–60; Surveyor-General of Works 1760–78, 407, 423.

Wright, Mr., surveyor, 296.

Wright, Dr. Thomas (1711–86), philosopher and mathematician, 130, 148.

Wycombe: visits to, 82, 83, 133, 319. *See also* Constituencies.

Wyndham, Miss, 105.

Wyndham, Thomas (1696–1777), of Hammersmith, D.'s cousin and heir; M.P. Poole 1732–41; eccentric, 9, 11, 30, 42, 80, 82, 143, 147, 169–70, 201, 225, 234–5, 247, 249, 251, 270–1, 278, 283, 290–1, 351, 378, 406, 412–13, 416, 442.

Yarmouth, Countess of (Amalie Sophie Marianne von Wendt) (1704–65), George II's official mistress from 1738; a Hanoverian; divorced by Colonel von Wallmoden 1739, 204, 236, 252.

Yonge, Sir William (d. 1755), 4th Bt.; Walpolian supporter; M.P. Honiton 1715–54; Tiverton 1754–5; Commissioner of Revenue in Ireland 1723; Lord of the Treasury 1724–7 and 1730; Lord of the Admiralty 1728; Secretary-at-War 1735; Joint Vice-Treasurer of Ireland 1746; F.R.S. 1748, 324.

York, Edward Augustus, Duke of, *see* Edward Augustus, Prince.

Yorke, Charles (1722–70), barrister and politician; M.P. Reigate 1747–68; Cambridge University 1768–70; son of 1st Earl of Hardwicke; Joint Clerk of